Takane & Hana

6

STORY AND ART BY

Yuki Shiwasu

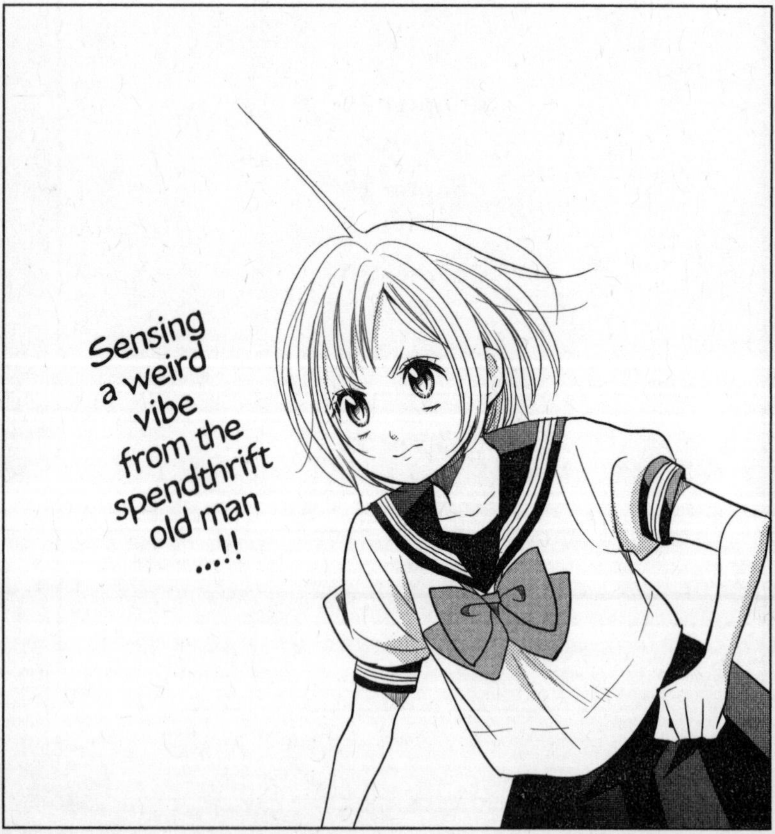
Sensing a weird vibe from the spendthrift old man ...!!

Takane
& Hana

6

Takane & Hana

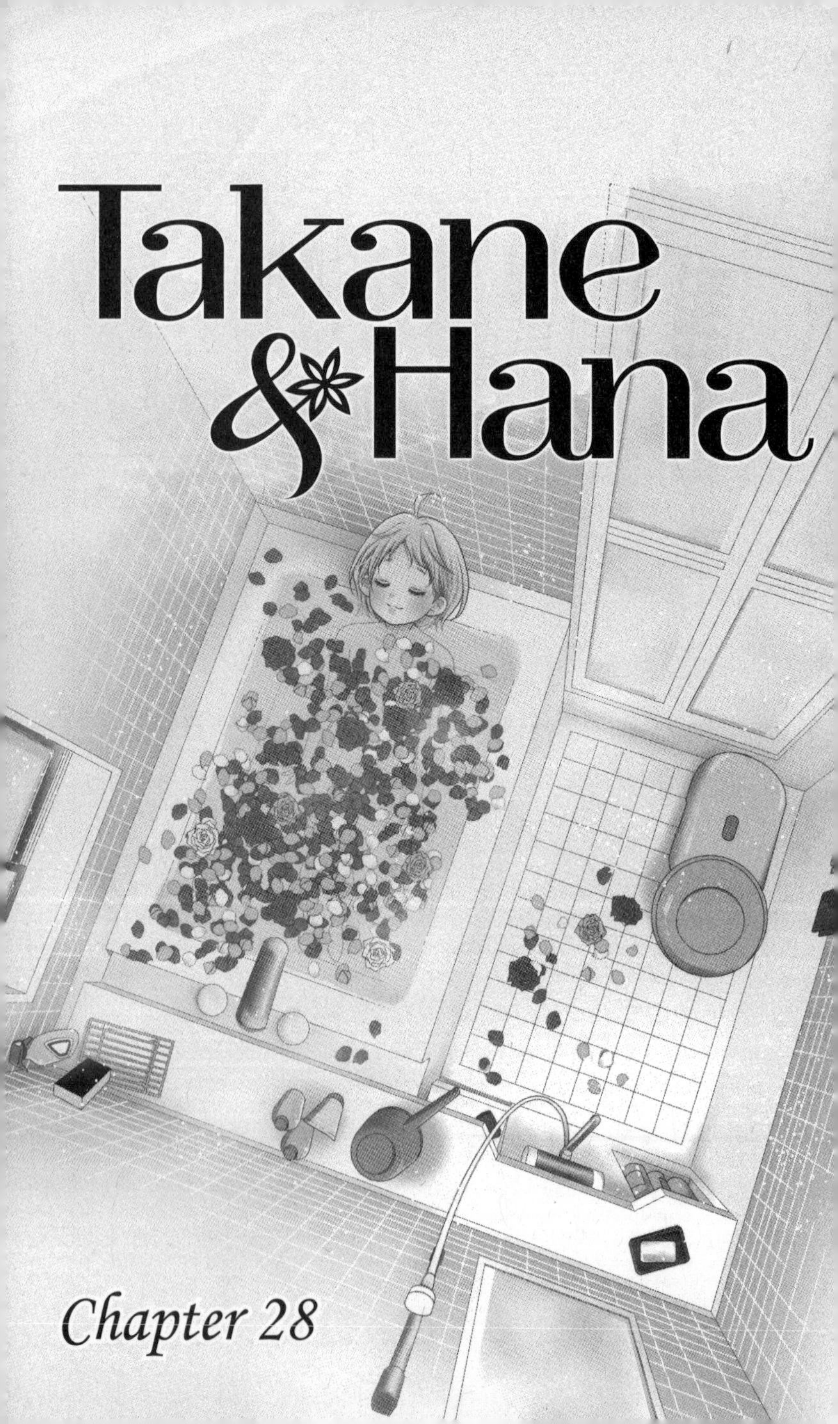

Chapter 28

Watch Out for Sharp Edges

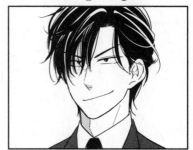

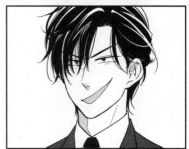

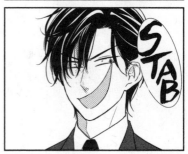

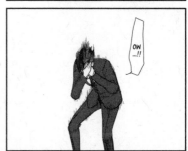

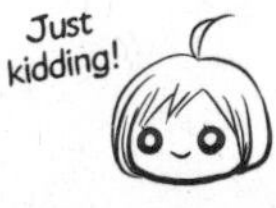

Just kidding!

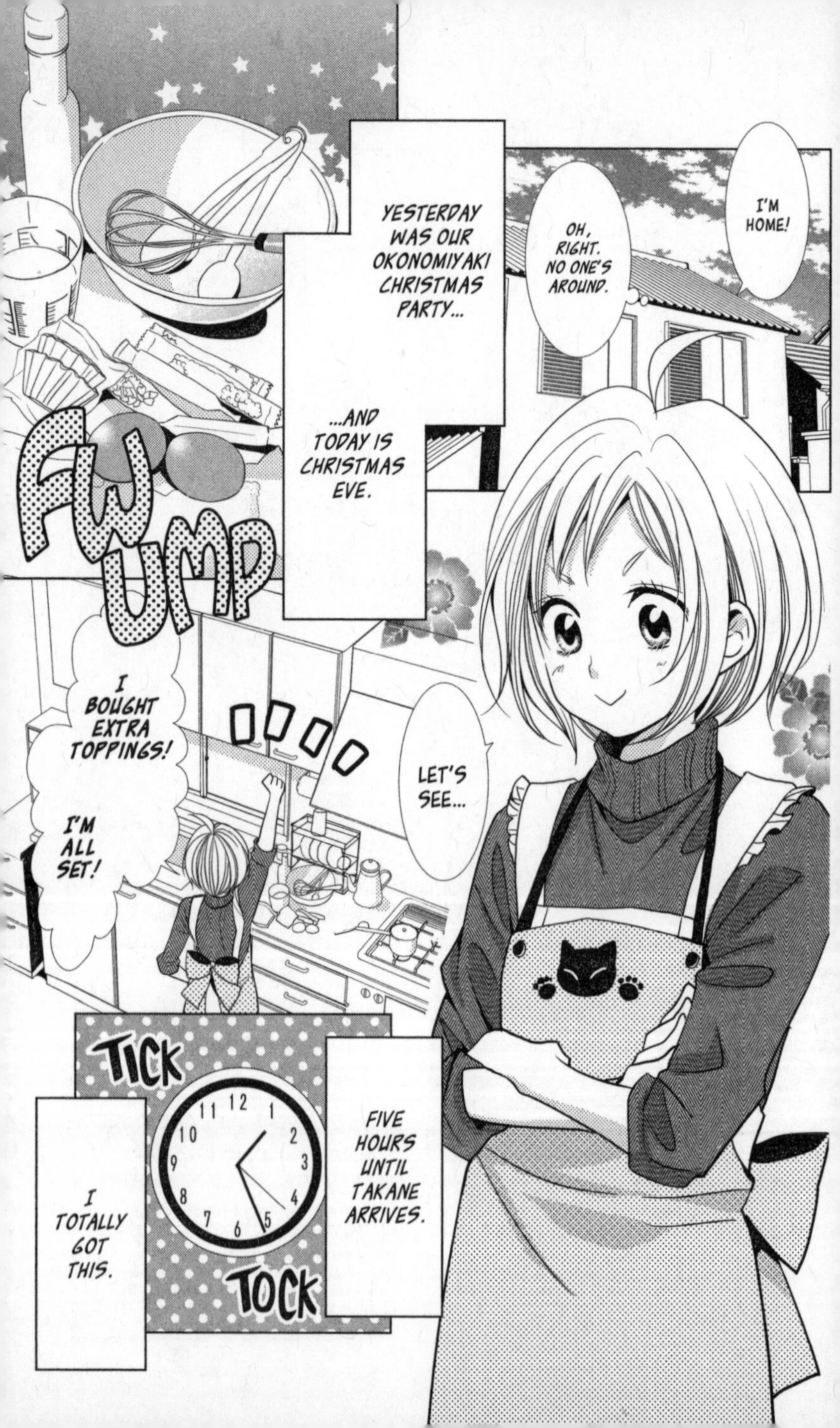
I'M HOME!
OH, RIGHT. NO ONE'S AROUND.
YESTERDAY WAS OUR OKONOMIYAKI CHRISTMAS PARTY...
...AND TODAY IS CHRISTMAS EVE.
FWUMP
LET'S SEE...
I BOUGHT EXTRA TOPPINGS!
I'M ALL SET!
FIVE HOURS UNTIL TAKANE ARRIVES.
TICK
TOCK
I TOTALLY GOT THIS.

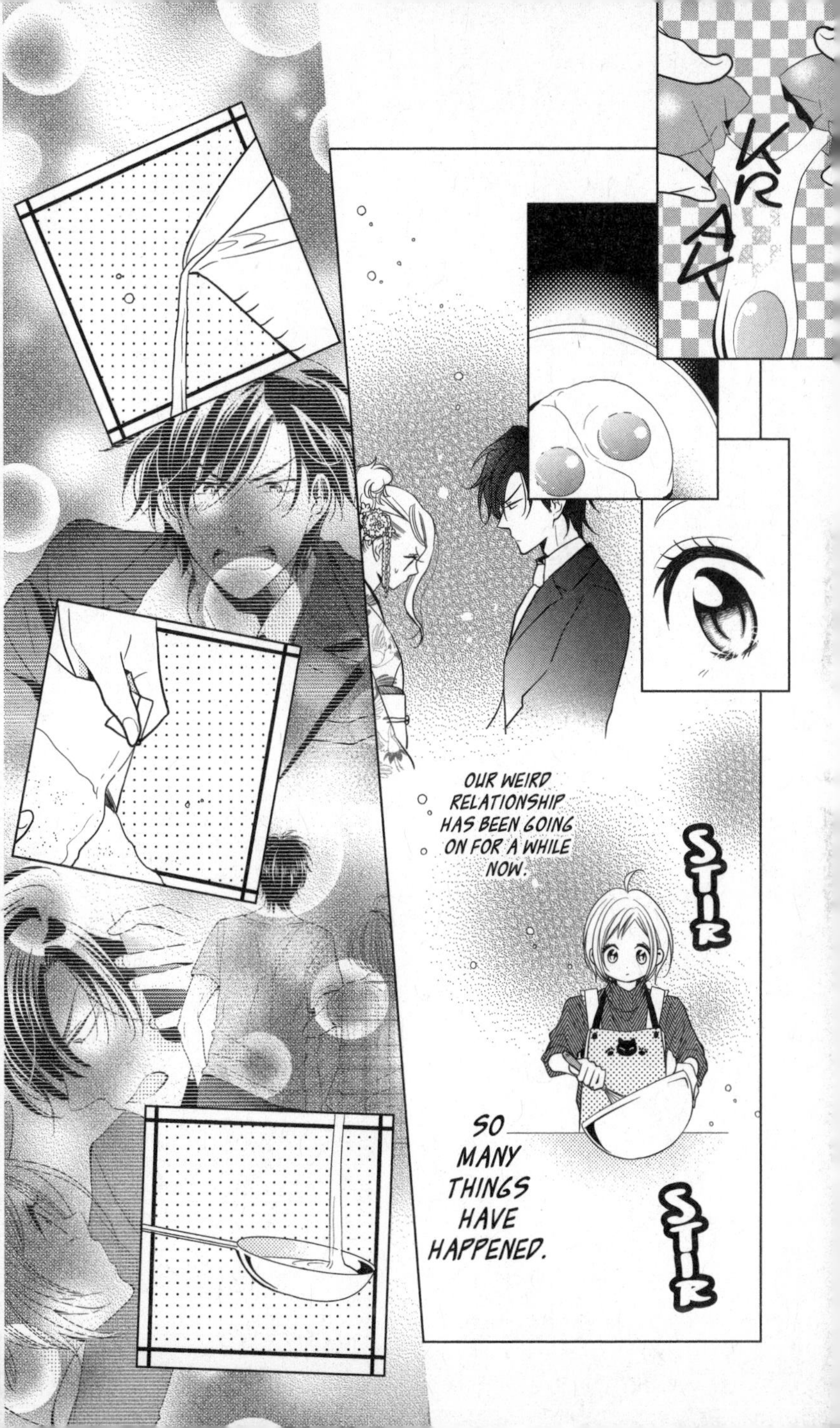
KRAK
OUR WEIRD RELATIONSHIP HAS BEEN GOING ON FOR A WHILE NOW.
STIR
SO MANY THINGS HAVE HAPPENED.
STIR

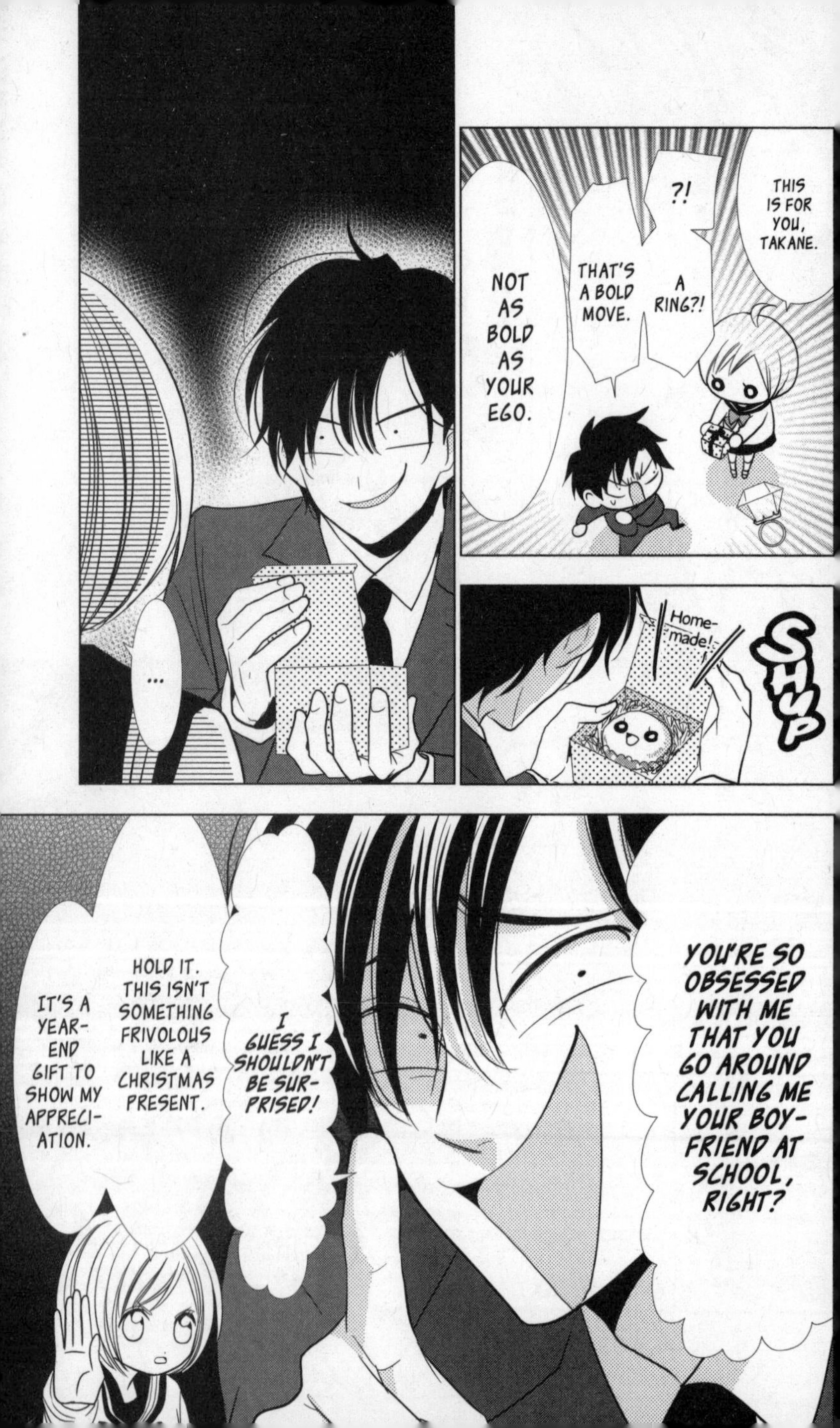
THIS IS FOR YOU, TAKANE.
?!
A RING?!
THAT'S A BOLD MOVE.
NOT AS BOLD AS YOUR EGO.
SHUP
Home-made!
...
YOU'RE SO OBSESSED WITH ME THAT YOU GO AROUND CALLING ME YOUR BOY-FRIEND AT SCHOOL, RIGHT?
I GUESS I SHOULDN'T BE SUR-PRISED!
HOLD IT. THIS ISN'T SOMETHING FRIVOLOUS LIKE A CHRISTMAS PRESENT.
IT'S A YEAR-END GIFT TO SHOW MY APPRECI-ATION.

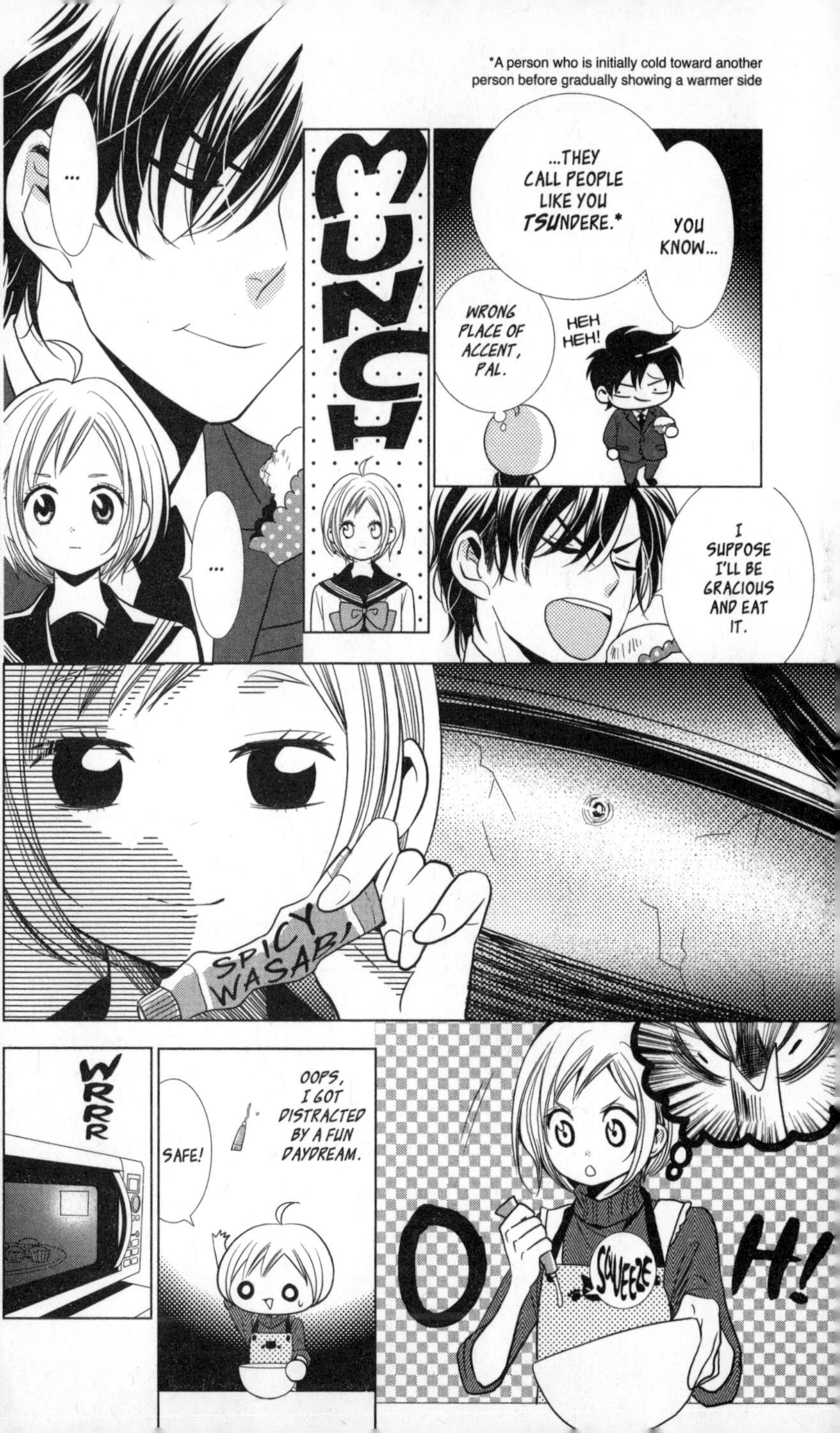
YOU KNOW...
...THEY CALL PEOPLE LIKE YOU TSUNDERE.*
HEH HEH!
WRONG PLACE OF ACCENT, PAL.
I SUPPOSE I'LL BE GRACIOUS AND EAT IT.
MUNCH
...
...
SPICY WASABI
OOH!
SQUEEZE
OOPS, I GOT DISTRACTED BY A FUN DAYDREAM.
SAFE!
WRRR

*A person who is initially cold toward another person before gradually showing a warmer side

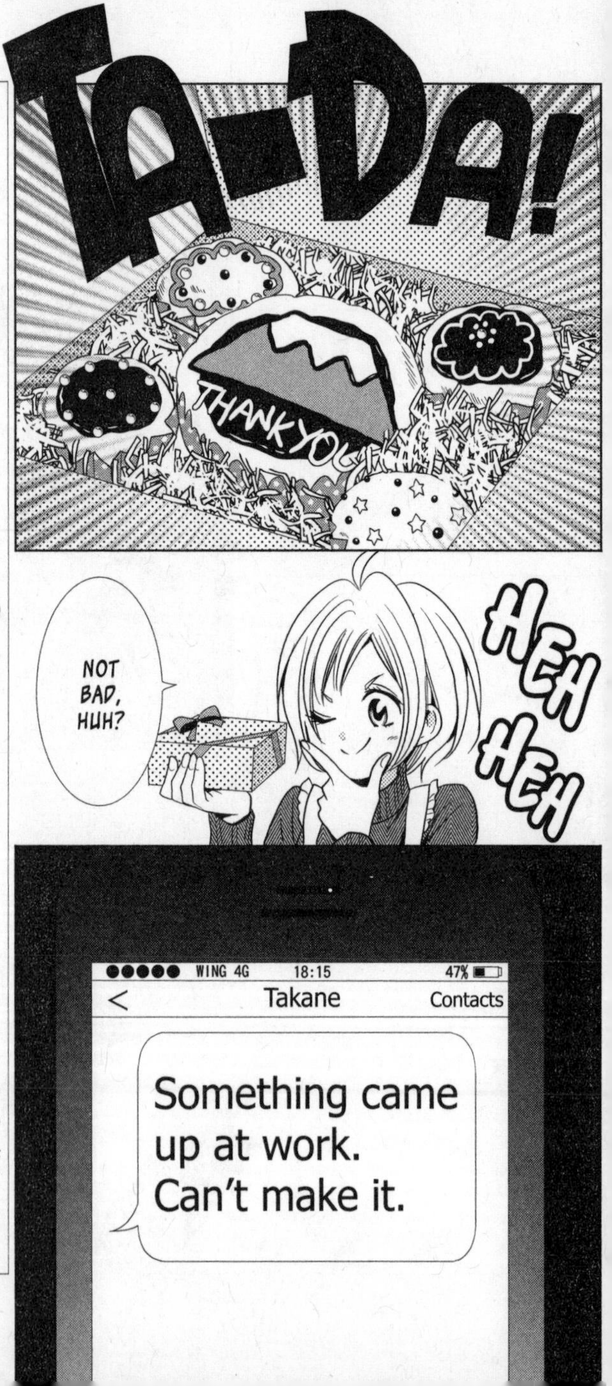
TA-DA!
THANK YOU
HEH HEH
NOT BAD, HUH?
WING 4G 18:15 47%
< Takane Contacts
Something came up at work. Can't make it.

Takane Rules the Whole Country

That's the name of a new campaign that's currently under way! (It'll be a year long, from April 2016 to March 2017.)

Each month, three or four bookstores around the country will get a cardboard cutout of Takane to display. Every prefecture will get one Takane, so 47 cutouts will be made overall. As I write this, it's October 2016, so we're halfway into the campaign.

Each Takane cutout will show him either holding a specialty product of that prefecture or doing cosplay with something associated with the area. Coming up with all the ideas is hard, but it's fun too!

In order to make a life-size cutout of Takane, I decided his official height would be six feet. I'd always thought the height difference between him and Hana would be one foot. But looking back, Hana often looks much shorter. There's no visual consistency. So if you could give me a break and just visualize Hana as being five feet, I'd appreciate it. Thank you! (Heh...)

The body/head ratios on these two are so different that it's really hard to draw them side by side. Who the heck designed them? Oh, right—that was me!

If drawn accurately, I think the top of Hana's head should come to the bottom of Takane's collarbone. I was focusing on the differences in their age and social status, not their height difference, so I didn't pay much attention to it. But the fact of the matter is that there's a huge height difference!

I kinda have set heights for the other characters too. Luciano is taller than Takane. Hikaruko is about average height. Okamon and Mizuki are about the same height right now, but Okamon is going through a growth spurt. When I have time, I'd love to draw them all lined up so I can finally decide on their heights.

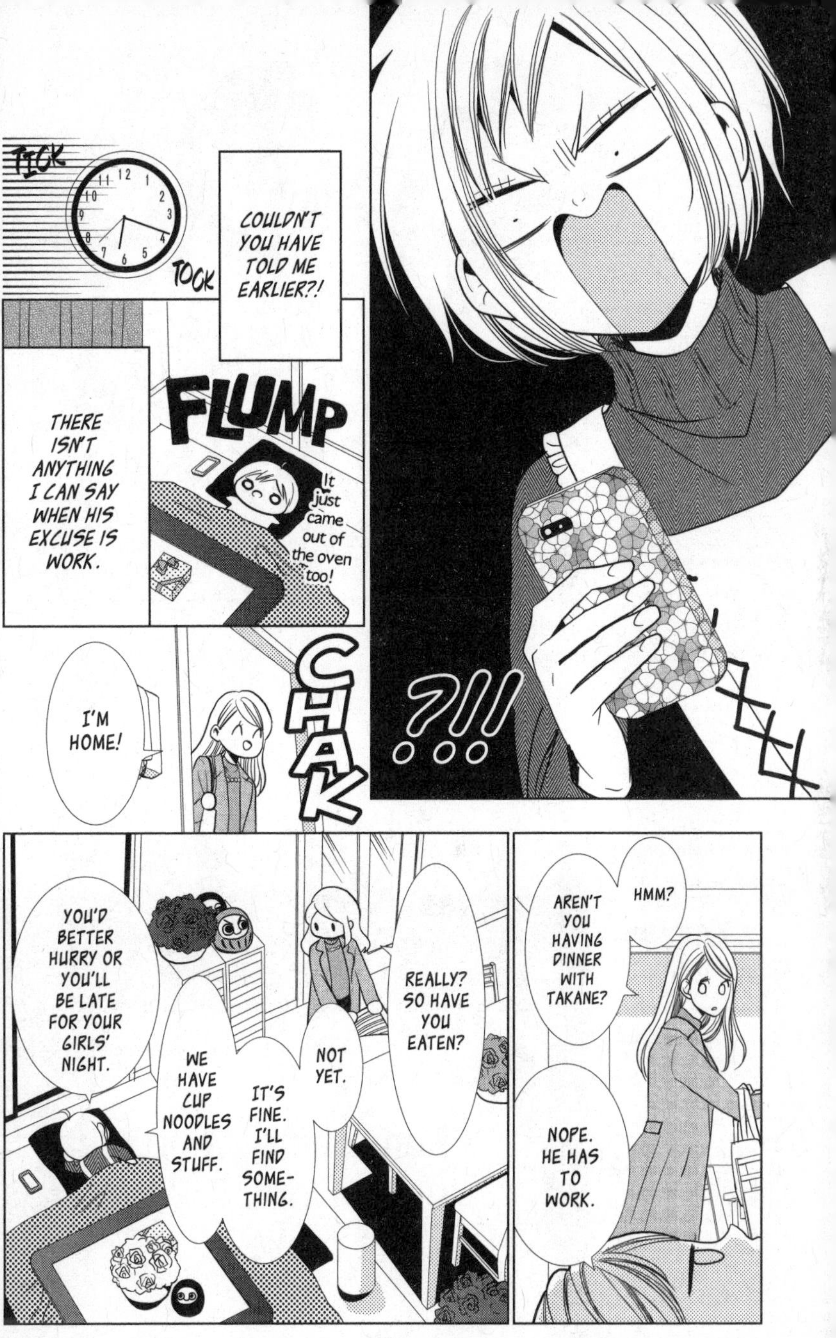
?!!...
TICK
TOCK
COULDN'T YOU HAVE TOLD ME EARLIER?!
THERE ISN'T ANYTHING I CAN SAY WHEN HIS EXCUSE IS WORK.
FLUMP
It just came out of the oven too!
CHAK
I'M HOME!
HMM?
AREN'T YOU HAVING DINNER WITH TAKANE?
NOPE. HE HAS TO WORK.
REALLY? SO HAVE YOU EATEN?
NOT YET.
IT'S FINE. I'LL FIND SOME-THING.
WE HAVE CUP NOODLES AND STUFF.
YOU'D BETTER HURRY OR YOU'LL BE LATE FOR YOUR GIRLS' NIGHT.

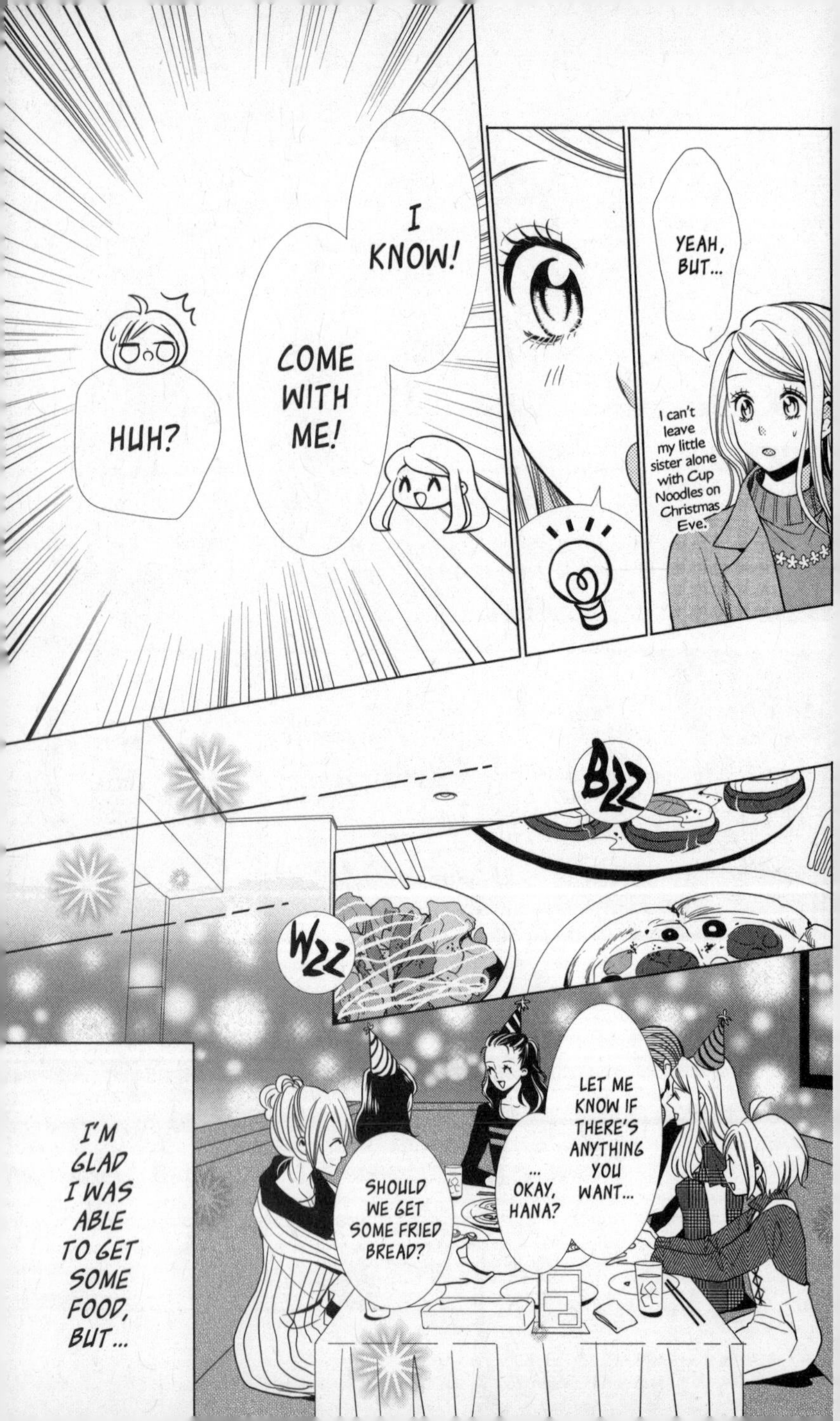

YEAH, BUT...
I can't leave my little sister alone with Cup Noodles on Christmas Eve.
I KNOW!
COME WITH ME!
HUH?
BZZ
WZZ
LET ME KNOW IF THERE'S ANYTHING YOU WANT...
... OKAY, HANA?
SHOULD WE GET SOME FRIED BREAD?
I'M GLAD I WAS ABLE TO GET SOME FOOD, BUT...

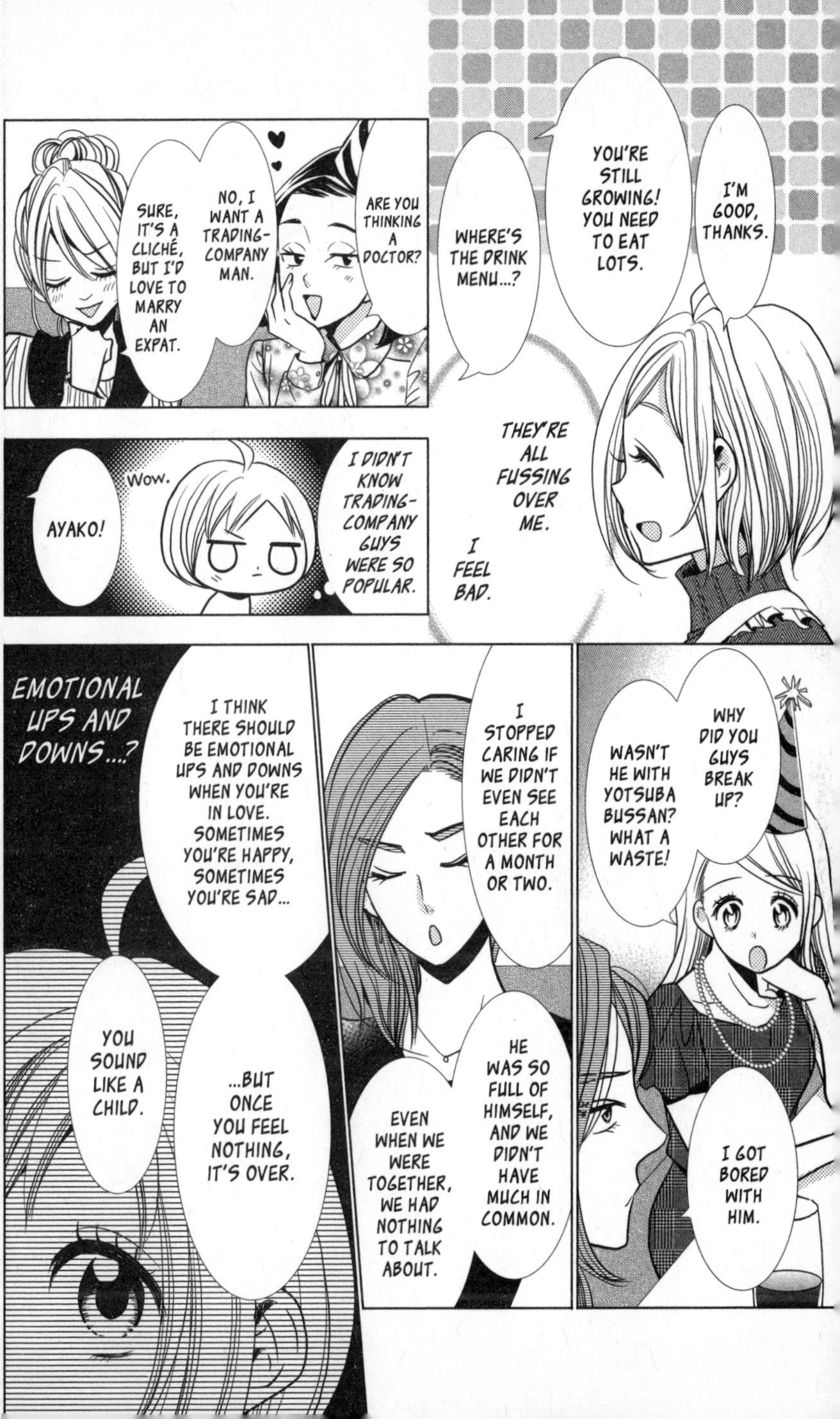
I'M GOOD, THANKS.
YOU'RE STILL GROWING! YOU NEED TO EAT LOTS.
WHERE'S THE DRINK MENU...?
THEY'RE ALL FUSSING OVER ME.
I FEEL BAD.
ARE YOU THINKING A DOCTOR?
NO, I WANT A TRADING-COMPANY MAN.
SURE, IT'S A CLICHÉ, BUT I'D LOVE TO MARRY AN EXPAT.
I DIDN'T KNOW TRADING-COMPANY GUYS WERE SO POPULAR.
Wow.
AYAKO!
WHY DID YOU GUYS BREAK UP?
WASN'T HE WITH YOTSUBA BUSSAN? WHAT A WASTE!
I GOT BORED WITH HIM.
I STOPPED CARING IF WE DIDN'T EVEN SEE EACH OTHER FOR A MONTH OR TWO.
HE WAS SO FULL OF HIMSELF, AND WE DIDN'T HAVE MUCH IN COMMON.
EVEN WHEN WE WERE TOGETHER, WE HAD NOTHING TO TALK ABOUT.
I THINK THERE SHOULD BE EMOTIONAL UPS AND DOWNS WHEN YOU'RE IN LOVE. SOMETIMES YOU'RE HAPPY, SOMETIMES YOU'RE SAD...
...BUT ONCE YOU FEEL NOTHING, IT'S OVER.
YOU SOUND LIKE A CHILD.
EMOTIONAL UPS AND DOWNS...?

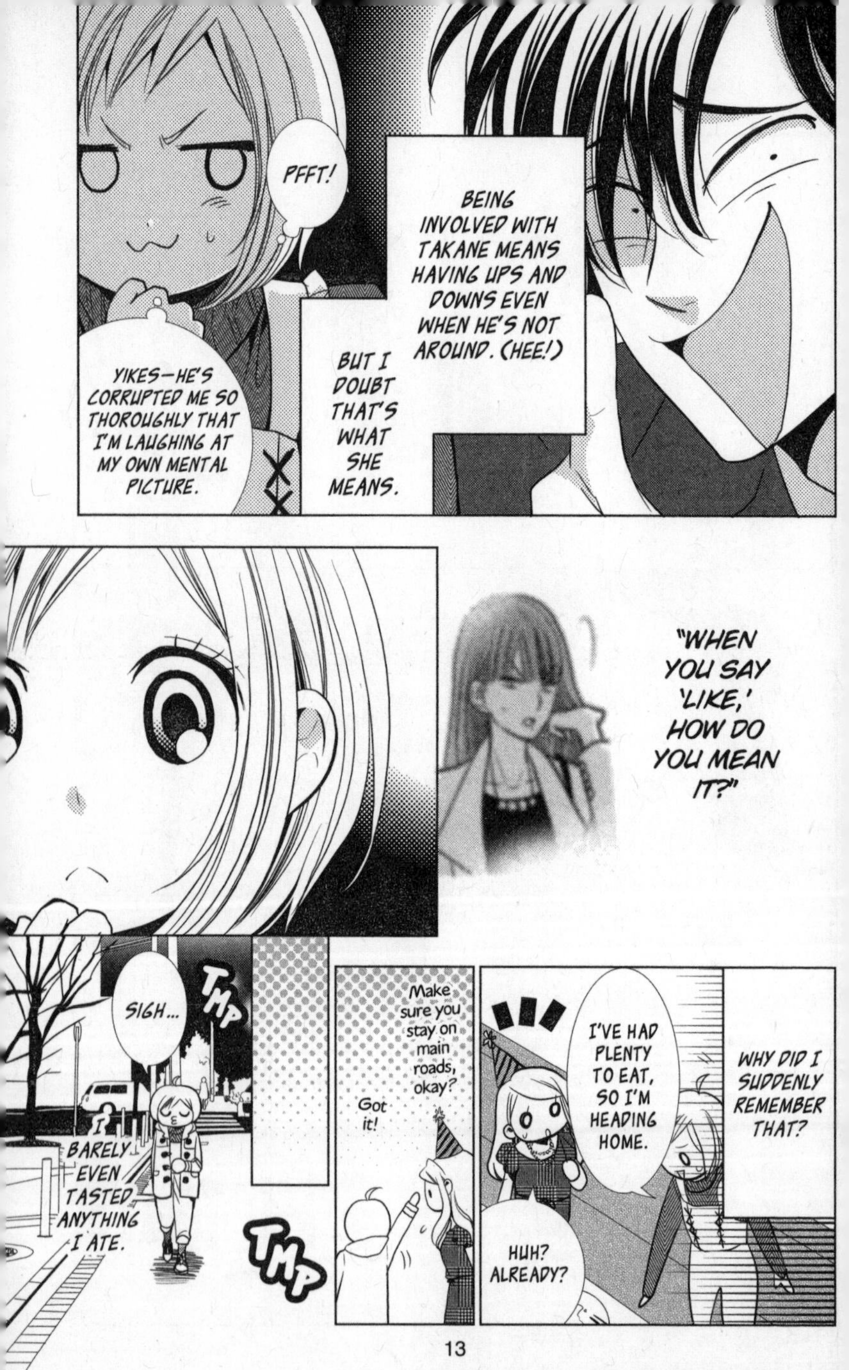
BEING INVOLVED WITH TAKANE MEANS HAVING UPS AND DOWNS EVEN WHEN HE'S NOT AROUND. (HEE!)
BUT I DOUBT THAT'S WHAT SHE MEANS.
PFFT!
YIKES—HE'S CORRUPTED ME SO THOROUGHLY THAT I'M LAUGHING AT MY OWN MENTAL PICTURE.
"WHEN YOU SAY 'LIKE,' HOW DO YOU MEAN IT?"
WHY DID I SUDDENLY REMEMBER THAT?
I'VE HAD PLENTY TO EAT, SO I'M HEADING HOME.
HUH? ALREADY?
Make sure you stay on main roads, okay?
Got it!
SIGH...
TMP
I BARELY EVEN TASTED ANYTHING I ATE.
TMP

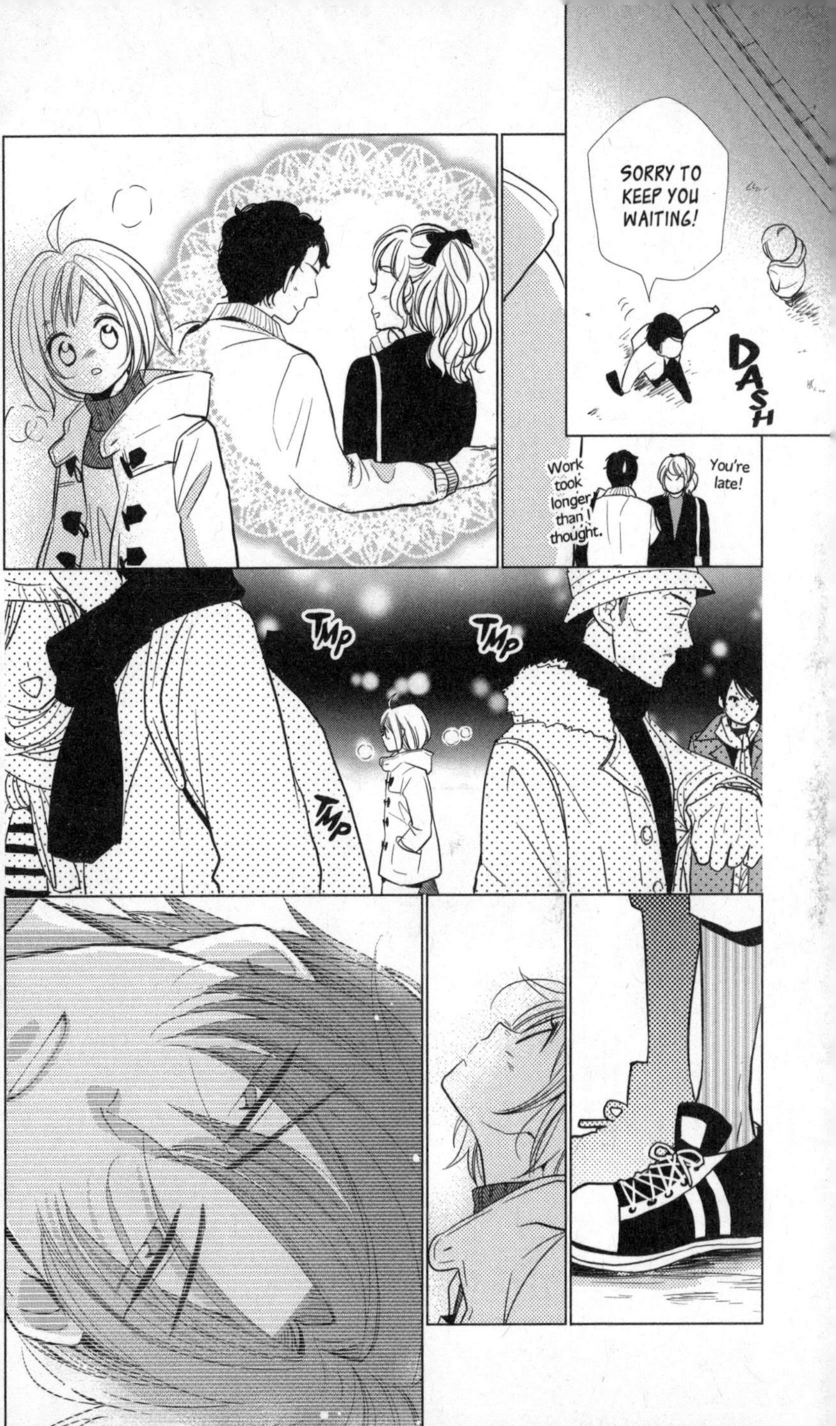
SORRY TO KEEP YOU WAITING!
DASH
You're late!
Work took longer than I thought.
TMP
TMP
TMP

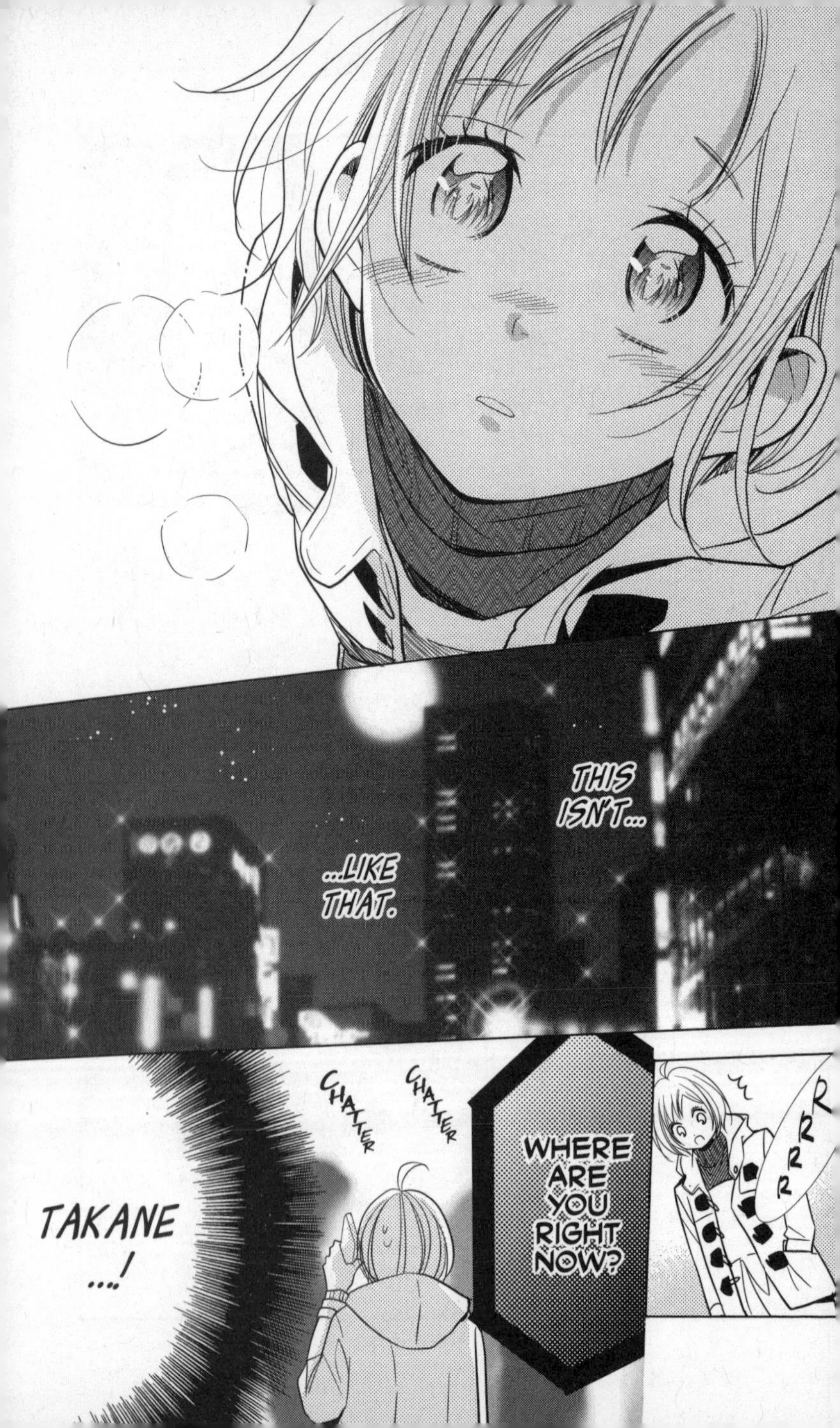
THIS ISN'T...
...LIKE THAT.
RRRRR
WHERE ARE YOU RIGHT NOW?
CHATTER
CHATTER
TAKANE ...!

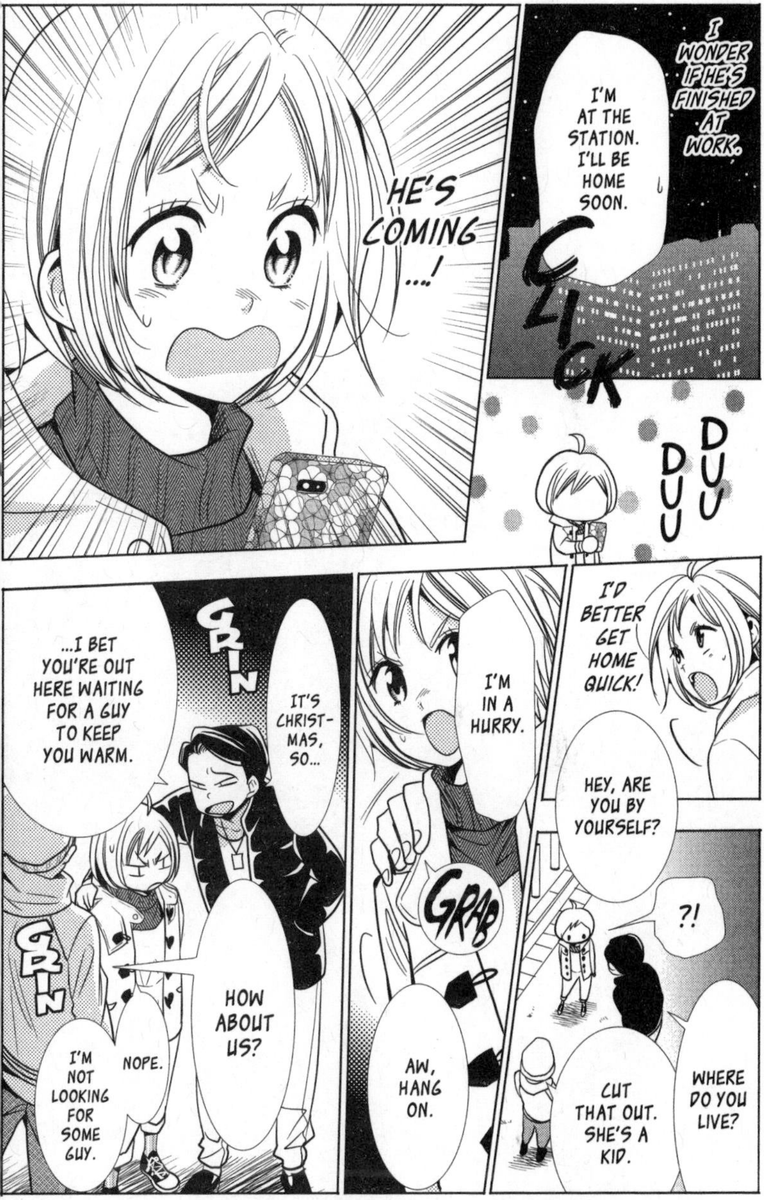
I WONDER IF HE'S FINISHED AT WORK.
I'M AT THE STATION. I'LL BE HOME SOON.
CLICK
DUU DUU
HE'S COMING ...!
I'D BETTER GET HOME QUICK!
HEY, ARE YOU BY YOURSELF?
?!
WHERE DO YOU LIVE?
CUT THAT OUT. SHE'S A KID.
I'M IN A HURRY.
GRAB
AW, HANG ON.
GRIN
IT'S CHRIST-MAS, SO...
...I BET YOU'RE OUT HERE WAITING FOR A GUY TO KEEP YOU WARM.
HOW ABOUT US?
GRIN
NOPE.
I'M NOT LOOKING FOR SOME GUY.

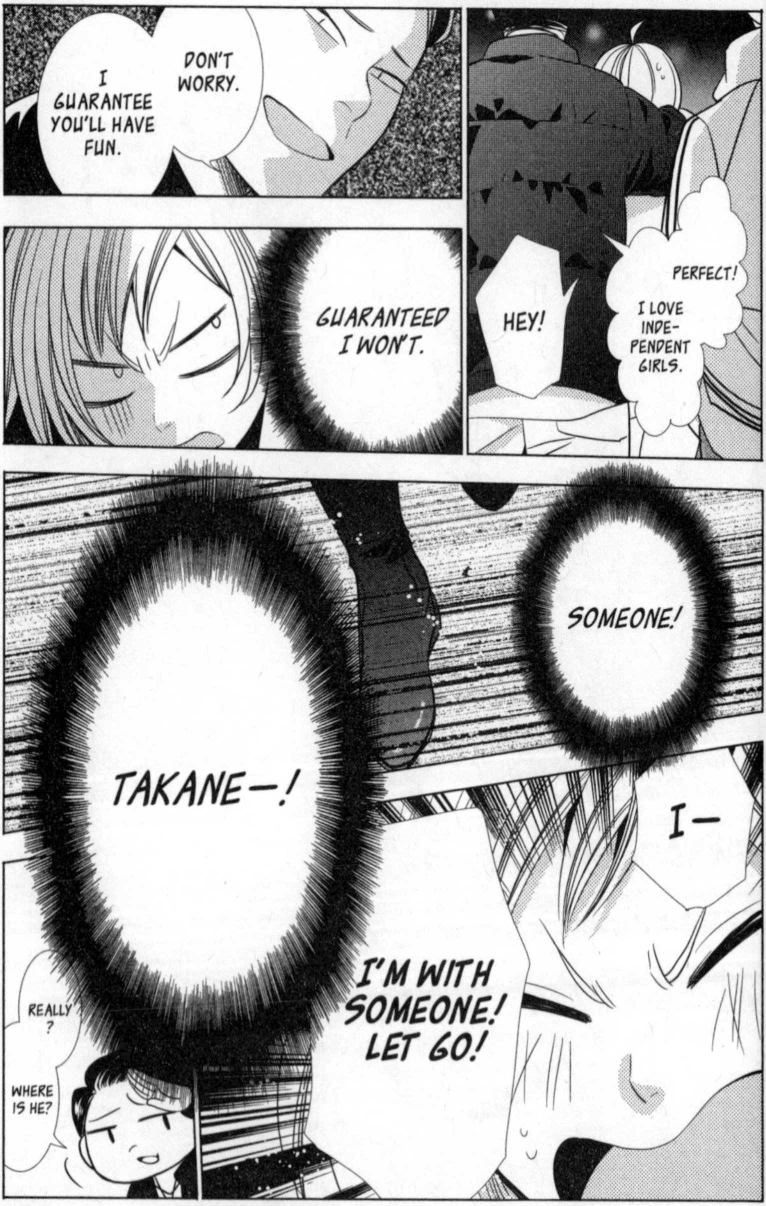
HEY!
PERFECT!
I LOVE INDE-PENDENT GIRLS.
DON'T WORRY.
I GUARANTEE YOU'LL HAVE FUN.
GUARANTEED I WON'T.
SOMEONE!
TAKANE—!
I—
I'M WITH SOMEONE! LET GO!
REALLY?
WHERE IS HE?

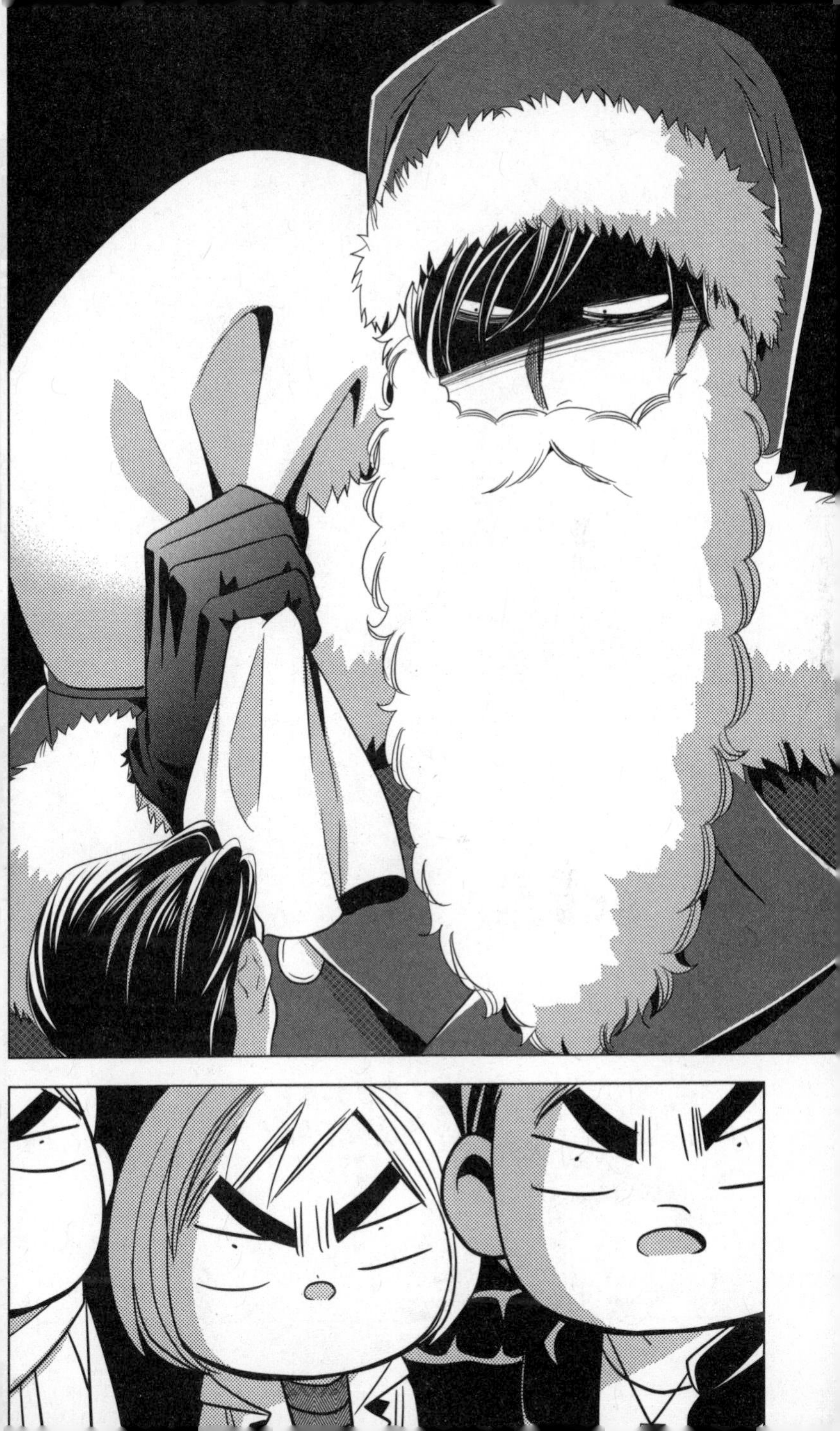

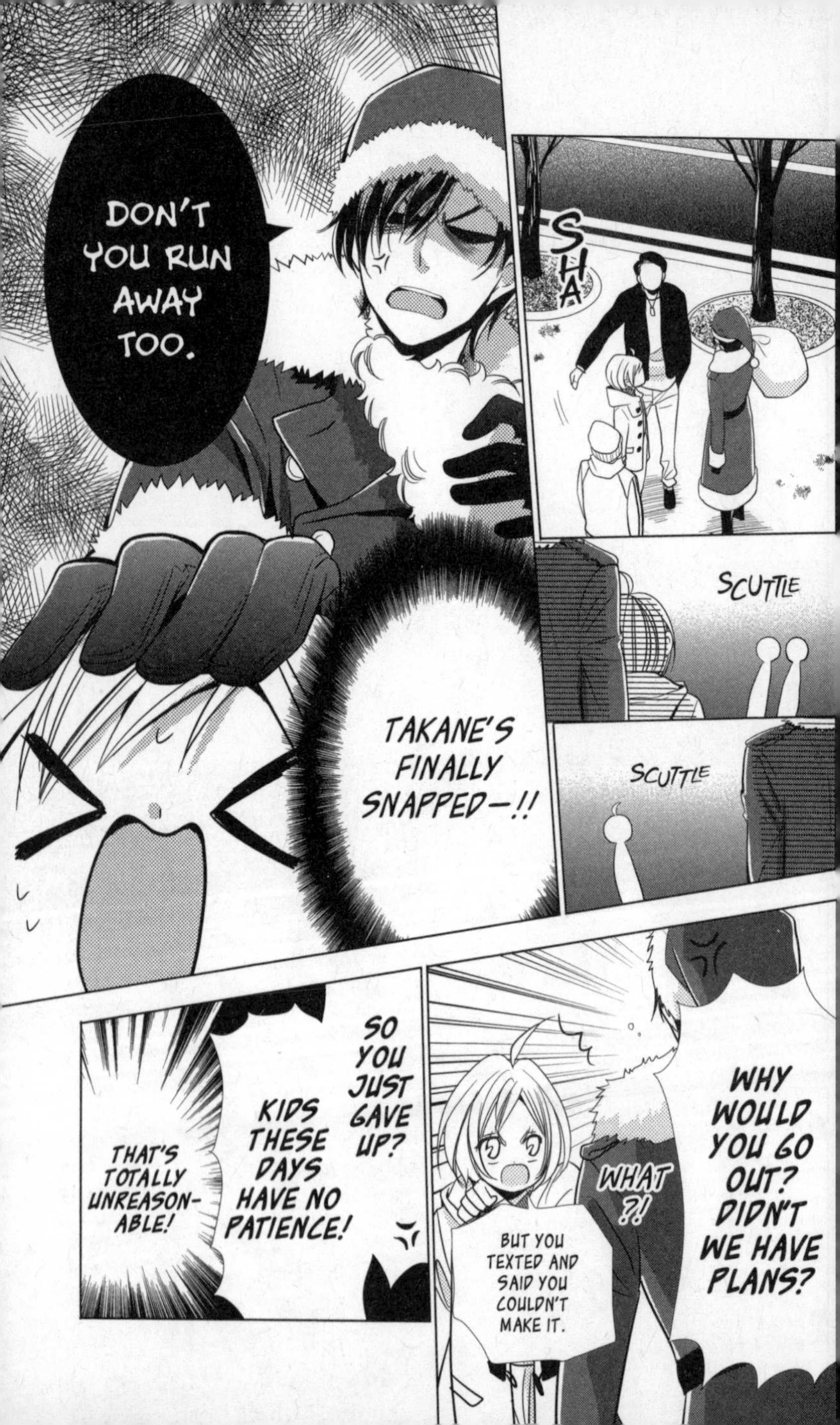
SHA
SCUTTLE
SCUTTLE
DON'T YOU RUN AWAY TOO.
TAKANE'S FINALLY SNAPPED—!!
WHY WOULD YOU GO OUT? DIDN'T WE HAVE PLANS?
WHAT?!
BUT YOU TEXTED AND SAID YOU COULDN'T MAKE IT.
SO YOU JUST GAVE UP?
KIDS THESE DAYS HAVE NO PATIENCE!
THAT'S TOTALLY UNREASONABLE!

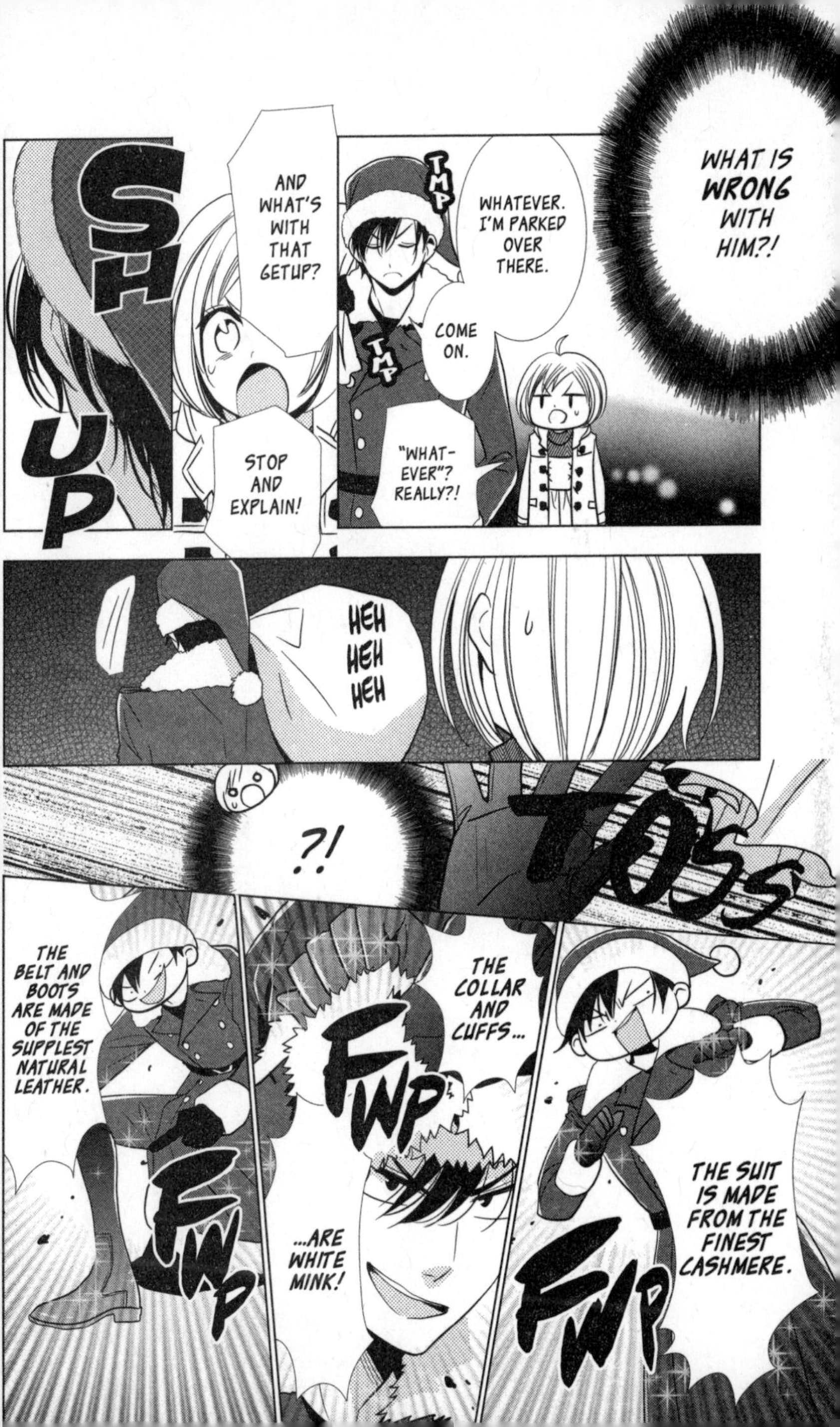
WHAT IS **WRONG** WITH HIM?!
WHATEVER. I'M PARKED OVER THERE.
TMP
COME ON.
TMP
"WHAT-EVER"? REALLY?!
AND WHAT'S WITH THAT GETUP?
STOP AND EXPLAIN!
SHUP
HEH HEH HEH
TOSS
?!
THE SUIT IS MADE FROM THE FINEST CASHMERE.
FWP
THE COLLAR AND CUFFS...
FWP
...ARE WHITE MINK!
THE BELT AND BOOTS ARE MADE OF THE SUPPLEST NATURAL LEATHER.
FWP

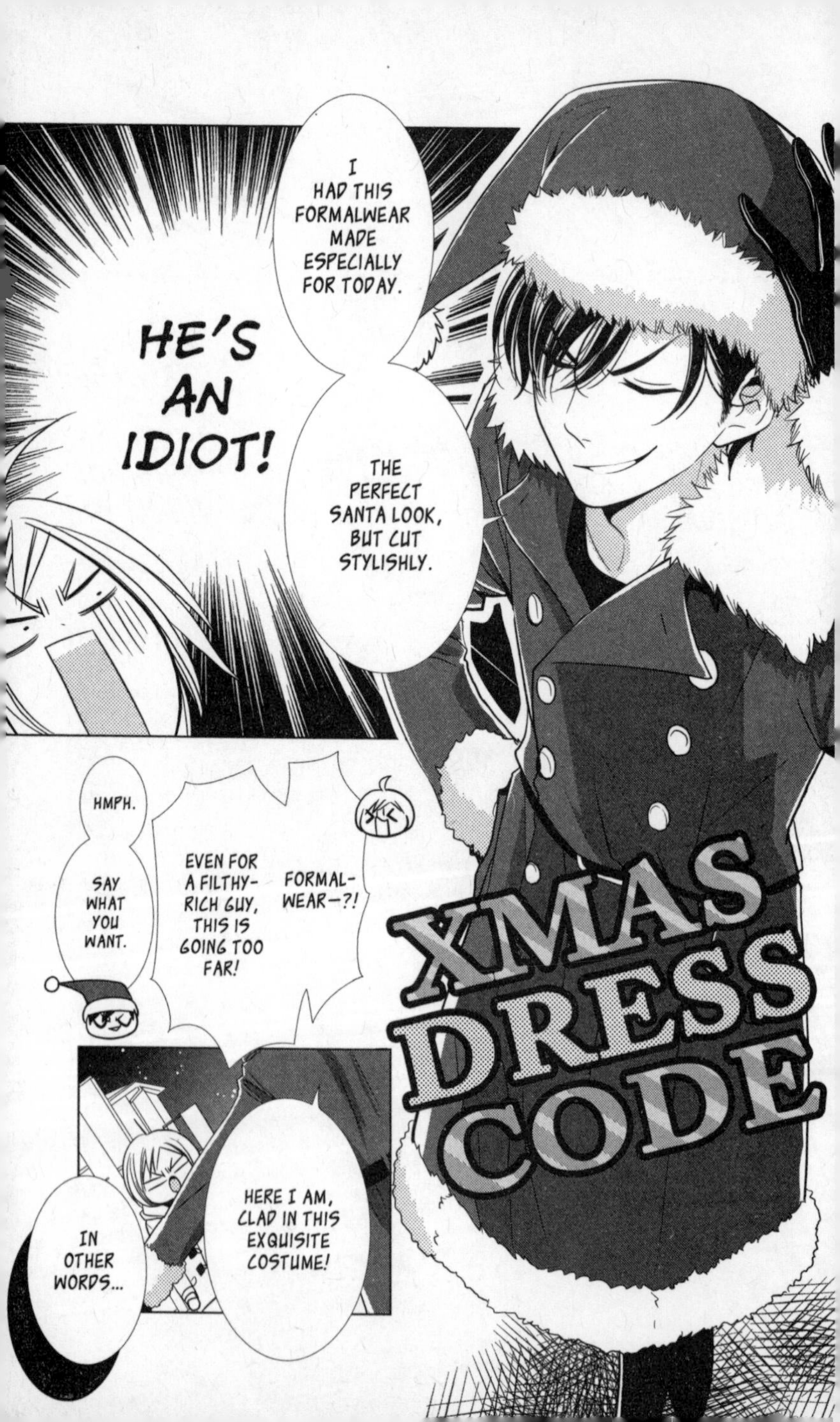
XMAS DRESS CODE
I HAD THIS FORMALWEAR MADE ESPECIALLY FOR TODAY.
THE PERFECT SANTA LOOK, BUT CUT STYLISHLY.
HE'S AN IDIOT!
FORMAL-WEAR—?!
EVEN FOR A FILTHY-RICH GUY, THIS IS GOING TOO FAR!
HMPH.
SAY WHAT YOU WANT.
HERE I AM, CLAD IN THIS EXQUISITE COSTUME!
IN OTHER WORDS...

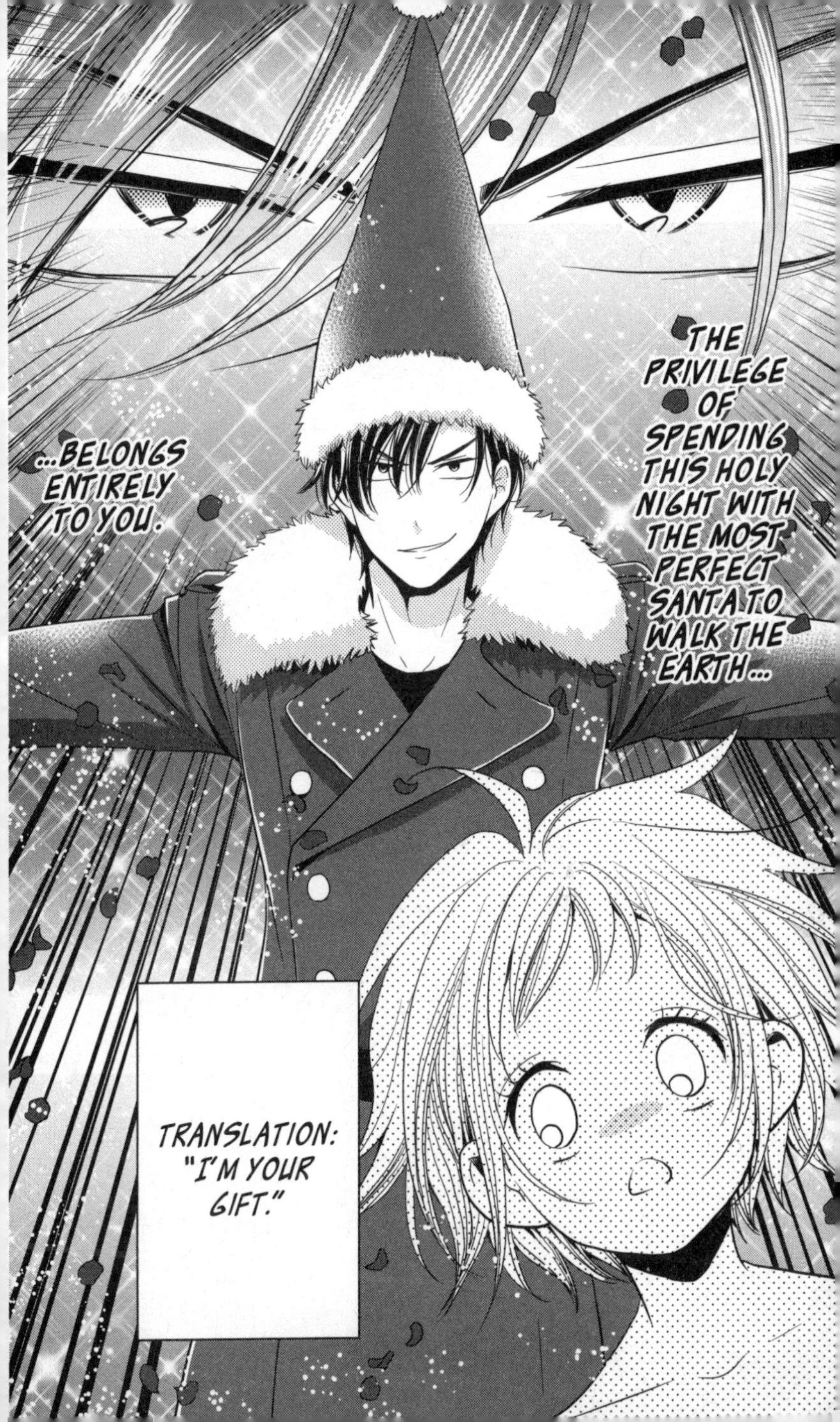
THE PRIVILEGE OF SPENDING THIS HOLY NIGHT WITH THE MOST PERFECT SANTA TO WALK THE EARTH...
...BELONGS ENTIRELY TO YOU.
TRANSLATION: "I'M YOUR GIFT."

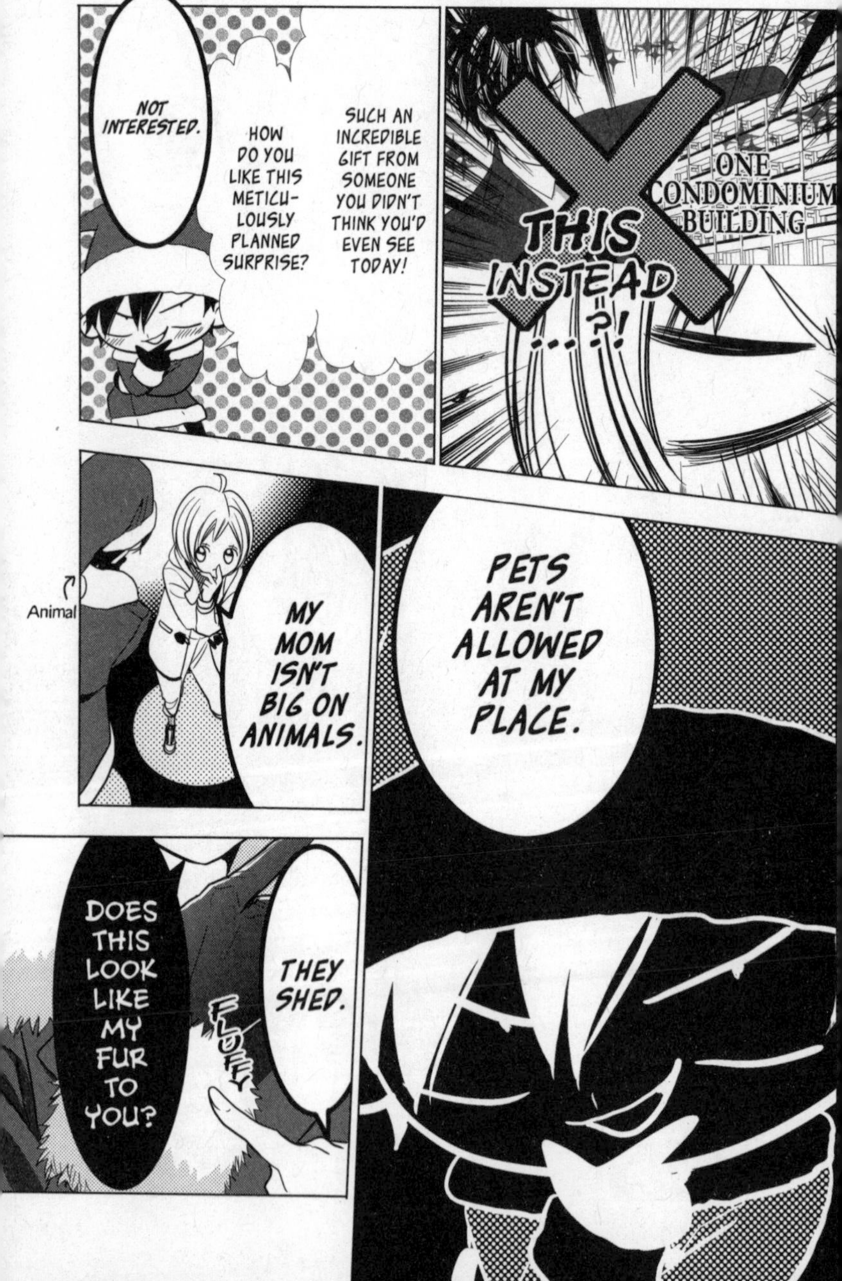
ONE CONDOMINIUM BUILDING
THIS INSTEAD
...?!
SUCH AN INCREDIBLE GIFT FROM SOMEONE YOU DIDN'T THINK YOU'D EVEN SEE TODAY!
HOW DO YOU LIKE THIS METICULOUSLY PLANNED SURPRISE?
NOT INTERESTED.
PETS AREN'T ALLOWED AT MY PLACE.
MY MOM ISN'T BIG ON ANIMALS.
Animal
THEY SHED.
FLUFFY
DOES THIS LOOK LIKE MY FUR TO YOU?

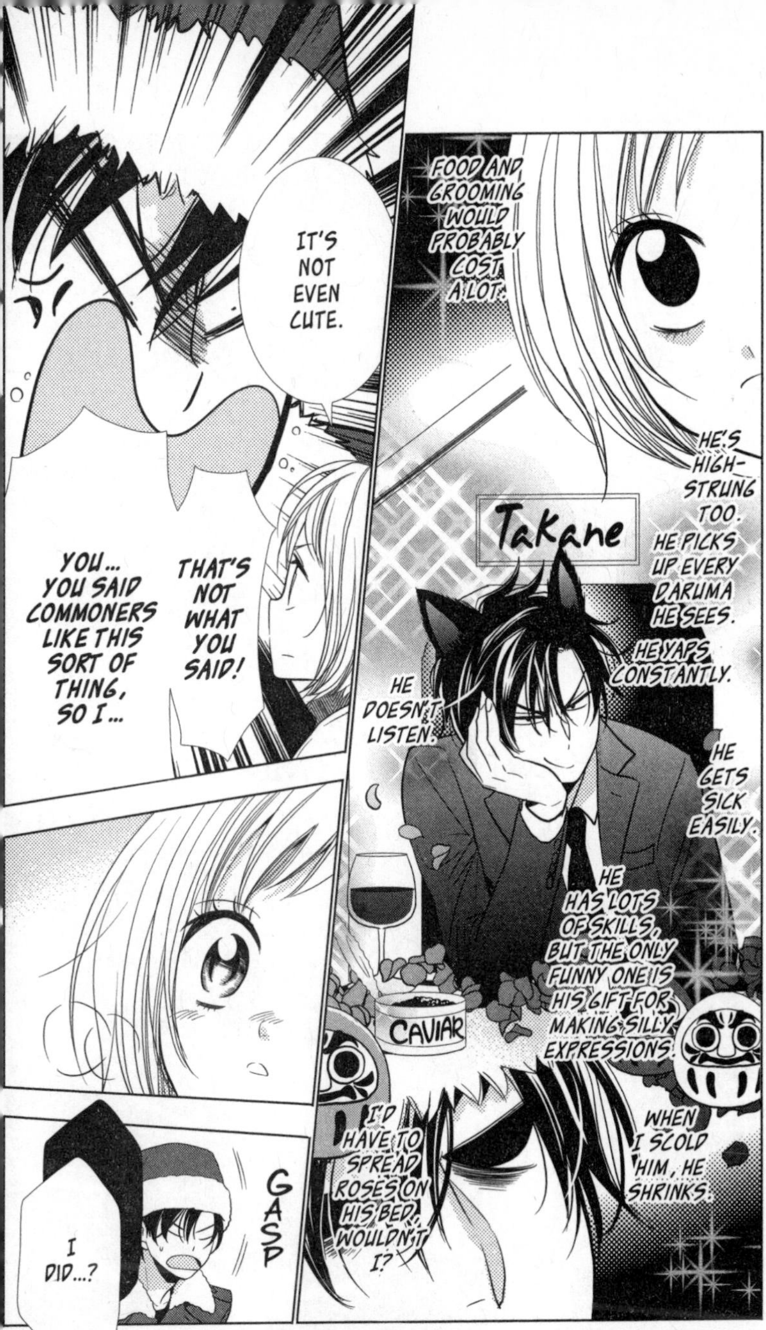
FOOD AND GROOMING WOULD PROBABLY COST A LOT.
HE'S HIGH-STRUNG TOO.
HE PICKS UP EVERY DARUMA HE SEES.
Takane
HE YAPS CONSTANTLY.
HE DOESN'T LISTEN.
HE GETS SICK EASILY.
HE HAS LOTS OF SKILLS, BUT THE ONLY FUNNY ONE IS HIS GIFT FOR MAKING SILLY EXPRESSIONS.
CAVIAR
WHEN I SCOLD HIM, HE SHRINKS.
I'D HAVE TO SPREAD ROSES ON HIS BED, WOULDN'T I?
IT'S NOT EVEN CUTE.
THAT'S NOT WHAT YOU SAID!
YOU... YOU SAID COMMONERS LIKE THIS SORT OF THING, SO I...
GASP
I DID...?

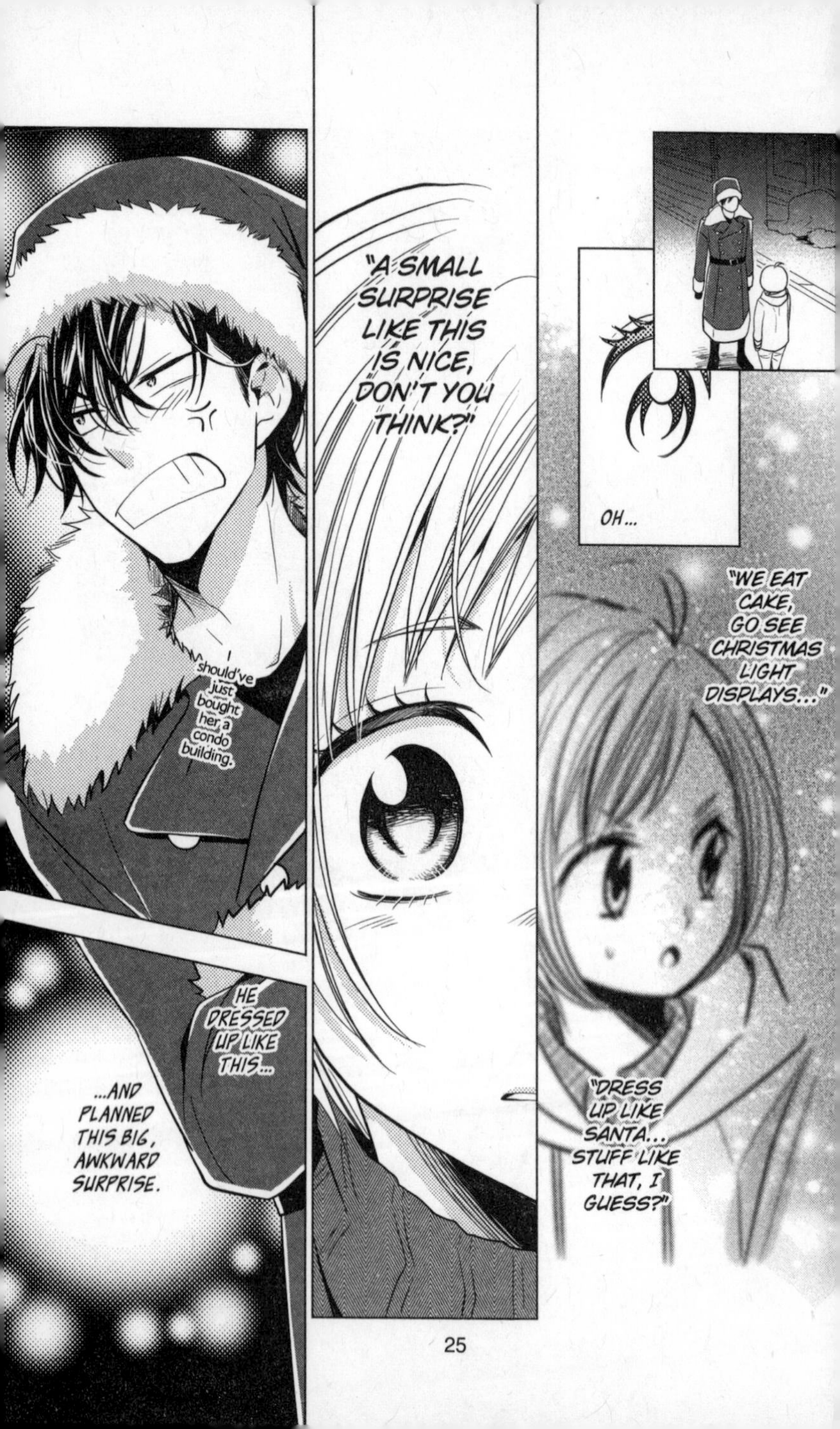
OH...
"WE EAT CAKE, GO SEE CHRISTMAS LIGHT DISPLAYS..."
"DRESS UP LIKE SANTA... STUFF LIKE THAT, I GUESS?"
"A SMALL SURPRISE LIKE THIS IS NICE, DON'T YOU THINK?"
I should've just bought her a condo building.
HE DRESSED UP LIKE THIS...
...AND PLANNED THIS BIG, AWKWARD SURPRISE.

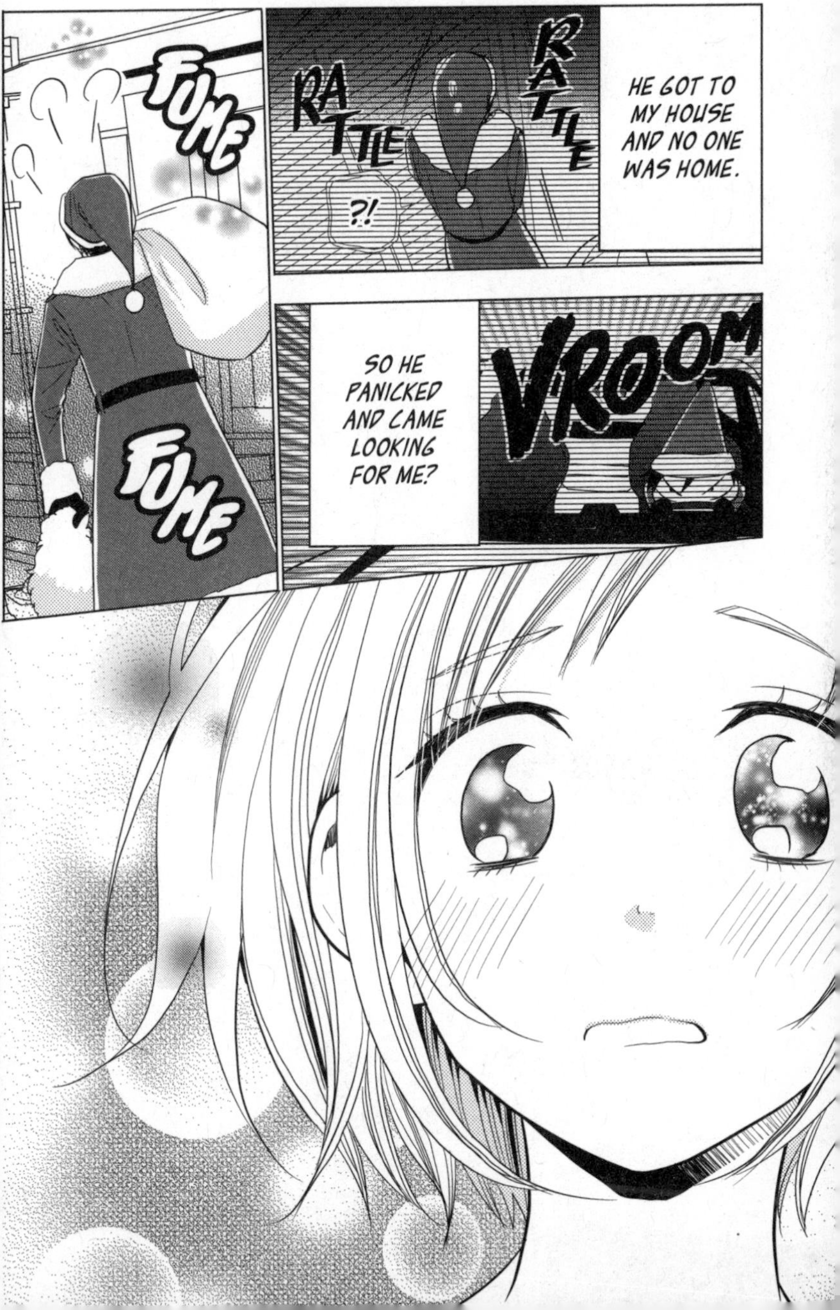
HE GOT TO MY HOUSE AND NO ONE WAS HOME.
RATTLE
RATTLE
?!
VROOM
SO HE PANICKED AND CAME LOOKING FOR ME?
FUME
FUME

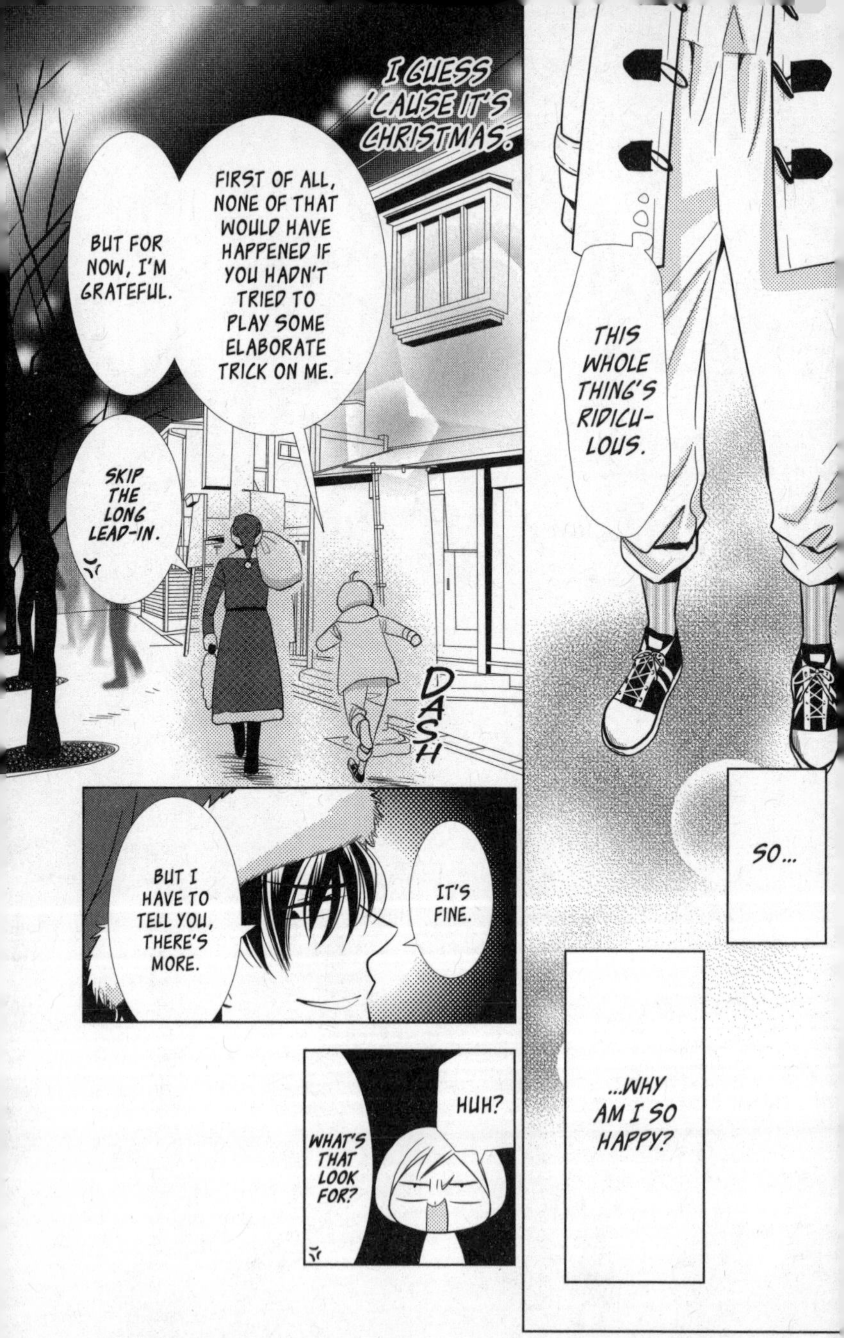
THIS WHOLE THING'S RIDICU-LOUS.
SO...
...WHY AM I SO HAPPY?
I GUESS 'CAUSE IT'S CHRISTMAS.
FIRST OF ALL, NONE OF THAT WOULD HAVE HAPPENED IF YOU HADN'T TRIED TO PLAY SOME ELABORATE TRICK ON ME.
BUT FOR NOW, I'M GRATEFUL.
SKIP THE LONG LEAD-IN.
DASH
IT'S FINE.
BUT I HAVE TO TELL YOU, THERE'S MORE.
HUH?
WHAT'S THAT LOOK FOR?

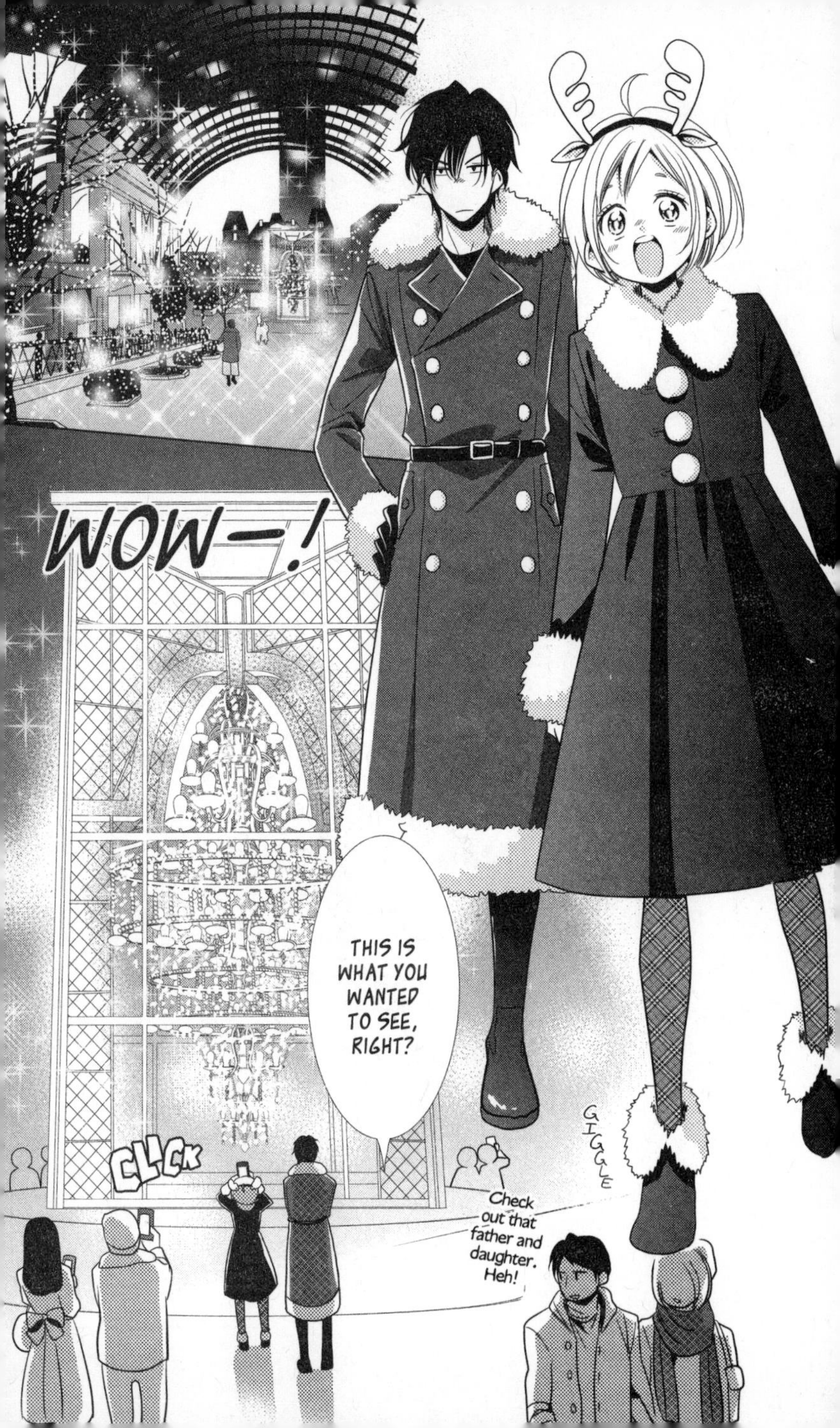
WOW—!
THIS IS WHAT YOU WANTED TO SEE, RIGHT?
GIGGLE
Check out that father and daughter. Heh!
CLICK

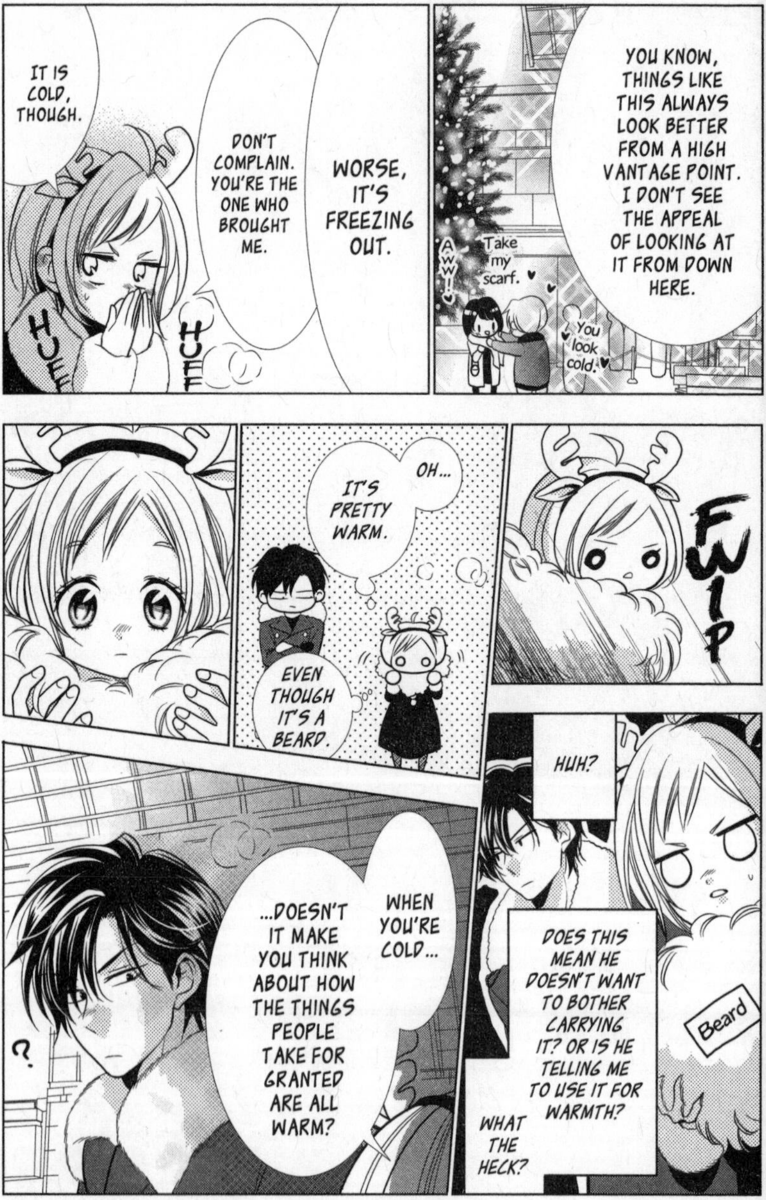
YOU KNOW, THINGS LIKE THIS ALWAYS LOOK BETTER FROM A HIGH VANTAGE POINT. I DON'T SEE THE APPEAL OF LOOKING AT IT FROM DOWN HERE.
Take my scarf.
Aww!
You look cold.
WORSE, IT'S FREEZING OUT.
DON'T COMPLAIN. YOU'RE THE ONE WHO BROUGHT ME.
IT IS COLD, THOUGH.
HUFF
HUFF
FWIP
OH...
IT'S PRETTY WARM.
EVEN THOUGH IT'S A BEARD.
HUH?
DOES THIS MEAN HE DOESN'T WANT TO BOTHER CARRYING IT? OR IS HE TELLING ME TO USE IT FOR WARMTH?
WHAT THE HECK?
Beard
WHEN YOU'RE COLD...
...DOESN'T IT MAKE YOU THINK ABOUT HOW THE THINGS PEOPLE TAKE FOR GRANTED ARE ALL WARM?
?

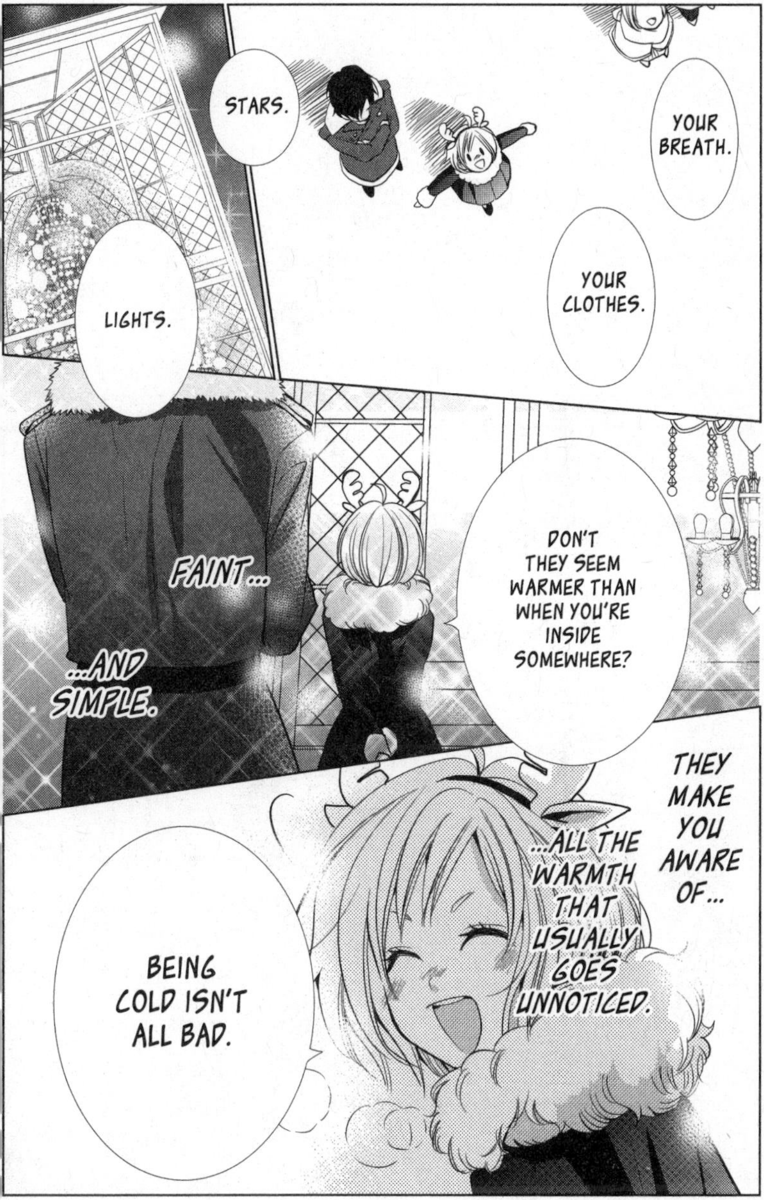
YOUR BREATH.
YOUR CLOTHES.
STARS.
LIGHTS.
DON'T THEY SEEM WARMER THAN WHEN YOU'RE INSIDE SOMEWHERE?
FAINT...
...AND SIMPLE.
THEY MAKE YOU AWARE OF...
...ALL THE WARMTH THAT USUALLY GOES UNNOTICED.
BEING COLD ISN'T ALL BAD.

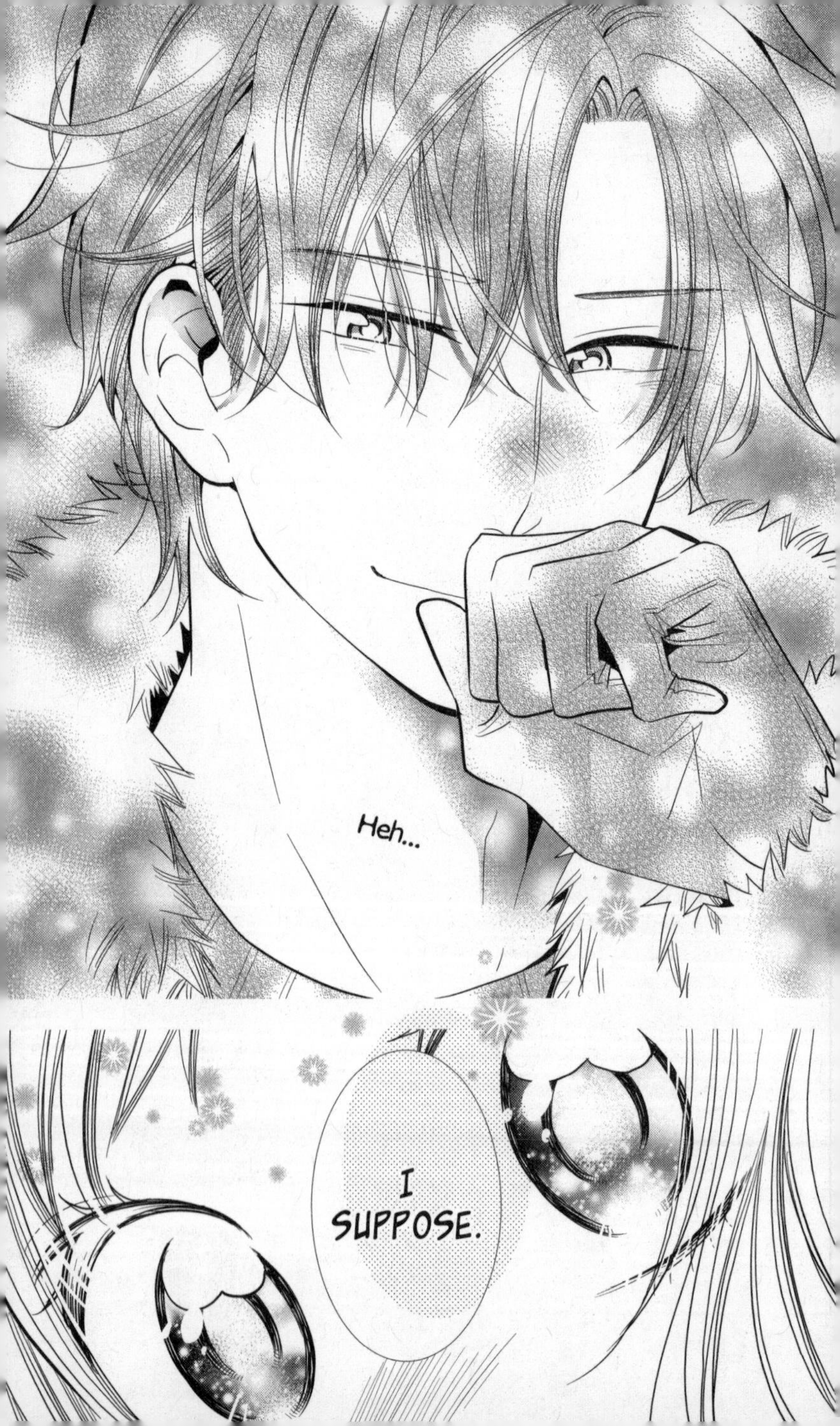
Heh...
I SUPPOSE.

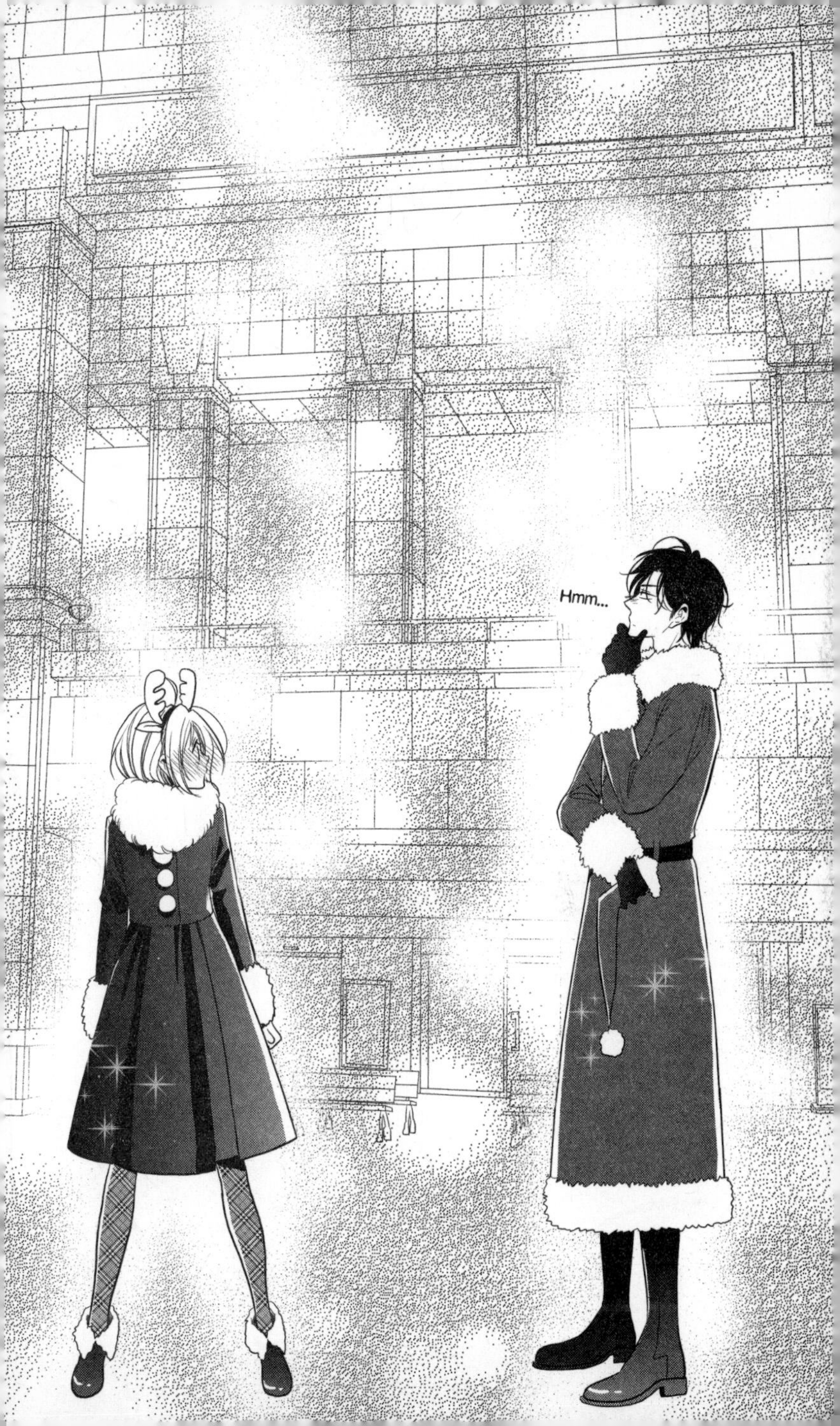
Hmm...

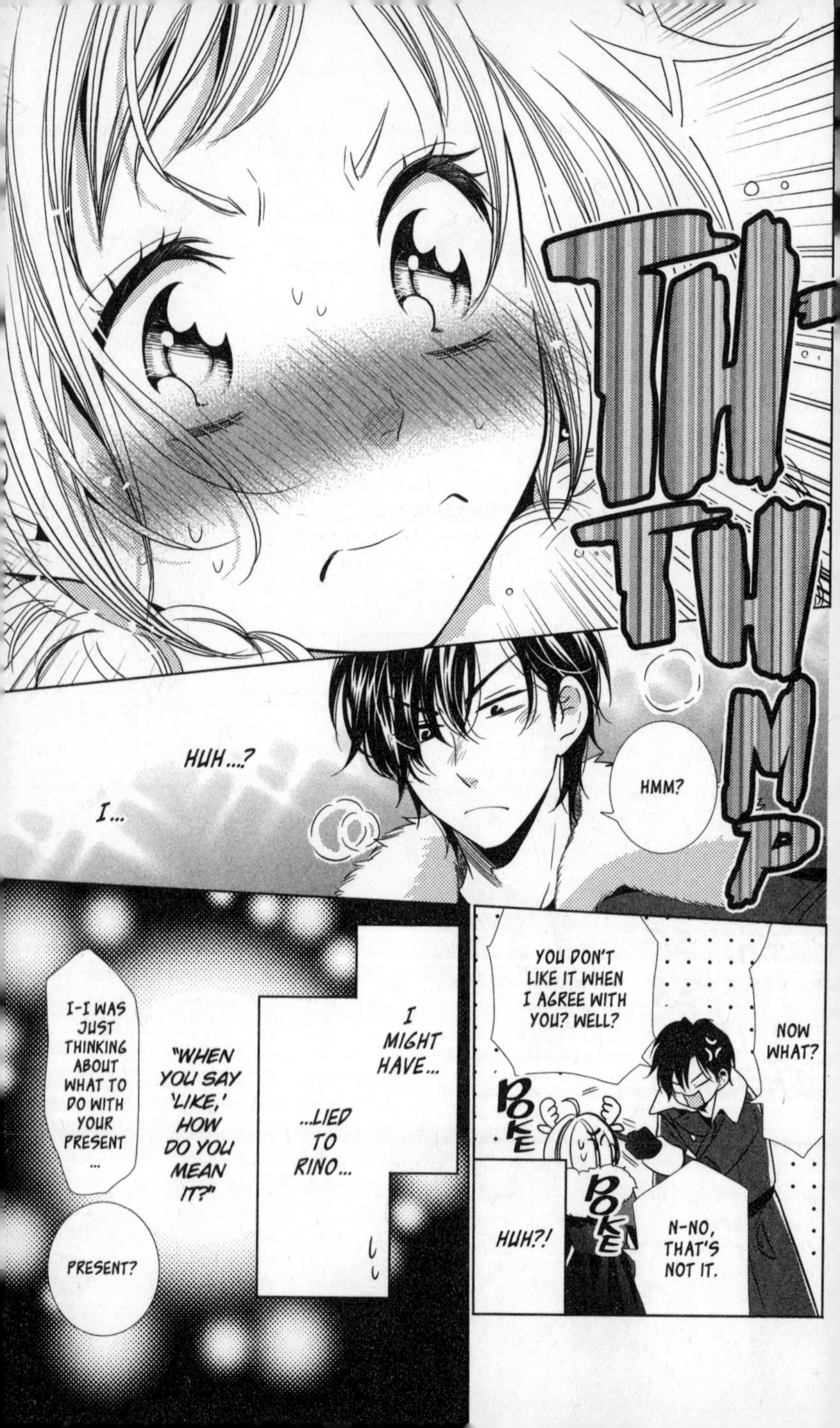
TH-THMP
HMM?
HUH...?
I...
NOW WHAT?
YOU DON'T LIKE IT WHEN I AGREE WITH YOU? WELL?
POKE
POKE
HUH?!
N-NO, THAT'S NOT IT.
I MIGHT HAVE...
...LIED TO RINO...
"WHEN YOU SAY 'LIKE,' HOW DO YOU MEAN IT?"
I-I WAS JUST THINKING ABOUT WHAT TO DO WITH YOUR PRESENT...
PRESENT?

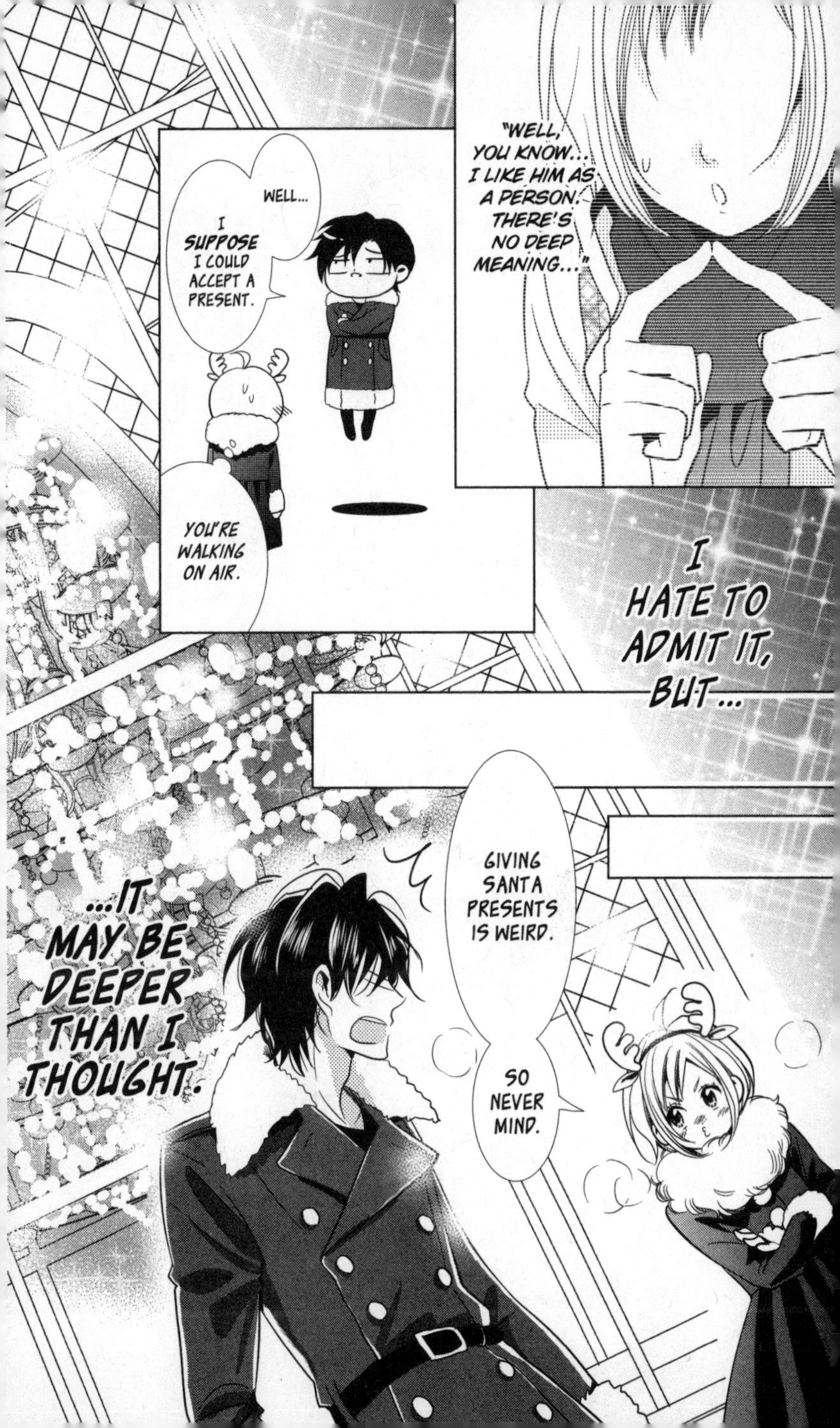
"WELL, YOU KNOW... I LIKE HIM AS A PERSON. THERE'S NO DEEP MEANING..."
WELL...
I SUPPOSE I COULD ACCEPT A PRESENT.
YOU'RE WALKING ON AIR.
I HATE TO ADMIT IT, BUT...
GIVING SANTA PRESENTS IS WEIRD.
SO NEVER MIND.
...IT MAY BE DEEPER THAN I THOUGHT.

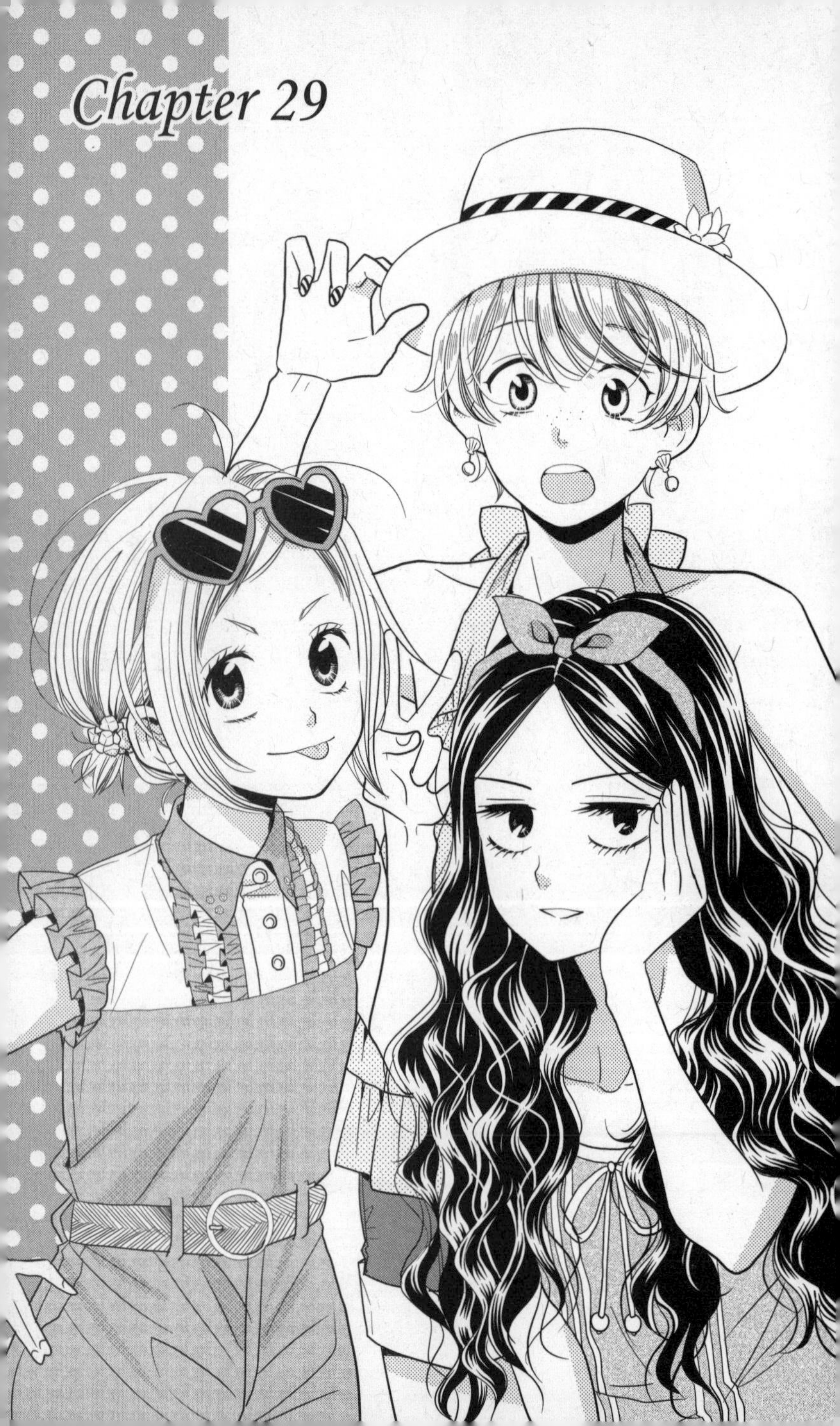
Chapter 29

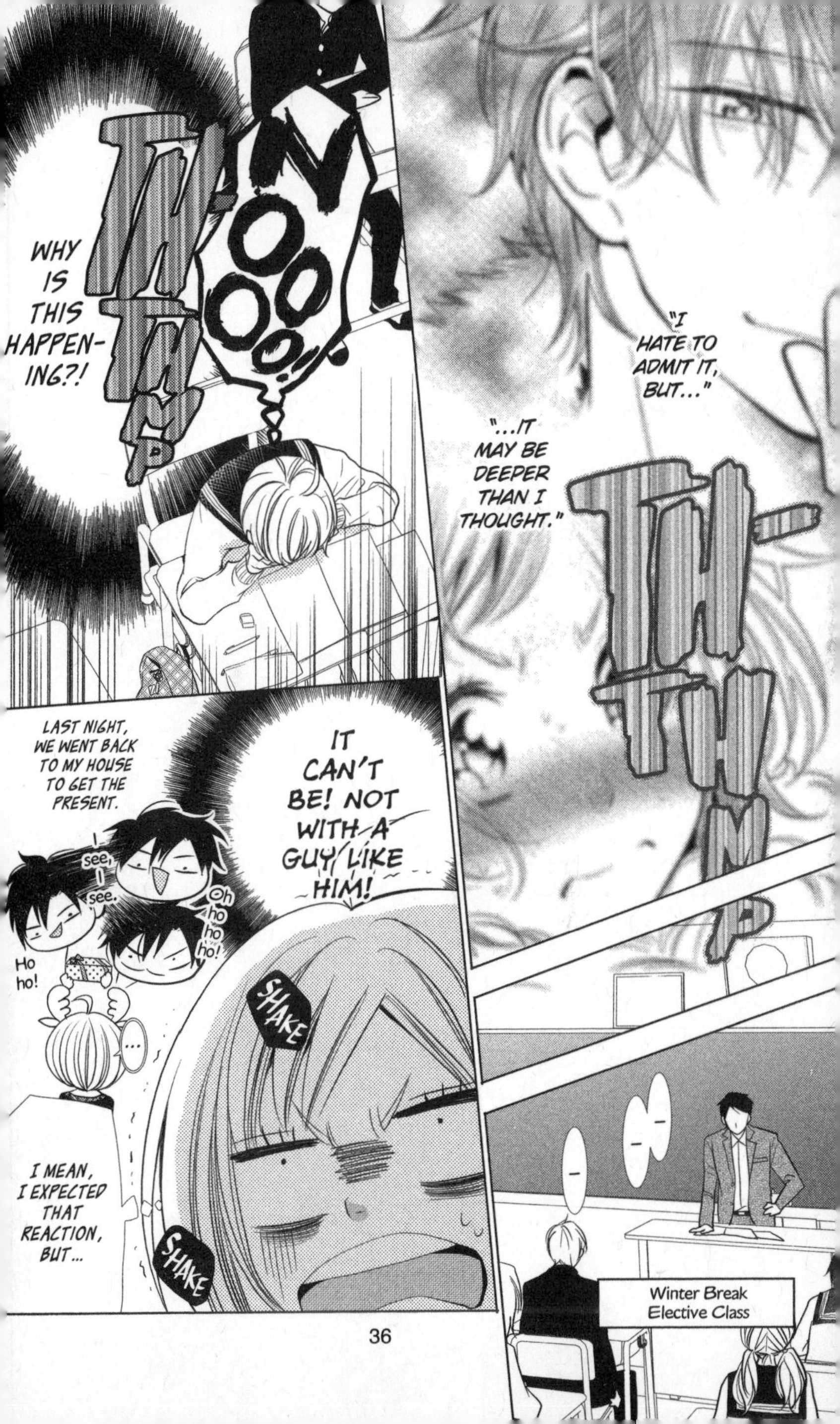
"I HATE TO ADMIT IT, BUT..."
"...IT MAY BE DEEPER THAN I THOUGHT."
THUMP
Winter Break Elective Class
—
—
—
WHOOOOO!
THUMP
WHY IS THIS HAPPEN-ING?!
IT CAN'T BE! NOT WITH A GUY LIKE HIM!
LAST NIGHT, WE WENT BACK TO MY HOUSE TO GET THE PRESENT.
I see, I see.
Oh ho ho ho!
Ho ho!
...
SHAKE
SHAKE
I MEAN, I EXPECTED THAT REACTION, BUT...

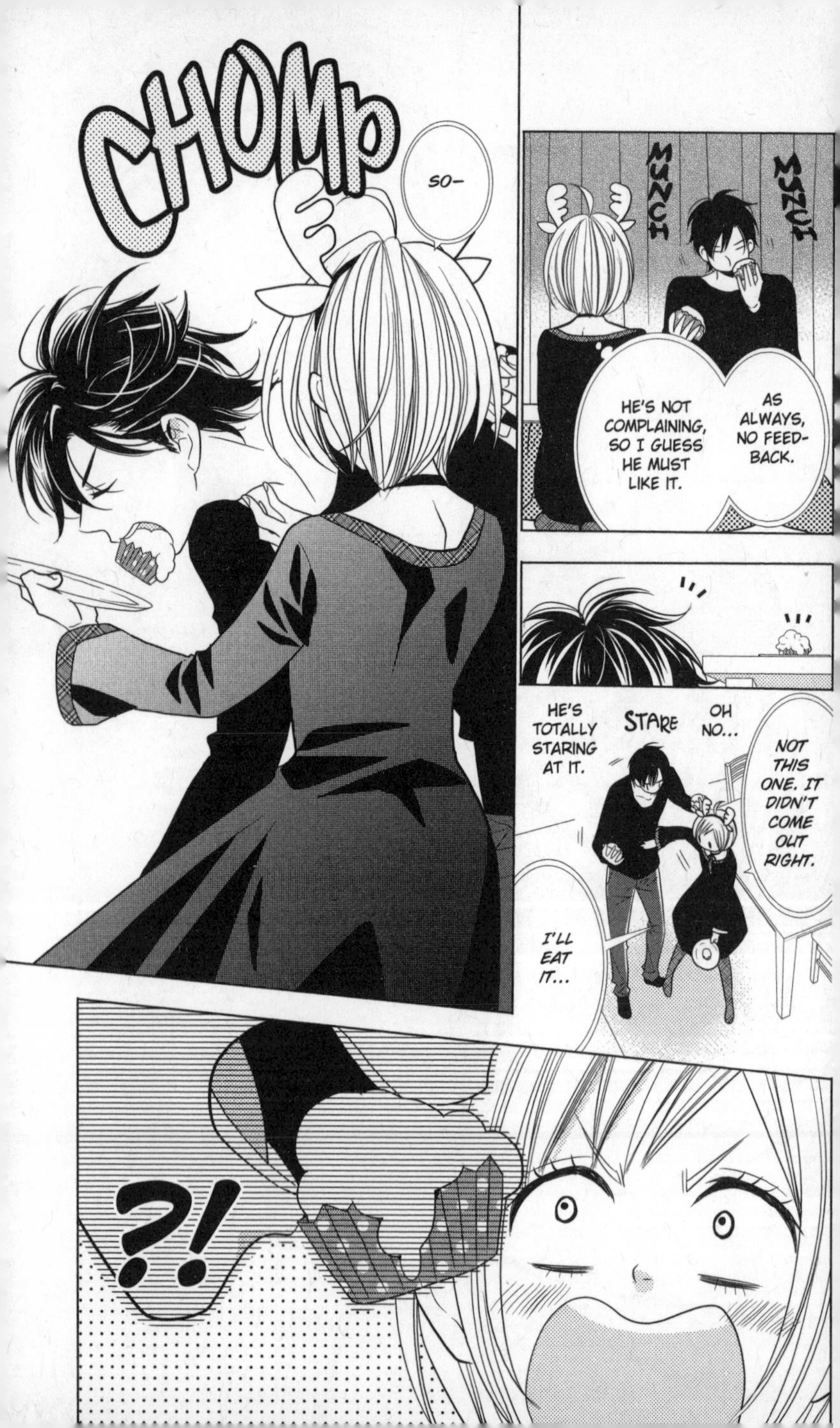

MUNCH
MUNCH
AS ALWAYS, NO FEED-BACK.
HE'S NOT COMPLAINING, SO I GUESS HE MUST LIKE IT.
NOT THIS ONE. IT DIDN'T COME OUT RIGHT.
OH NO...
STARE
HE'S TOTALLY STARING AT IT.
I'LL EAT IT...
SO–
CHOMP
?!

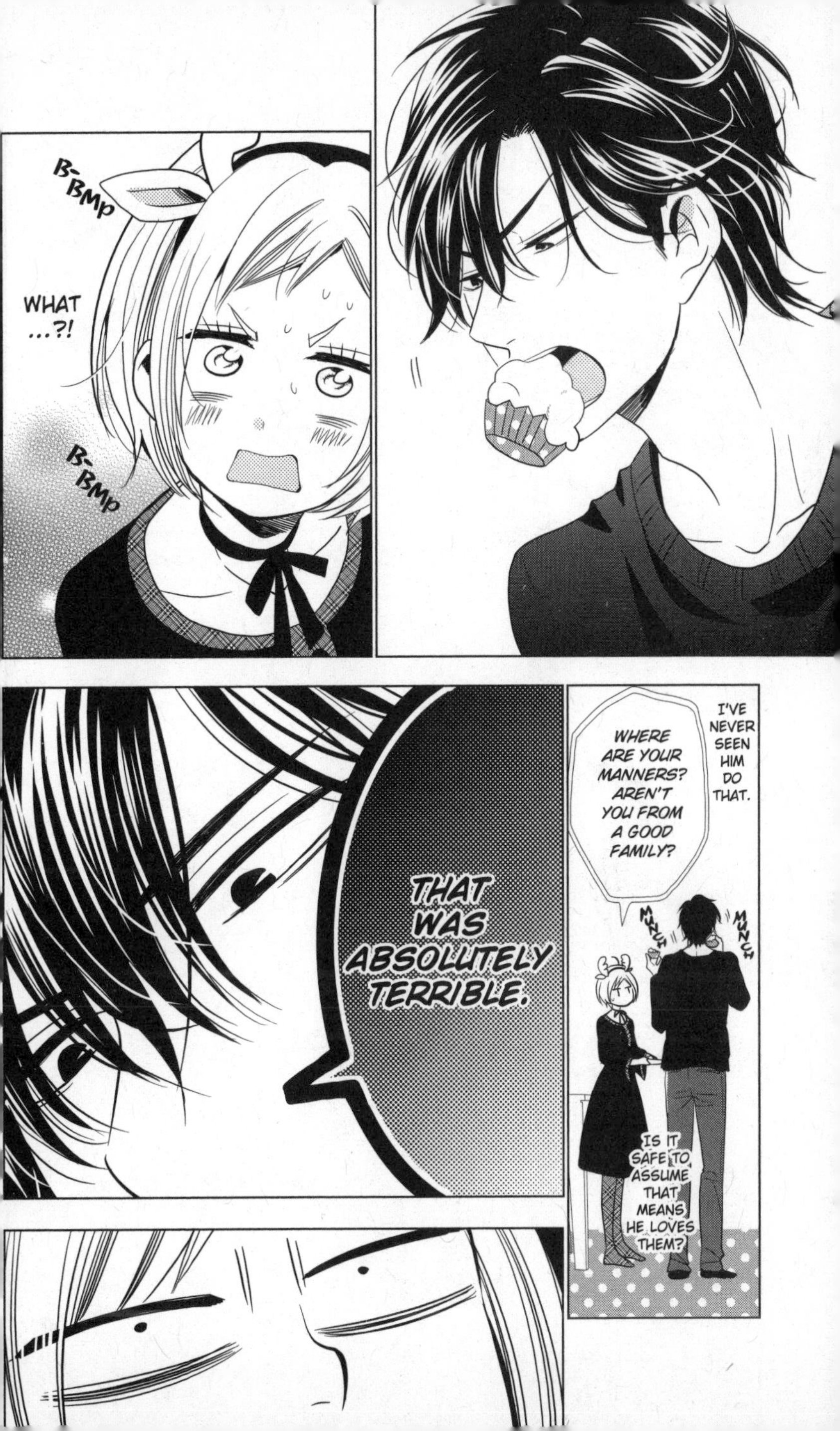
B-BMP
WHAT ...?!
B-BMP
I'VE NEVER SEEN HIM DO THAT.
WHERE ARE YOUR MANNERS? AREN'T YOU FROM A GOOD FAMILY?
MUNCH
MUNCH
IS IT SAFE TO ASSUME THAT MEANS HE LOVES THEM?
THAT WAS ABSOLUTELY TERRIBLE.

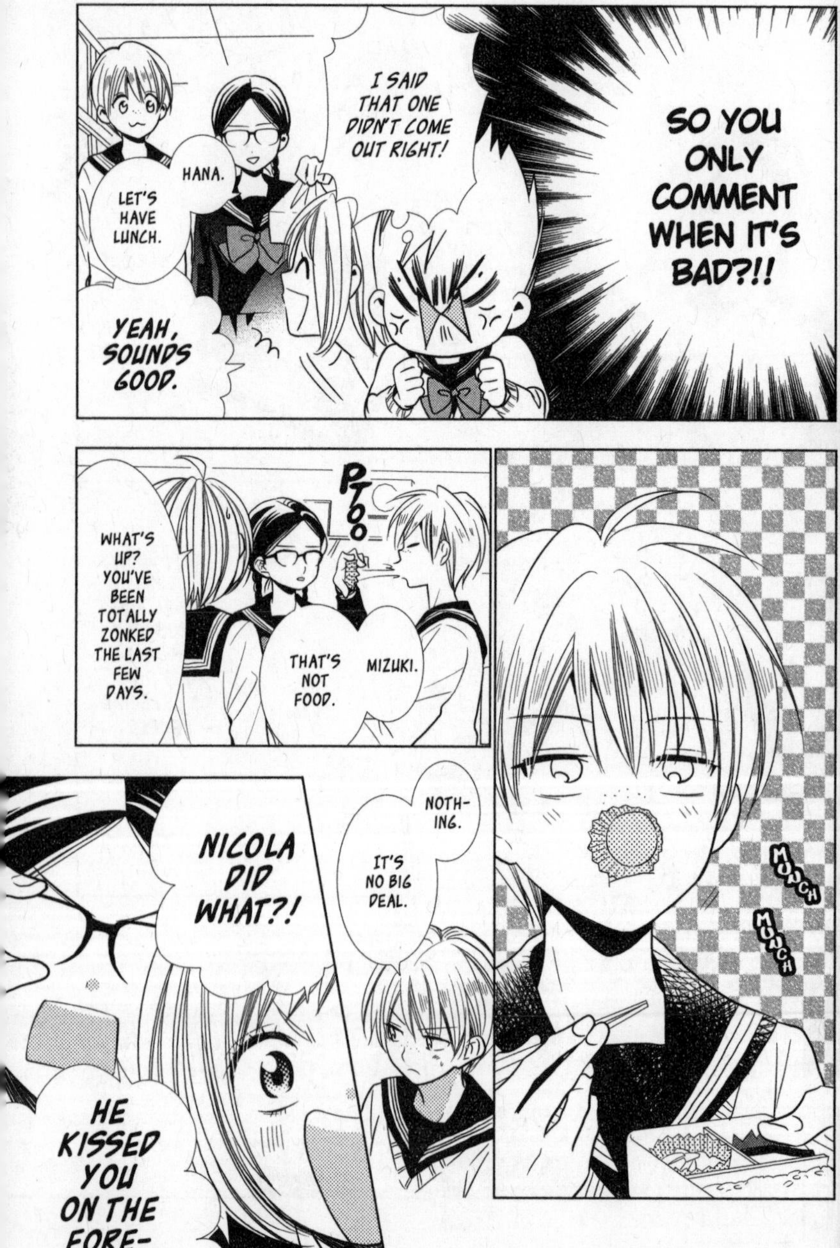
SO YOU ONLY COMMENT WHEN IT'S BAD?!!
I SAID THAT ONE DIDN'T COME OUT RIGHT!
HANA.
LET'S HAVE LUNCH.
YEAH, SOUNDS GOOD.
MUNCH
MUNCH
PTOO
MIZUKI.
THAT'S NOT FOOD.
WHAT'S UP? YOU'VE BEEN TOTALLY ZONKED THE LAST FEW DAYS.
NOTHING.
IT'S NO BIG DEAL.
NICOLA DID WHAT?!
HE KISSED YOU ON THE FOREHEAD?!

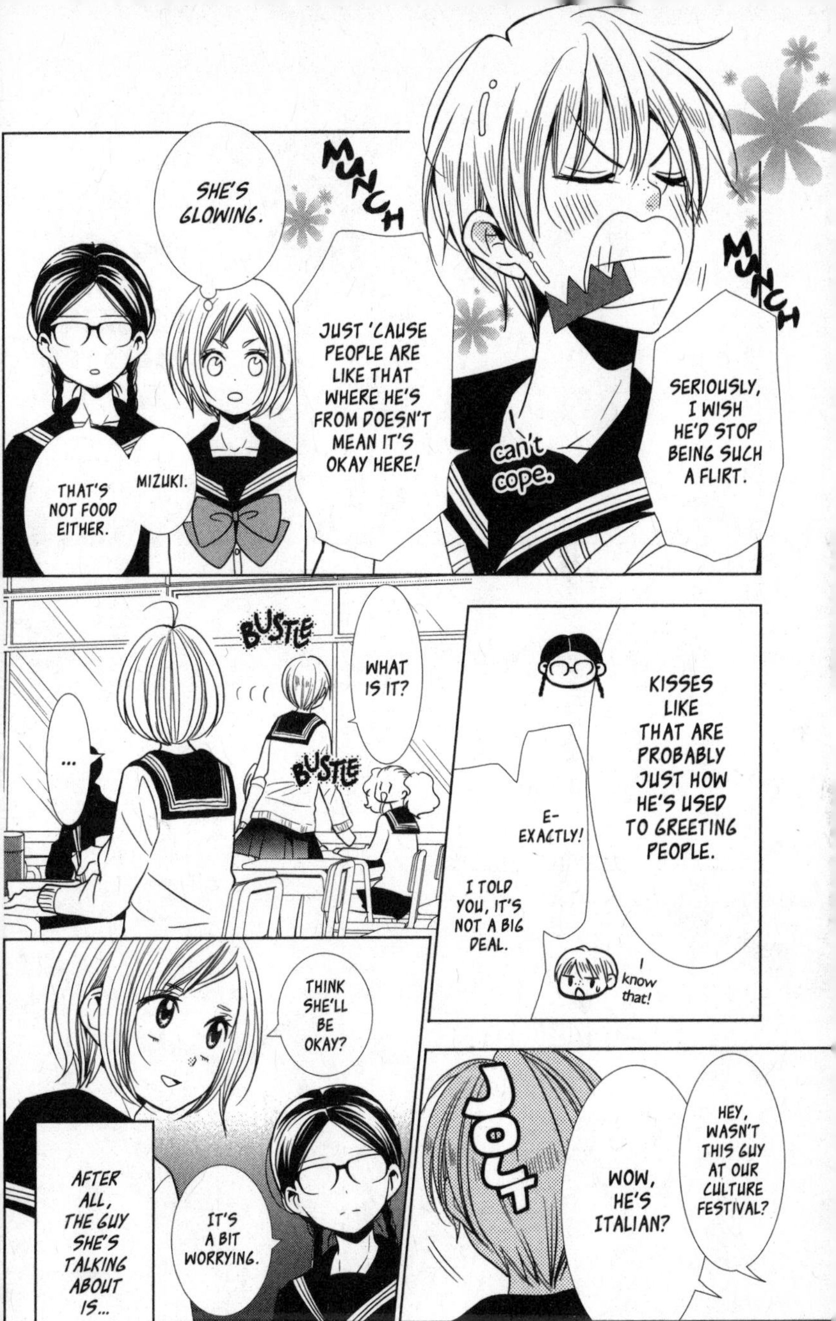
MUNCH
SERIOUSLY, I WISH HE'D STOP BEING SUCH A FLIRT.
I can't cope.
MUNCH
JUST 'CAUSE PEOPLE ARE LIKE THAT WHERE HE'S FROM DOESN'T MEAN IT'S OKAY HERE!
SHE'S GLOWING.
MIZUKI.
THAT'S NOT FOOD EITHER.
KISSES LIKE THAT ARE PROBABLY JUST HOW HE'S USED TO GREETING PEOPLE.
E-EXACTLY!
I TOLD YOU, IT'S NOT A BIG DEAL.
I know that!
BUSTLE
WHAT IS IT?
BUSTLE
...
HEY, WASN'T THIS GUY AT OUR CULTURE FESTIVAL?
WOW, HE'S ITALIAN?
JOLT
THINK SHE'LL BE OKAY?
IT'S A BIT WORRYING.
AFTER ALL, THE GUY SHE'S TALKING ABOUT IS...

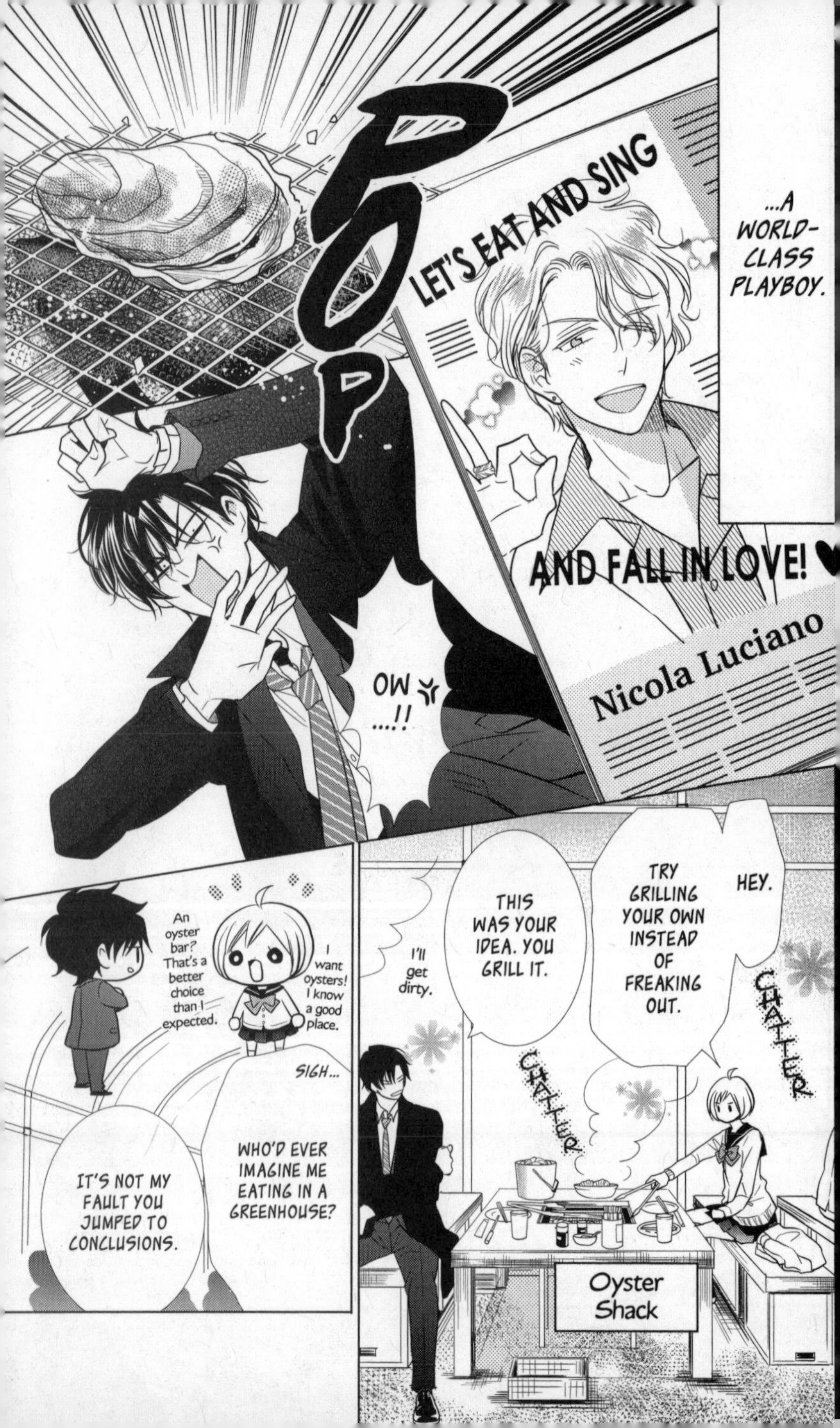
...A WORLD-CLASS PLAYBOY.
LET'S EAT AND SING
AND FALL IN LOVE! ♥
Nicola Luciano
POP
OW ...!!
HEY.
TRY GRILLING YOUR OWN INSTEAD OF FREAKING OUT.
THIS WAS YOUR IDEA. YOU GRILL IT.
I'll get dirty.
CHATTER
CHATTER
Oyster Shack
I want oysters! I know a good place.
An oyster bar? That's a better choice than I expected.
SIGH...
WHO'D EVER IMAGINE ME EATING IN A GREENHOUSE?
IT'S NOT MY FAULT YOU JUMPED TO CONCLUSIONS.

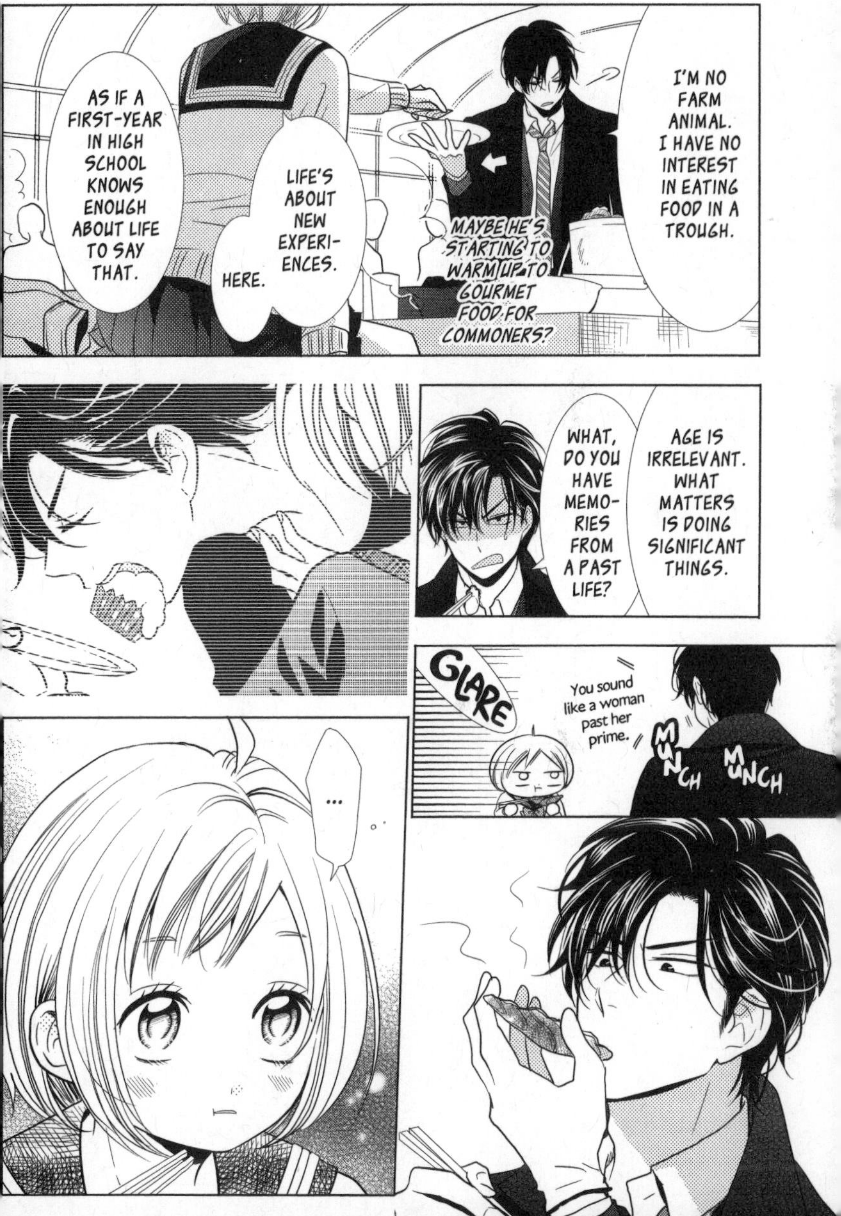
I'M NO FARM ANIMAL. I HAVE NO INTEREST IN EATING FOOD IN A TROUGH.
MAYBE HE'S STARTING TO WARM UP TO GOURMET FOOD FOR COMMONERS?
LIFE'S ABOUT NEW EXPERIENCES.
HERE.
AS IF A FIRST-YEAR IN HIGH SCHOOL KNOWS ENOUGH ABOUT LIFE TO SAY THAT.
AGE IS IRRELEVANT. WHAT MATTERS IS DOING SIGNIFICANT THINGS.
WHAT, DO YOU HAVE MEMORIES FROM A PAST LIFE?
MUNCH MUNCH
You sound like a woman past her prime.
GLARE
...

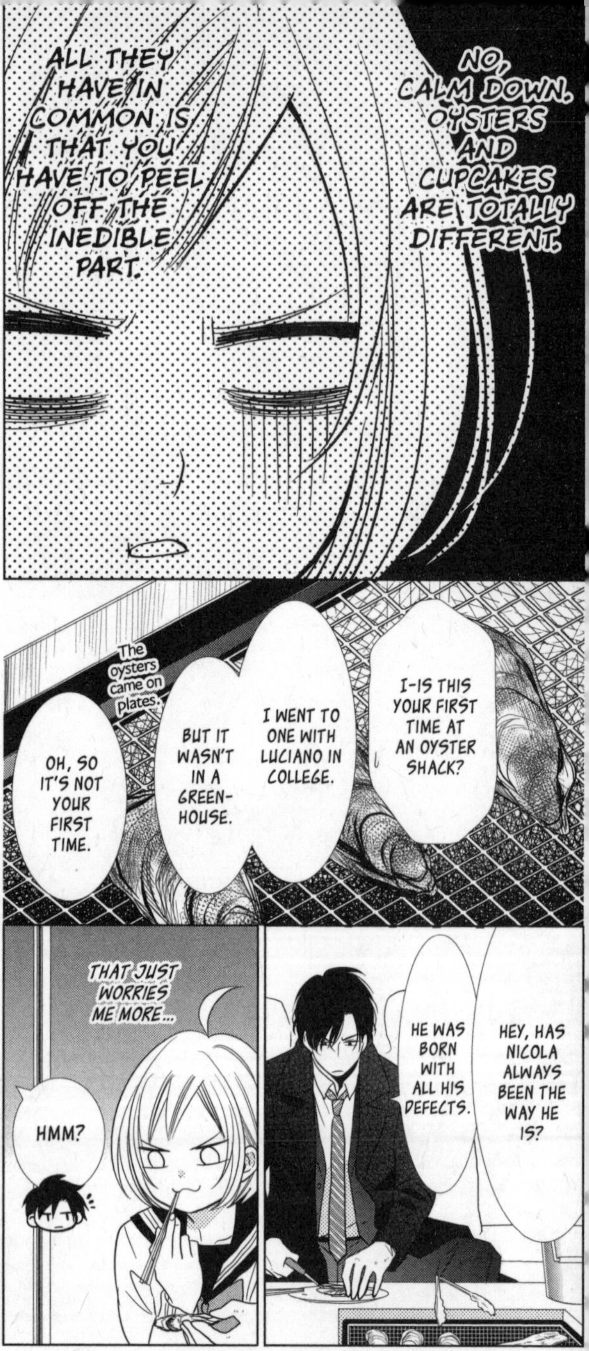
NO, CALM DOWN. OYSTERS AND CUPCAKES ARE TOTALLY DIFFERENT.
ALL THEY HAVE IN COMMON IS THAT YOU HAVE TO PEEL OFF THE INEDIBLE PART.
I-IS THIS YOUR FIRST TIME AT AN OYSTER SHACK?
I WENT TO ONE WITH LUCIANO IN COLLEGE.
BUT IT WASN'T IN A GREENHOUSE.
The oysters came on plates.
OH, SO IT'S NOT YOUR FIRST TIME.
HEY, HAS NICOLA ALWAYS BEEN THE WAY HE IS?
HE WAS BORN WITH ALL HIS DEFECTS.
THAT JUST WORRIES ME MORE...
HMM?

• Shigeru Nonomura •

Hana's father made his first appearance in the same panel in chapter 1 that introduced her.

In my initial rough draft, I drew him as a kind but weak father. He looked like this. But considering Hana's personality and her neuroses, I started thinking it'd be better if he was more unpleasant, so he wound up like this.

He's not a bad guy, though. He's just timid. His attitude changes to reflect who he's talking to, even with his children. Yukari's all smiles, so he always smiles at her, but since Hana's more sassy and glib, he acts facetious with her.

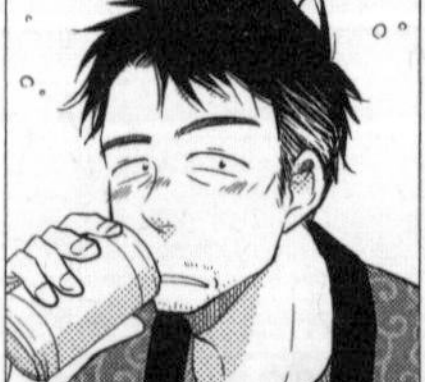

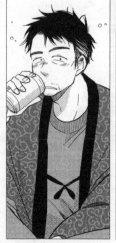

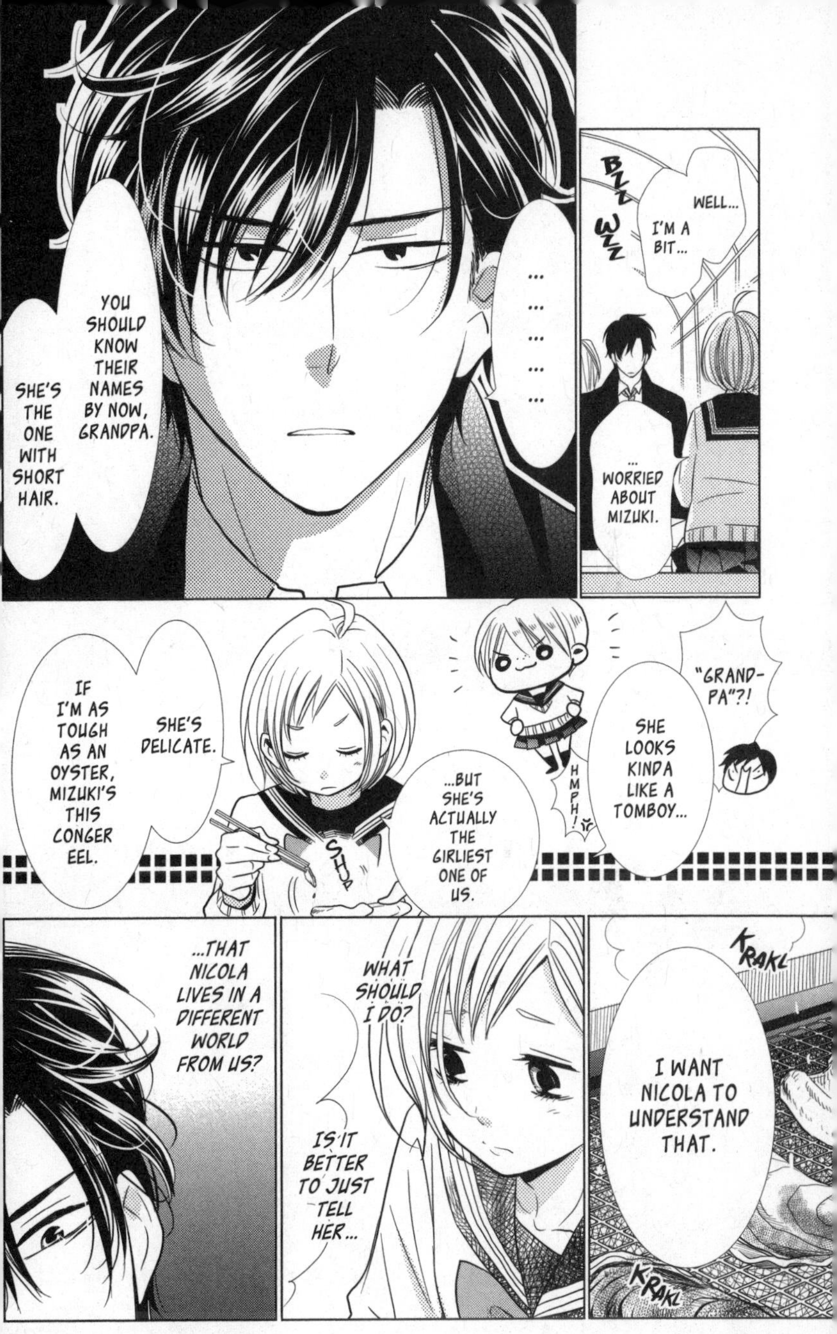
BZZ WZZ
WELL... I'M A BIT...
...WORRIED ABOUT MIZUKI.
....
YOU SHOULD KNOW THEIR NAMES BY NOW, GRANDPA.
SHE'S THE ONE WITH SHORT HAIR.
"GRAND-PA"?!
SHE LOOKS KINDA LIKE A TOMBOY...
HMPH!
...BUT SHE'S ACTUALLY THE GIRLIEST ONE OF US.
SHE'S DELICATE.
SHUP
IF I'M AS TOUGH AS AN OYSTER, MIZUKI'S THIS CONGER EEL.
KRAKL
I WANT NICOLA TO UNDERSTAND THAT.
KRAKL
WHAT SHOULD I DO?
IS IT BETTER TO JUST TELL HER...
...THAT NICOLA LIVES IN A DIFFERENT WORLD FROM US?

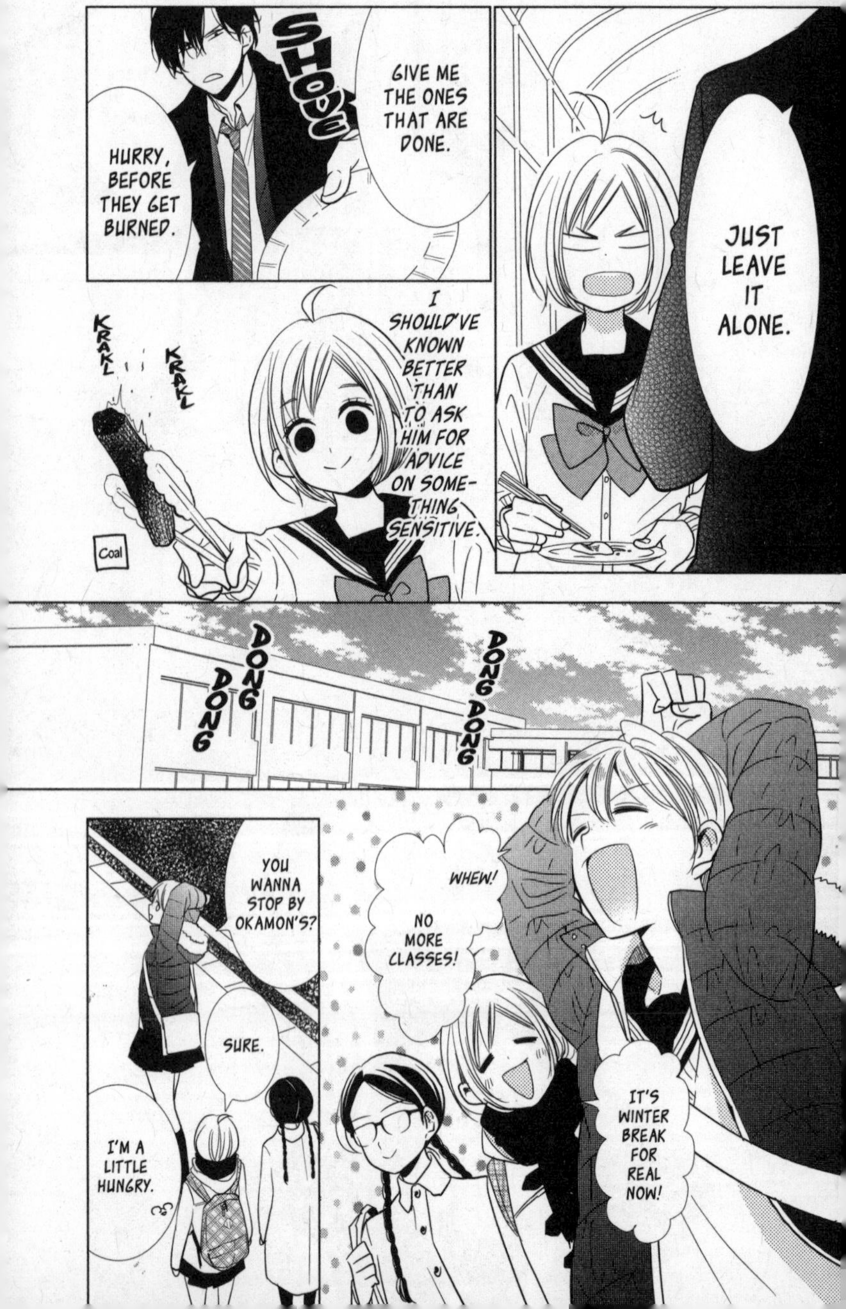
JUST LEAVE IT ALONE.
SHOVE
GIVE ME THE ONES THAT ARE DONE.
HURRY, BEFORE THEY GET BURNED.
I SHOULD'VE KNOWN BETTER THAN TO ASK HIM FOR ADVICE ON SOME-THING SENSITIVE.
KRAKL
KRAKL
Coal
DONG DONG
DONG DONG
WHEW!
NO MORE CLASSES!
IT'S WINTER BREAK FOR REAL NOW!
YOU WANNA STOP BY OKAMON'S?
SURE.
I'M A LITTLE HUNGRY.

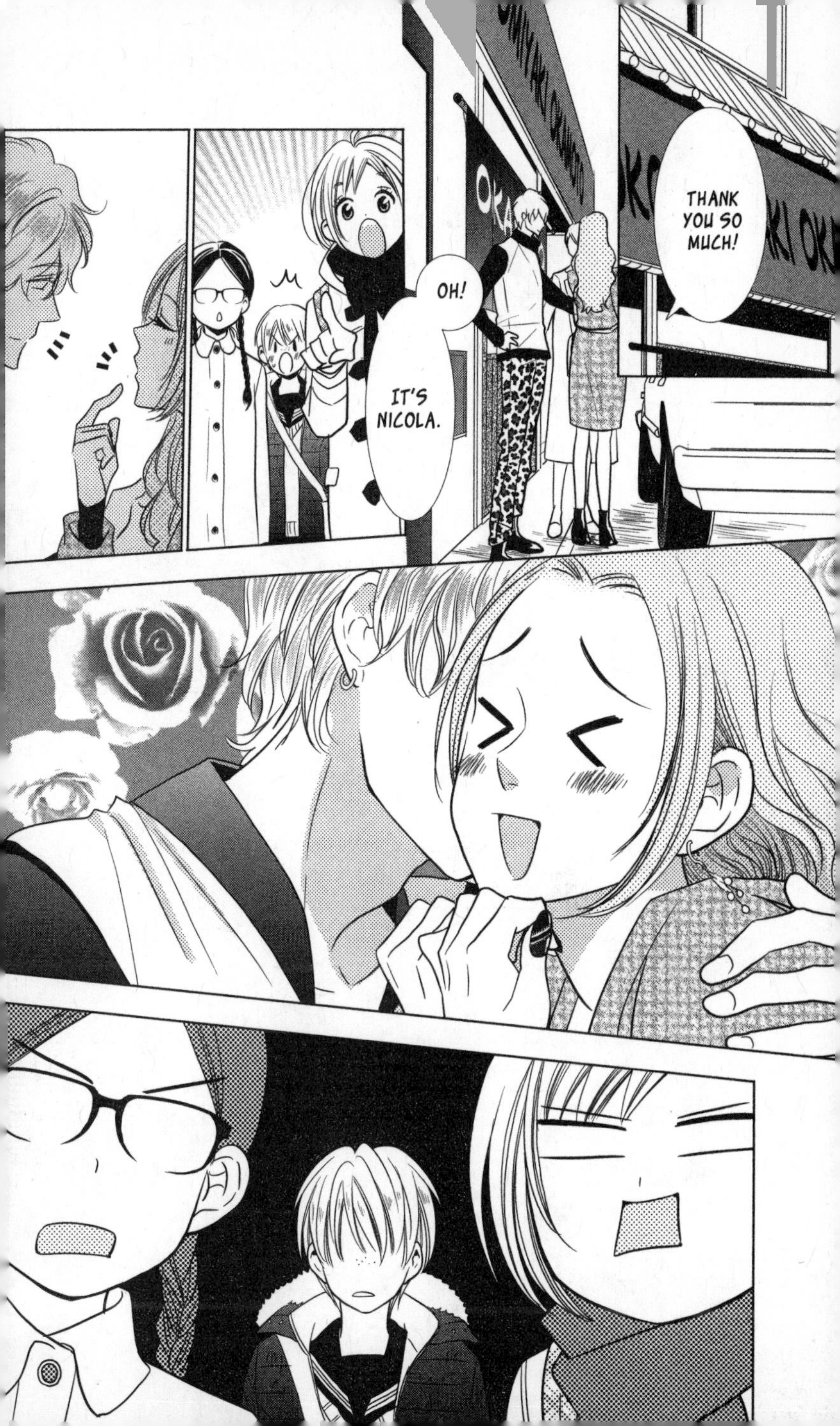
THANK YOU SO MUCH!
OH!
IT'S NICOLA.

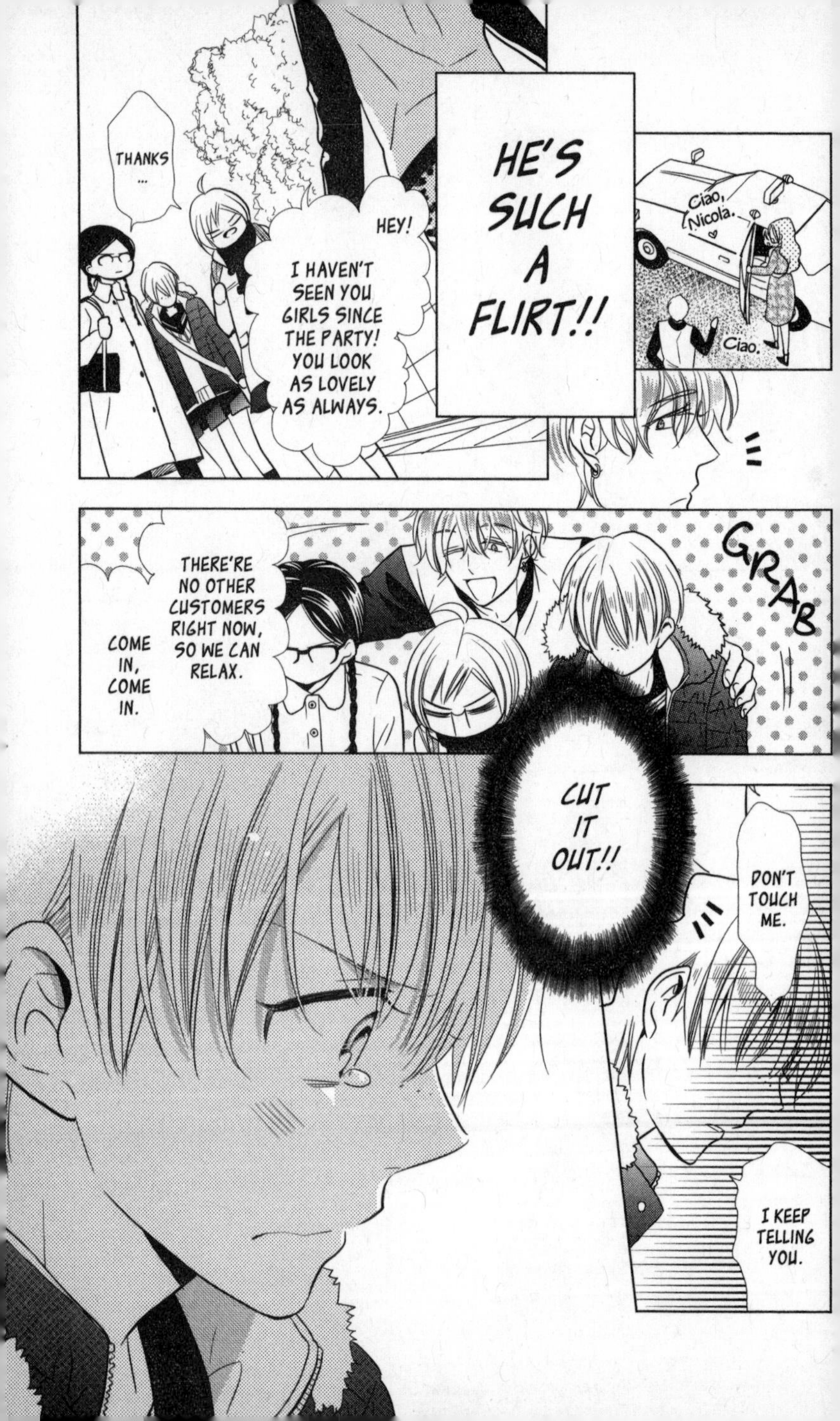
Ciao, Nicola. ♥
Ciao.
HE'S SUCH A FLIRT!!
HEY!
I HAVEN'T SEEN YOU GIRLS SINCE THE PARTY! YOU LOOK AS LOVELY AS ALWAYS.
THANKS ...
GRAB
COME IN, COME IN.
THERE'RE NO OTHER CUSTOMERS RIGHT NOW, SO WE CAN RELAX.
CUT IT OUT!!
DON'T TOUCH ME.
I KEEP TELLING YOU.

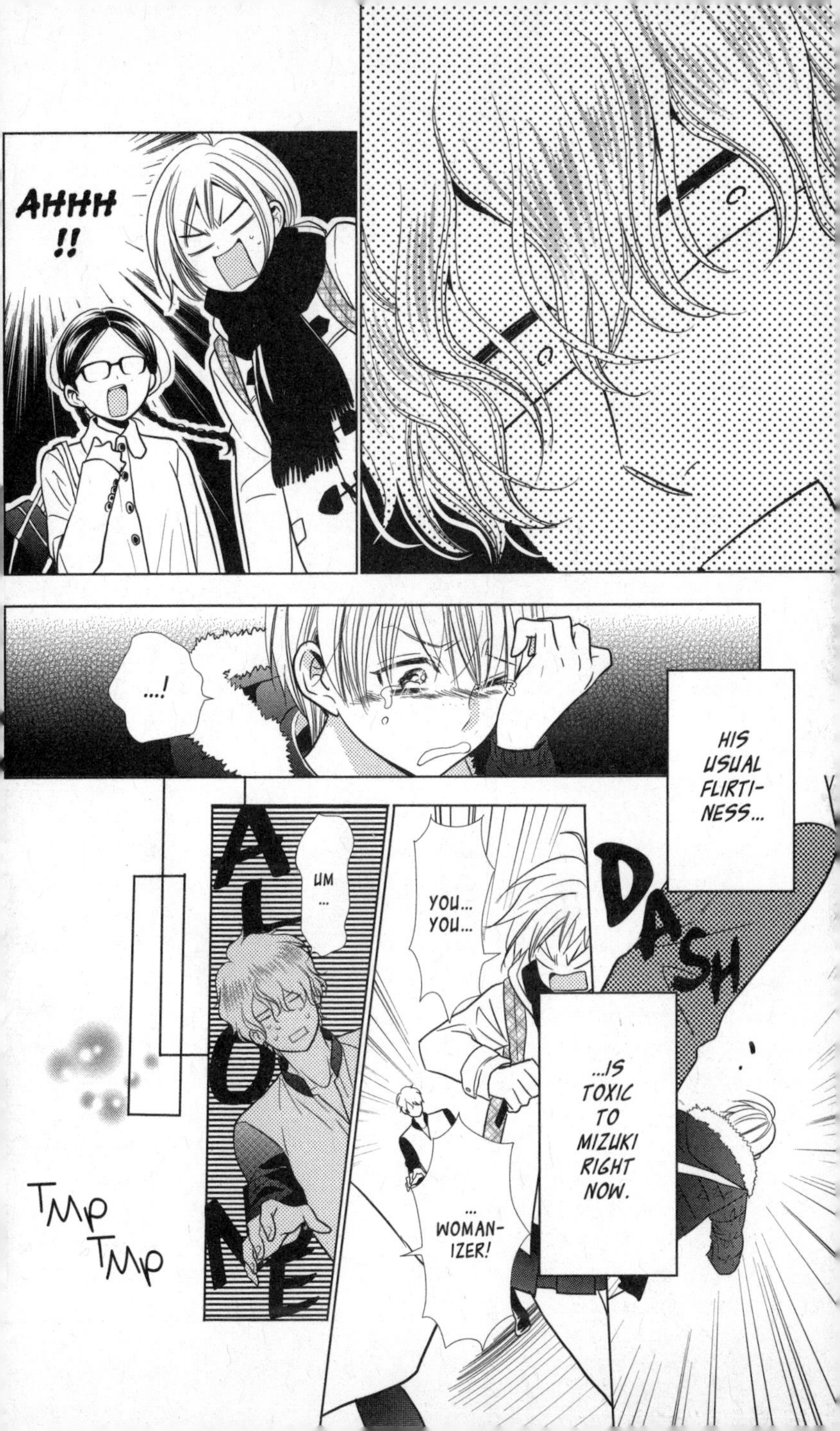
AHHH !!
...!
HIS USUAL FLIRTINESS...
DASH
...IS TOXIC TO MIZUKI RIGHT NOW.
YOU... YOU...
...WOMANIZER!
UM ...
ALONE
TMP TMP

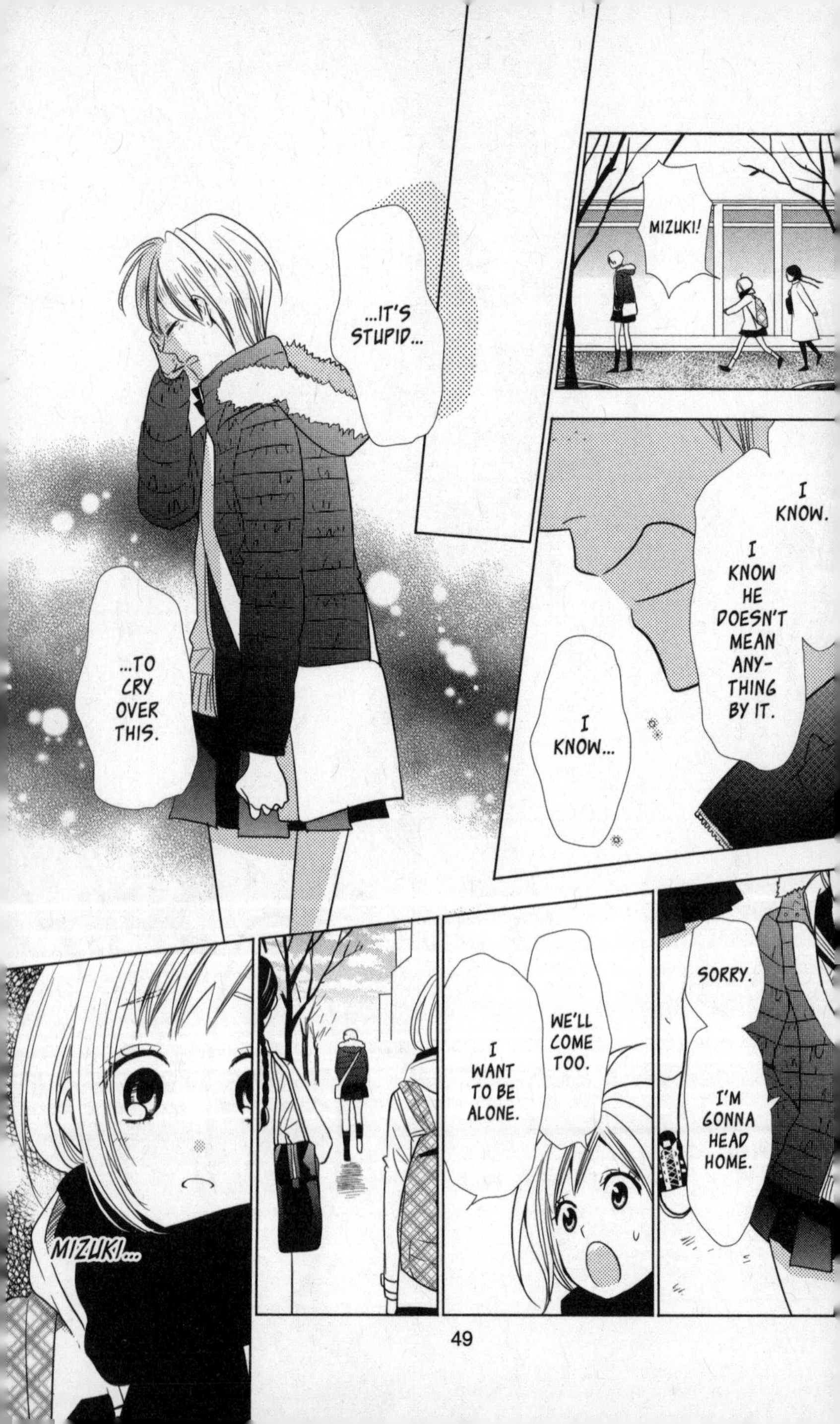
MIZUKI!
I KNOW.
I KNOW HE DOESN'T MEAN ANY-THING BY IT.
I KNOW...
...IT'S STUPID...
...TO CRY OVER THIS.
SORRY.
I'M GONNA HEAD HOME.
WE'LL COME TOO.
I WANT TO BE ALONE.
MIZUKI...

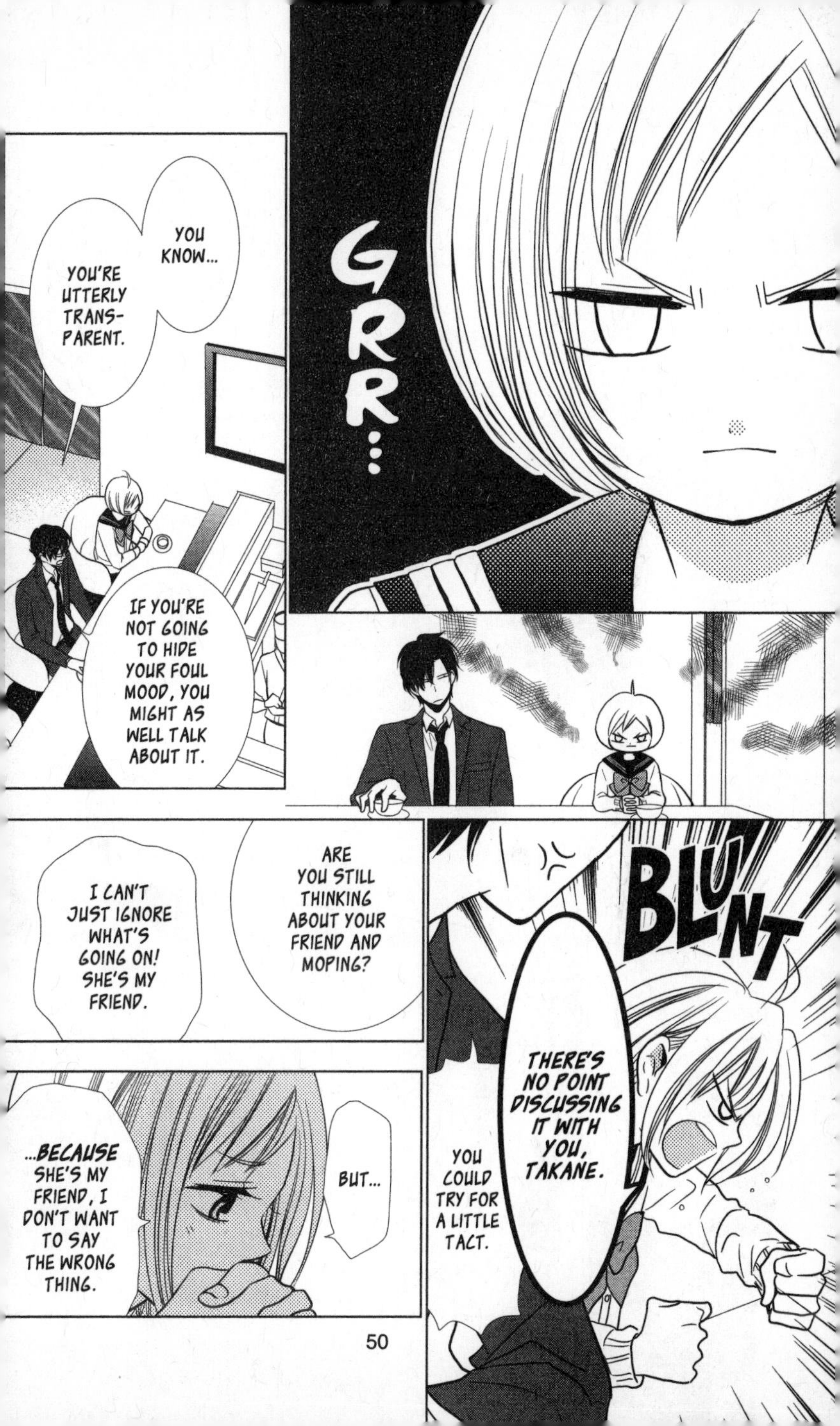
GRR...
YOU KNOW...
YOU'RE UTTERLY TRANS-PARENT.
IF YOU'RE NOT GOING TO HIDE YOUR FOUL MOOD, YOU MIGHT AS WELL TALK ABOUT IT.
BLUNT
THERE'S NO POINT DISCUSSING IT WITH YOU, TAKANE.
YOU COULD TRY FOR A LITTLE TACT.
ARE YOU STILL THINKING ABOUT YOUR FRIEND AND MOPING?
I CAN'T JUST IGNORE WHAT'S GOING ON! SHE'S MY FRIEND.
BUT...
...BECAUSE SHE'S MY FRIEND, I DON'T WANT TO SAY THE WRONG THING.

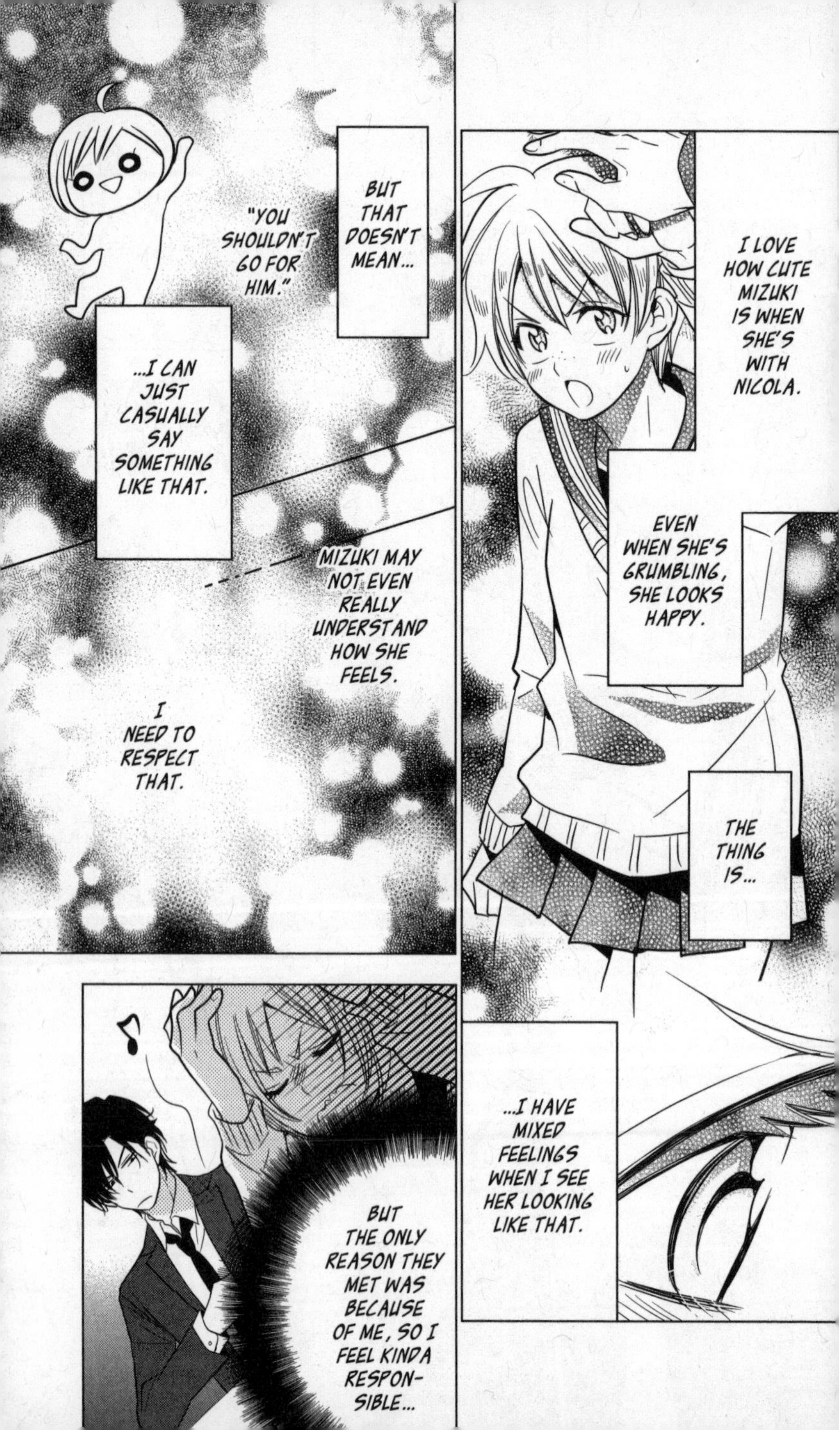
I LOVE HOW CUTE MIZUKI IS WHEN SHE'S WITH NICOLA.
EVEN WHEN SHE'S GRUMBLING, SHE LOOKS HAPPY.
THE THING IS...
...I HAVE MIXED FEELINGS WHEN I SEE HER LOOKING LIKE THAT.
BUT THAT DOESN'T MEAN...
"YOU SHOULDN'T GO FOR HIM."
...I CAN JUST CASUALLY SAY SOMETHING LIKE THAT.
MIZUKI MAY NOT EVEN REALLY UNDERSTAND HOW SHE FEELS.
I NEED TO RESPECT THAT.
BUT THE ONLY REASON THEY MET WAS BECAUSE OF ME, SO I FEEL KINDA RESPON-SIBLE...

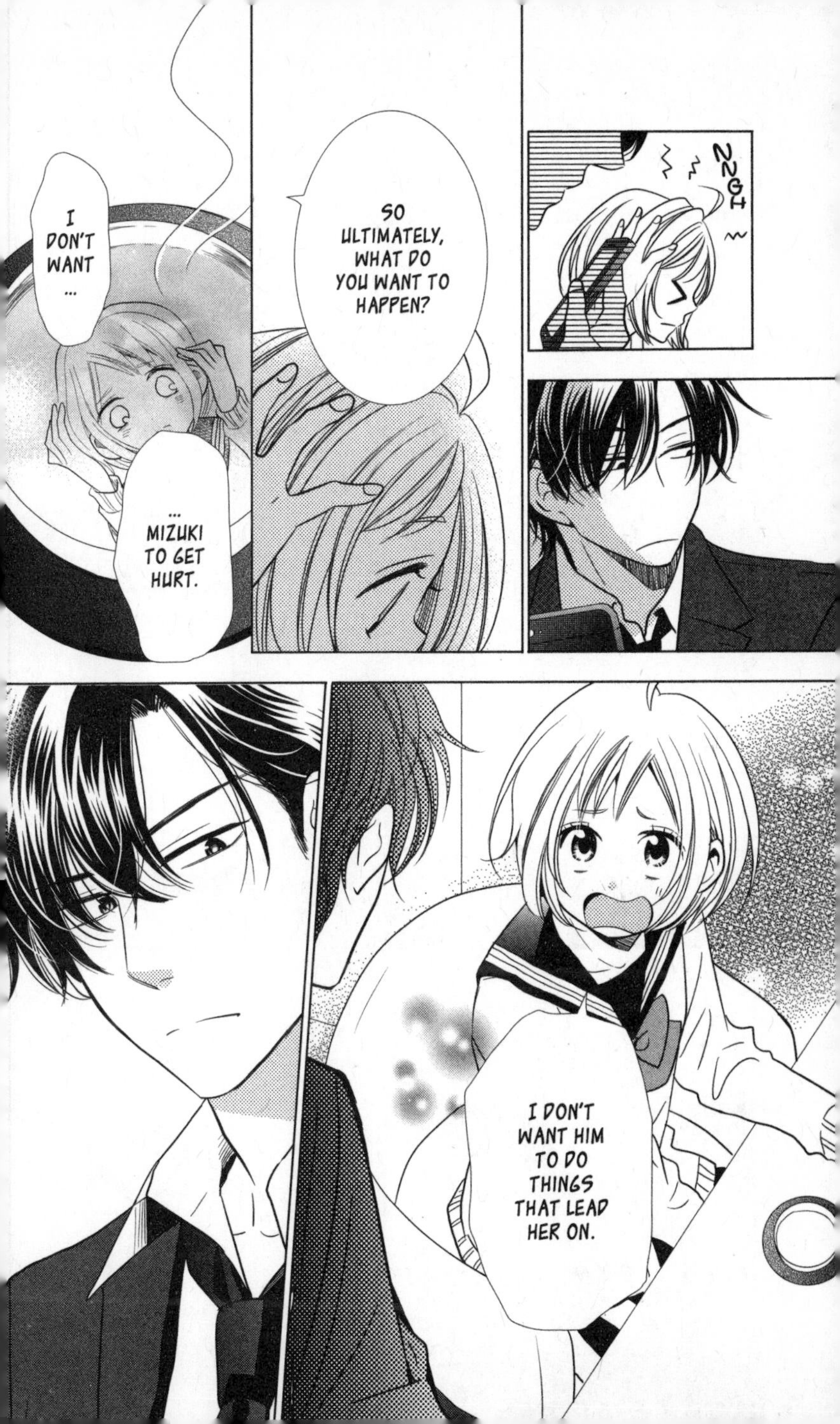
NNGH
SO ULTIMATELY, WHAT DO YOU WANT TO HAPPEN?
I DON'T WANT ...
... MIZUKI TO GET HURT.
I DON'T WANT HIM TO DO THINGS THAT LEAD HER ON.

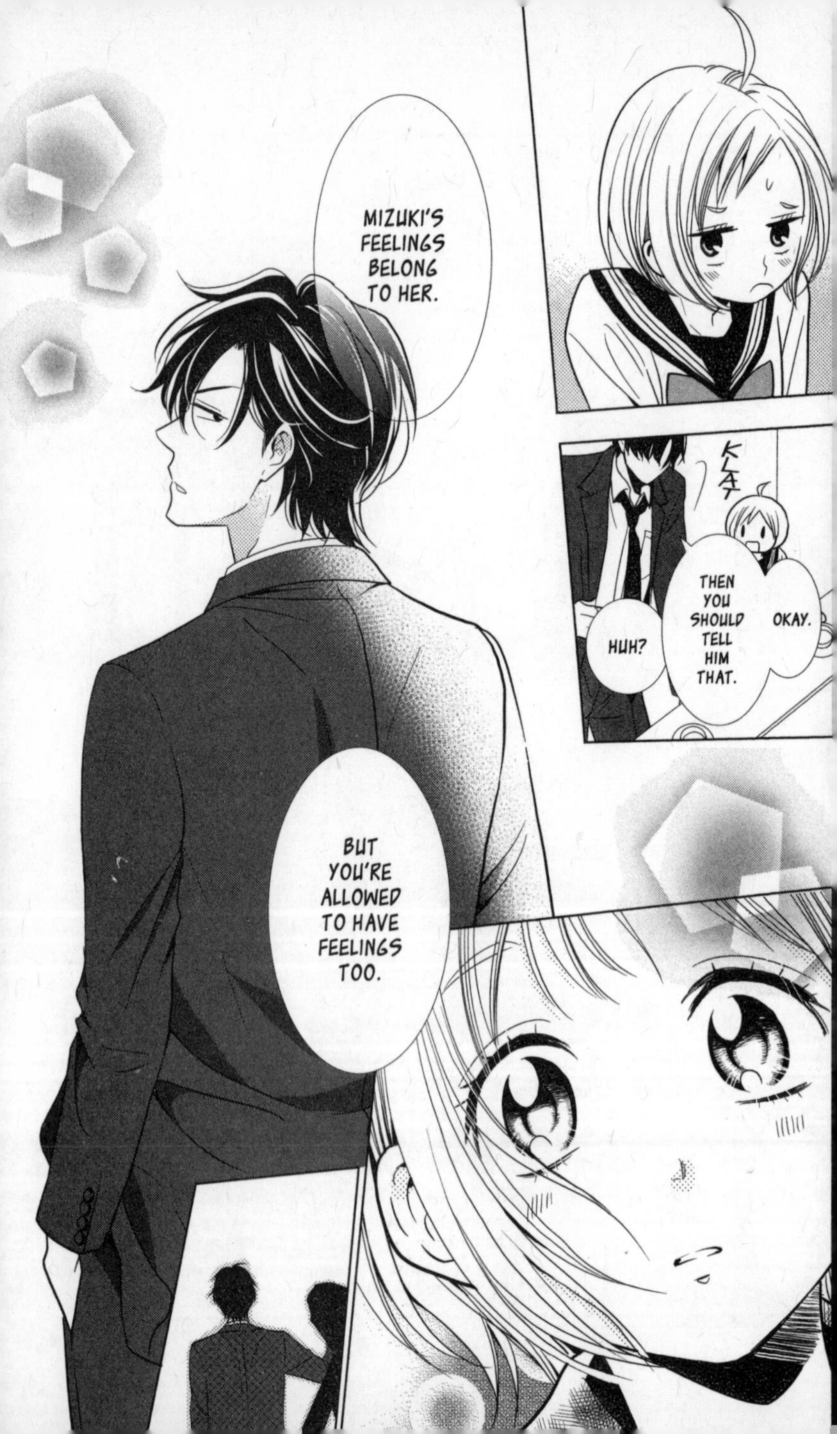
KLAT
OKAY.
THEN YOU SHOULD TELL HIM THAT.
HUH?
MIZUKI'S FEELINGS BELONG TO HER.
BUT YOU'RE ALLOWED TO HAVE FEELINGS TOO.

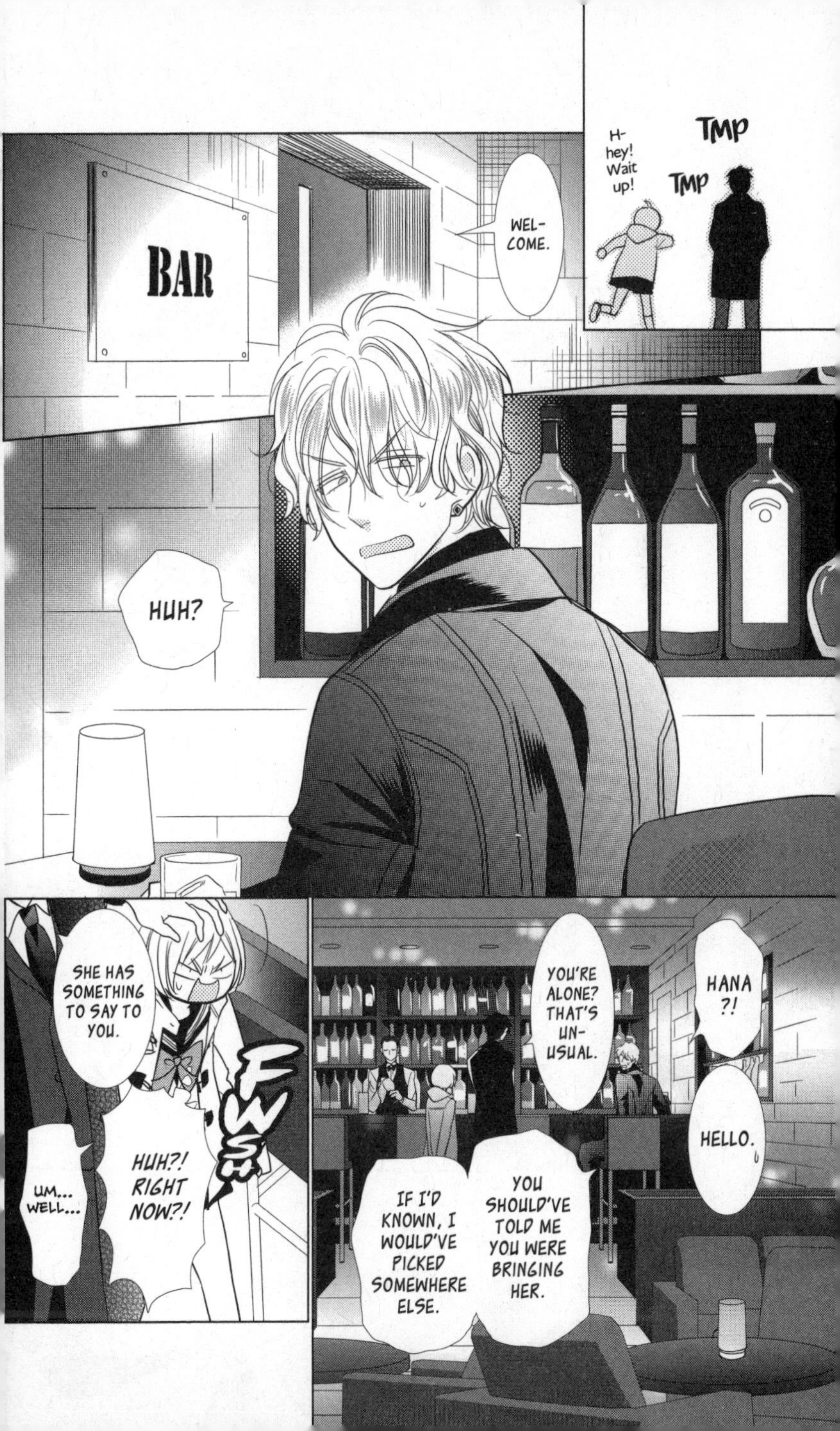
TMP
TMP
H-hey! Wait up!
BAR
WEL-COME.
HUH?
HANA?!
HELLO.
YOU'RE ALONE? THAT'S UN-USUAL.
YOU SHOULD'VE TOLD ME YOU WERE BRINGING HER.
IF I'D KNOWN, I WOULD'VE PICKED SOMEWHERE ELSE.
SHE HAS SOMETHING TO SAY TO YOU.
FWSH
HUH?! RIGHT NOW?!
UM... WELL...

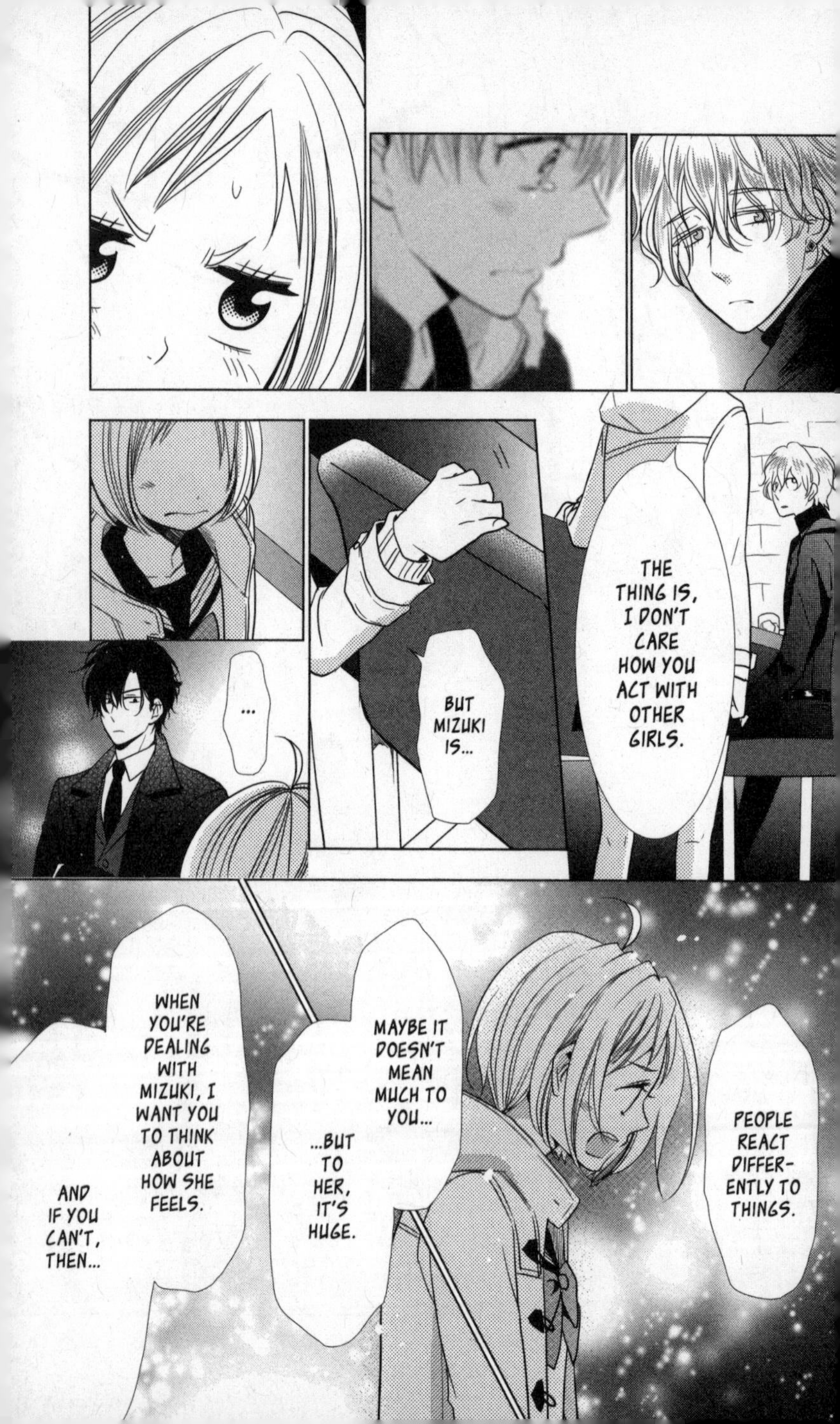
THE THING IS, I DON'T CARE HOW YOU ACT WITH OTHER GIRLS.
BUT MIZUKI IS...
...
PEOPLE REACT DIFFERENTLY TO THINGS.
MAYBE IT DOESN'T MEAN MUCH TO YOU...
...BUT TO HER, IT'S HUGE.
WHEN YOU'RE DEALING WITH MIZUKI, I WANT YOU TO THINK ABOUT HOW SHE FEELS.
AND IF YOU CAN'T, THEN...

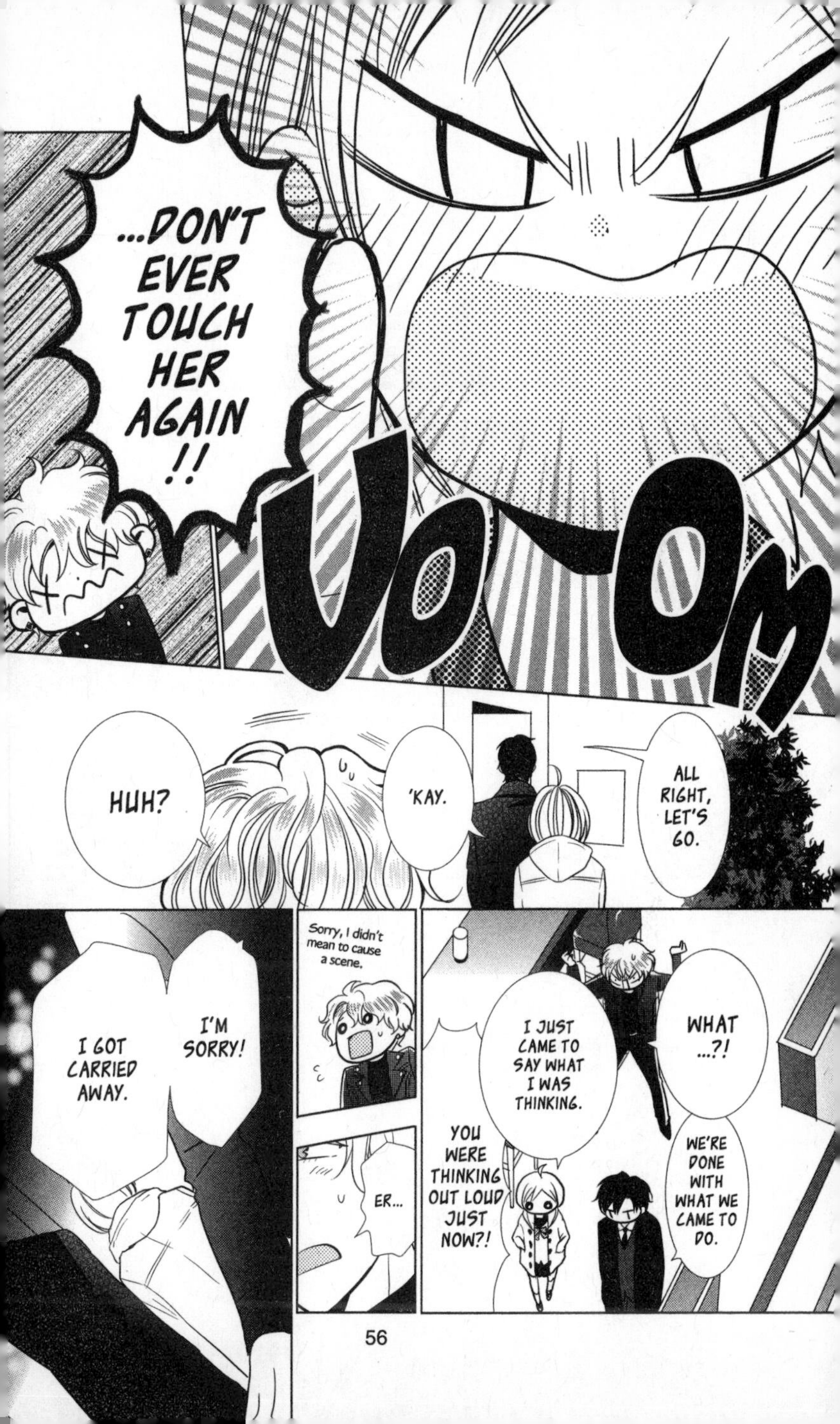
...DON'T EVER TOUCH HER AGAIN!!
VO-OM
ALL RIGHT, LET'S GO.
'KAY.
HUH?
WHAT ...?!
I JUST CAME TO SAY WHAT I WAS THINKING.
WE'RE DONE WITH WHAT WE CAME TO DO.
YOU WERE THINKING OUT LOUD JUST NOW?!
Sorry, I didn't mean to cause a scene.
ER...
I'M SORRY!
I GOT CARRIED AWAY.

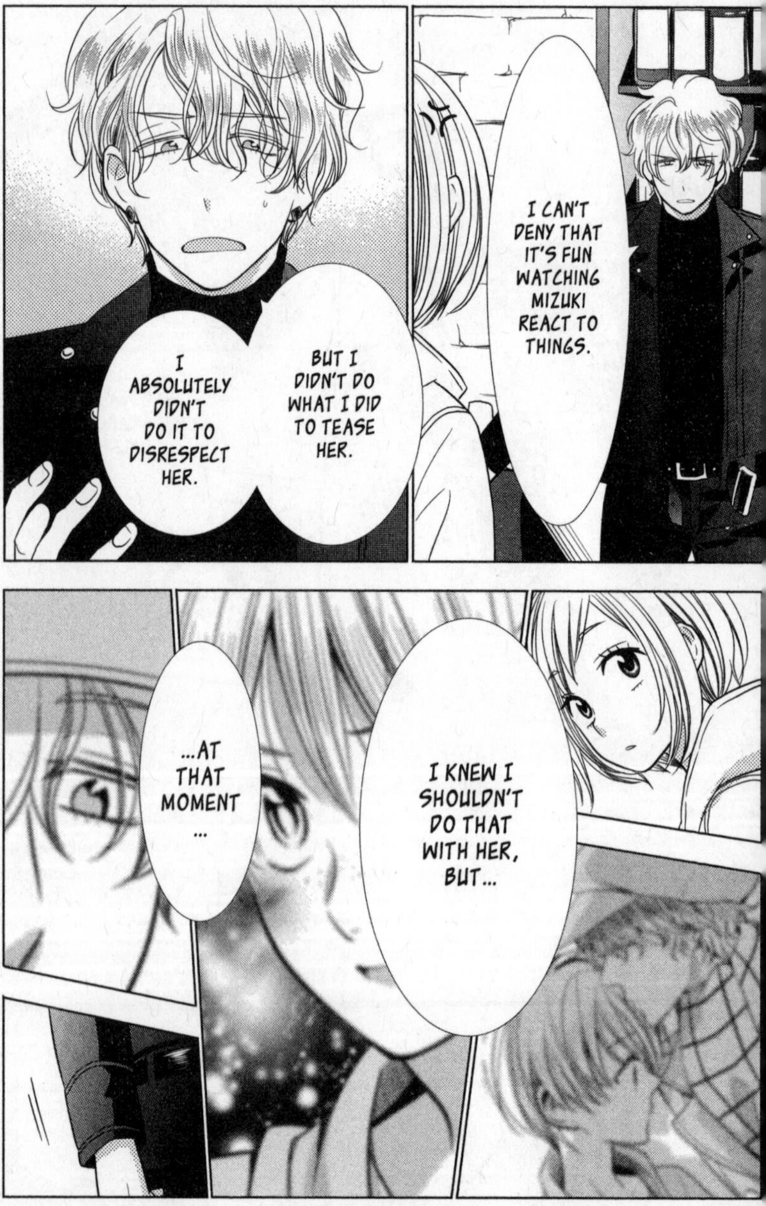
I CAN'T DENY THAT IT'S FUN WATCHING MIZUKI REACT TO THINGS.
BUT I DIDN'T DO WHAT I DID TO TEASE HER.
I ABSOLUTELY DIDN'T DO IT TO DISRESPECT HER.
I KNEW I SHOULDN'T DO THAT WITH HER, BUT...
...AT THAT MOMENT...

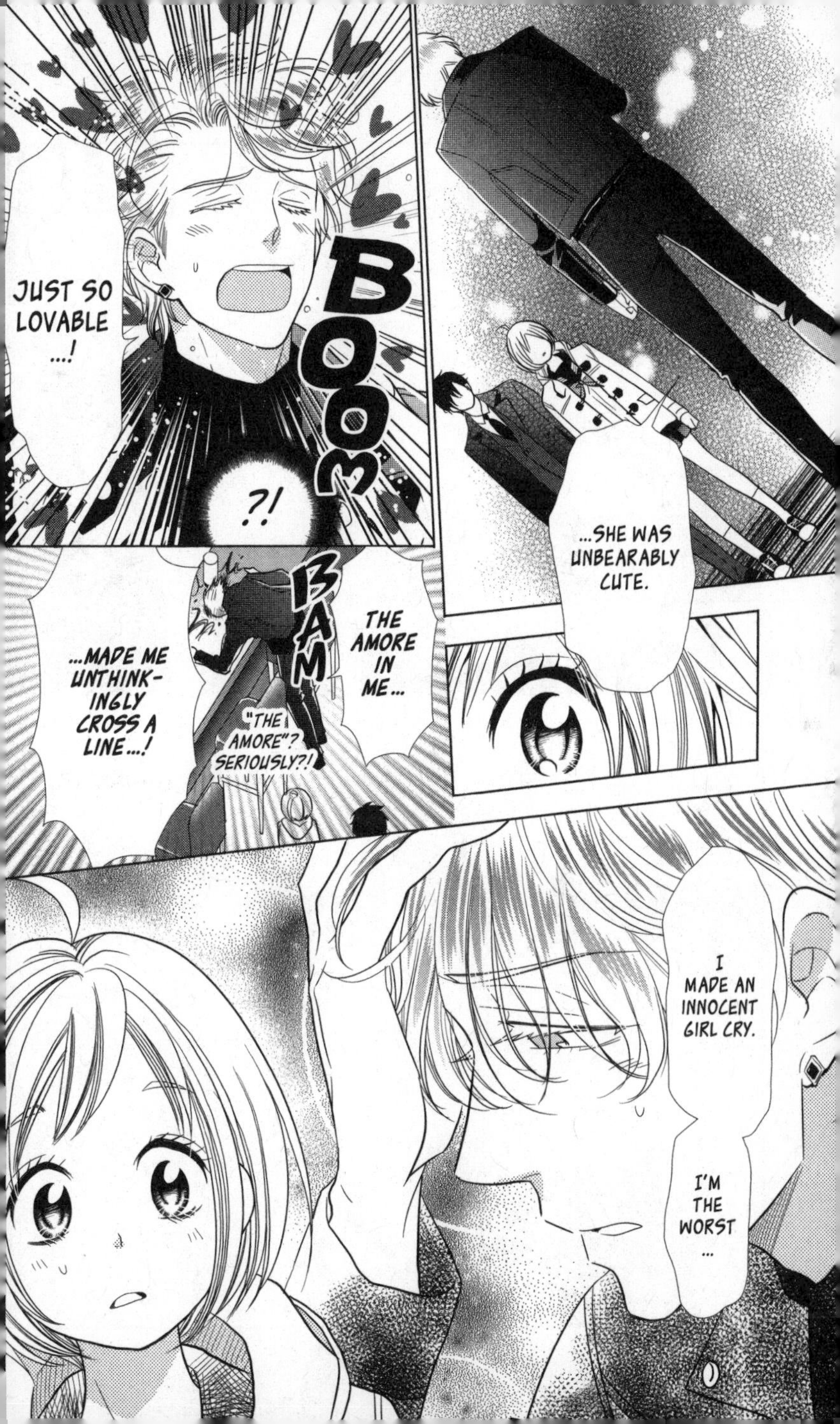
...SHE WAS UNBEARABLY CUTE.
JUST SO LOVABLE ...!
BOOM
?!
THE AMORE IN ME...
BAM
...MADE ME UNTHINKINGLY CROSS A LINE...!
"THE AMORE"? SERIOUSLY?!
I MADE AN INNOCENT GIRL CRY.
I'M THE WORST ...

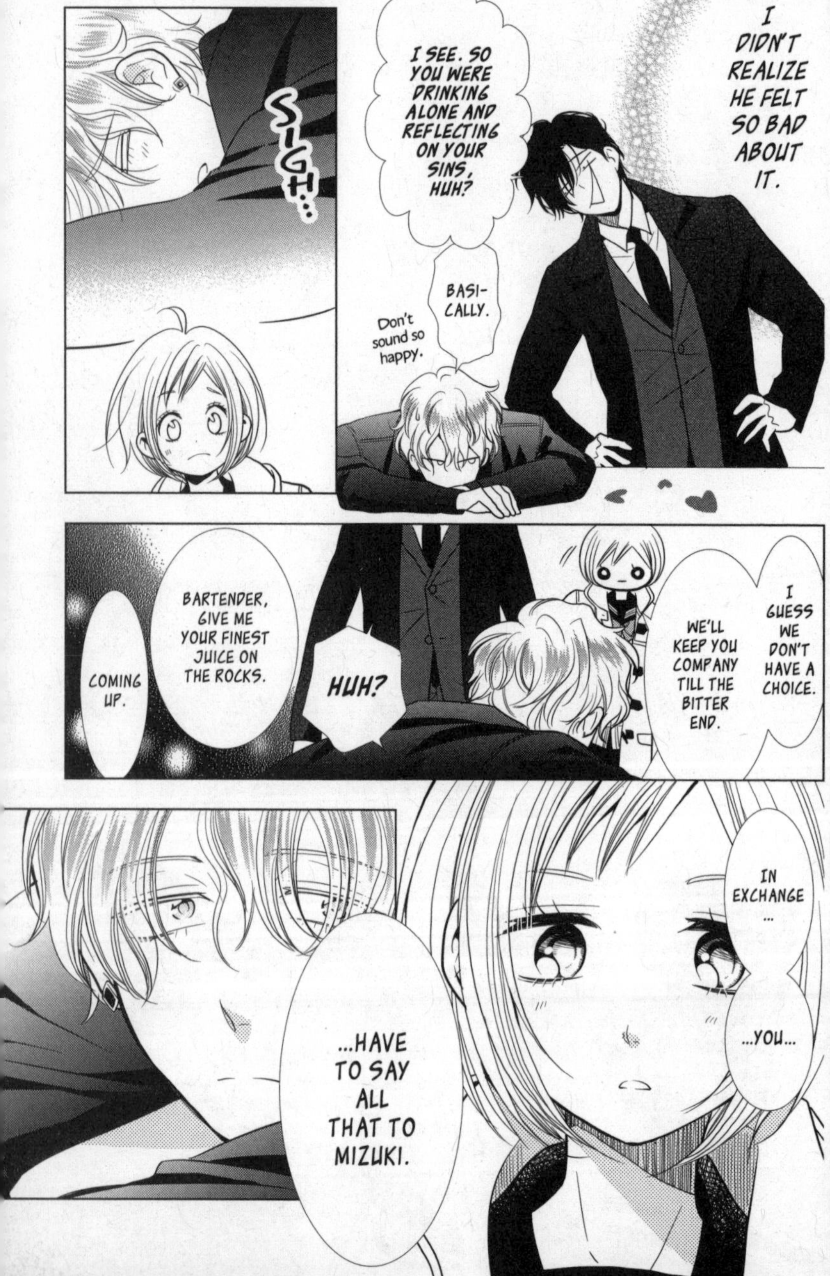
I DIDN'T REALIZE HE FELT SO BAD ABOUT IT.
I SEE. SO YOU WERE DRINKING ALONE AND REFLECTING ON YOUR SINS, HUH?
BASI-CALLY.
Don't sound so happy.
SIGH...
I GUESS WE DON'T HAVE A CHOICE.
WE'LL KEEP YOU COMPANY TILL THE BITTER END.
HUH?
BARTENDER, GIVE ME YOUR FINEST JUICE ON THE ROCKS.
COMING UP.
IN EXCHANGE...
...YOU...
...HAVE TO SAY ALL THAT TO MIZUKI.

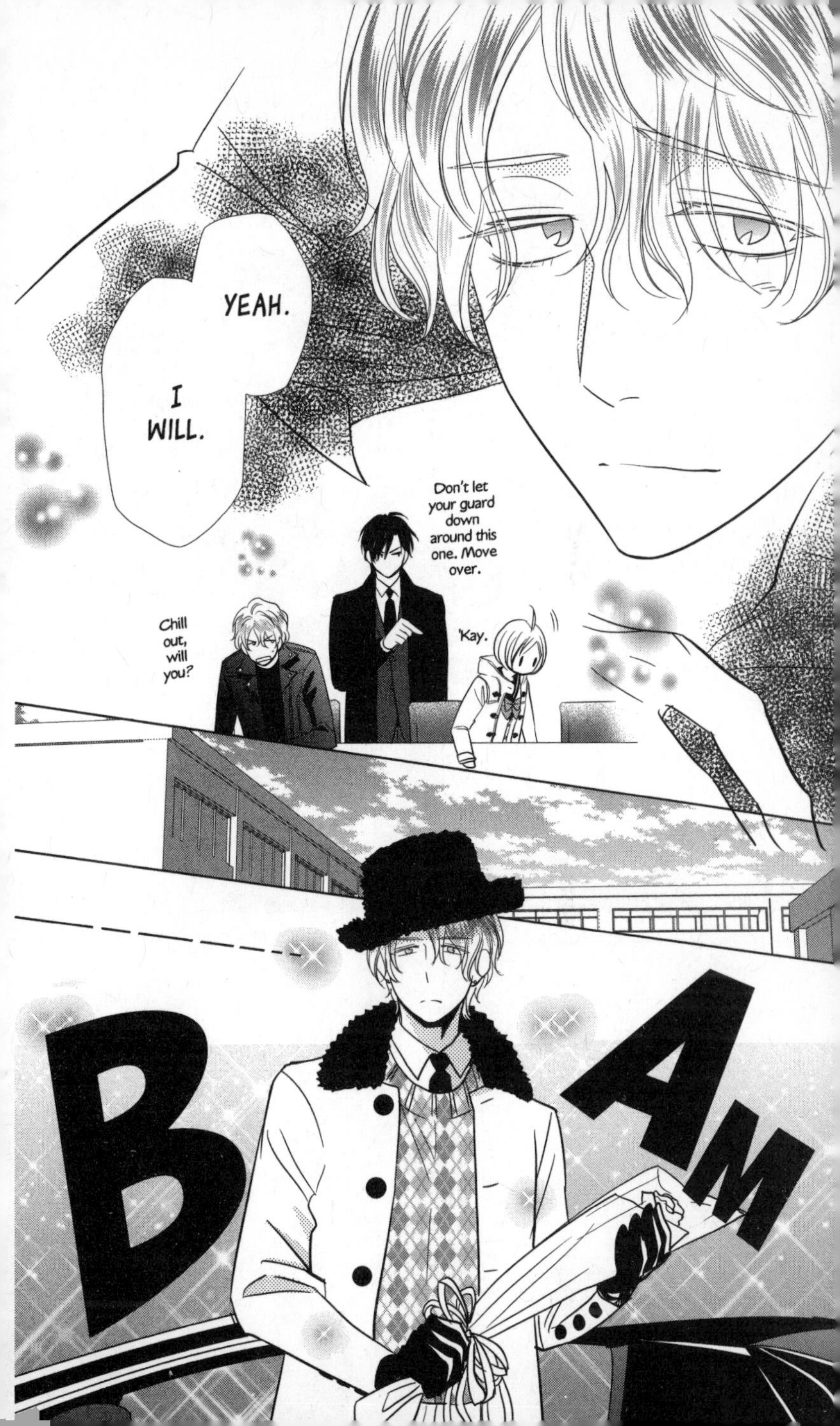
YEAH.
I WILL.
Don't let your guard down around this one. Move over.
'Kay.
Chill out, will you?
BAM

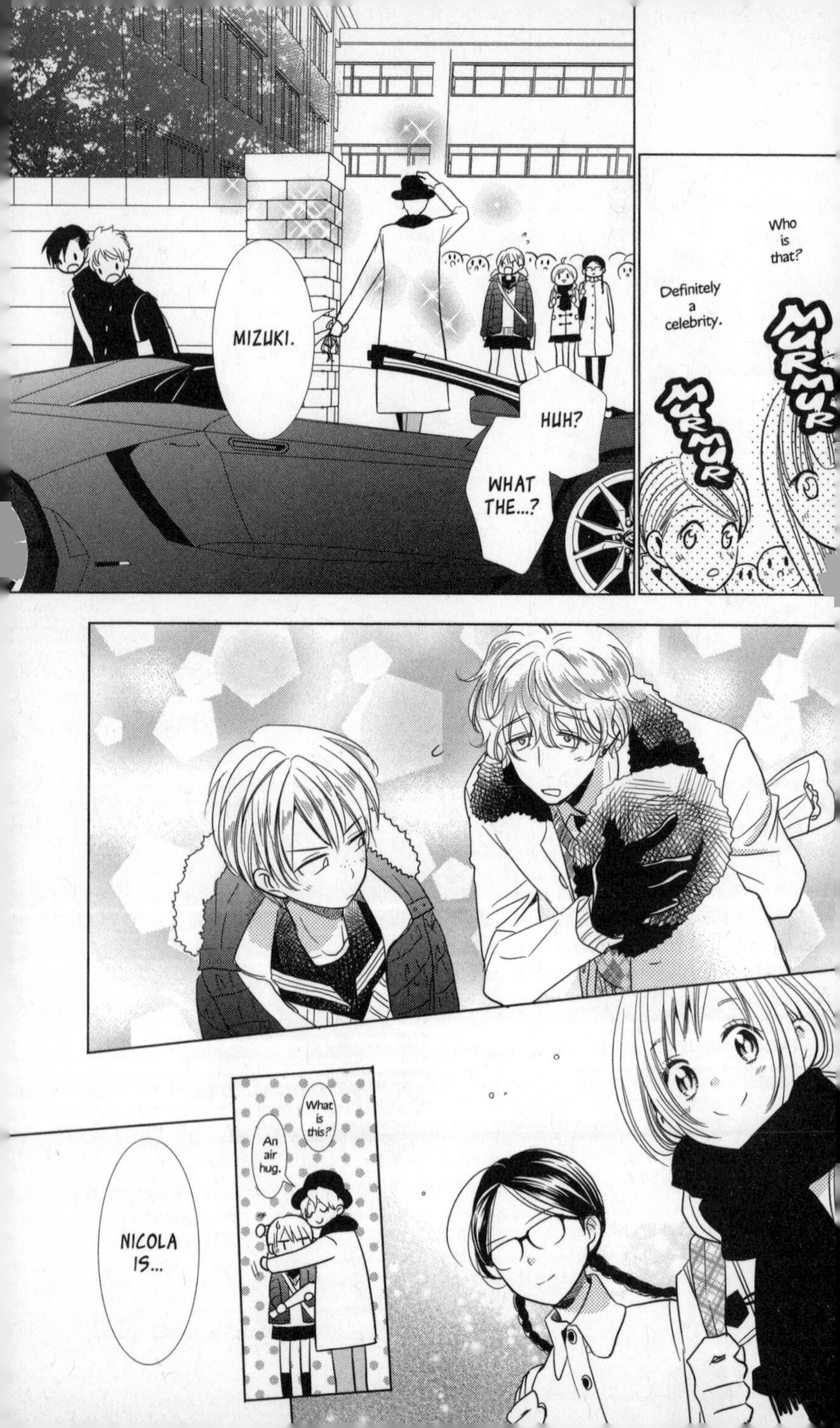
Who is that?
Definitely a celebrity.
MURMUR
MURMUR
MIZUKI.
HUH?
WHAT THE...?
What is this?
An air hug.
NICOLA IS...

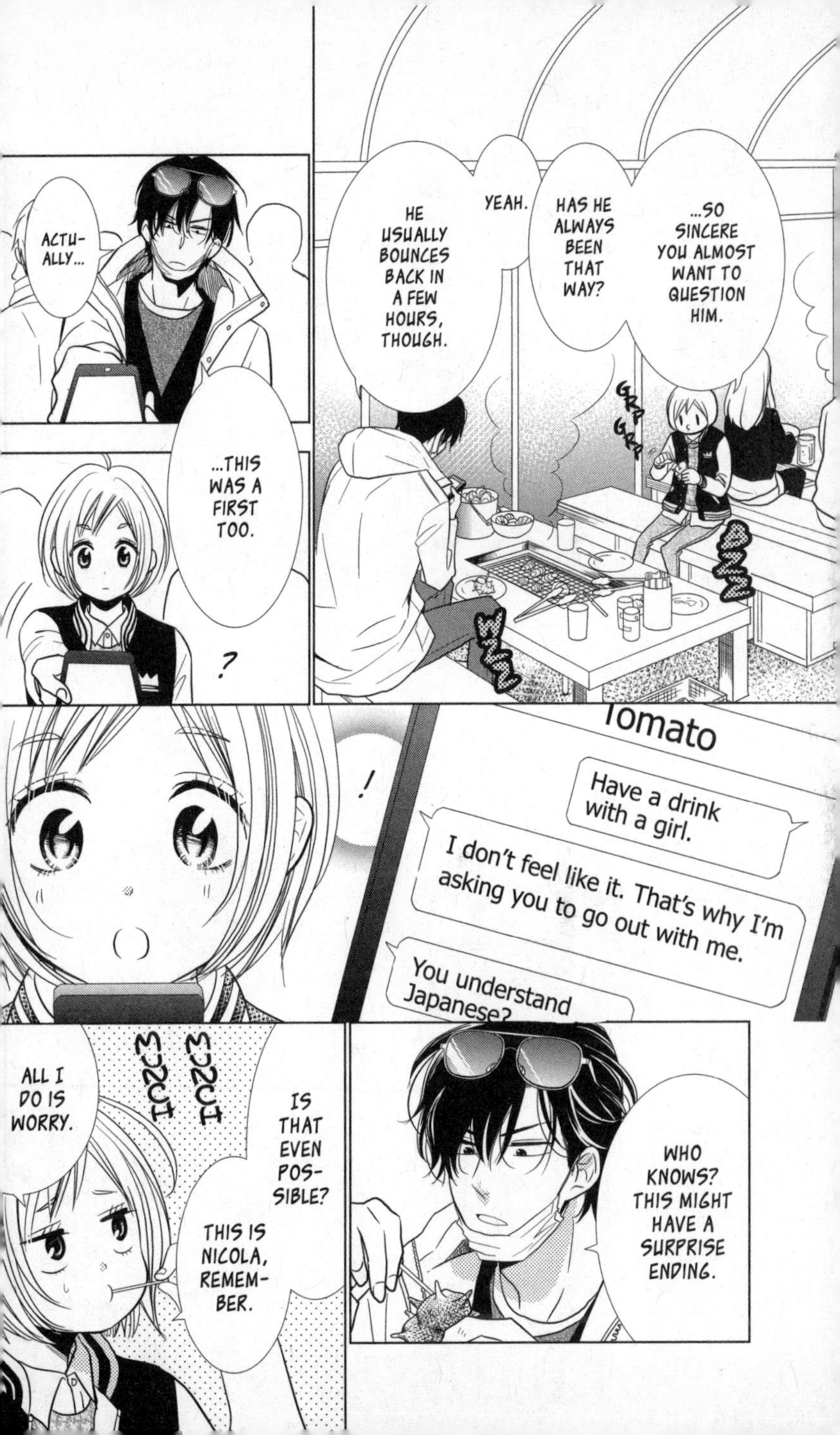
...SO SINCERE YOU ALMOST WANT TO QUESTION HIM.
HAS HE ALWAYS BEEN THAT WAY?
YEAH.
HE USUALLY BOUNCES BACK IN A FEW HOURS, THOUGH.
GRR GRR
ACTU-ALLY...
...THIS WAS A FIRST TOO.
?
Tomato
Have a drink with a girl.
I don't feel like it. That's why I'm asking you to go out with me.
You understand Japanese?
!
WHO KNOWS? THIS MIGHT HAVE A SURPRISE ENDING.
IS THAT EVEN POS-SIBLE?
THIS IS NICOLA, REMEM-BER.
ALL I DO IS WORRY.

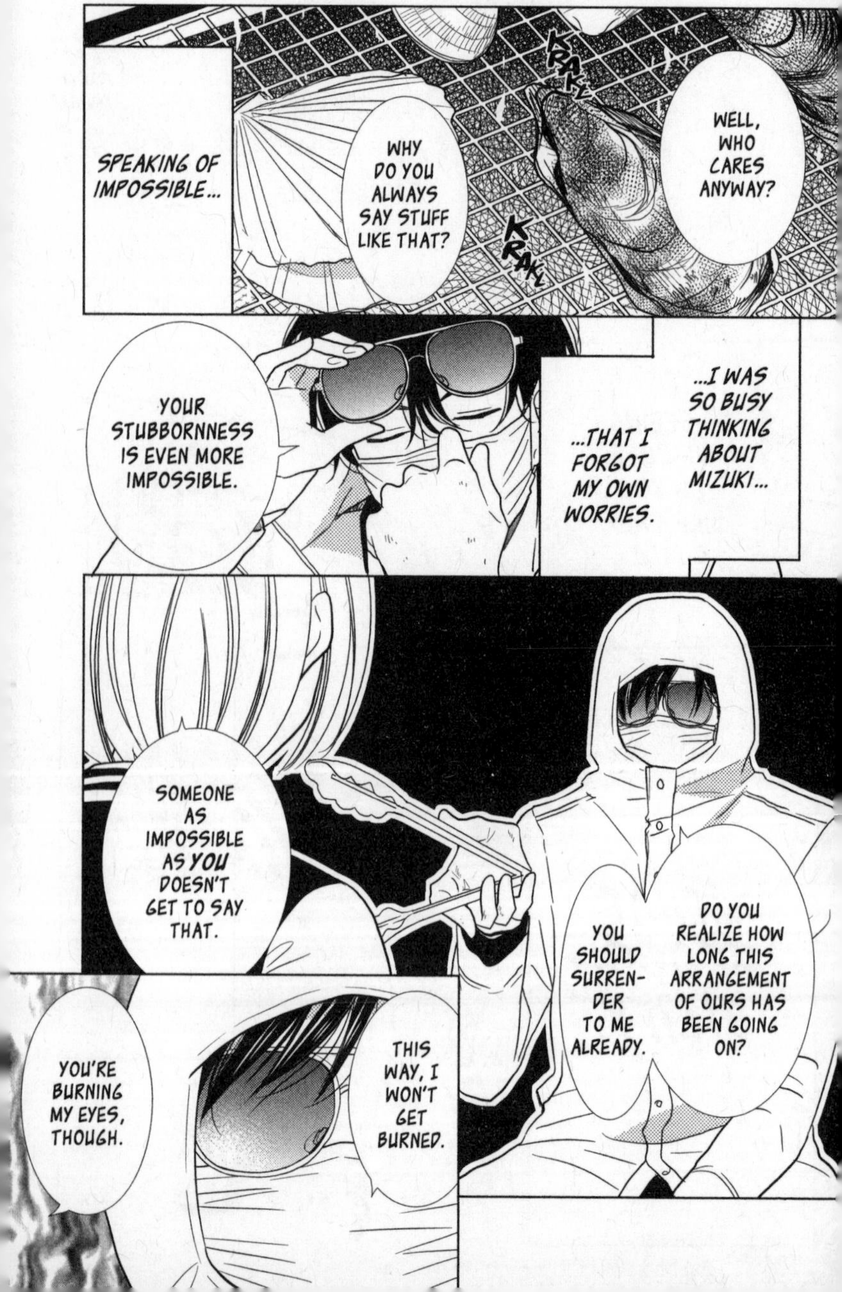
WELL, WHO CARES ANYWAY?
KRAK
KRAK
WHY DO YOU ALWAYS SAY STUFF LIKE THAT?
SPEAKING OF IMPOSSIBLE...
...I WAS SO BUSY THINKING ABOUT MIZUKI...
...THAT I FORGOT MY OWN WORRIES.
YOUR STUBBORNNESS IS EVEN MORE IMPOSSIBLE.
DO YOU REALIZE HOW LONG THIS ARRANGEMENT OF OURS HAS BEEN GOING ON?
YOU SHOULD SURREN-DER TO ME ALREADY.
SOMEONE AS IMPOSSIBLE AS *YOU* DOESN'T GET TO SAY THAT.
THIS WAY, I WON'T GET BURNED.
YOU'RE BURNING MY EYES, THOUGH.

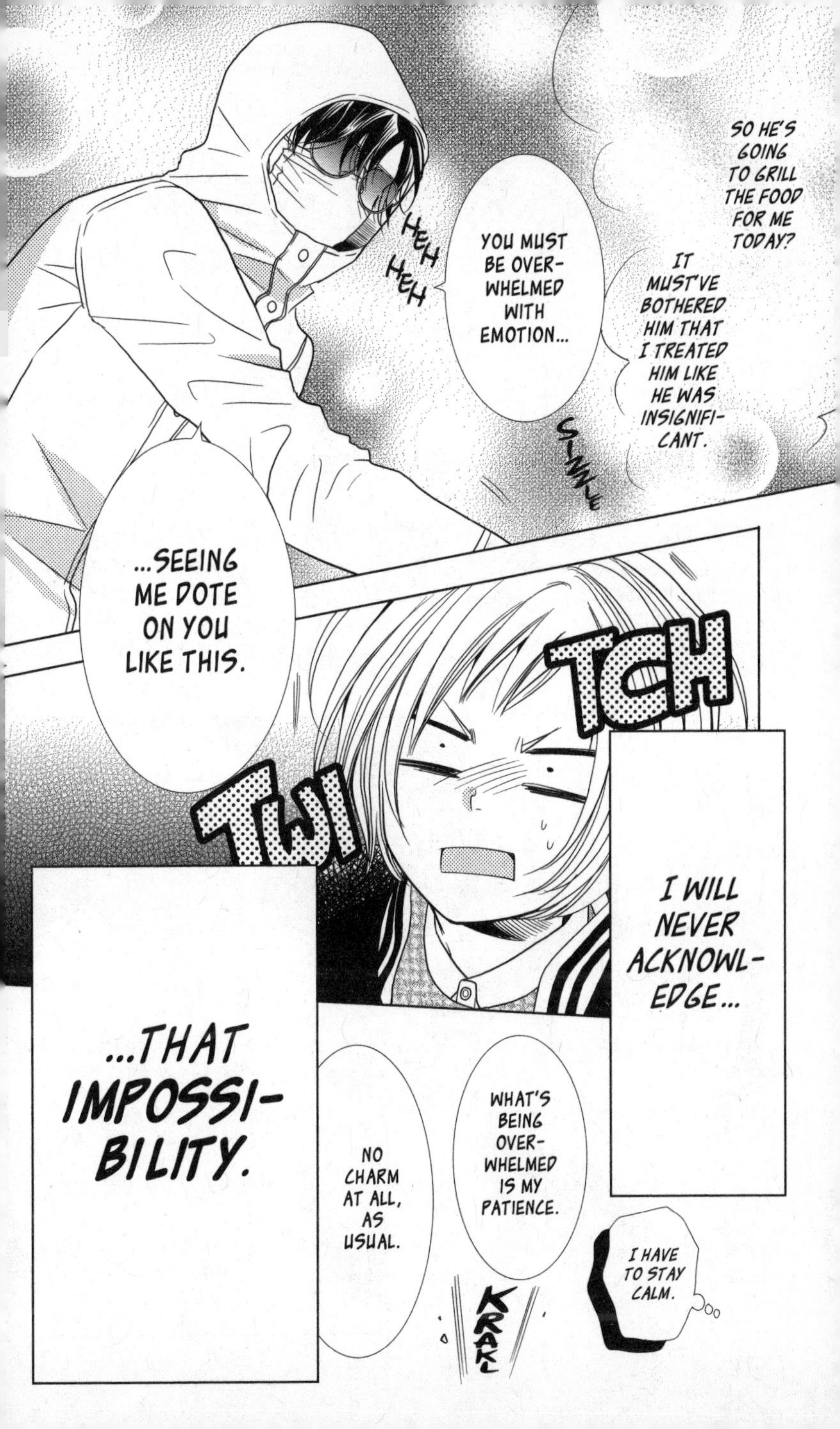
SO HE'S GOING TO GRILL THE FOOD FOR ME TODAY?
IT MUST'VE BOTHERED HIM THAT I TREATED HIM LIKE HE WAS INSIGNIFICANT.
YOU MUST BE OVERWHELMED WITH EMOTION...
HEH HEH
SIZZLE
...SEEING ME DOTE ON YOU LIKE THIS.
TWI TCH
I WILL NEVER ACKNOWLEDGE...
...THAT IMPOSSIBILITY.
I HAVE TO STAY CALM.
KRAK
WHAT'S BEING OVERWHELMED IS MY PATIENCE.
NO CHARM AT ALL, AS USUAL.

Takane Levitated

WELL ...
I SUPPOSE I COULD ACCEPT A PRESENT.
YOU'RE WALKING ON AIR.

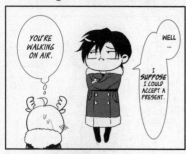

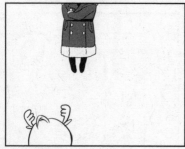

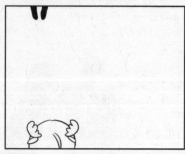

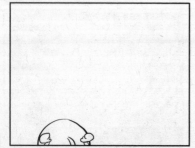

It's Been Decided

MIZUKI'S FEELINGS BELONG TO HER.
BUT YOU'RE ALLOWED TO HAVE FEELINGS TOO.
SMIRK

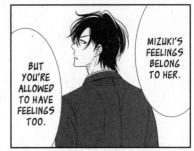

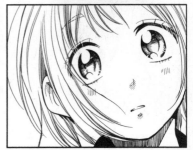

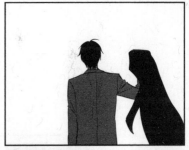

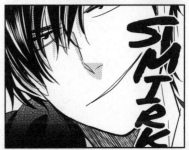

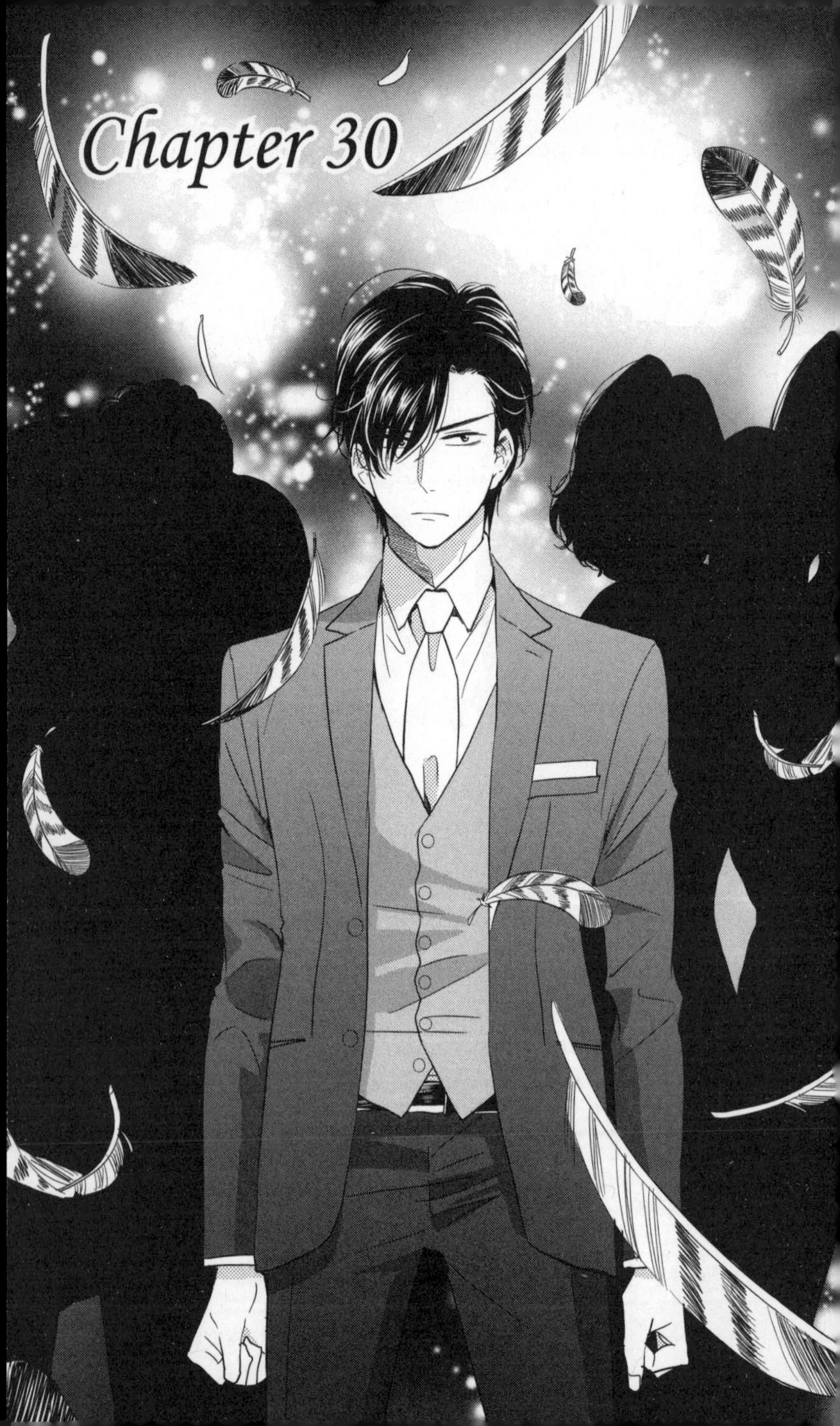
Chapter 30

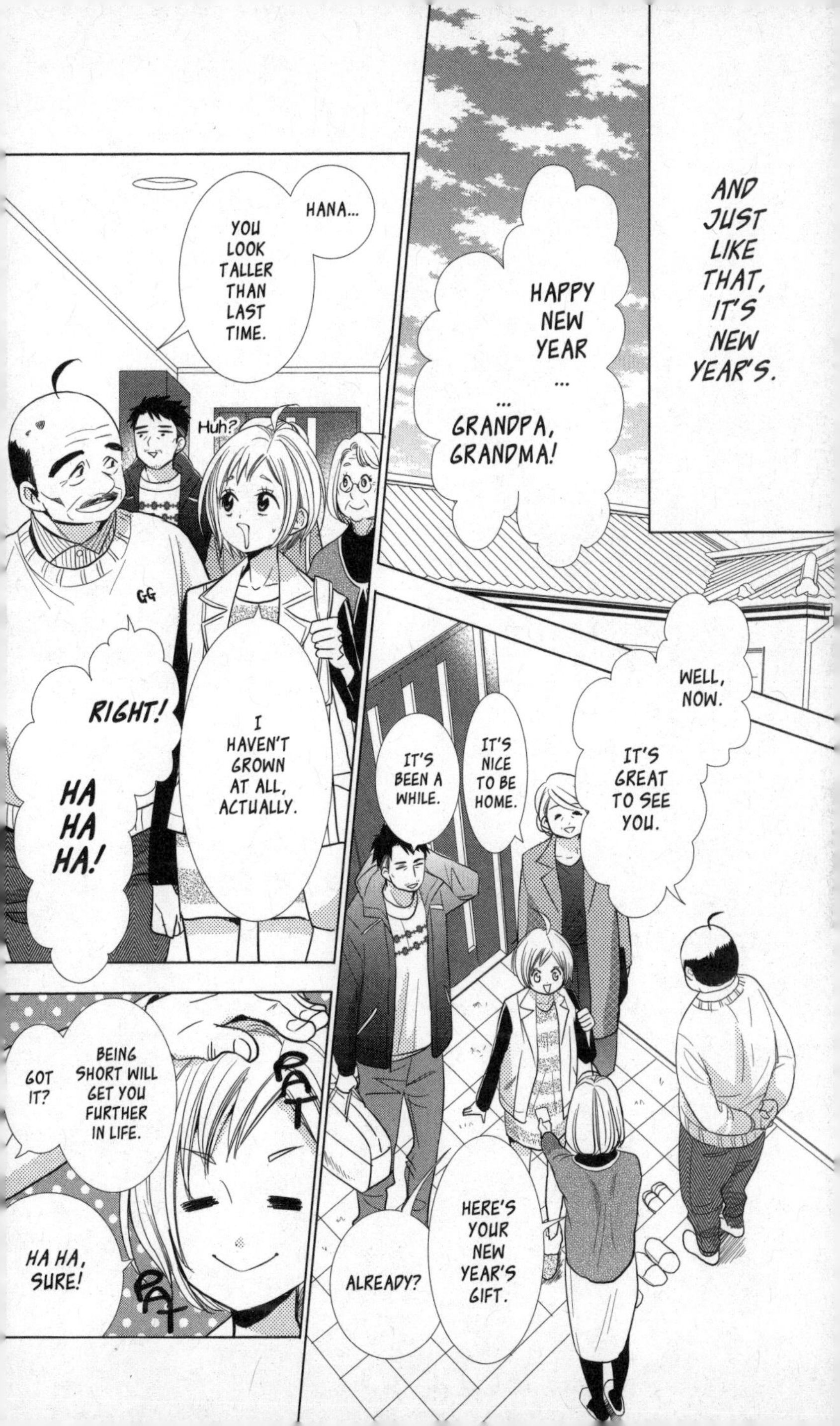
AND JUST LIKE THAT, IT'S NEW YEAR'S.
HAPPY NEW YEAR... ...GRANDPA, GRANDMA!
HANA...
YOU LOOK TALLER THAN LAST TIME.
Huh?
I HAVEN'T GROWN AT ALL, ACTUALLY.
RIGHT!
HA HA HA!
WELL, NOW.
IT'S GREAT TO SEE YOU.
IT'S NICE TO BE HOME.
IT'S BEEN A WHILE.
HERE'S YOUR NEW YEAR'S GIFT.
ALREADY?
BEING SHORT WILL GET YOU FURTHER IN LIFE.
GOT IT?
PAT
HA HA, SURE!
PAT

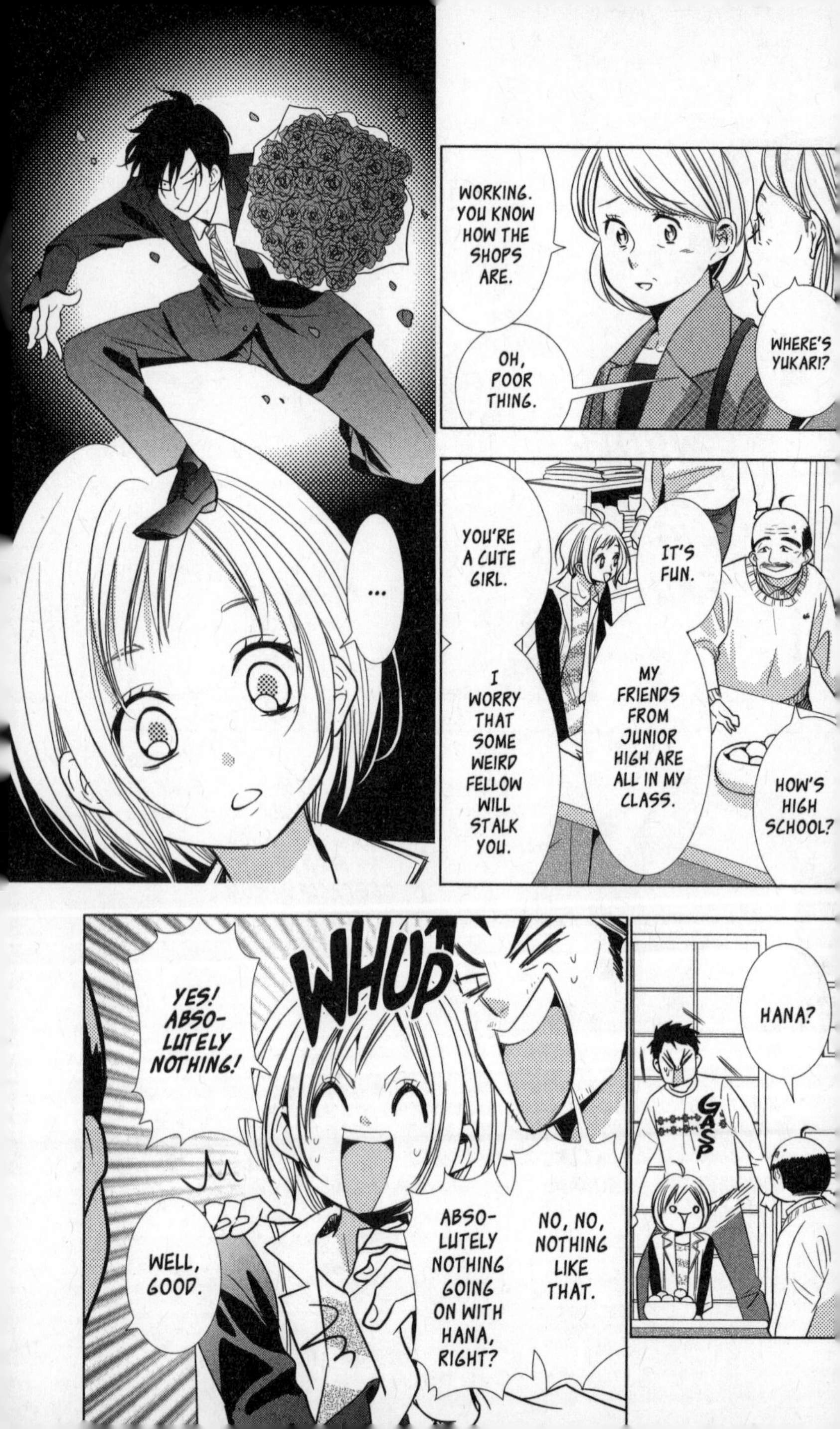
WHERE'S YUKARI?
WORKING. YOU KNOW HOW THE SHOPS ARE.
OH, POOR THING.
HOW'S HIGH SCHOOL?
IT'S FUN.
MY FRIENDS FROM JUNIOR HIGH ARE ALL IN MY CLASS.
YOU'RE A CUTE GIRL.
I WORRY THAT SOME WEIRD FELLOW WILL STALK YOU.
...
HANA?
GASP
WHUP
NO, NO, NOTHING LIKE THAT.
ABSOLUTELY NOTHING GOING ON WITH HANA, RIGHT?
YES! ABSOLUTELY NOTHING!
WELL, GOOD.

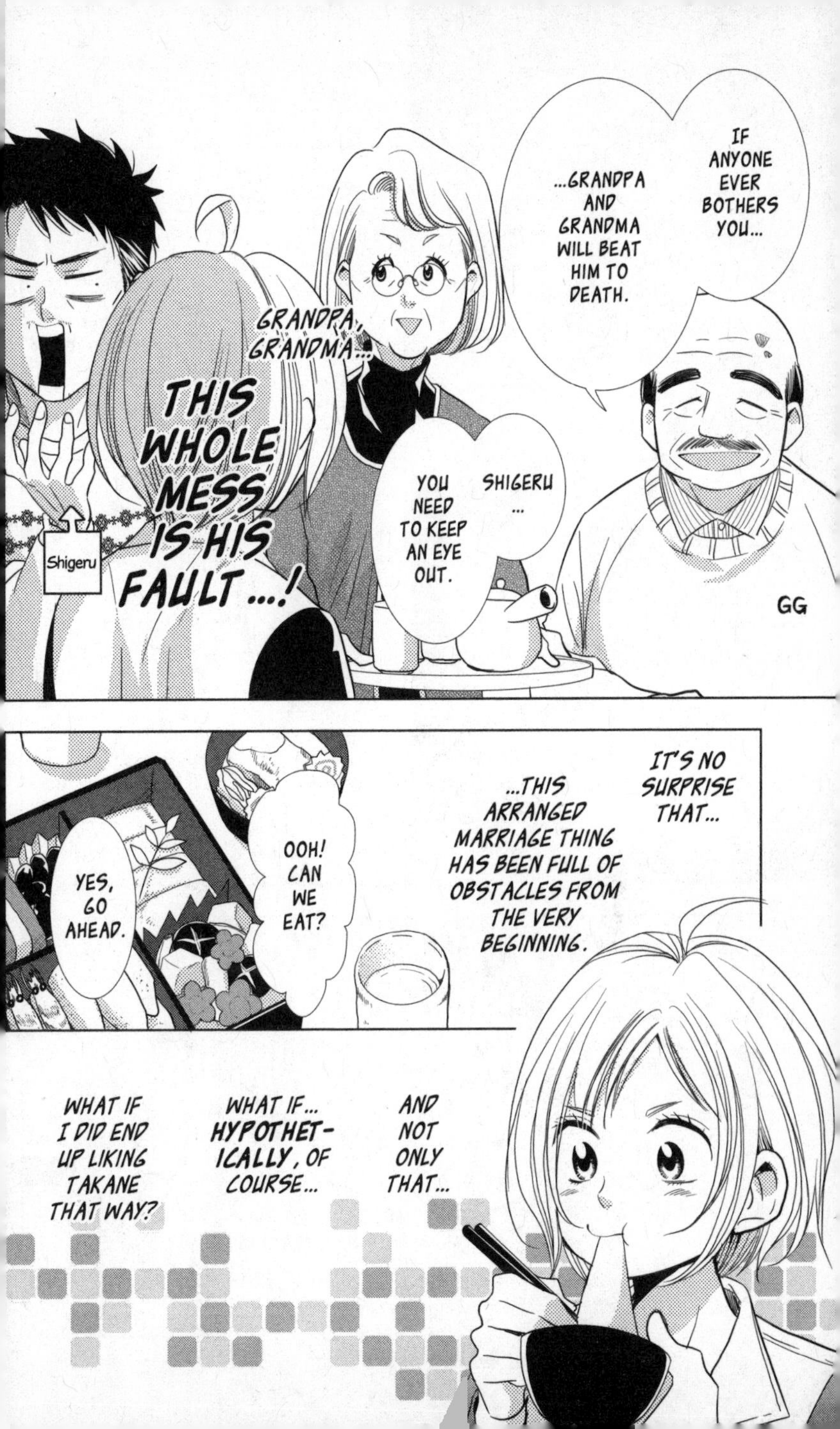
IF ANYONE EVER BOTHERS YOU...
...GRANDPA AND GRANDMA WILL BEAT HIM TO DEATH.
GG
SHIGERU ...
YOU NEED TO KEEP AN EYE OUT.
GRANDPA, GRANDMA...
THIS WHOLE MESS IS HIS FAULT...!
Shigeru
IT'S NO SURPRISE THAT...
...THIS ARRANGED MARRIAGE THING HAS BEEN FULL OF OBSTACLES FROM THE VERY BEGINNING.
OOH! CAN WE EAT?
YES, GO AHEAD.
AND NOT ONLY THAT...
WHAT IF... HYPOTHET-ICALLY, OF COURSE...
WHAT IF I DID END UP LIKING TAKANE THAT WAY?

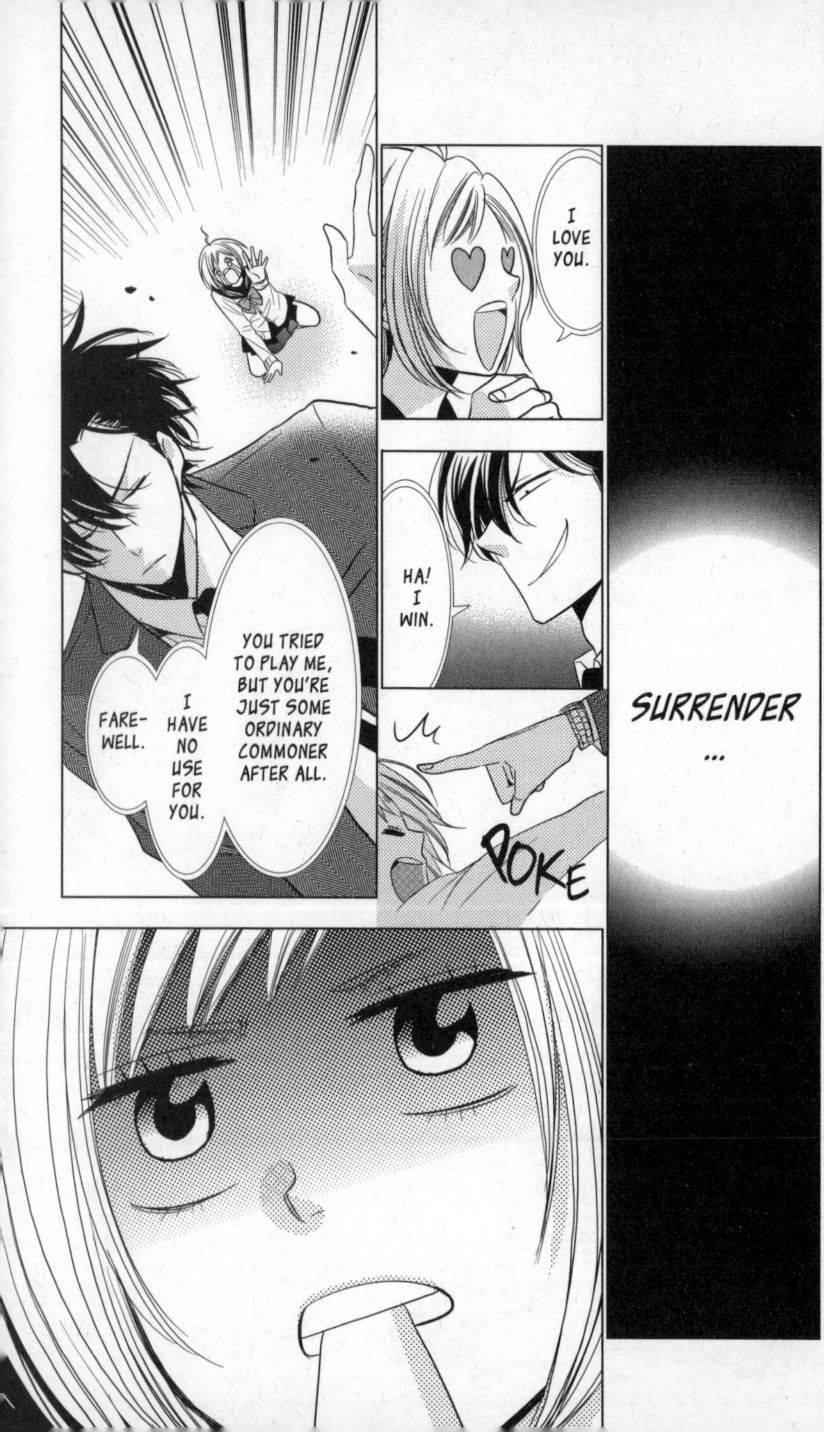
SURRENDER ...
I LOVE YOU.
HA! I WIN.
POKE
YOU TRIED TO PLAY ME, BUT YOU'RE JUST SOME ORDINARY COMMONER AFTER ALL.
I HAVE NO USE FOR YOU.
FARE-WELL.

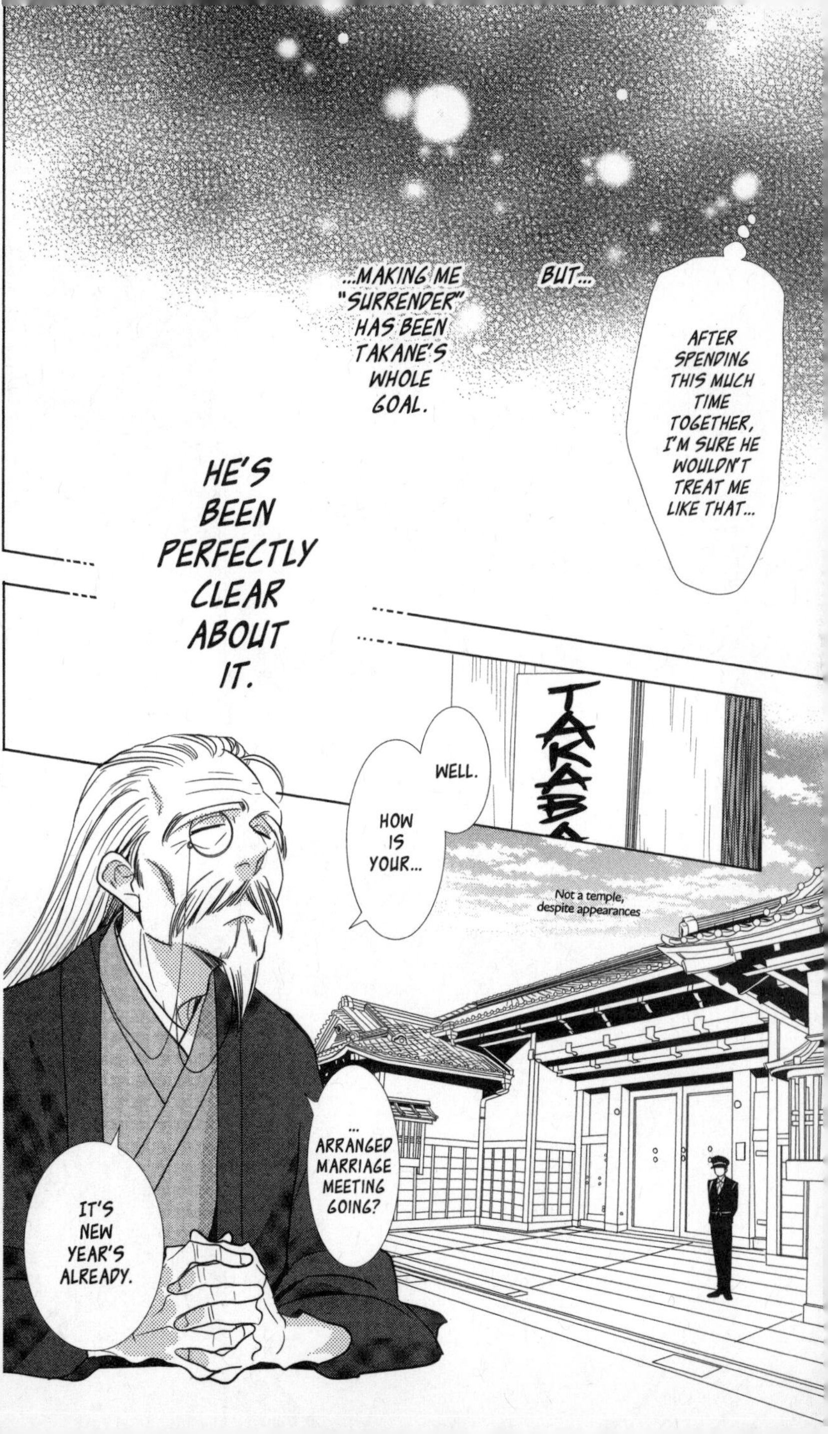

AFTER SPENDING THIS MUCH TIME TOGETHER, I'M SURE HE WOULDN'T TREAT ME LIKE THAT...
BUT...
...MAKING ME "SURRENDER" HAS BEEN TAKANE'S WHOLE GOAL.
HE'S BEEN PERFECTLY CLEAR ABOUT IT.
WELL.
HOW IS YOUR...
Not a temple, despite appearances
...ARRANGED MARRIAGE MEETING GOING?
IT'S NEW YEAR'S ALREADY.

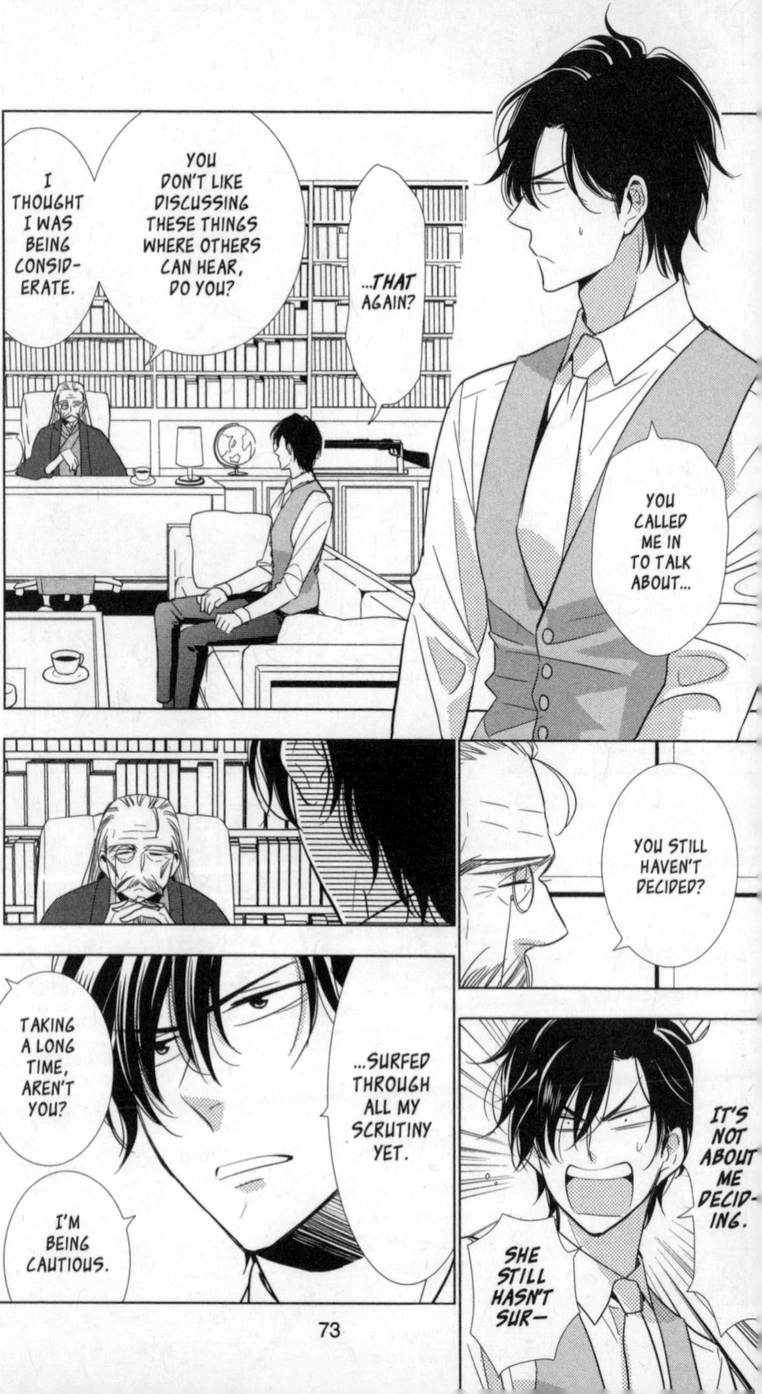
YOU CALLED ME IN TO TALK ABOUT...
...THAT AGAIN?
YOU DON'T LIKE DISCUSSING THESE THINGS WHERE OTHERS CAN HEAR, DO YOU?
I THOUGHT I WAS BEING CONSID-ERATE.
YOU STILL HAVEN'T DECIDED?
IT'S NOT ABOUT ME DECID-ING.
SHE STILL HASN'T SUR—
...SURFED THROUGH ALL MY SCRUTINY YET.
TAKING A LONG TIME, AREN'T YOU?
I'M BEING CAUTIOUS.

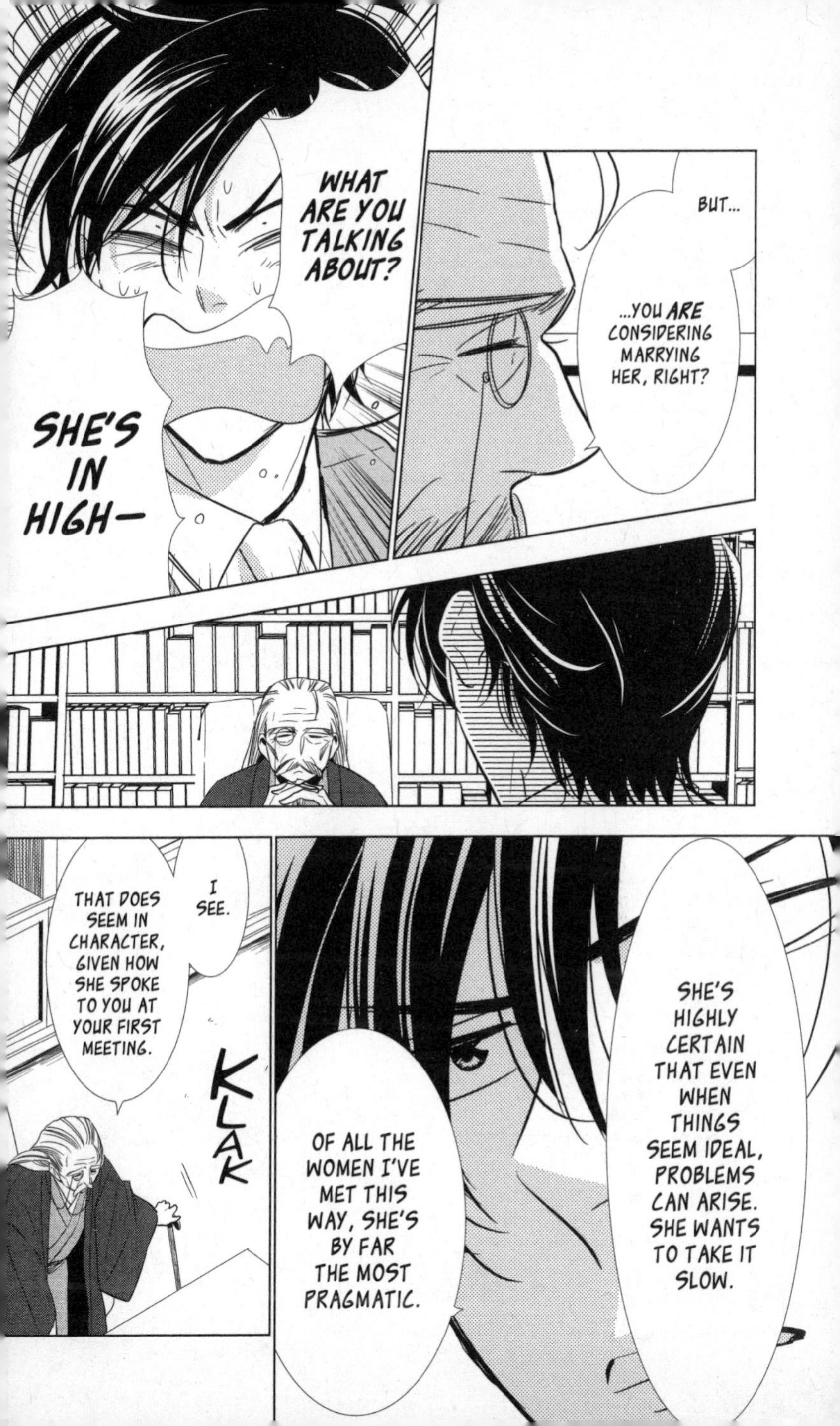
BUT...
...YOU ARE CONSIDERING MARRYING HER, RIGHT?
WHAT ARE YOU TALKING ABOUT?
SHE'S IN HIGH—
SHE'S HIGHLY CERTAIN THAT EVEN WHEN THINGS SEEM IDEAL, PROBLEMS CAN ARISE. SHE WANTS TO TAKE IT SLOW.
OF ALL THE WOMEN I'VE MET THIS WAY, SHE'S BY FAR THE MOST PRAGMATIC.
I SEE.
THAT DOES SEEM IN CHARACTER, GIVEN HOW SHE SPOKE TO YOU AT YOUR FIRST MEETING.
KLAK

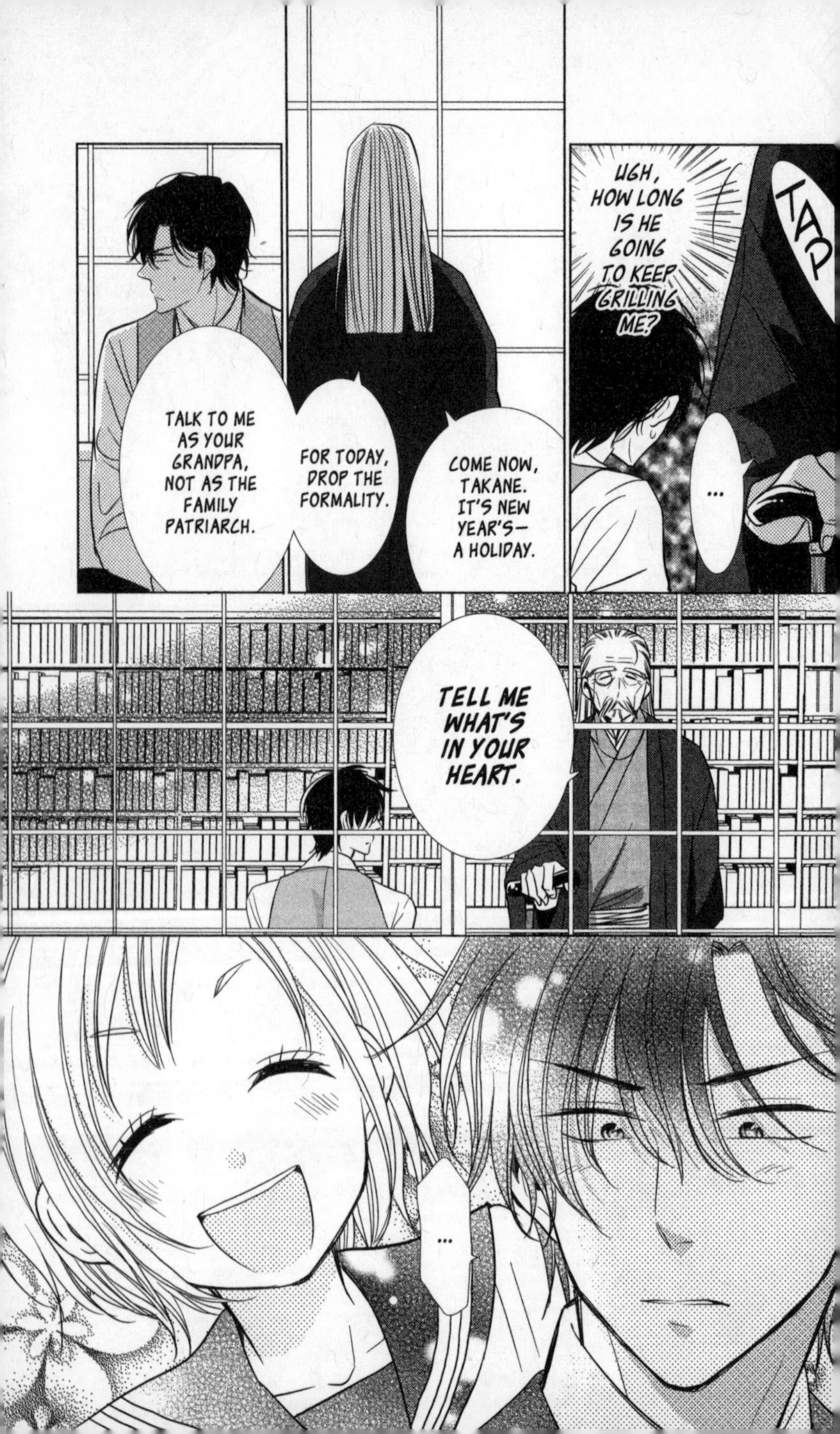
TAP
UGH, HOW LONG IS HE GOING TO KEEP GRILLING ME?
...
COME NOW, TAKANE. IT'S NEW YEAR'S— A HOLIDAY.
FOR TODAY, DROP THE FORMALITY.
TALK TO ME AS YOUR GRANDPA, NOT AS THE FAMILY PATRIARCH.
TELL ME WHAT'S IN YOUR HEART.
...

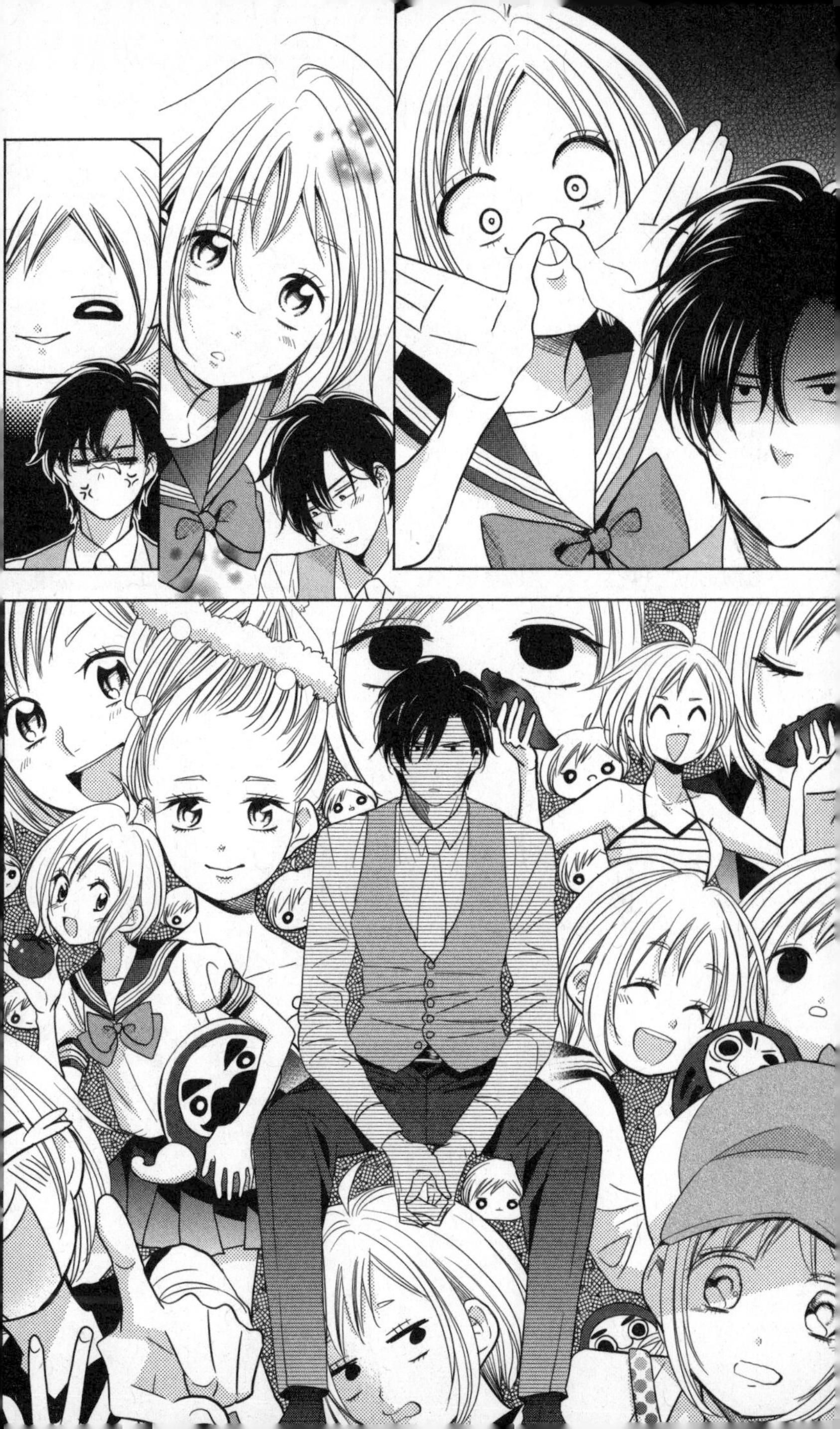

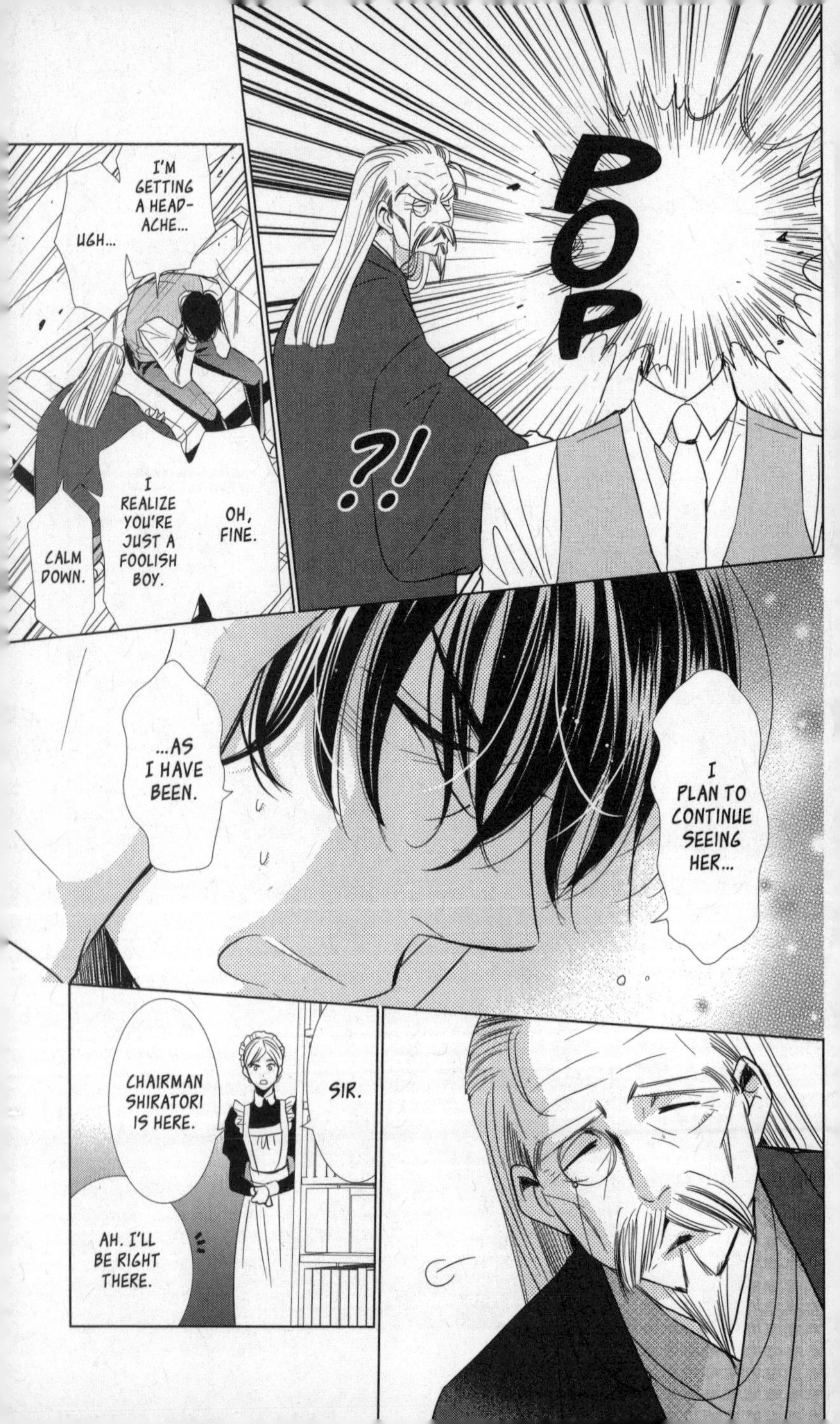
POP
?!
I'M GETTING A HEAD-ACHE...
UGH...
OH, FINE.
I REALIZE YOU'RE JUST A FOOLISH BOY.
CALM DOWN.
I PLAN TO CONTINUE SEEING HER...
...AS I HAVE BEEN.
SIR.
CHAIRMAN SHIRATORI IS HERE.
AH. I'LL BE RIGHT THERE.

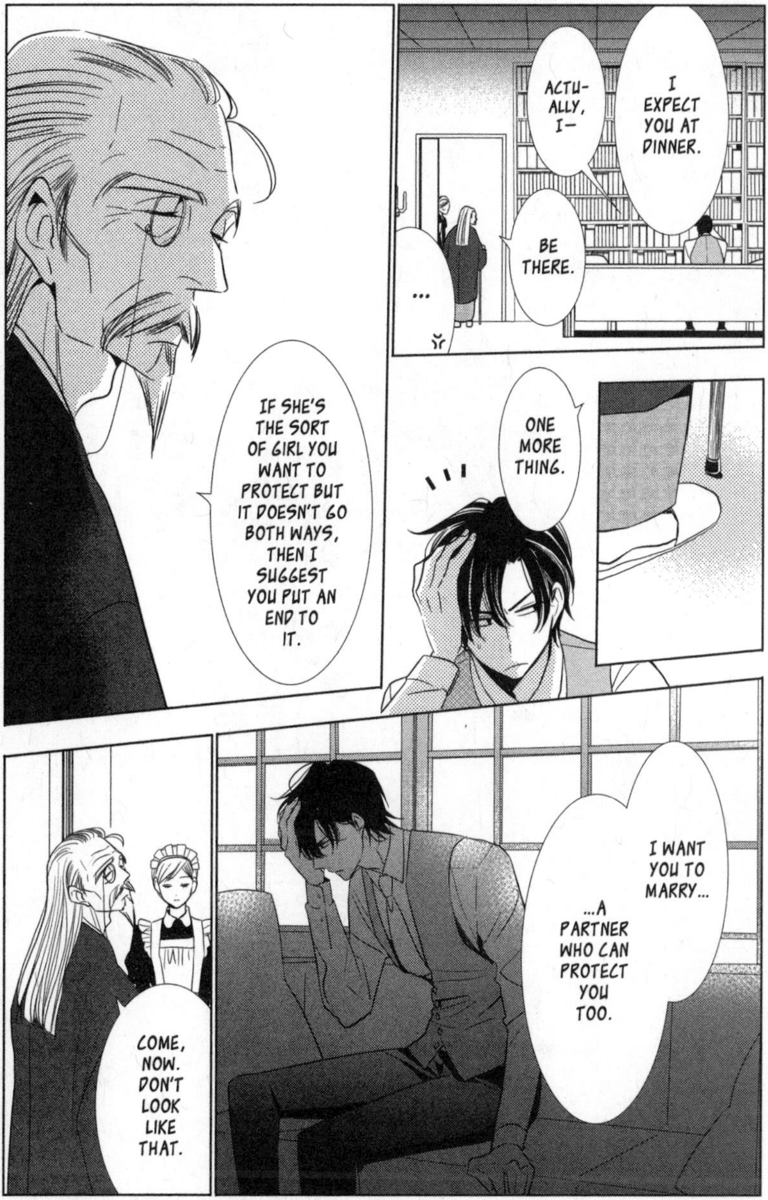
I EXPECT YOU AT DINNER.
ACTUALLY, I—
BE THERE.
...
ONE MORE THING.
IF SHE'S THE SORT OF GIRL YOU WANT TO PROTECT BUT IT DOESN'T GO BOTH WAYS, THEN I SUGGEST YOU PUT AN END TO IT.
I WANT YOU TO MARRY...
...A PARTNER WHO CAN PROTECT YOU TOO.
COME, NOW. DON'T LOOK LIKE THAT.

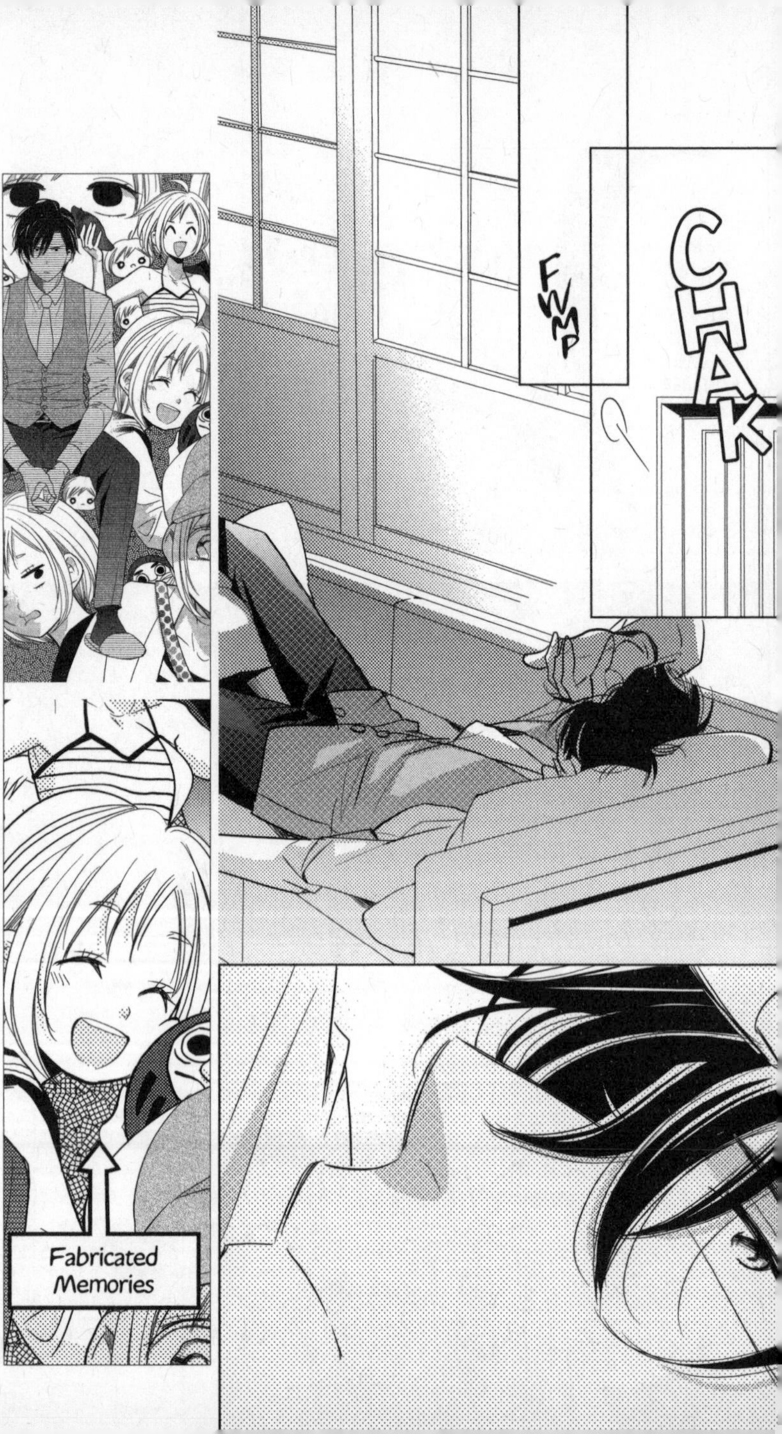
CHAK
FWMP
Fabricated Memories

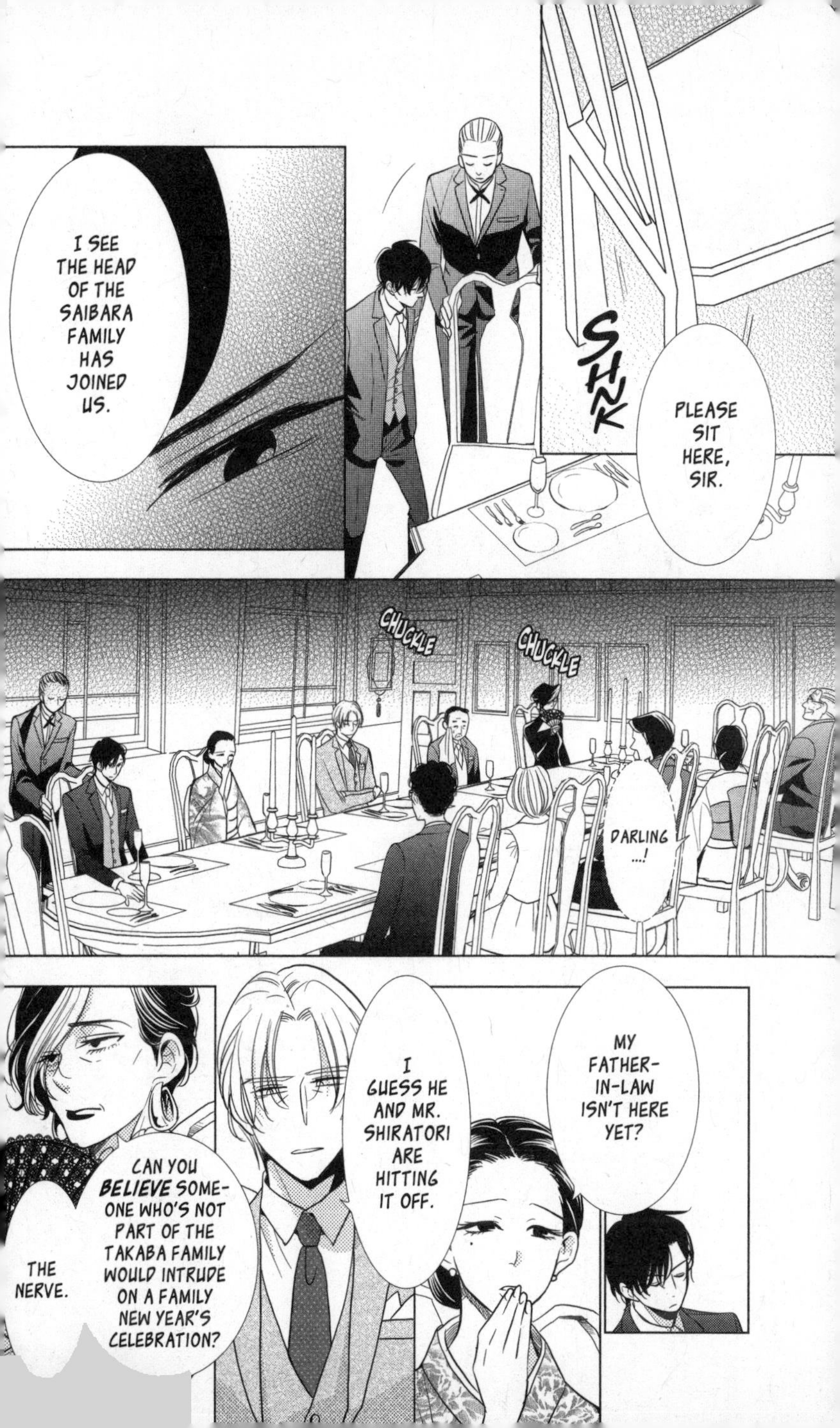
SHNK
PLEASE SIT HERE, SIR.
I SEE THE HEAD OF THE SAIBARA FAMILY HAS JOINED US.
CHUCKLE
CHUCKLE
DARLING ...!
MY FATHER-IN-LAW ISN'T HERE YET?
I GUESS HE AND MR. SHIRATORI ARE HITTING IT OFF.
CAN YOU *BELIEVE* SOME-ONE WHO'S NOT PART OF THE TAKABA FAMILY WOULD INTRUDE ON A FAMILY NEW YEAR'S CELEBRATION?
THE NERVE.

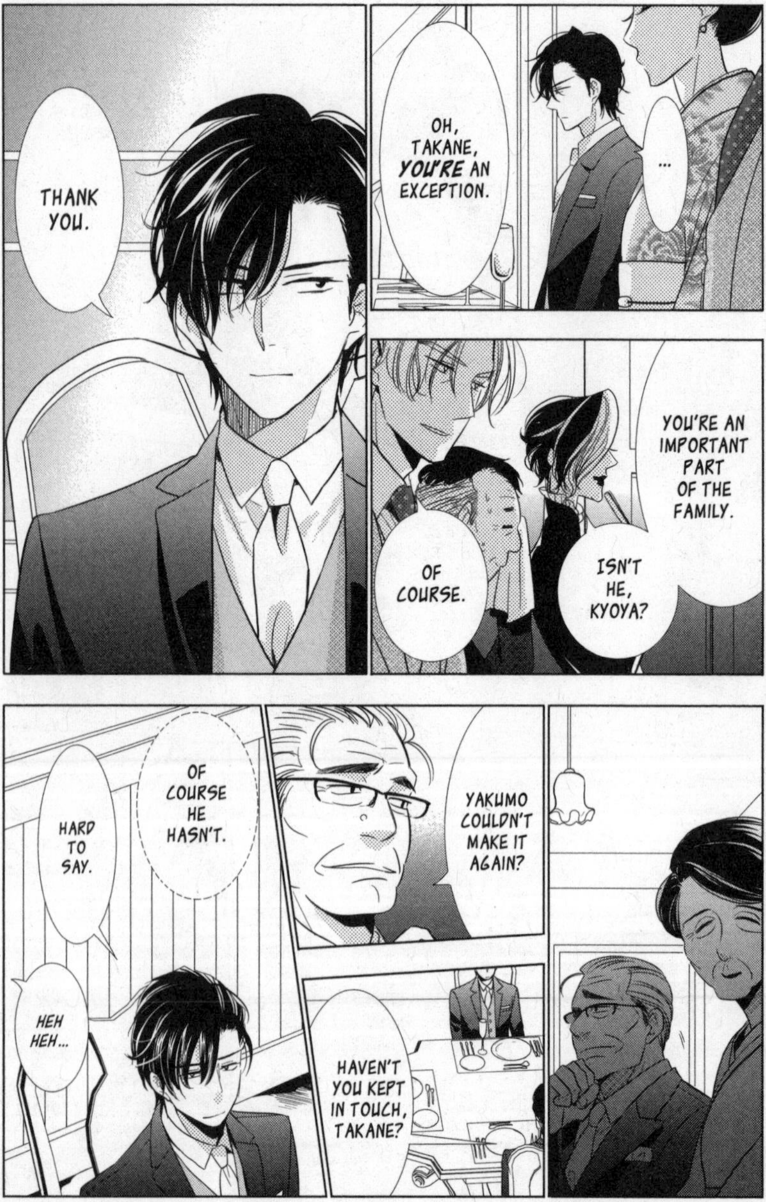
...
OH, TAKANE, *YOU'RE* AN EXCEPTION.
YOU'RE AN IMPORTANT PART OF THE FAMILY.
ISN'T HE, KYOYA?
OF COURSE.
THANK YOU.
YAKUMO COULDN'T MAKE IT AGAIN?
HAVEN'T YOU KEPT IN TOUCH, TAKANE?
OF COURSE HE HASN'T.
HARD TO SAY.
HEH HEH...

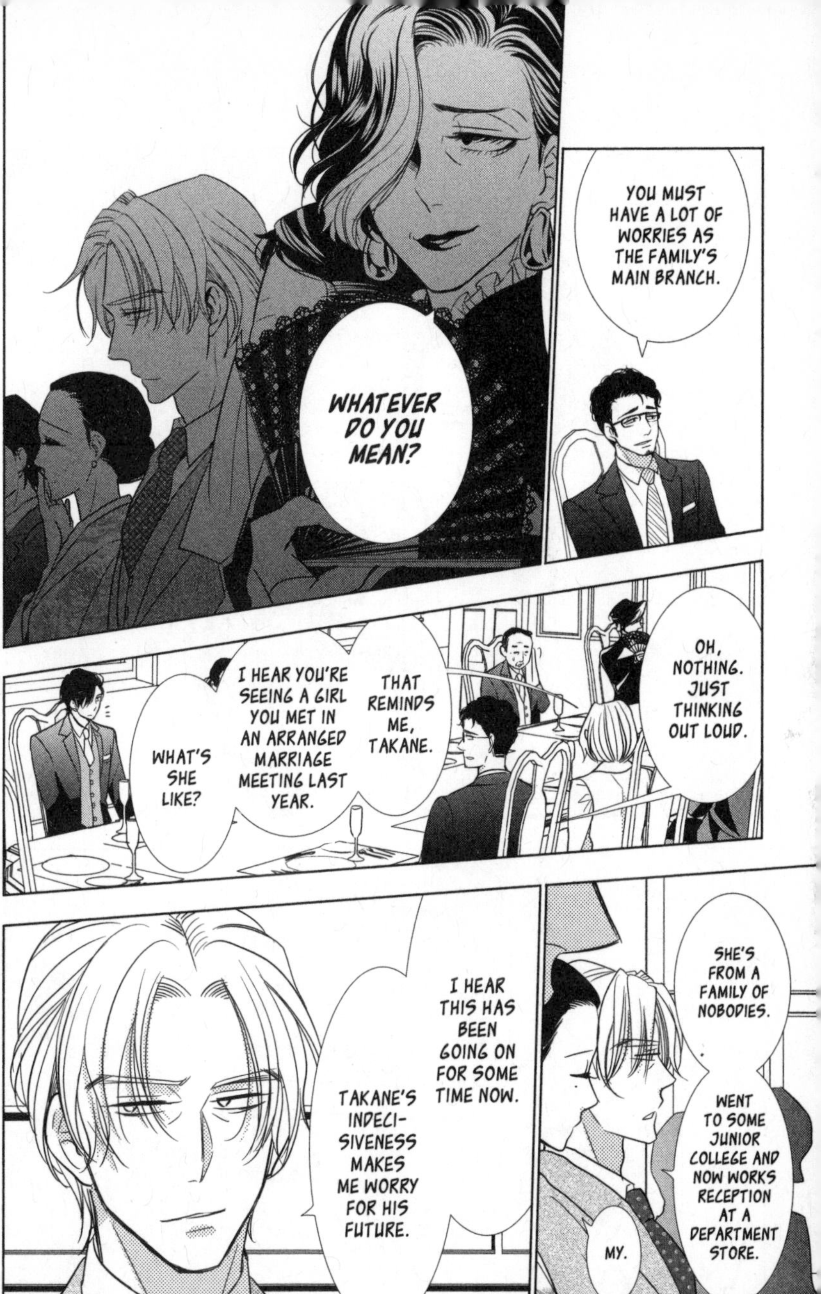
YOU MUST HAVE A LOT OF WORRIES AS THE FAMILY'S MAIN BRANCH.
WHATEVER DO YOU MEAN?
OH, NOTHING. JUST THINKING OUT LOUD.
THAT REMINDS ME, TAKANE.
I HEAR YOU'RE SEEING A GIRL YOU MET IN AN ARRANGED MARRIAGE MEETING LAST YEAR.
WHAT'S SHE LIKE?
SHE'S FROM A FAMILY OF NOBODIES.
WENT TO SOME JUNIOR COLLEGE AND NOW WORKS RECEPTION AT A DEPARTMENT STORE.
MY.
I HEAR THIS HAS BEEN GOING ON FOR SOME TIME NOW.
TAKANE'S INDECI-SIVENESS MAKES ME WORRY FOR HIS FUTURE.

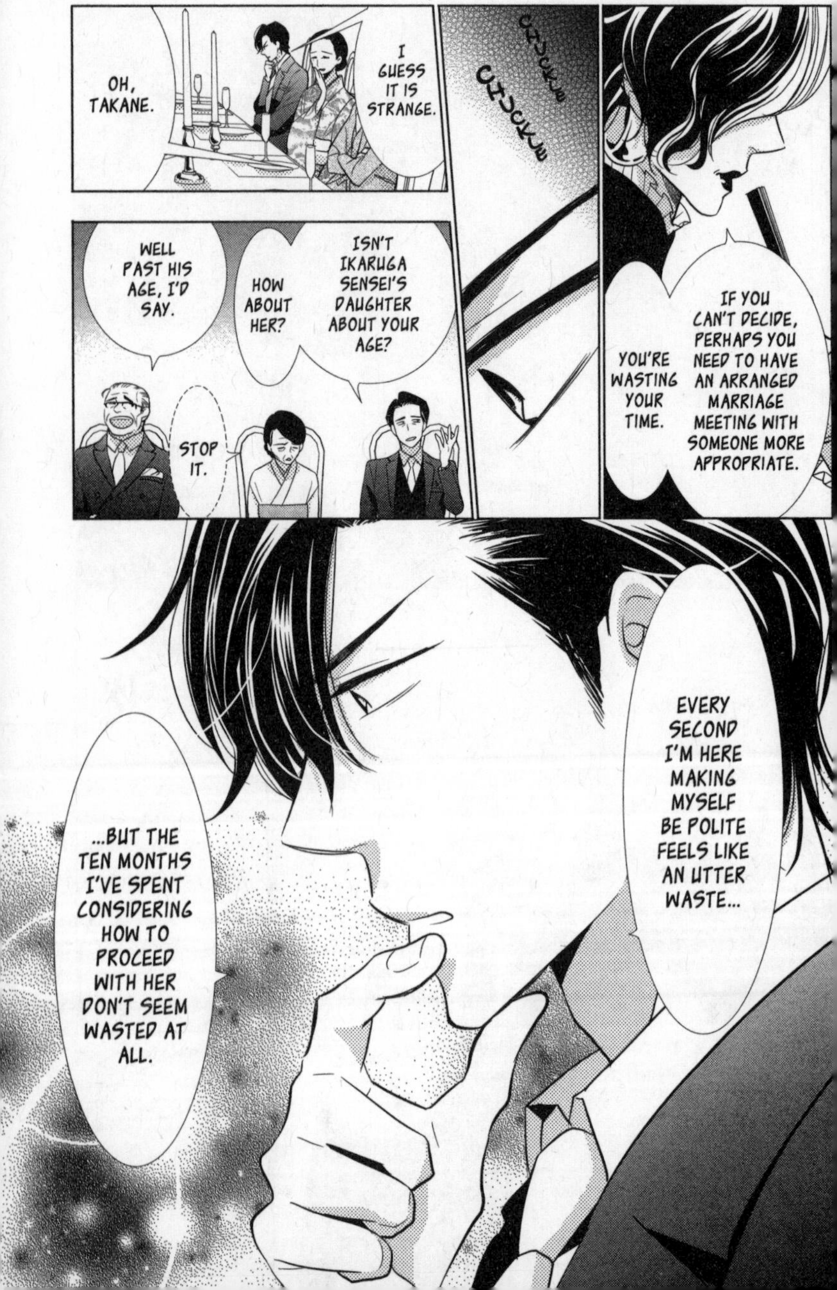
IF YOU CAN'T DECIDE, PERHAPS YOU NEED TO HAVE AN ARRANGED MARRIAGE MEETING WITH SOMEONE MORE APPROPRIATE.
YOU'RE WASTING YOUR TIME.
CHUCKLE
CHUCKLE
I GUESS IT IS STRANGE.
OH, TAKANE.
ISN'T IKARUGA SENSEI'S DAUGHTER ABOUT YOUR AGE?
HOW ABOUT HER?
WELL PAST HIS AGE, I'D SAY.
STOP IT.
EVERY SECOND I'M HERE MAKING MYSELF BE POLITE FEELS LIKE AN UTTER WASTE...
...BUT THE TEN MONTHS I'VE SPENT CONSIDERING HOW TO PROCEED WITH HER DON'T SEEM WASTED AT ALL.

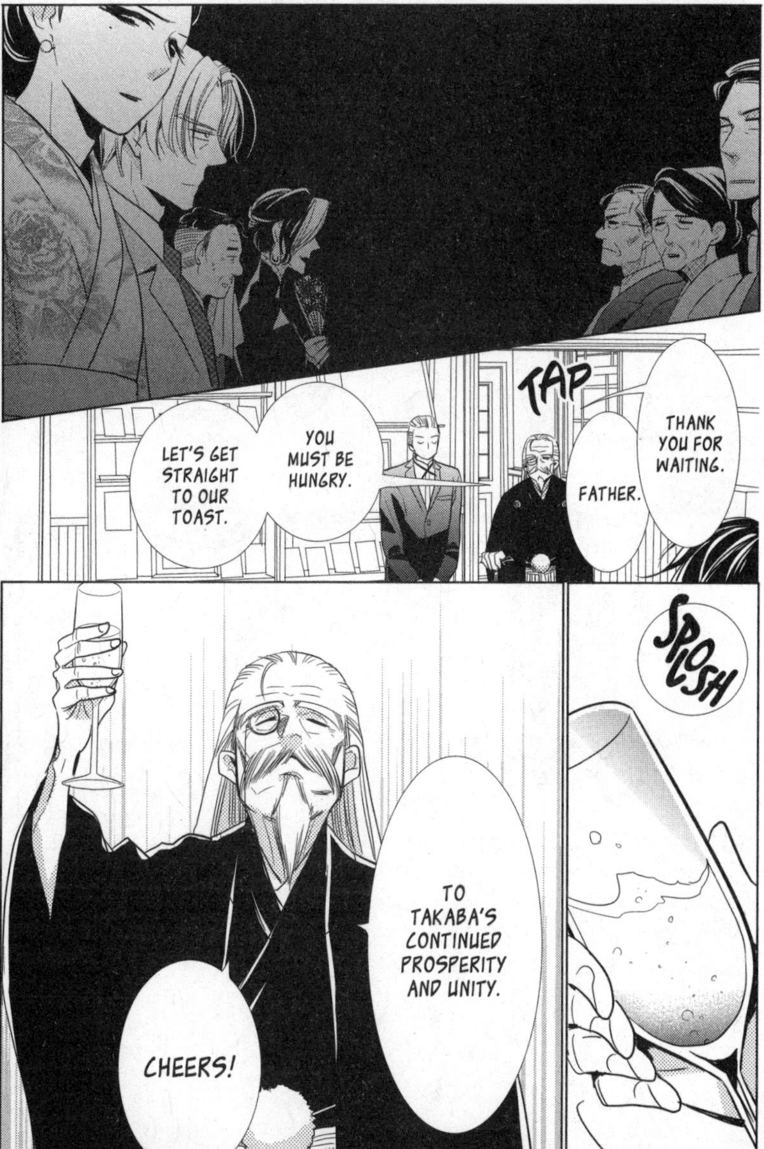
THANK YOU FOR WAITING.
TAP
FATHER.
YOU MUST BE HUNGRY.
LET'S GET STRAIGHT TO OUR TOAST.
SPLOSH
TO TAKABA'S CONTINUED PROSPERITY AND UNITY.
CHEERS!

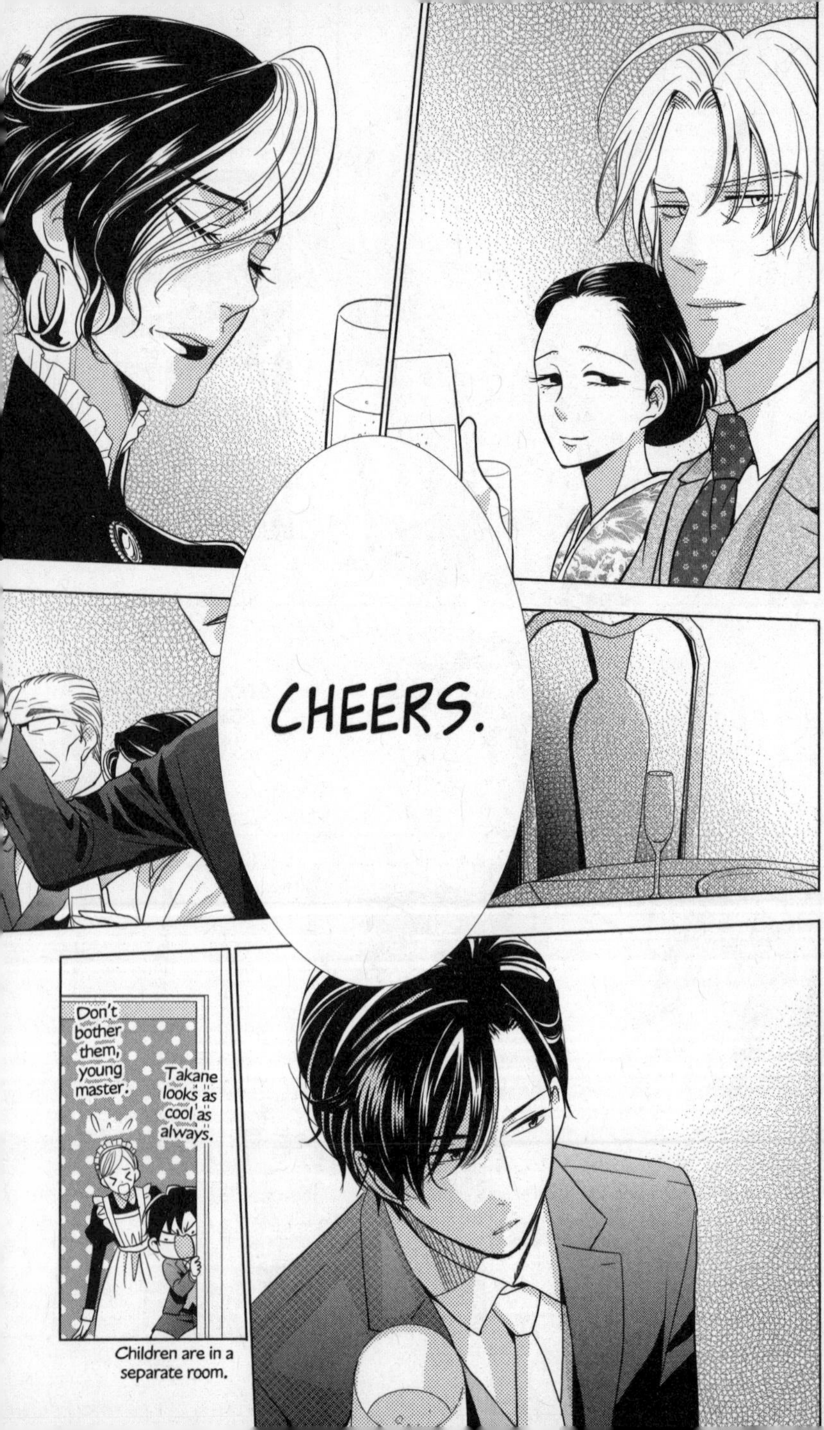
CHEERS.
Takane looks as cool as always.
Don't bother them, young master.
Children are in a separate room.

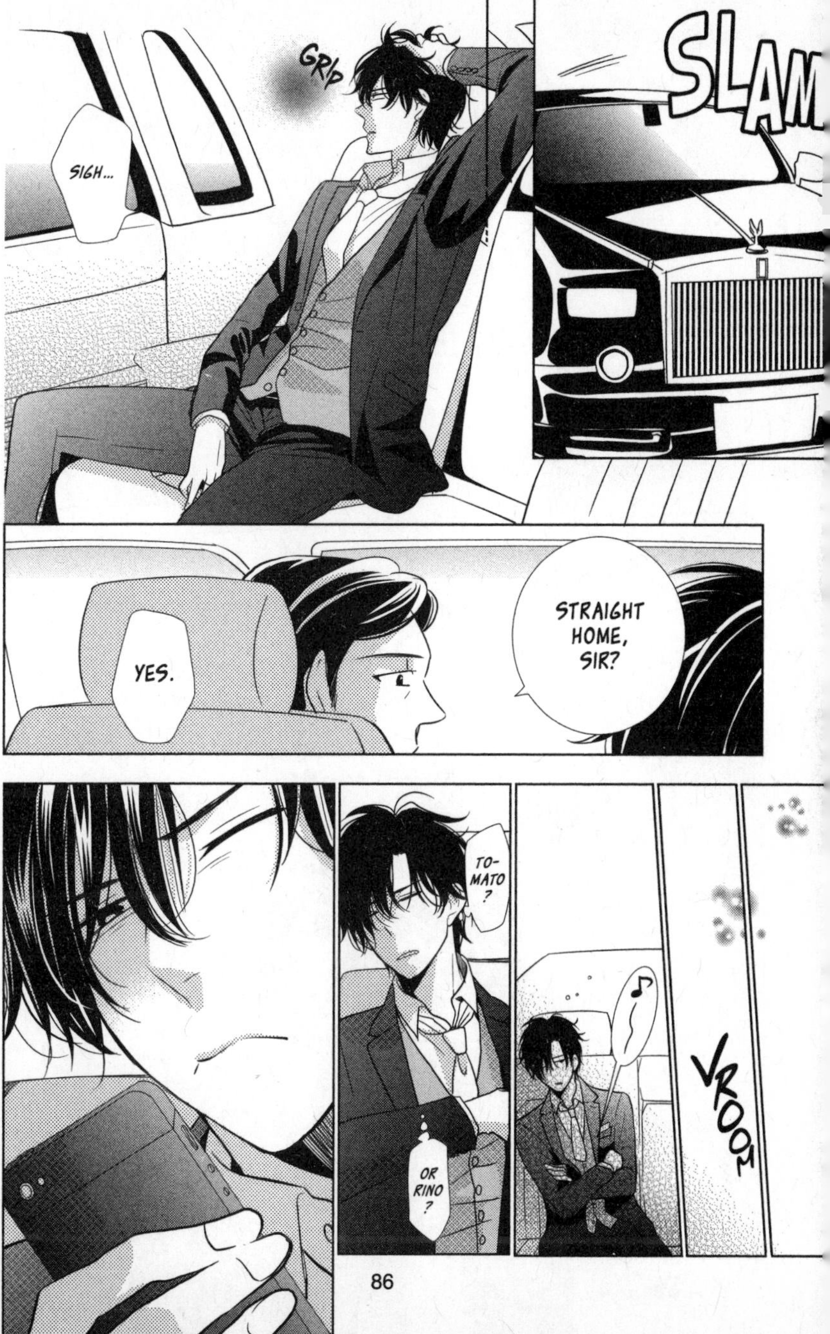
SLAM
GRIP
SIGH...
STRAIGHT HOME, SIR?
YES.
VROOM
♪
TO-MATO?
OR RINO?

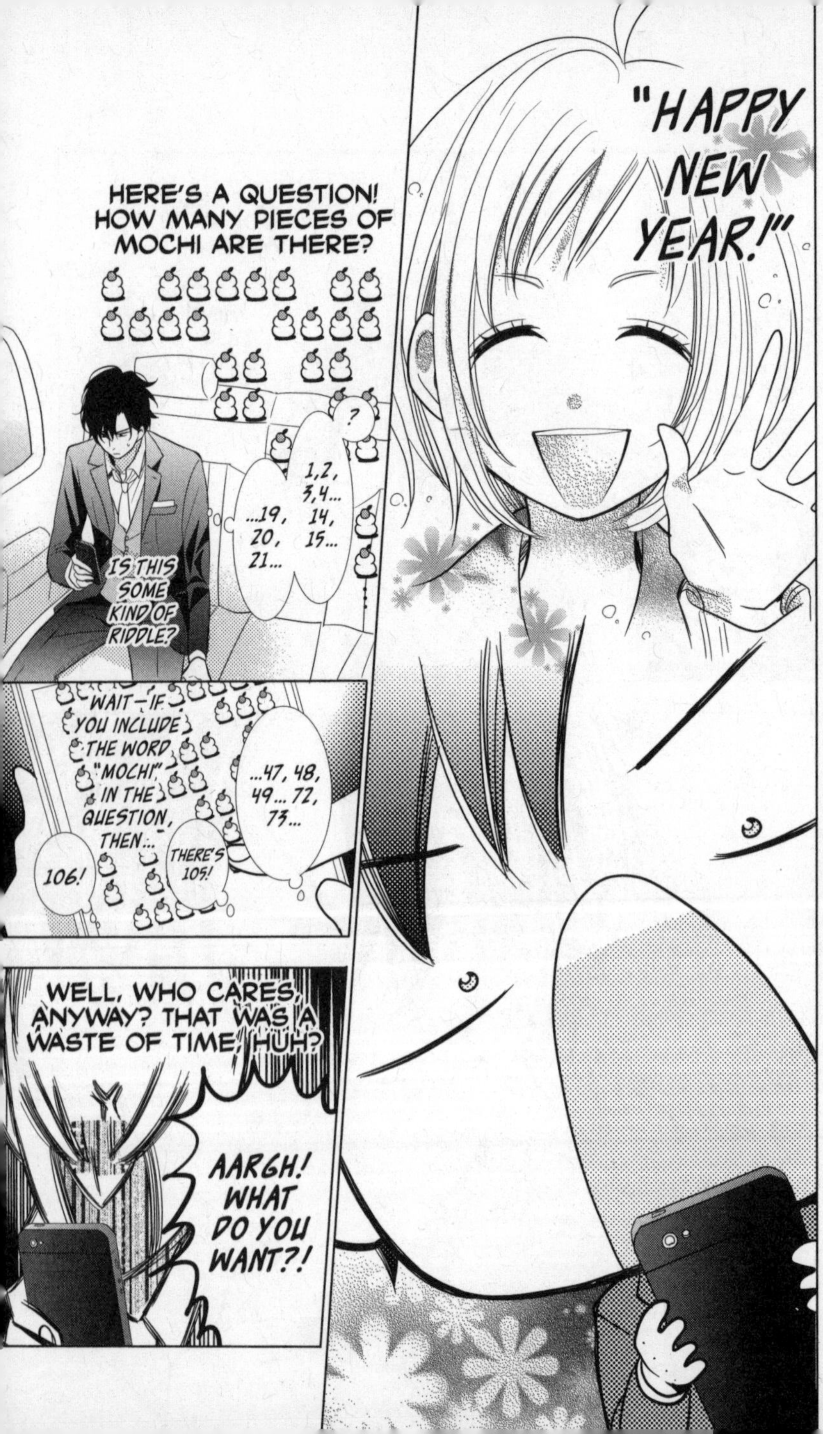
"HAPPY NEW YEAR!"
HERE'S A QUESTION! HOW MANY PIECES OF MOCHI ARE THERE?
?
1,2, 3,4... 14, 15...
...19, 20, 21...
IS THIS SOME KIND OF RIDDLE?
...47, 48, 49... 72, 73...
WAIT—IF YOU INCLUDE THE WORD "MOCHI" IN THE QUESTION, THEN...
THERE'S 105!
106!
WELL, WHO CARES, ANYWAY? THAT WAS A WASTE OF TIME, HUH?
AARGH! WHAT DO YOU WANT?!

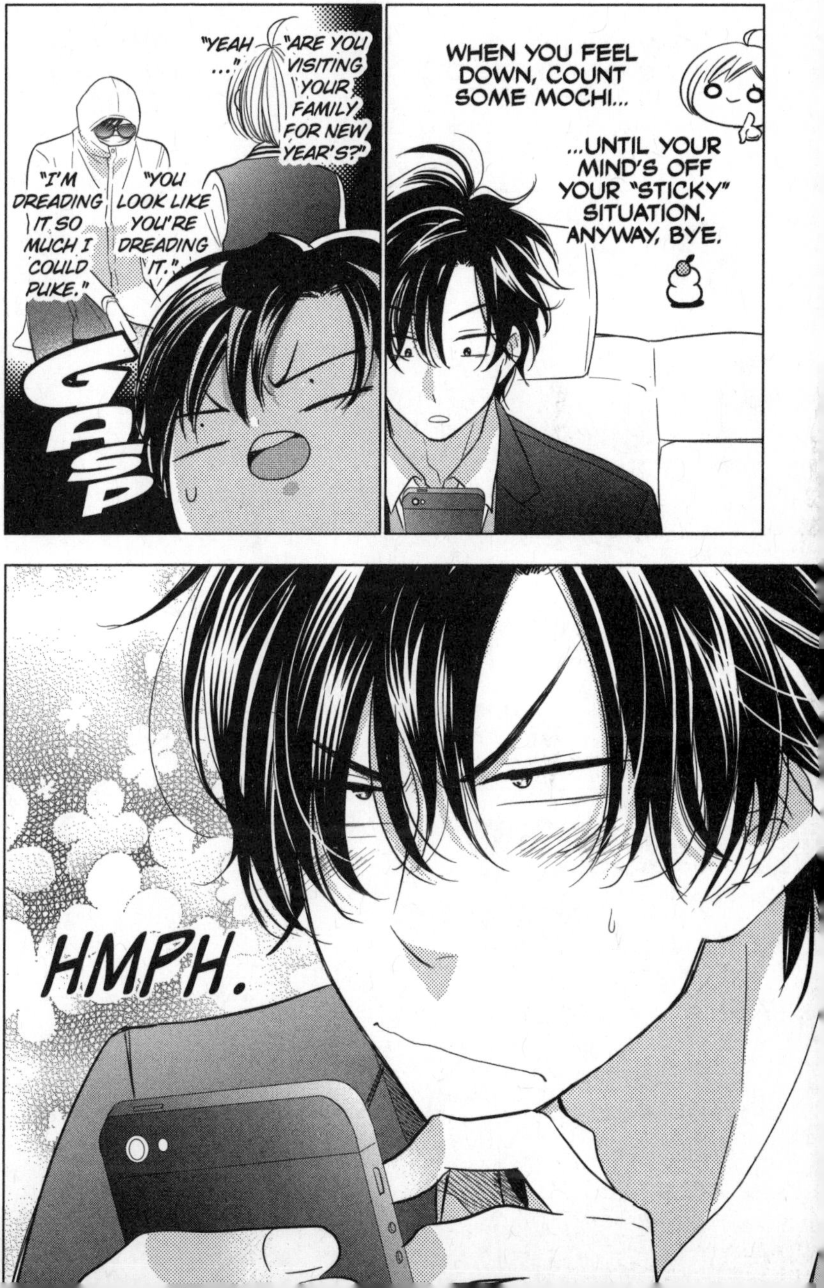
WHEN YOU FEEL DOWN, COUNT SOME MOCHI...
...UNTIL YOUR MIND'S OFF YOUR "STICKY" SITUATION. ANYWAY, BYE.
"ARE YOU VISITING YOUR FAMILY FOR NEW YEAR'S?"
"YEAH..."
"YOU LOOK LIKE YOU'RE DREADING IT."
"I'M DREADING IT SO MUCH I COULD PUKE."
GASP
HMPH.

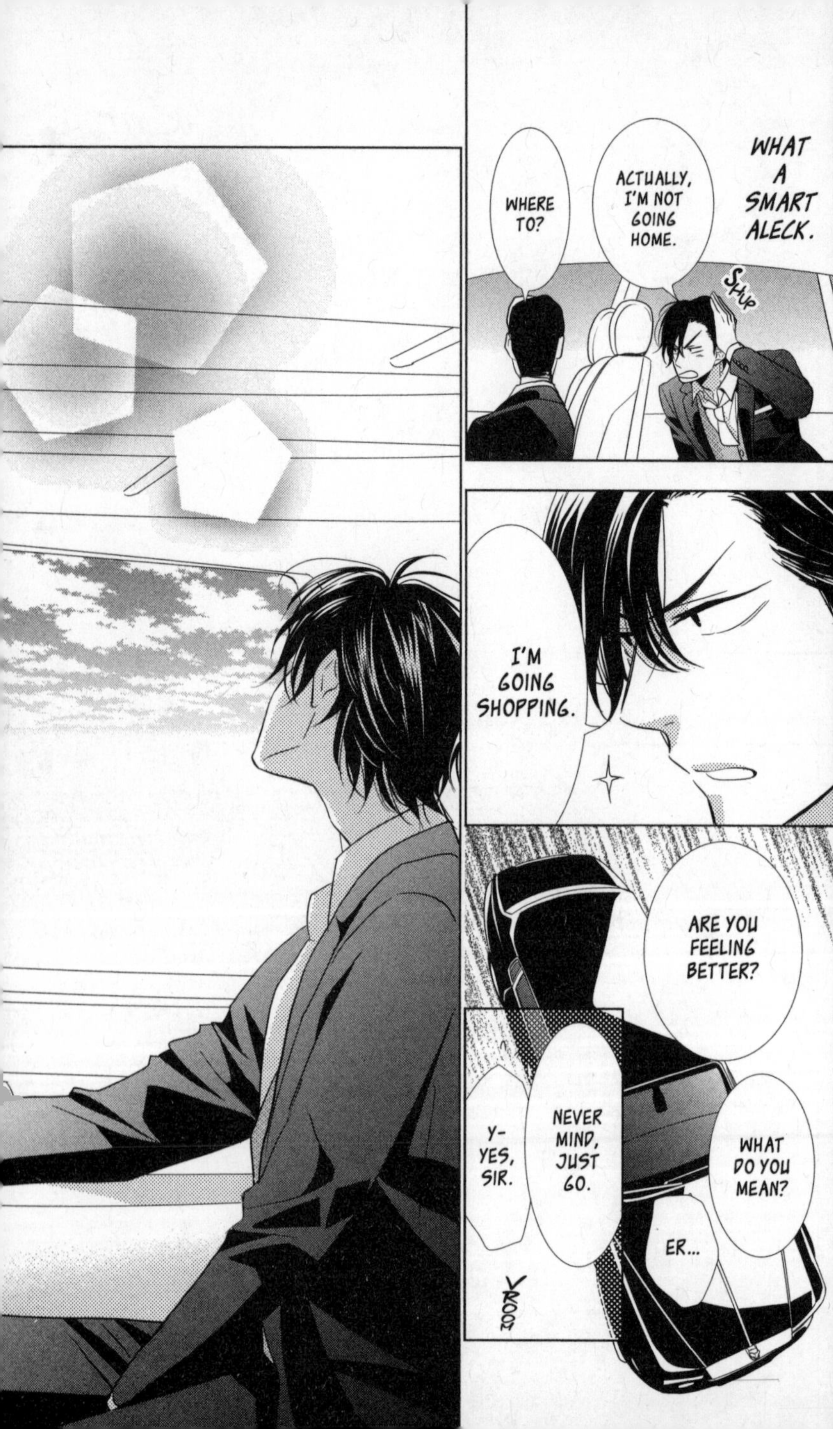
WHAT A SMART ALECK.
SHUP
ACTUALLY, I'M NOT GOING HOME.
WHERE TO?
I'M GOING SHOPPING.
ARE YOU FEELING BETTER?
WHAT DO YOU MEAN?
ER...
NEVER MIND, JUST GO.
Y-YES, SIR.
VROOM

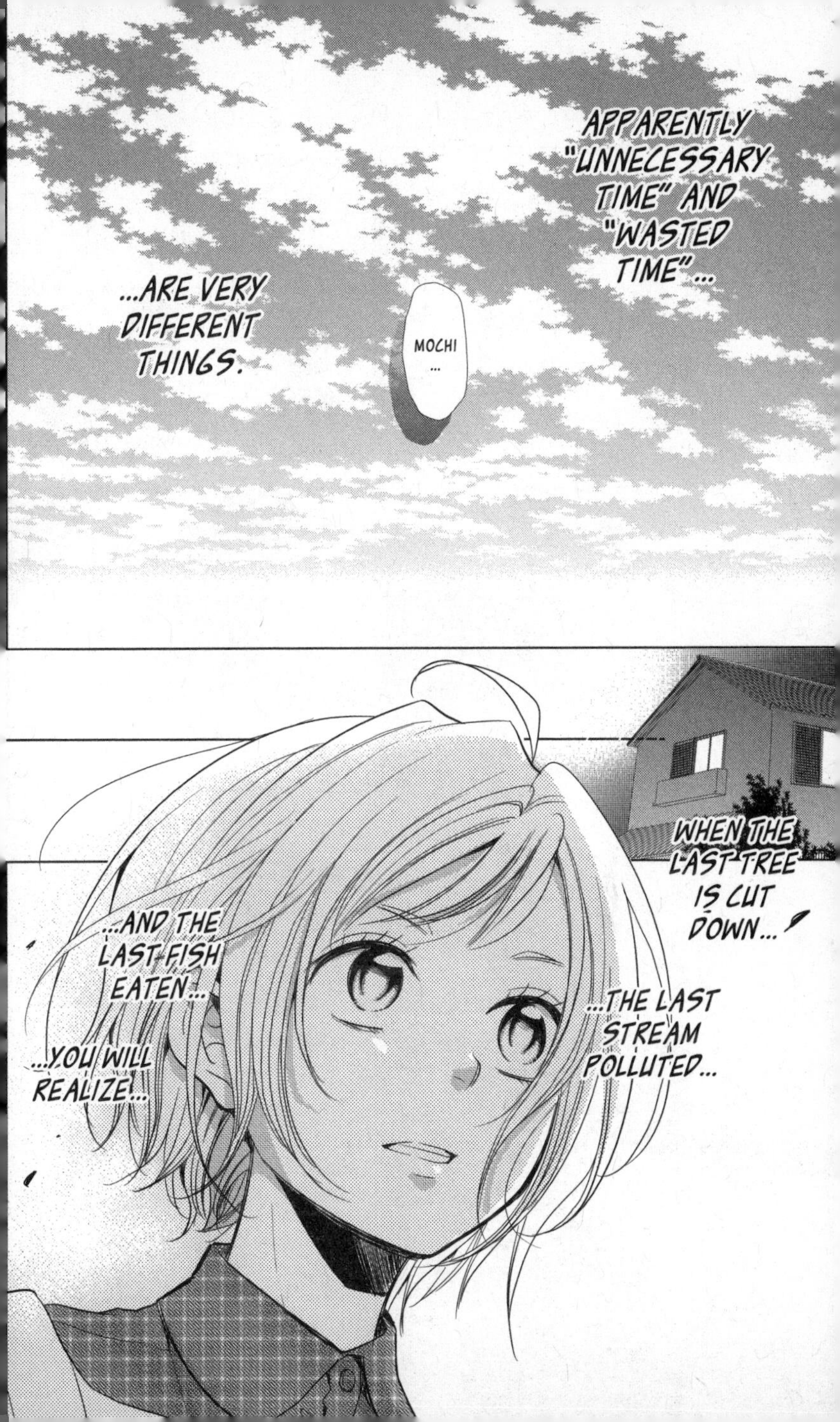
APPARENTLY "UNNECESSARY TIME" AND "WASTED TIME"...
...ARE VERY DIFFERENT THINGS.
MOCHI ...
WHEN THE LAST TREE IS CUT DOWN...
...THE LAST STREAM POLLUTED...
...AND THE LAST FISH EATEN...
...YOU WILL REALIZE...

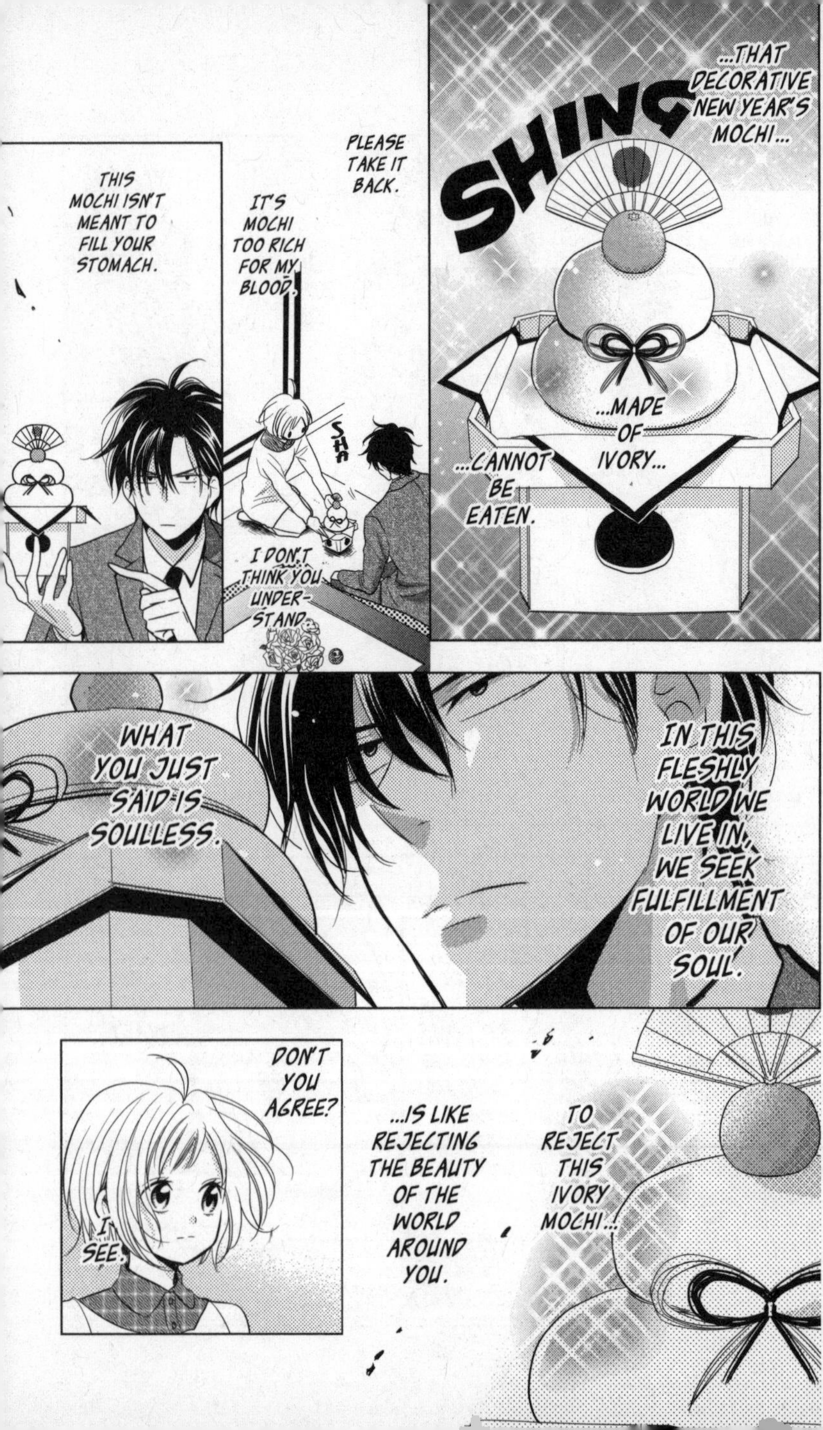

...THAT DECORATIVE NEW YEAR'S MOCHI...
SHING
...MADE OF IVORY...
...CANNOT BE EATEN.
PLEASE TAKE IT BACK.
IT'S MOCHI TOO RICH FOR MY BLOOD.
SHA
I DON'T THINK YOU UNDERSTAND.
THIS MOCHI ISN'T MEANT TO FILL YOUR STOMACH.
IN THIS FLESHLY WORLD WE LIVE IN, WE SEEK FULFILLMENT OF OUR SOUL.
WHAT YOU JUST SAID IS SOULLESS.
TO REJECT THIS IVORY MOCHI...
...IS LIKE REJECTING THE BEAUTY OF THE WORLD AROUND YOU.
DON'T YOU AGREE?
I SEE.

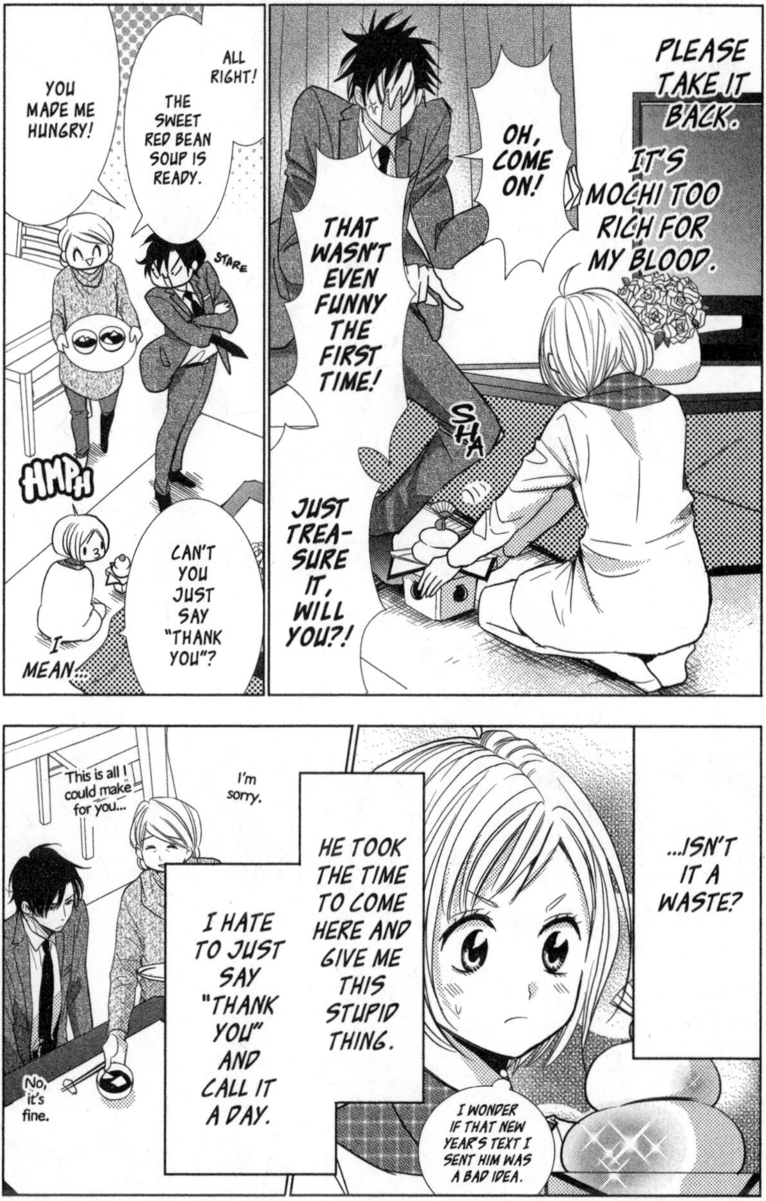
PLEASE TAKE IT BACK.
IT'S MOCHI TOO RICH FOR MY BLOOD.
OH, COME ON!
THAT WASN'T EVEN FUNNY THE FIRST TIME!
SHA
JUST TREASURE IT, WILL YOU?!
ALL RIGHT! THE SWEET RED BEAN SOUP IS READY.
YOU MADE ME HUNGRY!
STARE
CAN'T YOU JUST SAY "THANK YOU"?
HMPH
I MEAN...
...ISN'T IT A WASTE?
I WONDER IF THAT NEW YEAR'S TEXT I SENT HIM WAS A BAD IDEA.
HE TOOK THE TIME TO COME HERE AND GIVE ME THIS STUPID THING.
I HATE TO JUST SAY "THANK YOU" AND CALL IT A DAY.
I'm sorry.
This is all I could make for you...
No, it's fine.

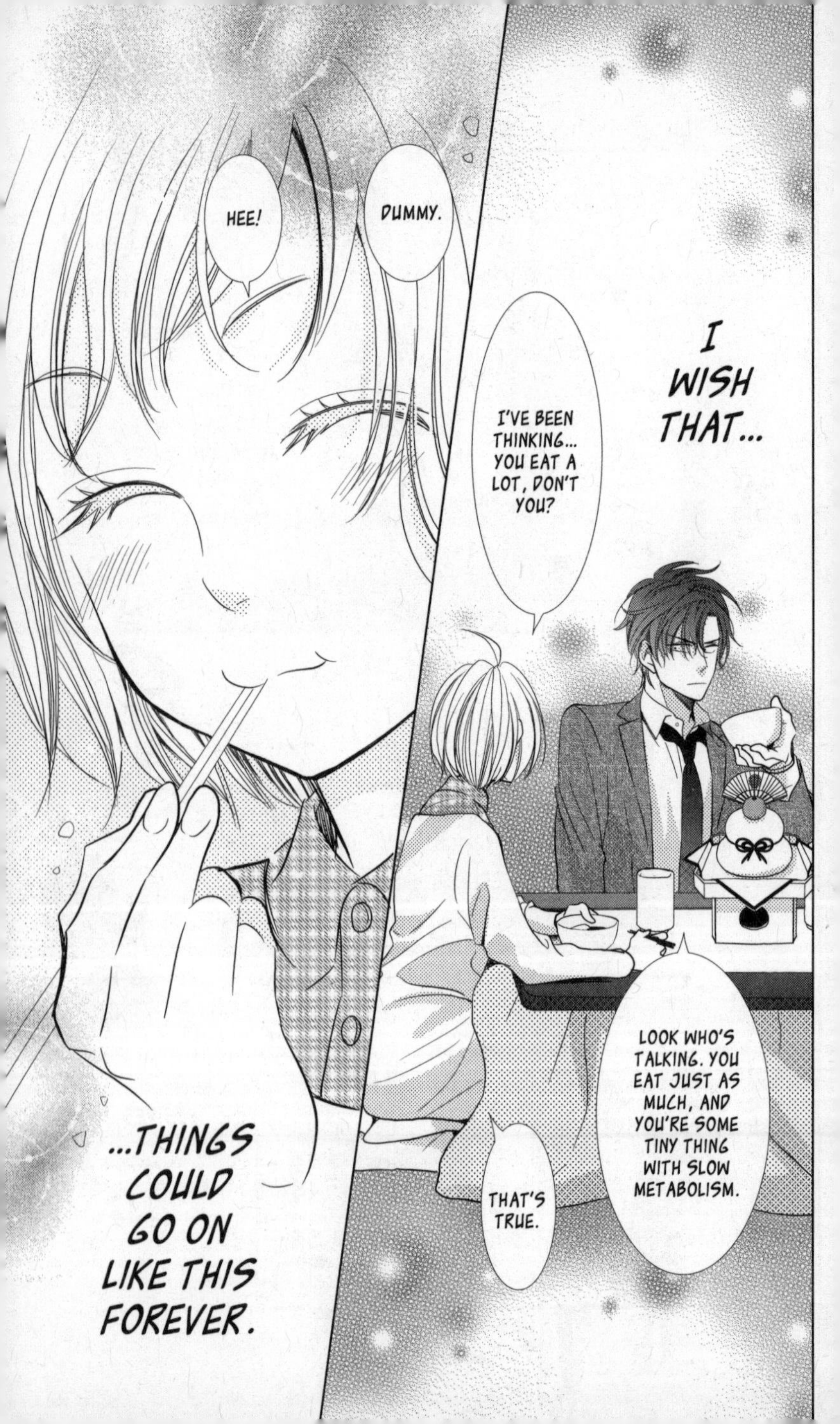
I WISH THAT...
I'VE BEEN THINKING... YOU EAT A LOT, DON'T YOU?
LOOK WHO'S TALKING. YOU EAT JUST AS MUCH, AND YOU'RE SOME TINY THING WITH SLOW METABOLISM.
THAT'S TRUE.
DUMMY.
HEE!
...THINGS COULD GO ON LIKE THIS FOREVER.

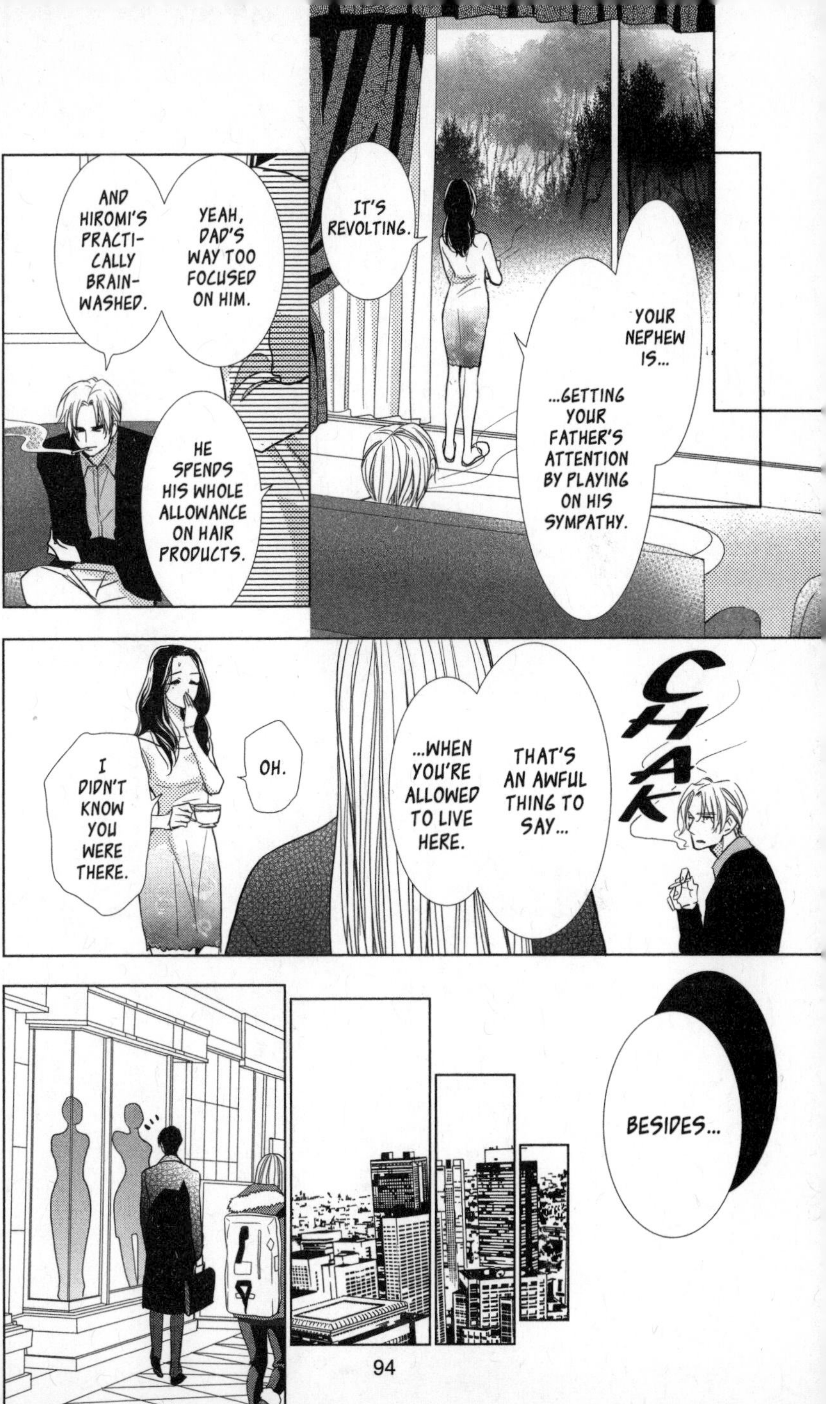
YOUR NEPHEW IS...
...GETTING YOUR FATHER'S ATTENTION BY PLAYING ON HIS SYMPATHY.
IT'S REVOLTING.
YEAH, DAD'S WAY TOO FOCUSED ON HIM.
AND HIROMI'S PRACTICALLY BRAINWASHED.
HE SPENDS HIS WHOLE ALLOWANCE ON HAIR PRODUCTS.
CHAK
THAT'S AN AWFUL THING TO SAY...
...WHEN YOU'RE ALLOWED TO LIVE HERE.
OH.
I DIDN'T KNOW YOU WERE THERE.
BESIDES...

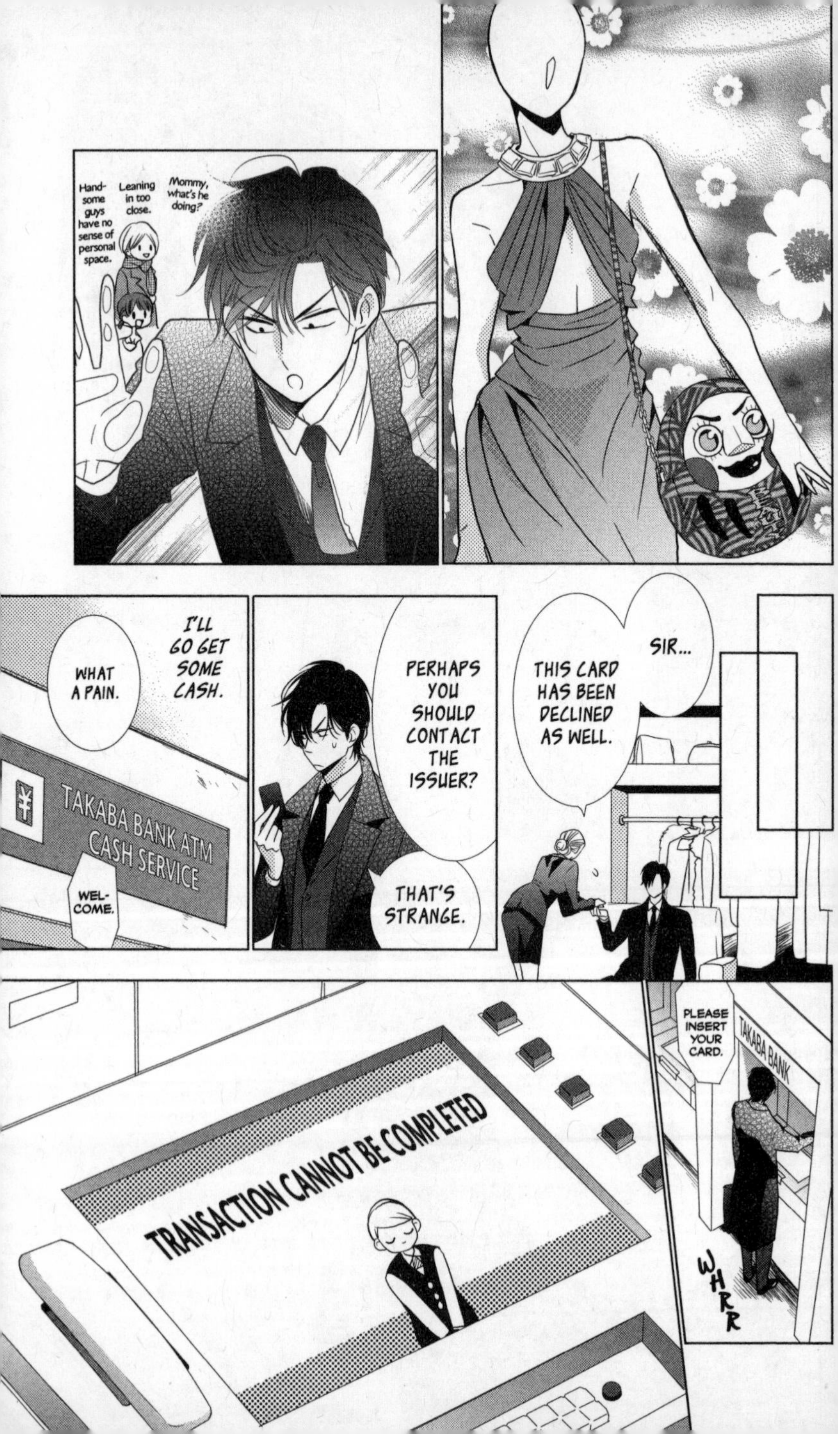
Mommy, what's he doing?
Leaning in too close.
Hand-some guys have no sense of personal space.
SIR...
THIS CARD HAS BEEN DECLINED AS WELL.
PERHAPS YOU SHOULD CONTACT THE ISSUER?
THAT'S STRANGE.
I'LL GO GET SOME CASH.
WHAT A PAIN.
¥ TAKABA BANK ATM CASH SERVICE
WEL-COME.
PLEASE INSERT YOUR CARD.
TAKABA BANK
WHRR
TRANSACTION CANNOT BE COMPLETED

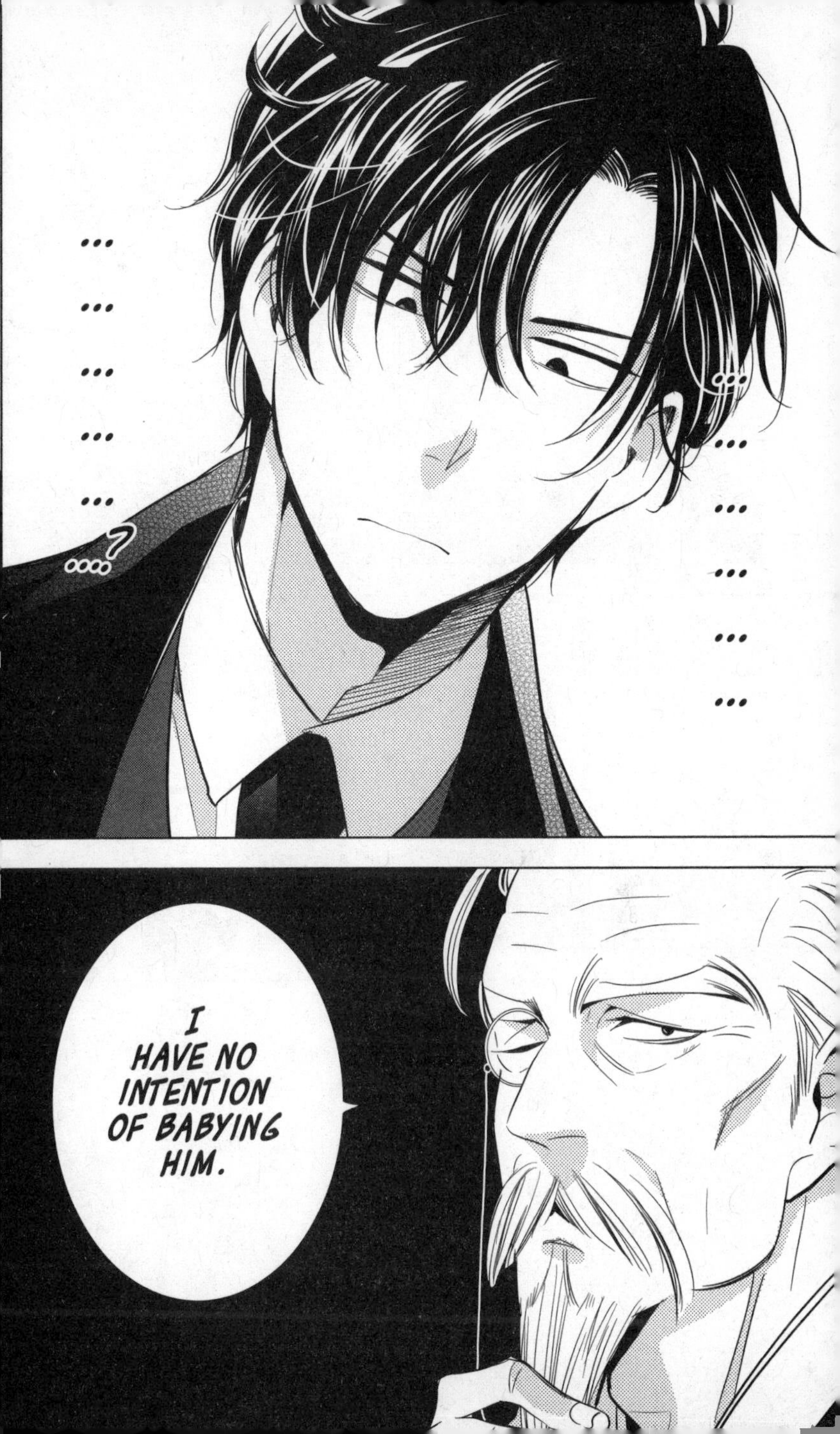

...
...
...
...
...
...
...
...
...
...
...
....?
I HAVE NO INTENTION OF BABYING HIM.

Chapter 31

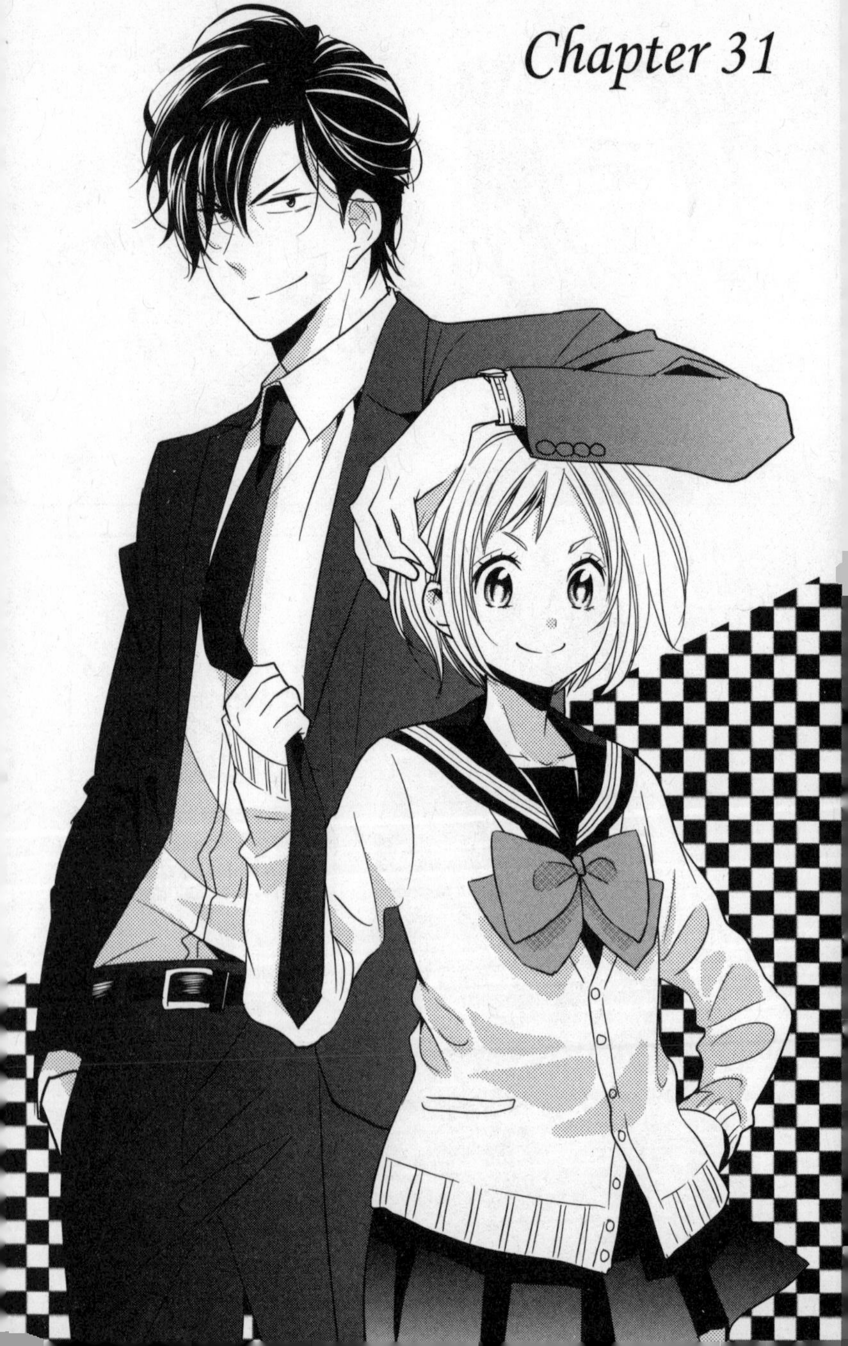

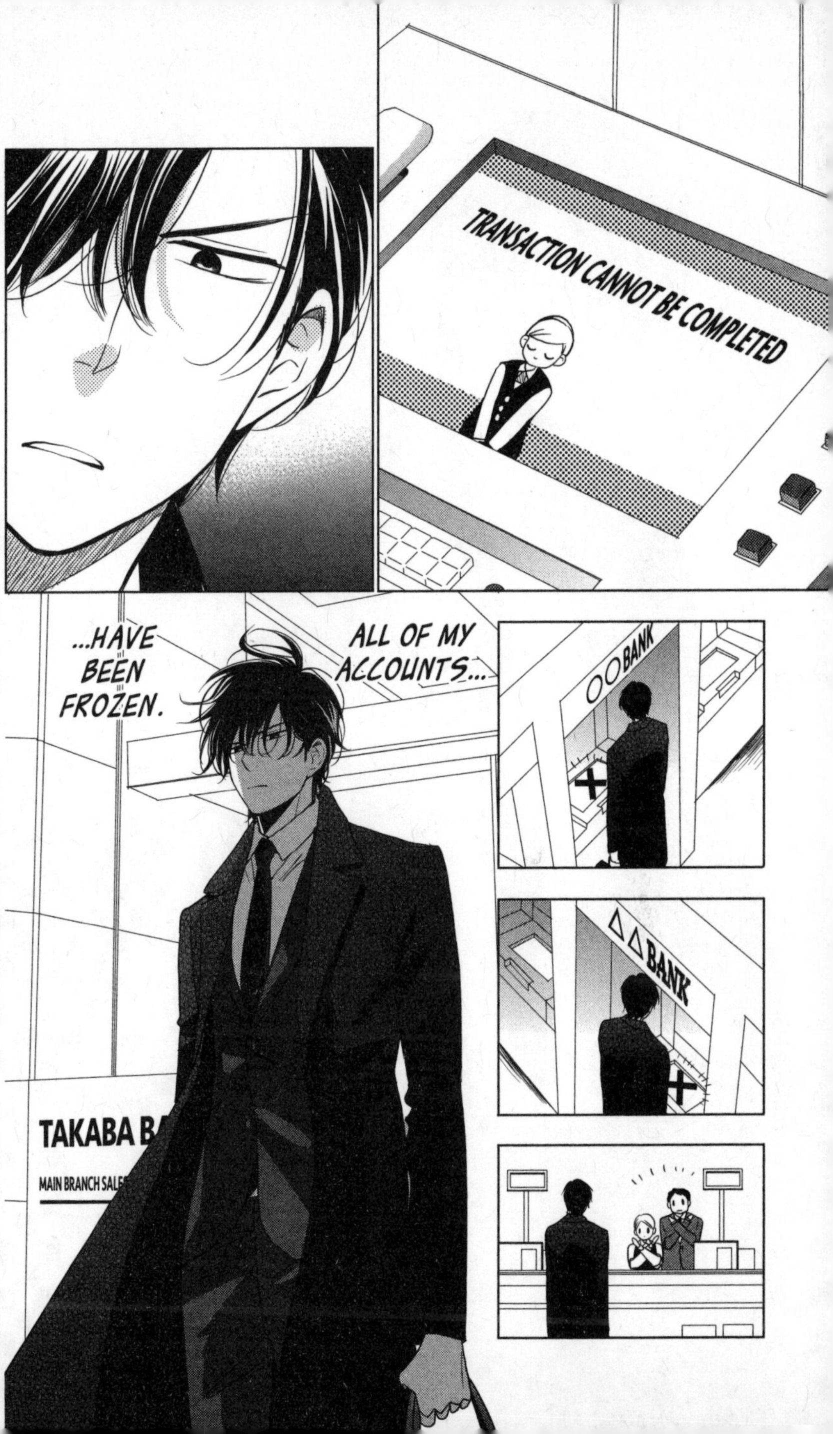
TRANSACTION CANNOT BE COMPLETED
○○BANK
△△BANK
ALL OF MY ACCOUNTS...
...HAVE BEEN FROZEN.
TAKABA BA
MAIN BRANCH SALE

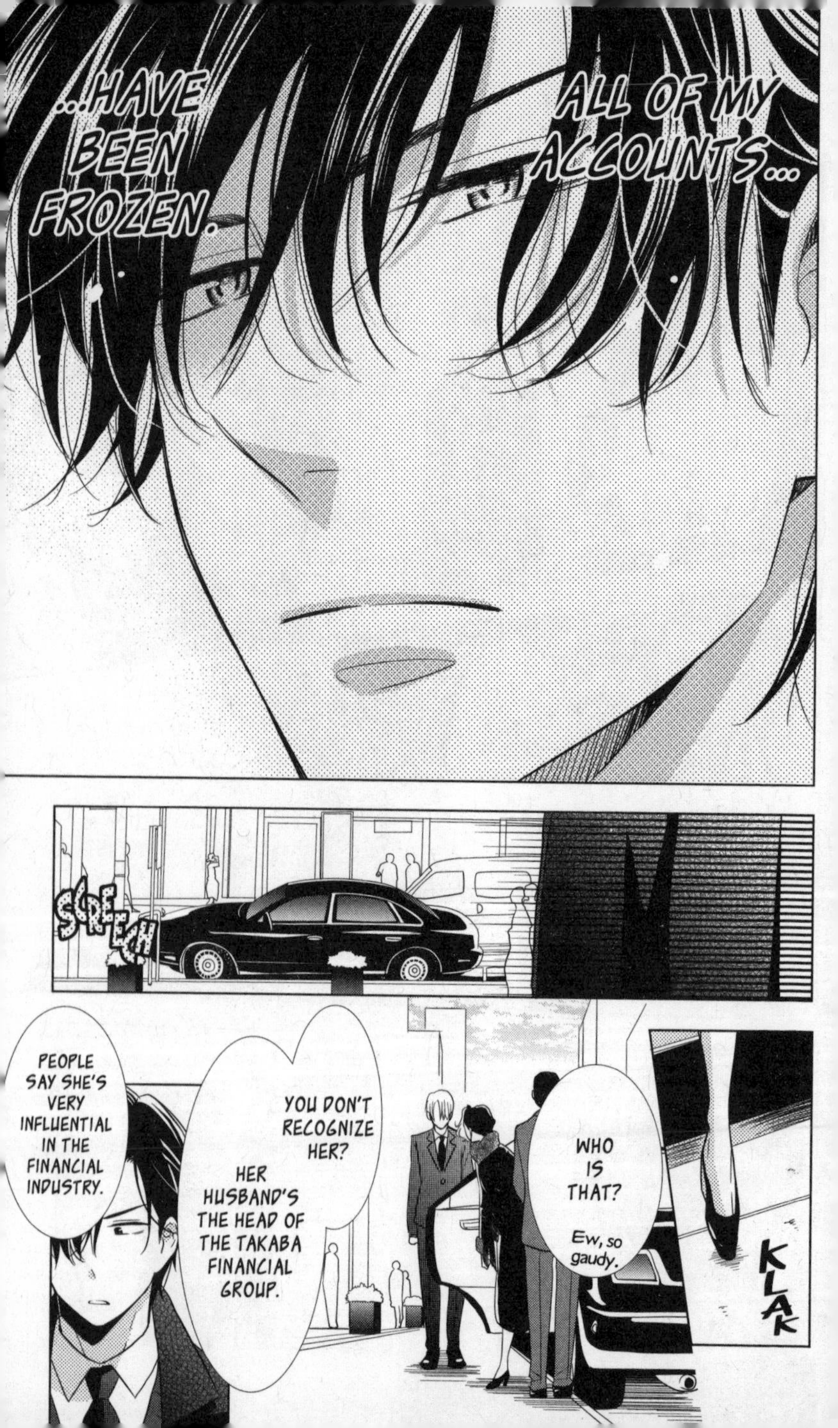
ALL OF MY ACCOUNTS...
...HAVE BEEN FROZEN.
SCREECH
KLAK
WHO IS THAT?
Ew, so gaudy.
YOU DON'T RECOGNIZE HER?
HER HUSBAND'S THE HEAD OF THE TAKABA FINANCIAL GROUP.
PEOPLE SAY SHE'S VERY INFLUENTIAL IN THE FINANCIAL INDUSTRY.

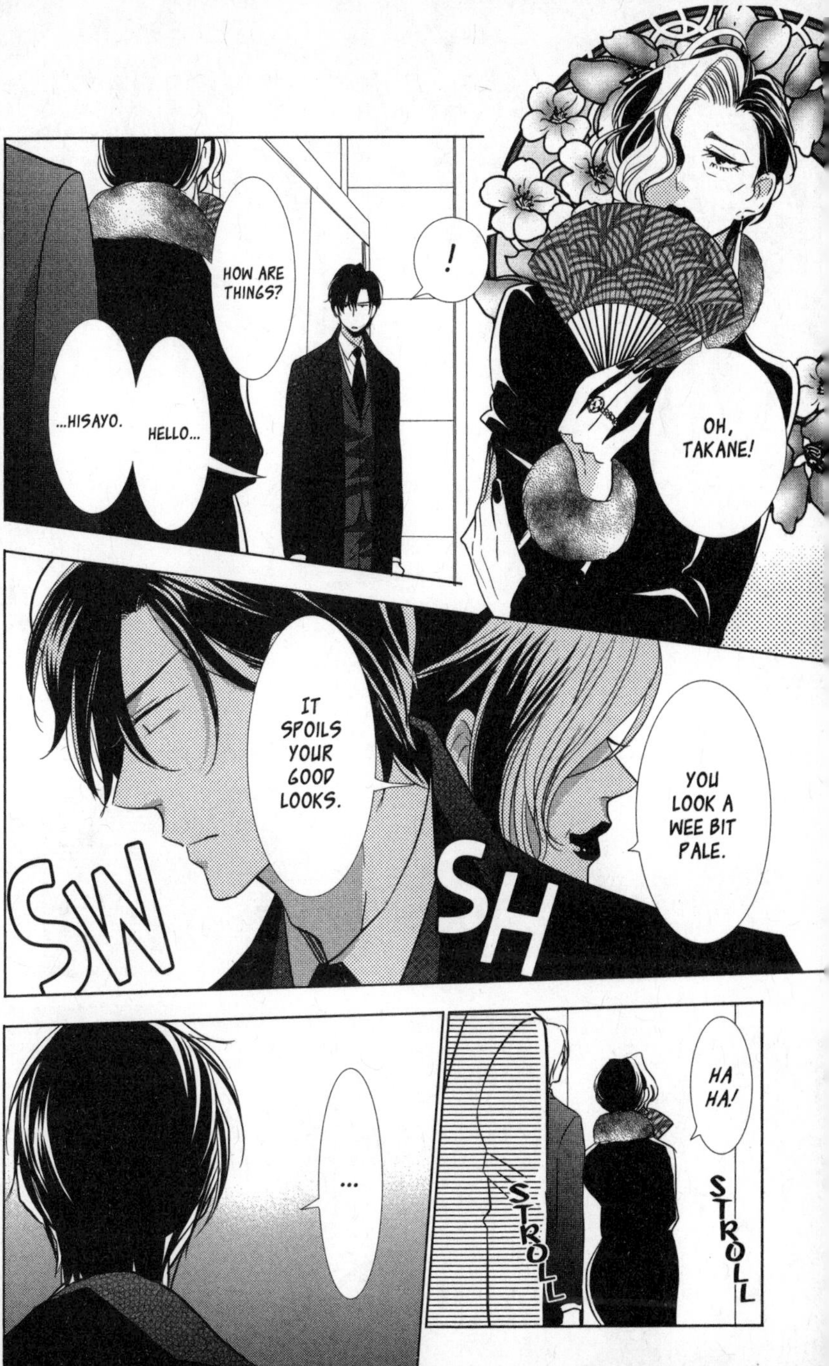
OH, TAKANE!
!
HOW ARE THINGS?
HELLO...
...HISAYO.
YOU LOOK A WEE BIT PALE.
IT SPOILS YOUR GOOD LOOKS.
SWSH
HA HA!
STROLL
STROLL
...

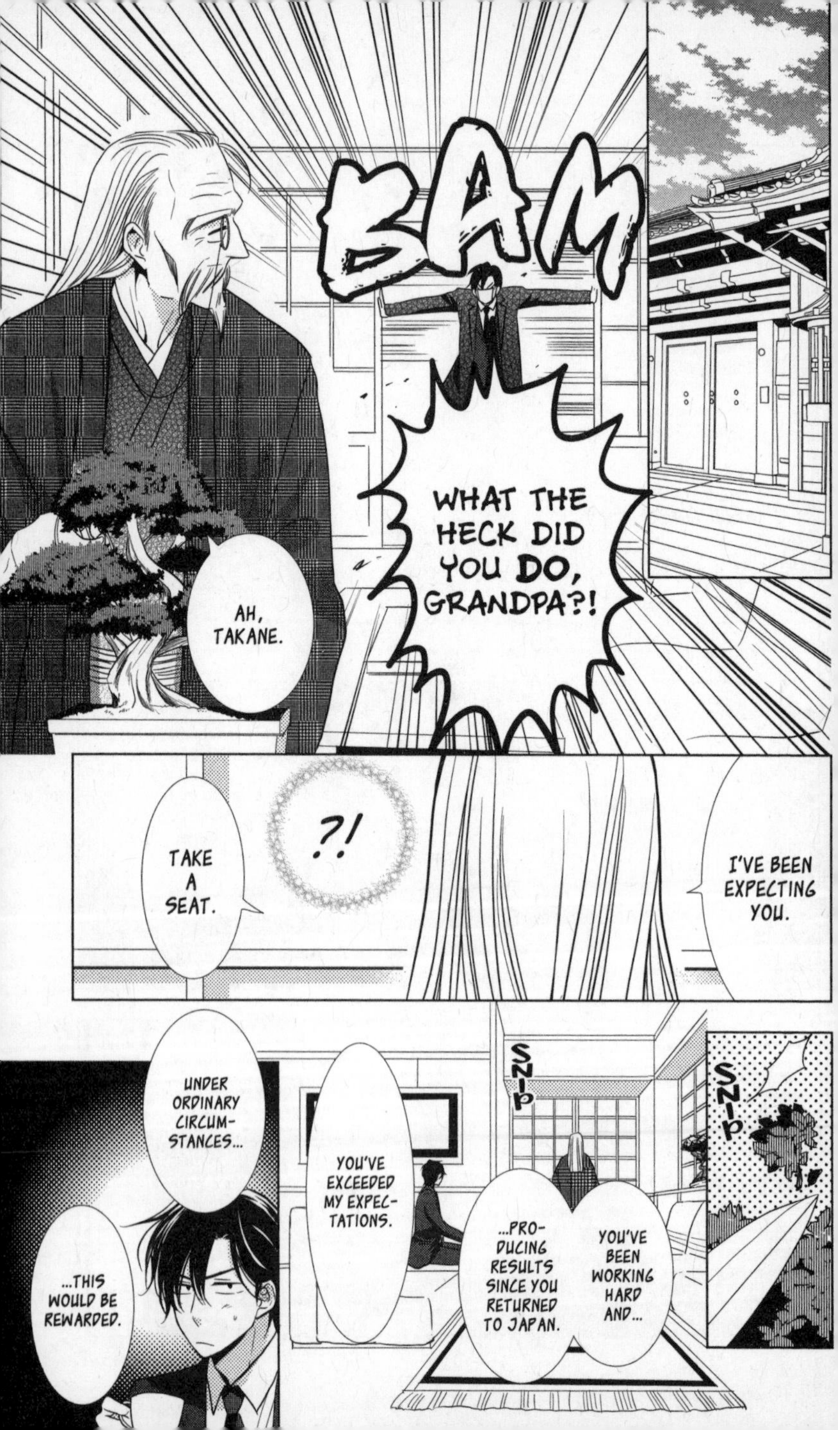
SAM
WHAT THE HECK DID YOU DO, GRANDPA?!
AH, TAKANE.
I'VE BEEN EXPECTING YOU.
?!
TAKE A SEAT.
SNIP
SNIP
YOU'VE BEEN WORKING HARD AND...
...PRO-DUCING RESULTS SINCE YOU RETURNED TO JAPAN.
YOU'VE EXCEEDED MY EXPEC-TATIONS.
UNDER ORDINARY CIRCUM-STANCES...
...THIS WOULD BE REWARDED.

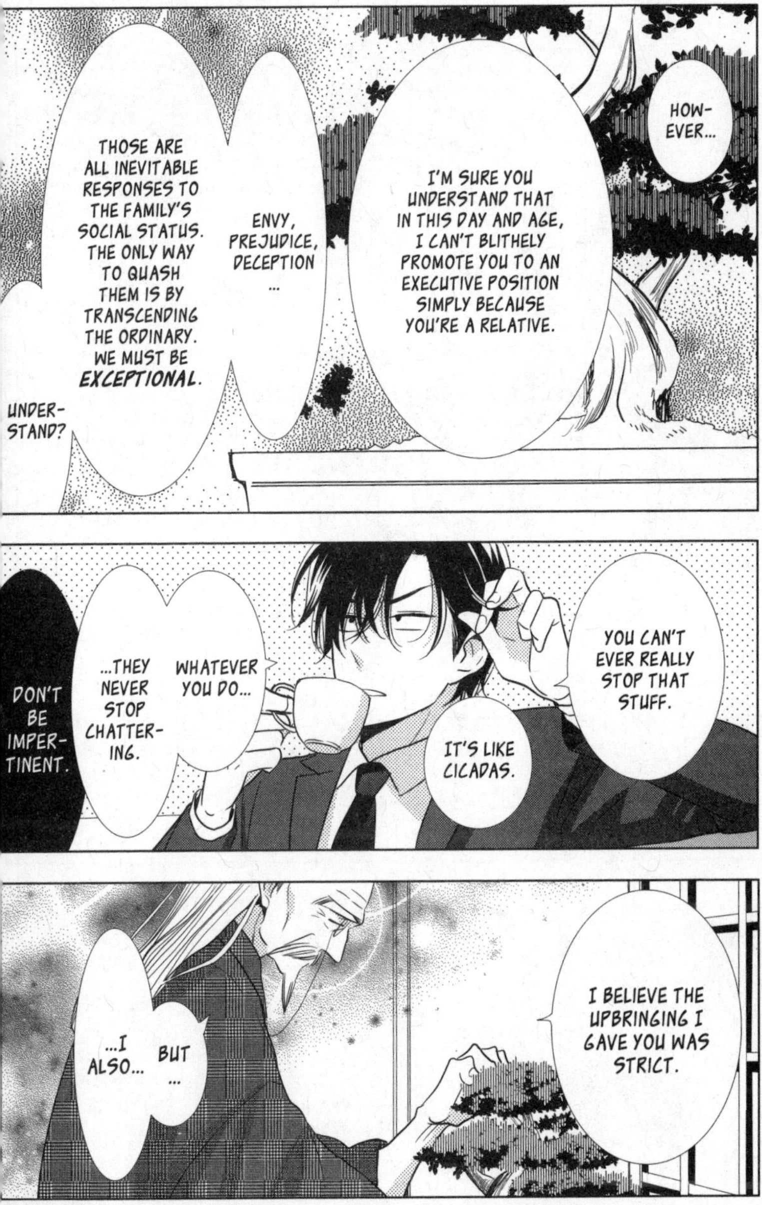
HOW-EVER...
I'M SURE YOU UNDERSTAND THAT IN THIS DAY AND AGE, I CAN'T BLITHELY PROMOTE YOU TO AN EXECUTIVE POSITION SIMPLY BECAUSE YOU'RE A RELATIVE.
ENVY, PREJUDICE, DECEPTION...
THOSE ARE ALL INEVITABLE RESPONSES TO THE FAMILY'S SOCIAL STATUS. THE ONLY WAY TO QUASH THEM IS BY TRANSCENDING THE ORDINARY. WE MUST BE *EXCEPTIONAL*.
UNDER-STAND?
YOU CAN'T EVER REALLY STOP THAT STUFF.
IT'S LIKE CICADAS.
WHATEVER YOU DO...
...THEY NEVER STOP CHATTER-ING.
DON'T BE IMPER-TINENT.
I BELIEVE THE UPBRINGING I GAVE YOU WAS STRICT.
BUT...
...I ALSO...

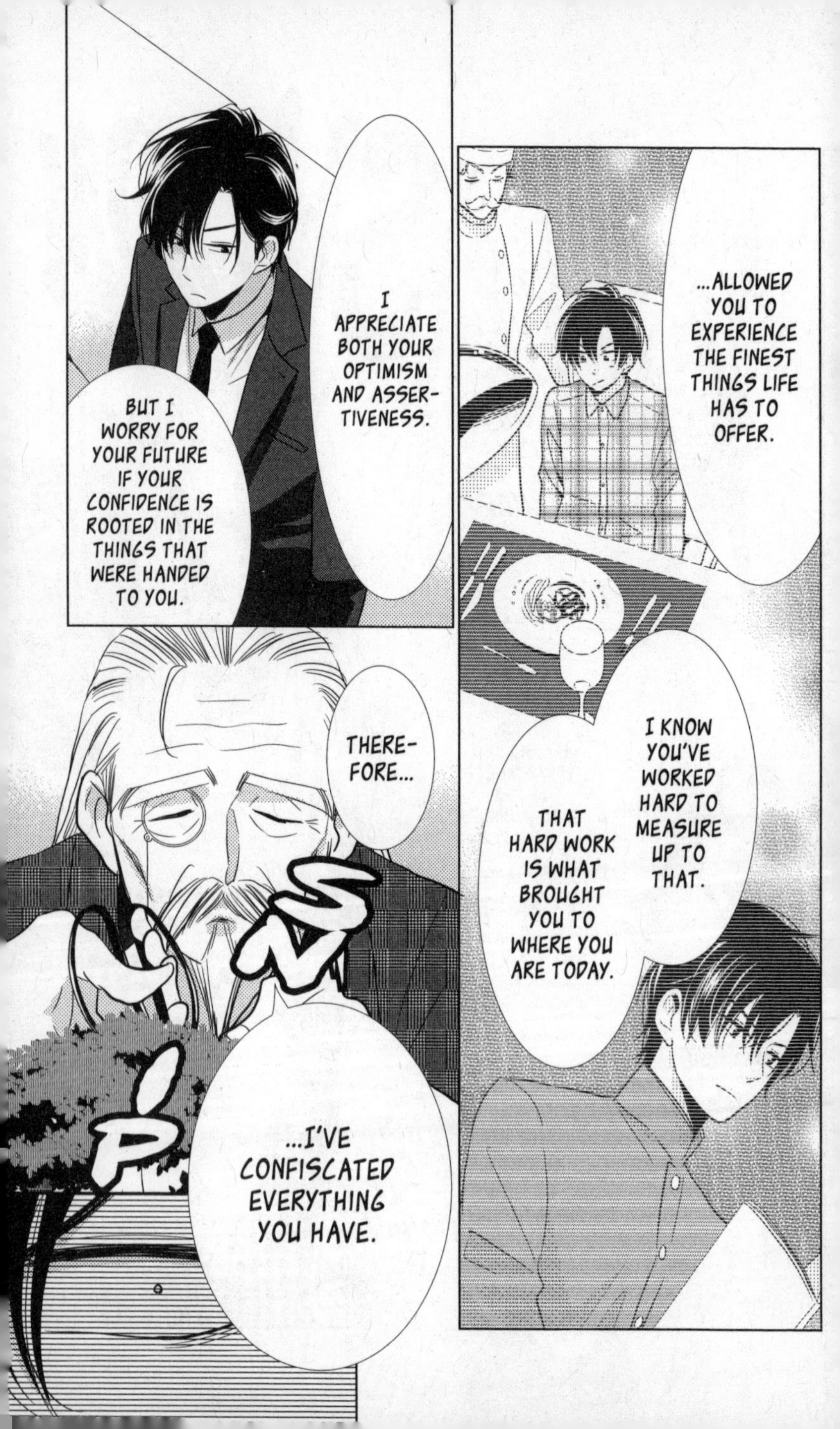
...ALLOWED YOU TO EXPERIENCE THE FINEST THINGS LIFE HAS TO OFFER.
I KNOW YOU'VE WORKED HARD TO MEASURE UP TO THAT.
THAT HARD WORK IS WHAT BROUGHT YOU TO WHERE YOU ARE TODAY.
I APPRECIATE BOTH YOUR OPTIMISM AND ASSER-TIVENESS.
BUT I WORRY FOR YOUR FUTURE IF YOUR CONFIDENCE IS ROOTED IN THE THINGS THAT WERE HANDED TO YOU.
THERE-FORE...
SNIP
...I'VE CONFISCATED EVERYTHING YOU HAVE.

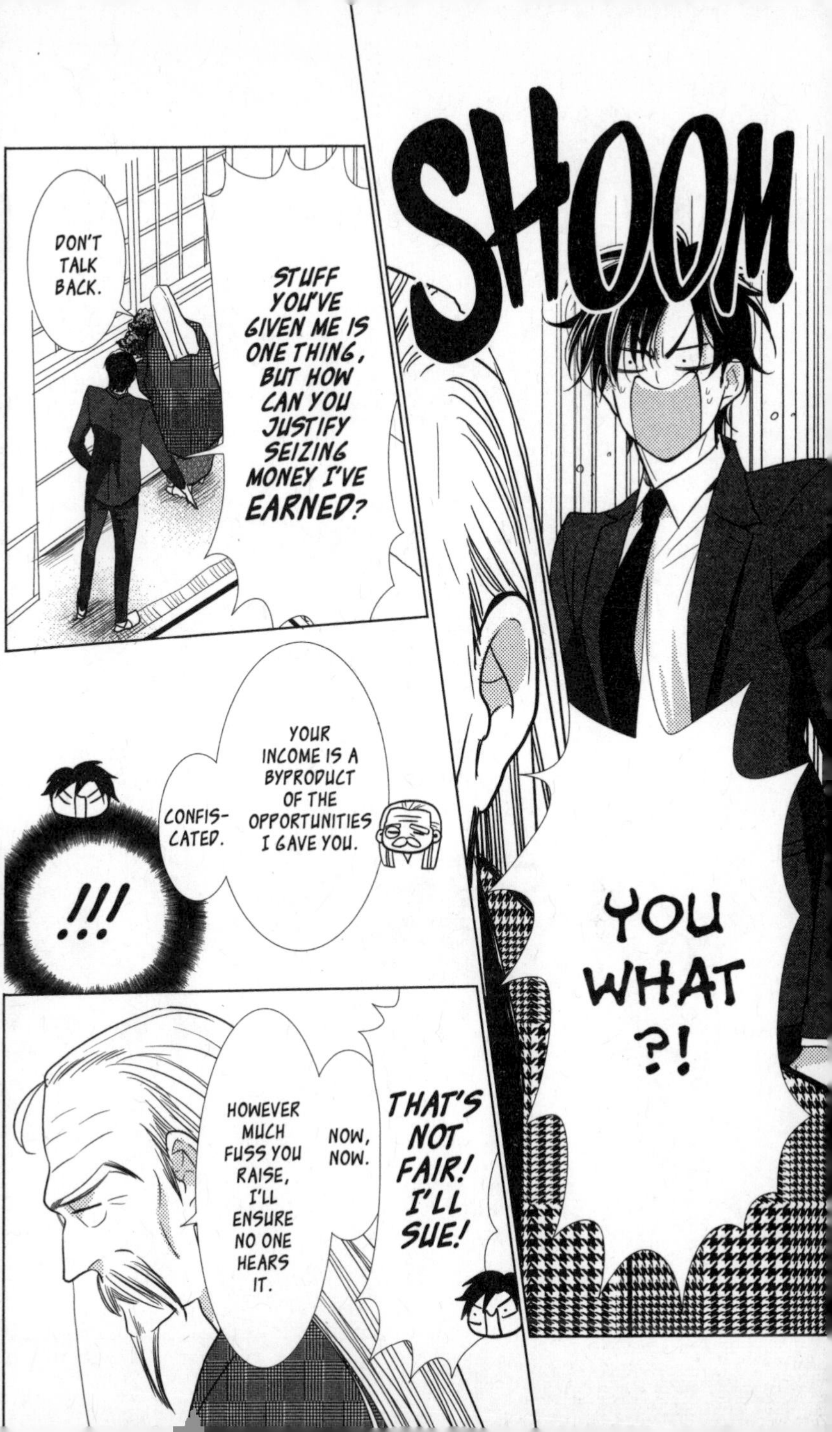
SHOOM
YOU WHAT?!
STUFF YOU'VE GIVEN ME IS ONE THING, BUT HOW CAN YOU JUSTIFY SEIZING MONEY I'VE EARNED?
DON'T TALK BACK.
YOUR INCOME IS A BYPRODUCT OF THE OPPORTUNITIES I GAVE YOU.
CONFIS-CATED.
!!!
THAT'S NOT FAIR! I'LL SUE!
NOW, NOW.
HOWEVER MUCH FUSS YOU RAISE, I'LL ENSURE NO ONE HEARS IT.

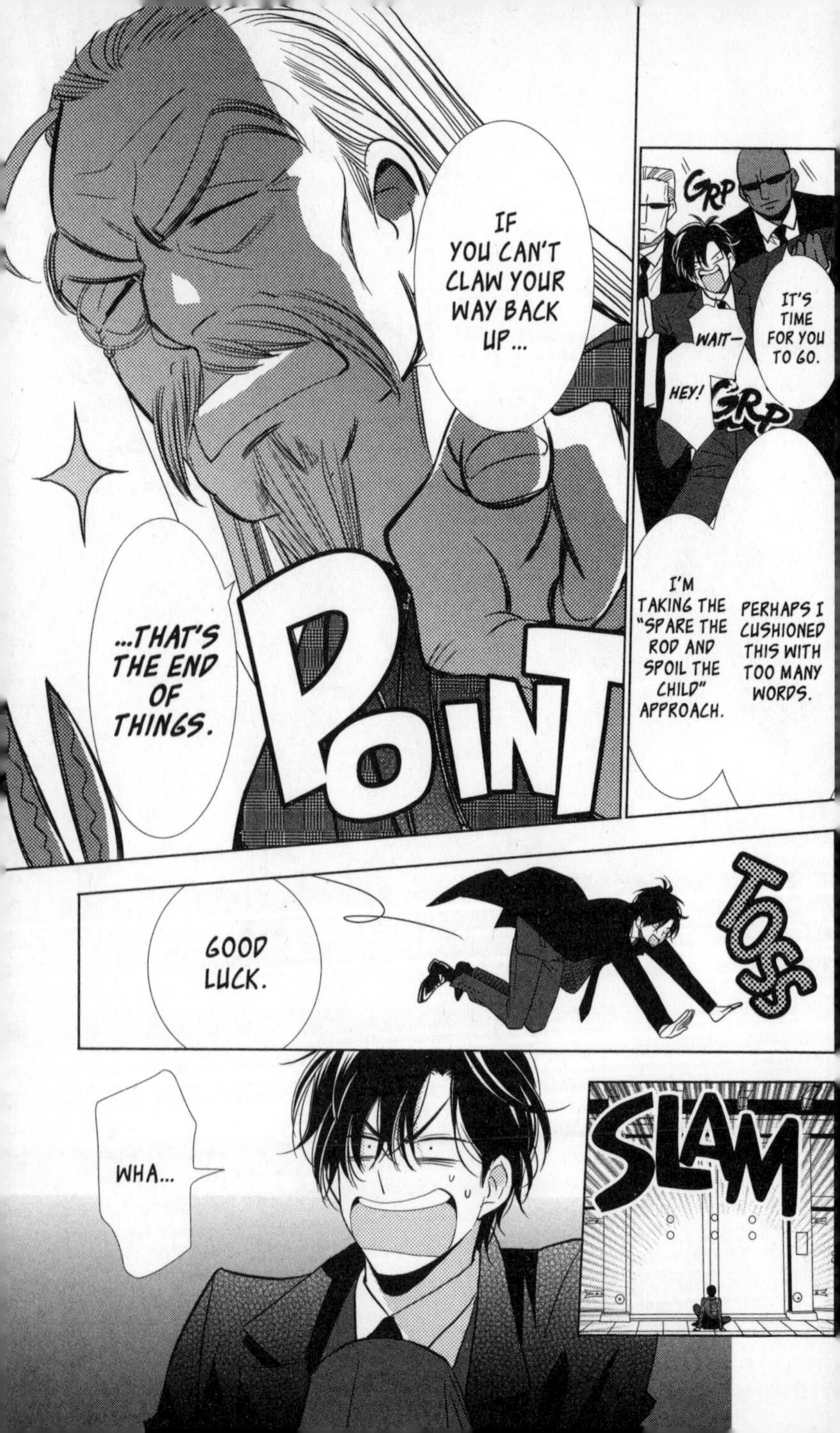
GRP
IT'S TIME FOR YOU TO GO.
WAIT—
HEY!
GRP
PERHAPS I CUSHIONED THIS WITH TOO MANY WORDS.
I'M TAKING THE "SPARE THE ROD AND SPOIL THE CHILD" APPROACH.
IF YOU CAN'T CLAW YOUR WAY BACK UP...
POINT
...THAT'S THE END OF THINGS.
TOSS
GOOD LUCK.
SLAM
WHA...

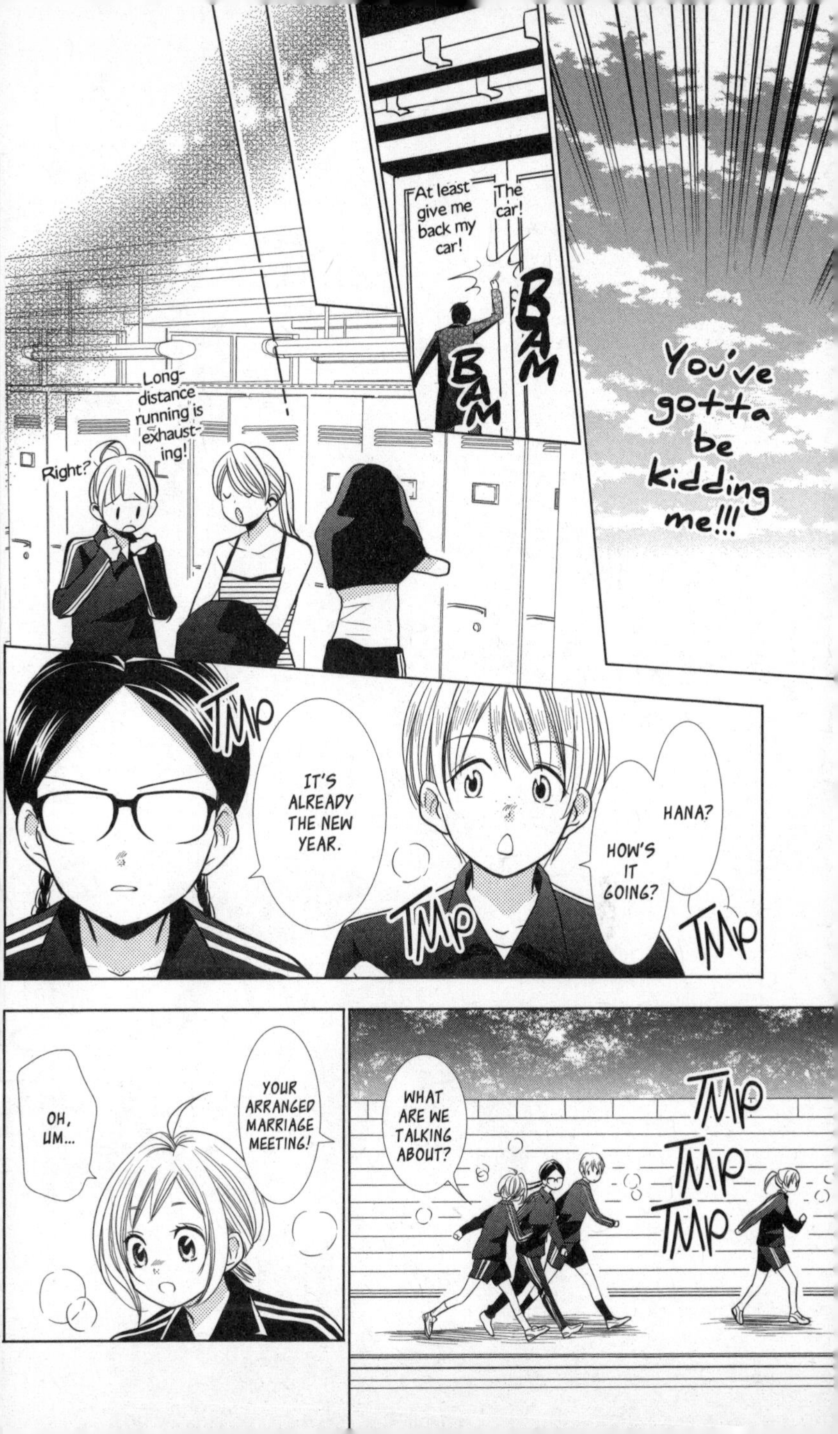
You've gotta be kidding me!!!
The car!
At least give me back my car!
BAM BAM
BAM
Long-distance running is exhausting!
Right?
TMP
HANA?
HOW'S IT GOING?
TMP
IT'S ALREADY THE NEW YEAR.
TMP
TMP TMP TMP
WHAT ARE WE TALKING ABOUT?
YOUR ARRANGED MARRIAGE MEETING!
OH, UM...

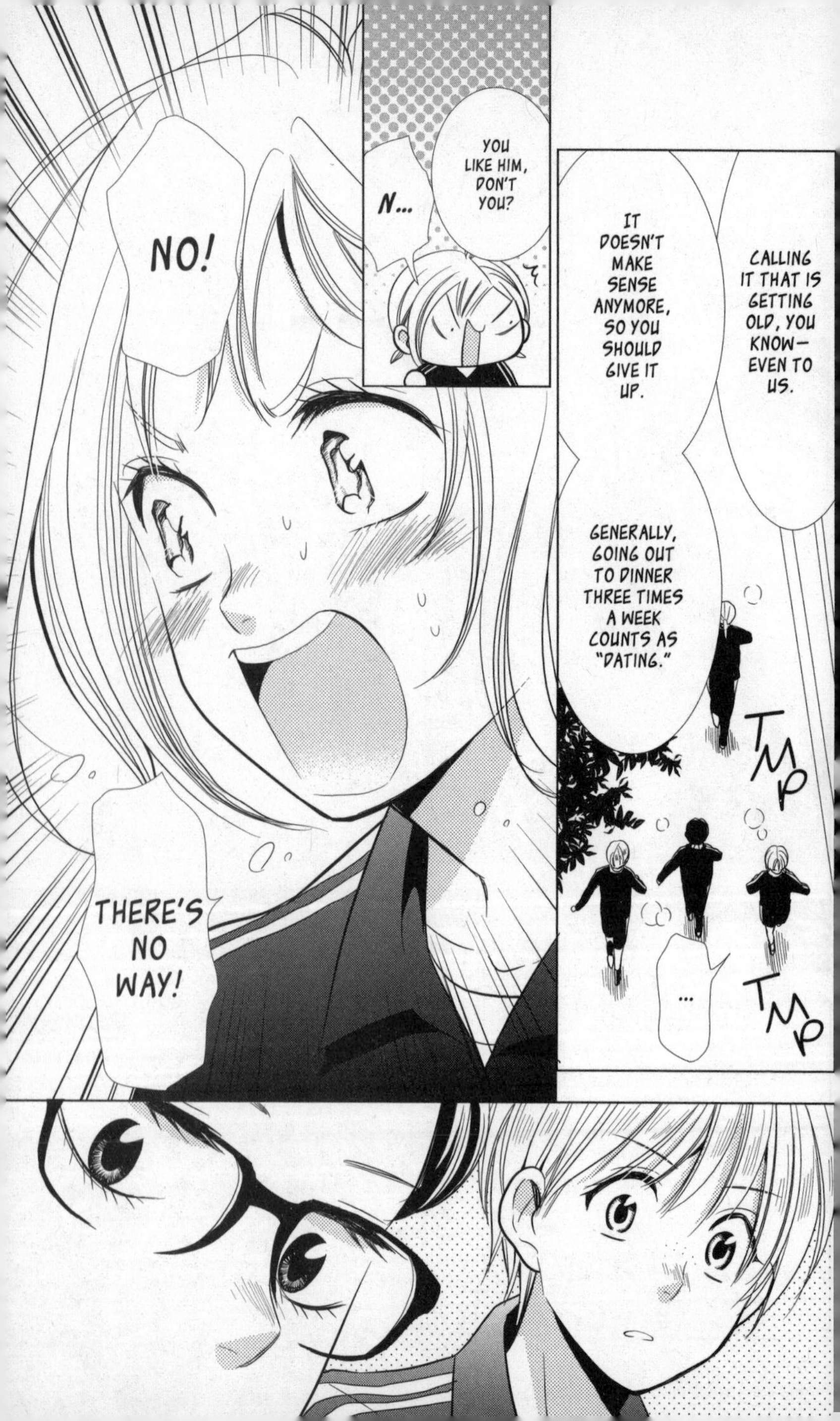
CALLING IT THAT IS GETTING OLD, YOU KNOW—EVEN TO US.
IT DOESN'T MAKE SENSE ANYMORE, SO YOU SHOULD GIVE IT UP.
GENERALLY, GOING OUT TO DINNER THREE TIMES A WEEK COUNTS AS "DATING."
TMP
TMP
...
YOU LIKE HIM, DON'T YOU?
N...
NO!
THERE'S NO WAY!

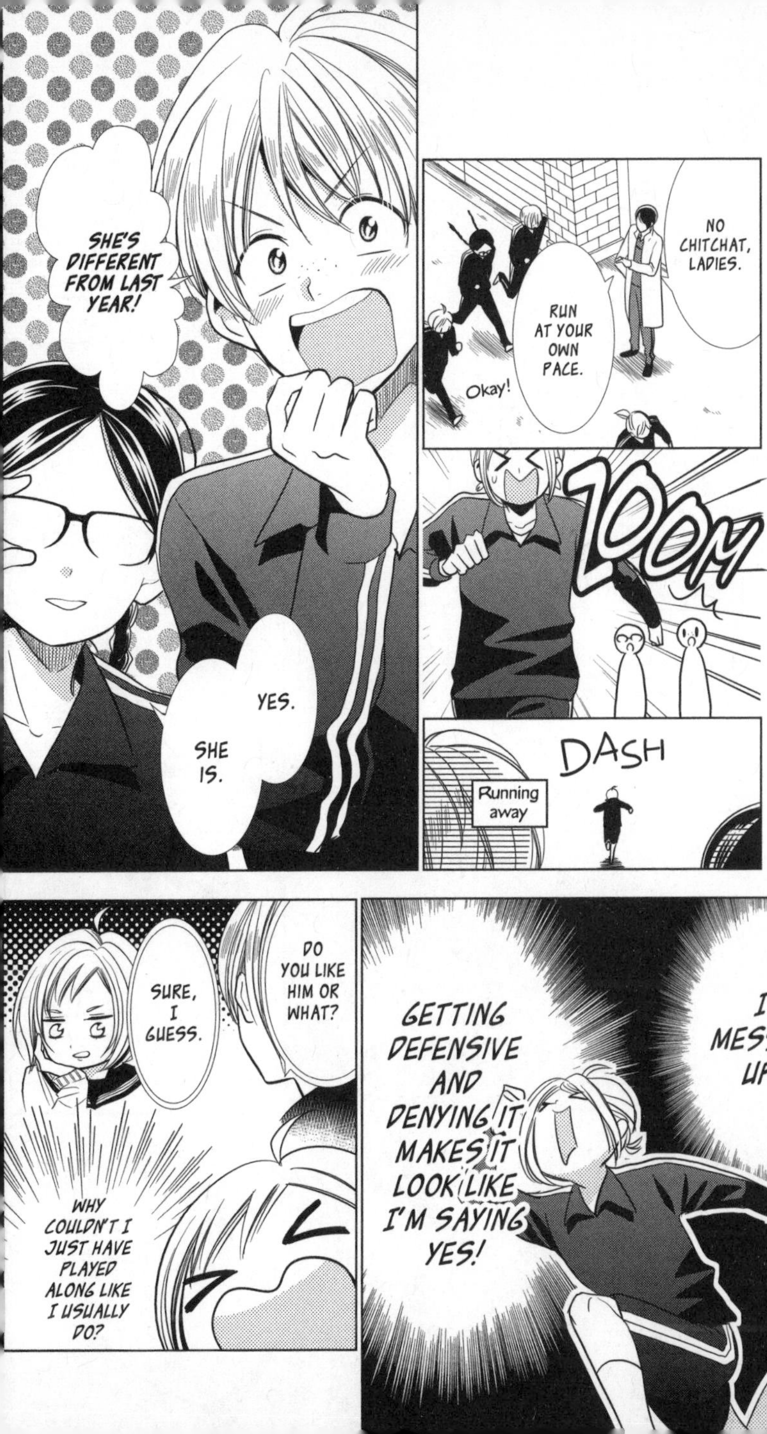
NO CHITCHAT, LADIES.
RUN AT YOUR OWN PACE.
Okay!
ZOOM
DASH
Running away
SHE'S DIFFERENT FROM LAST YEAR!
YES.
SHE IS.
I MESSED UP.
GETTING DEFENSIVE AND DENYING IT MAKES IT LOOK LIKE I'M SAYING YES!
DO YOU LIKE HIM OR WHAT?
SURE, I GUESS.
WHY COULDN'T I JUST HAVE PLAYED ALONG LIKE I USUALLY DO?

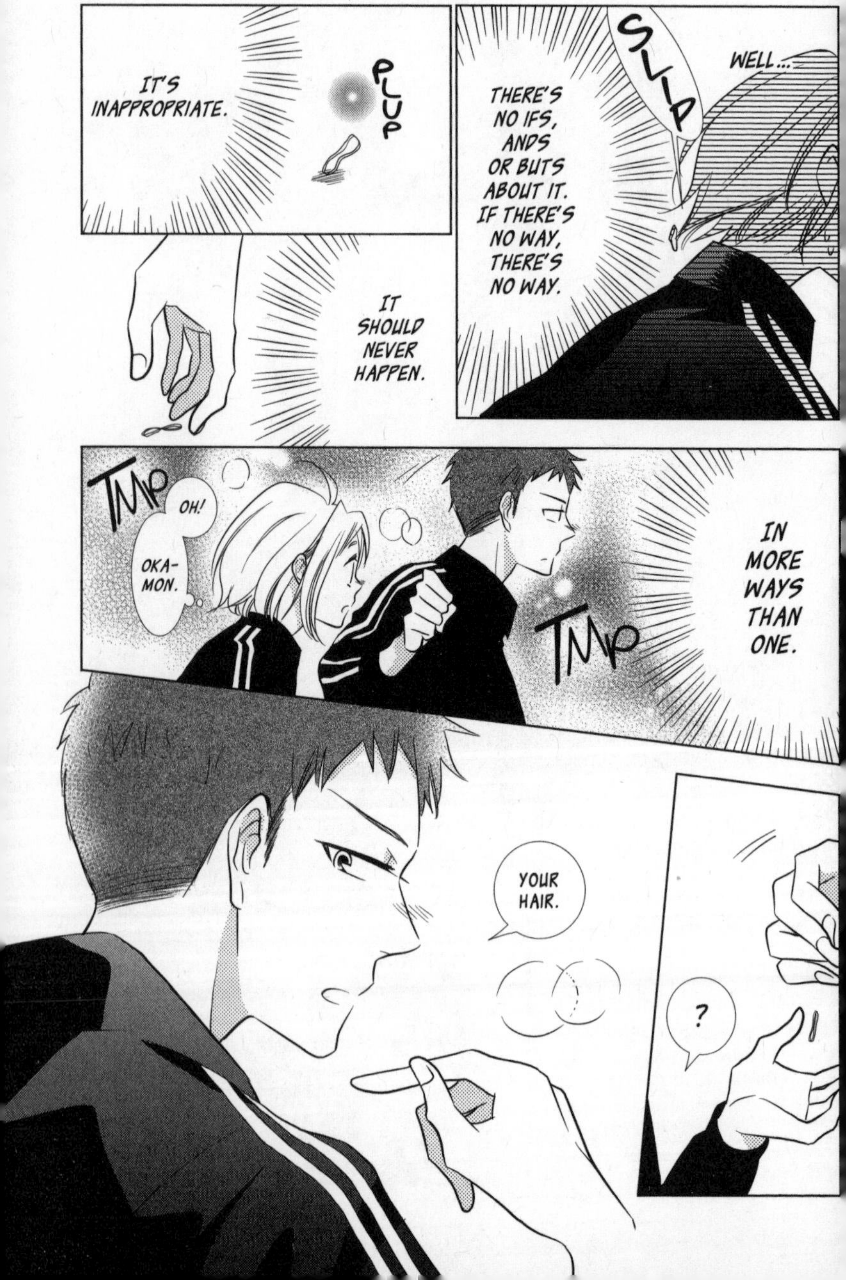
SLIP
WELL...
THERE'S NO IFS, ANDS OR BUTS ABOUT IT. IF THERE'S NO WAY, THERE'S NO WAY.
IT'S INAPPROPRIATE.
PLUP
IT SHOULD NEVER HAPPEN.
IN MORE WAYS THAN ONE.
TMP
OH!
OKA-MON.
TMP
?
YOUR HAIR.

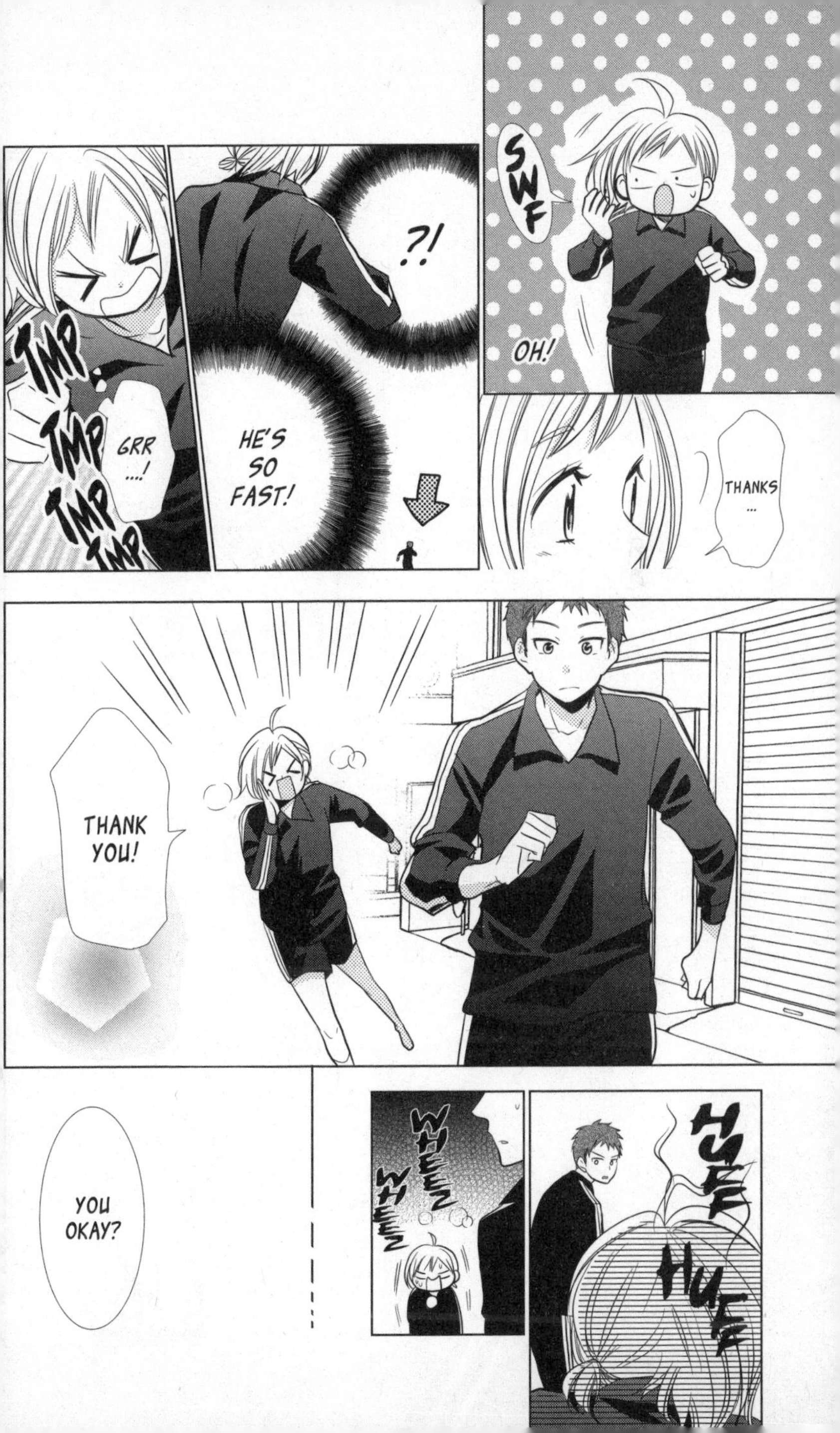
SWF
OH!
THANKS ...
?!
HE'S SO FAST!
TMP TMP TMP TMP
GRR ...!
THANK YOU!
HUFF HUFF
WHEEZ WHEEZ
YOU OKAY?

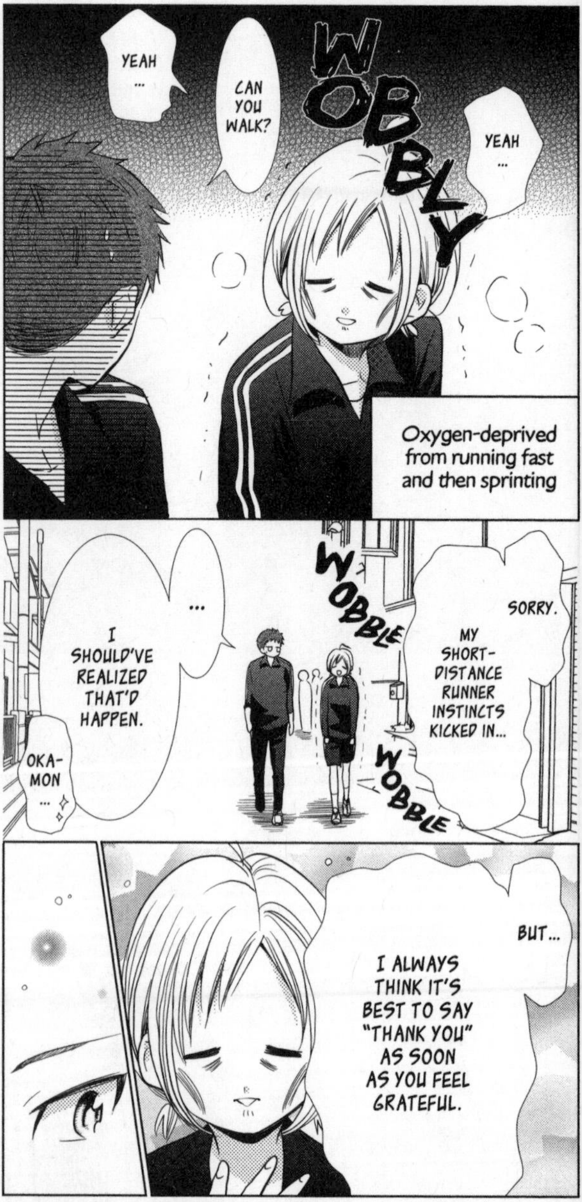
WOBBLY
YEAH...
CAN YOU WALK?
YEAH...
Oxygen-deprived from running fast and then sprinting
SORRY.
MY SHORT-DISTANCE RUNNER INSTINCTS KICKED IN...
WOBBLE
WOBBLE
...
I SHOULD'VE REALIZED THAT'D HAPPEN.
OKA-MON...
BUT...
I ALWAYS THINK IT'S BEST TO SAY "THANK YOU" AS SOON AS YOU FEEL GRATEFUL.

● Emi Nonomura ●

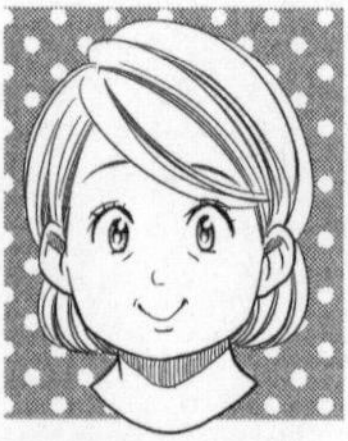

The Nonomura family's conscience. I just came up with her first name right now. (*Ha ha.*) Of all the adults in Hana's life, she's the only decent one. Maybe Hana's attraction to flawed men comes from her mother.

● Hana's Grandparents ●

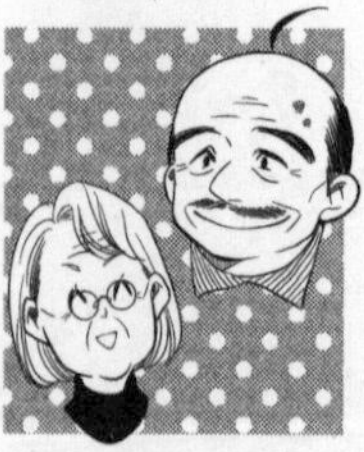

Her mother's parents. They live in Fukuoka. Maybe some of you have noticed that Hana's inherited a lot of traits from her grandparents.

Unlike the Takaba family—for better or worse—they're blunt people who don't hide their feelings. Some of you were shocked at Grandpa's remarks! (*Hee hee.*)

But when he said, "Grandpa and Grandma will beat him to death," that just meant "I'll teach him a lesson" in Grandpa's terms. All you good boys and girls out there, don't copy him, okay?

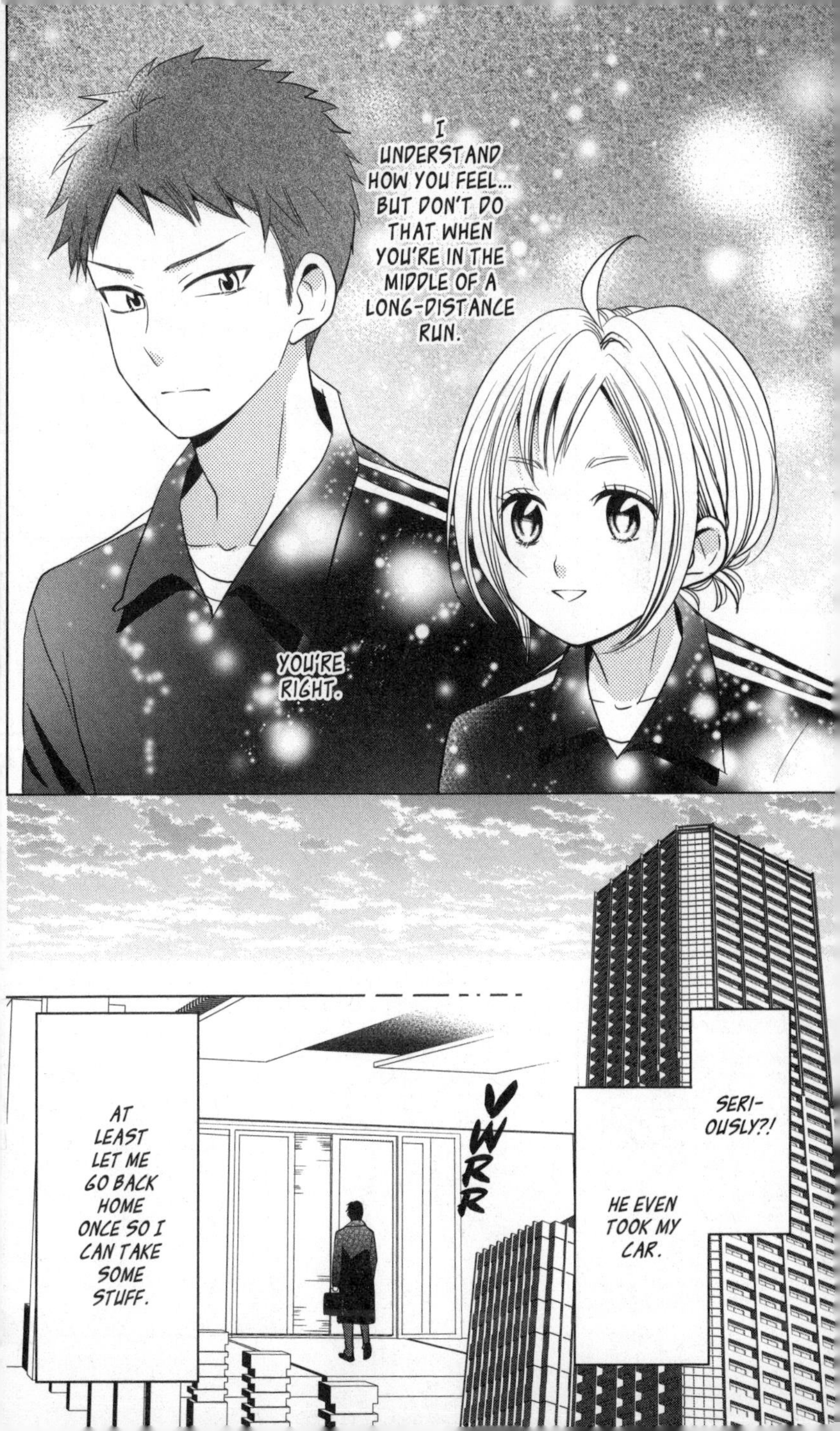
I UNDERSTAND HOW YOU FEEL... BUT DON'T DO THAT WHEN YOU'RE IN THE MIDDLE OF A LONG-DISTANCE RUN.
YOU'RE RIGHT.
SERI-OUSLY?!
HE EVEN TOOK MY CAR.
VWRR
AT LEAST LET ME GO BACK HOME ONCE SO I CAN TAKE SOME STUFF.

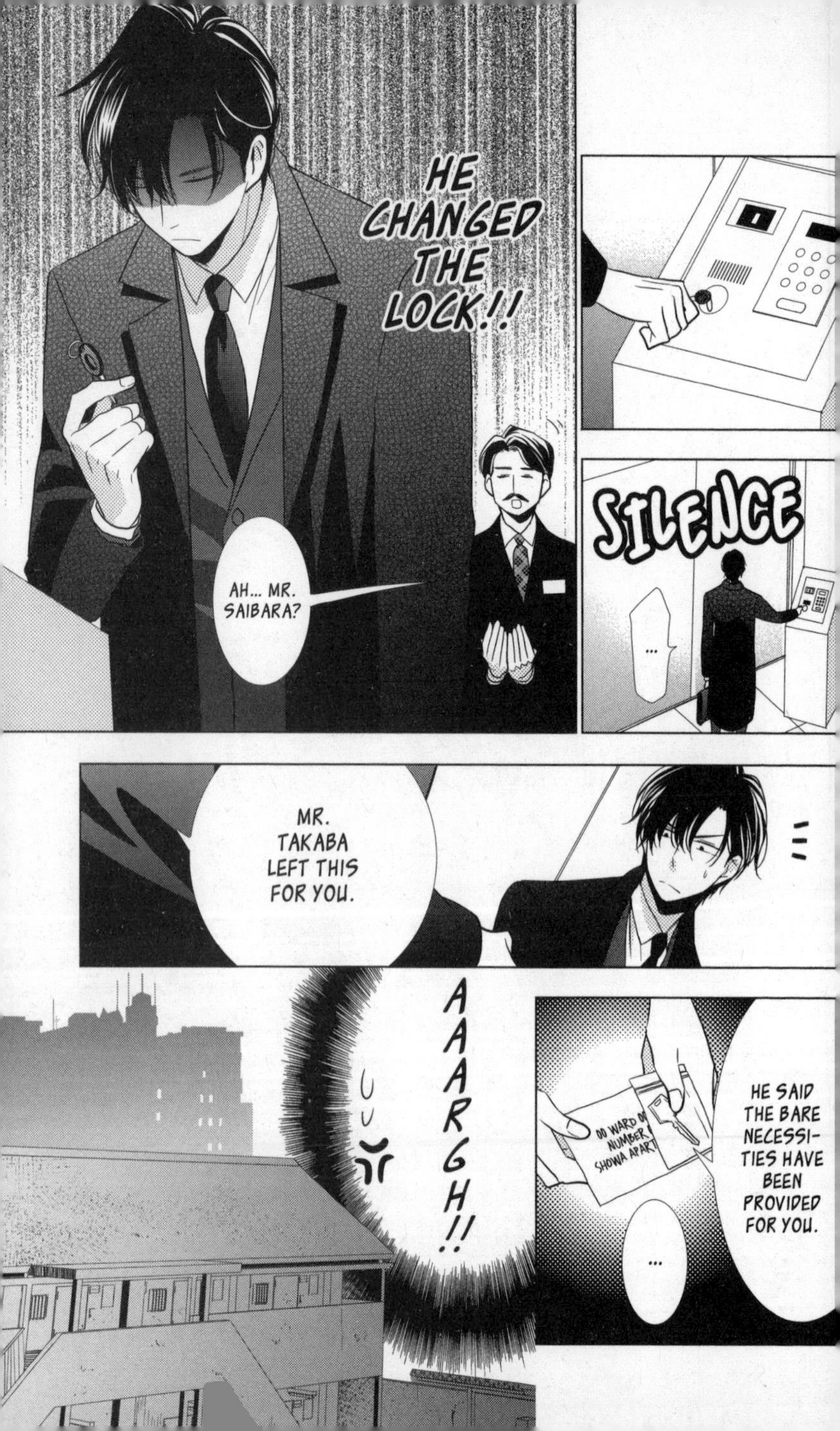

SILENCE
...
HE CHANGED THE LOCK!!
AH... MR. SAIBARA?
MR. TAKABA LEFT THIS FOR YOU.
HE SAID THE BARE NECESSI-TIES HAVE BEEN PROVIDED FOR YOU.
...
AAAARGH!!

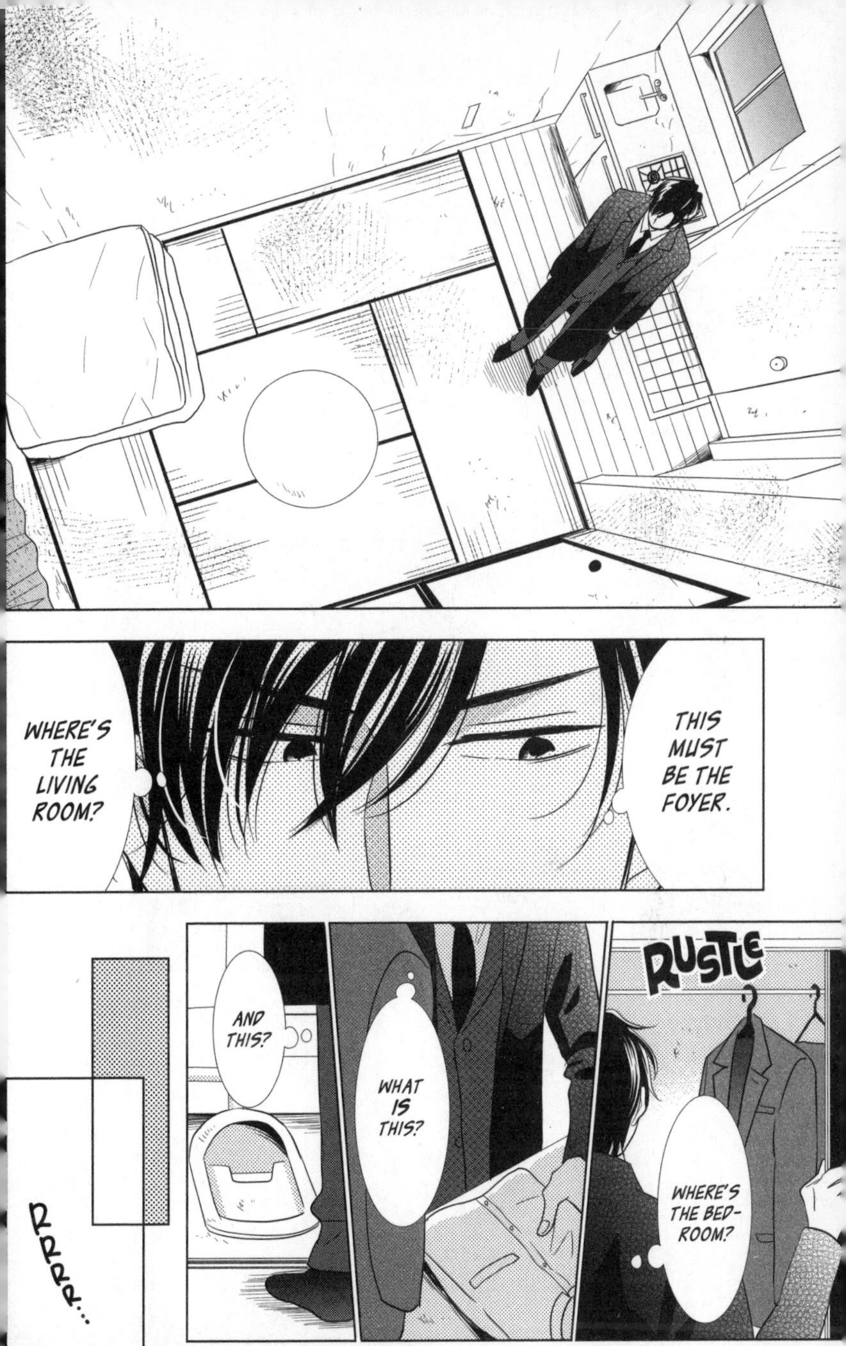
THIS MUST BE THE FOYER.
WHERE'S THE LIVING ROOM?
RUSTLE
WHERE'S THE BED-ROOM?
WHAT IS THIS?
AND THIS?
RRRRR...

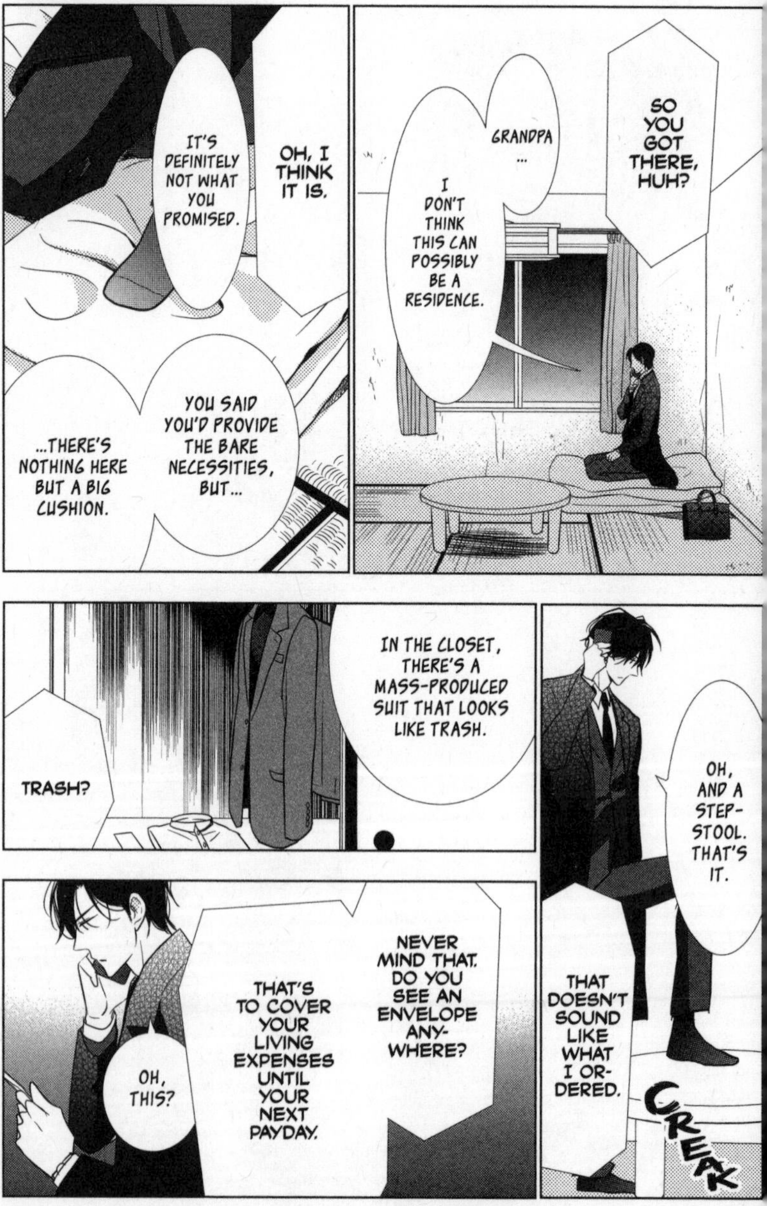
SO YOU GOT THERE, HUH?
GRANDPA...
I DON'T THINK THIS CAN POSSIBLY BE A RESIDENCE.
OH, I THINK IT IS.
IT'S DEFINITELY NOT WHAT YOU PROMISED.
YOU SAID YOU'D PROVIDE THE BARE NECESSITIES, BUT...
...THERE'S NOTHING HERE BUT A BIG CUSHION.
OH, AND A STEP-STOOL. THAT'S IT.
THAT DOESN'T SOUND LIKE WHAT I ORDERED.
CREAK
IN THE CLOSET, THERE'S A MASS-PRODUCED SUIT THAT LOOKS LIKE TRASH.
TRASH?
NEVER MIND THAT. DO YOU SEE AN ENVELOPE ANYWHERE?
OH, THIS?
THAT'S TO COVER YOUR LIVING EXPENSES UNTIL YOUR NEXT PAYDAY.

*10,000 yen = about $91

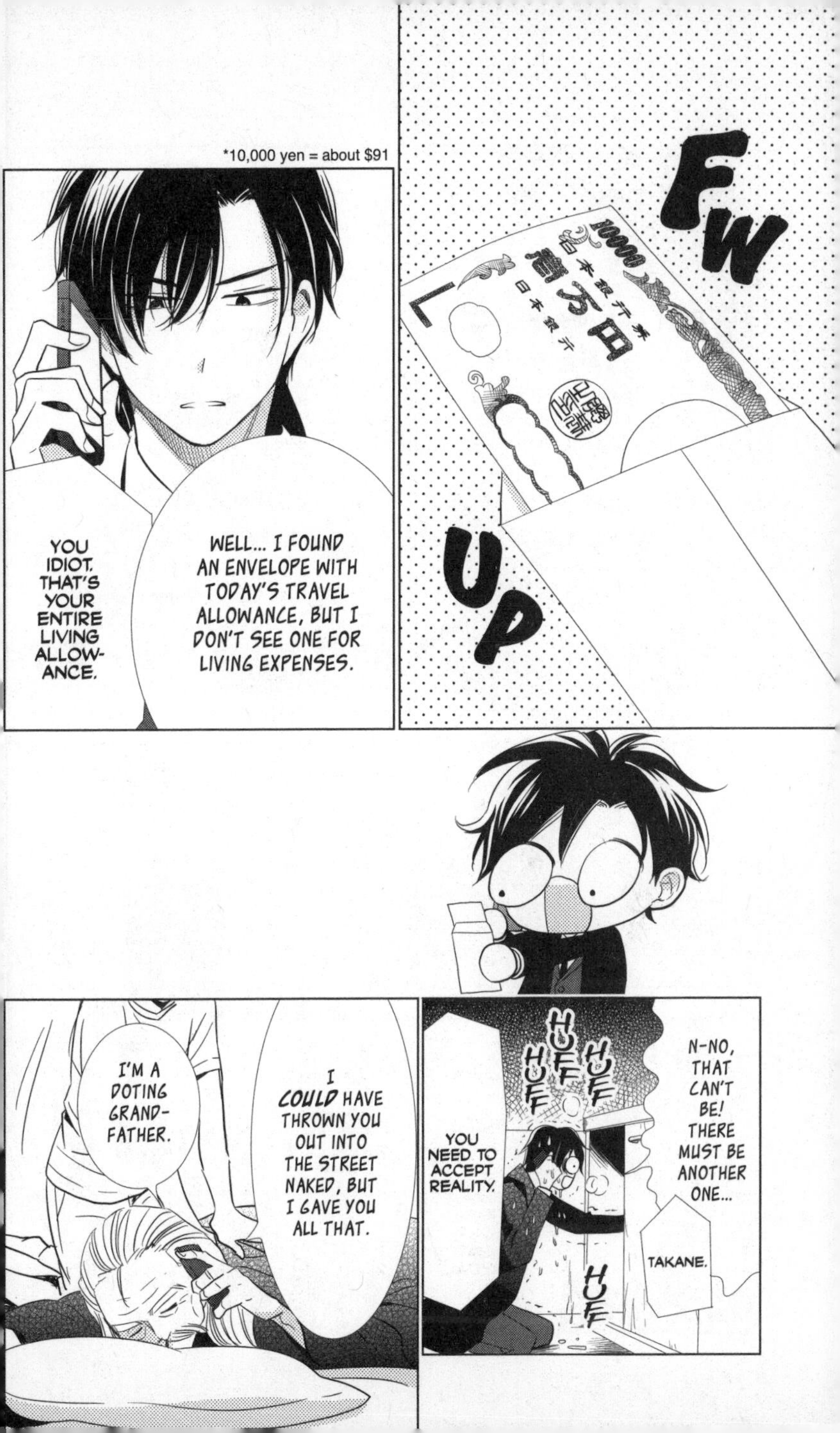
FW
UP
WELL... I FOUND AN ENVELOPE WITH TODAY'S TRAVEL ALLOWANCE, BUT I DON'T SEE ONE FOR LIVING EXPENSES.
YOU IDIOT. THAT'S YOUR ENTIRE LIVING ALLOWANCE.
N-NO, THAT CAN'T BE! THERE MUST BE ANOTHER ONE...
HUFF HUFF
HUFF HUFF
TAKANE.
YOU NEED TO ACCEPT REALITY.
HUFF
I *COULD* HAVE THROWN YOU OUT INTO THE STREET NAKED, BUT I GAVE YOU ALL THAT.
I'M A DOTING GRANDFATHER.

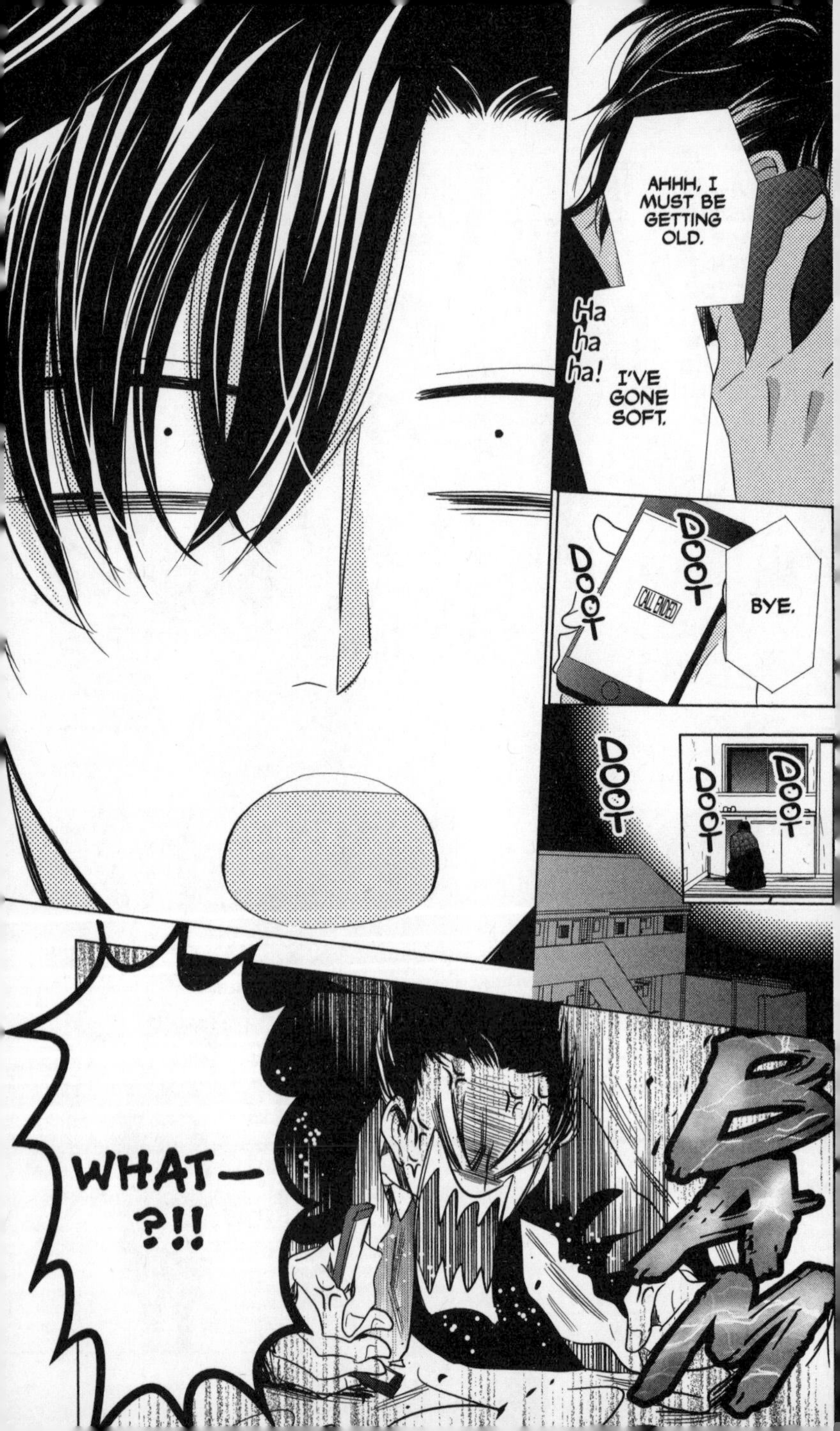
AHHH, I MUST BE GETTING OLD.
Ha ha ha!
I'VE GONE SOFT.
BYE.
DOOT
DOOT
CALL ENDED
DOOT
DOOT
DOOT
WHAT— ?!!

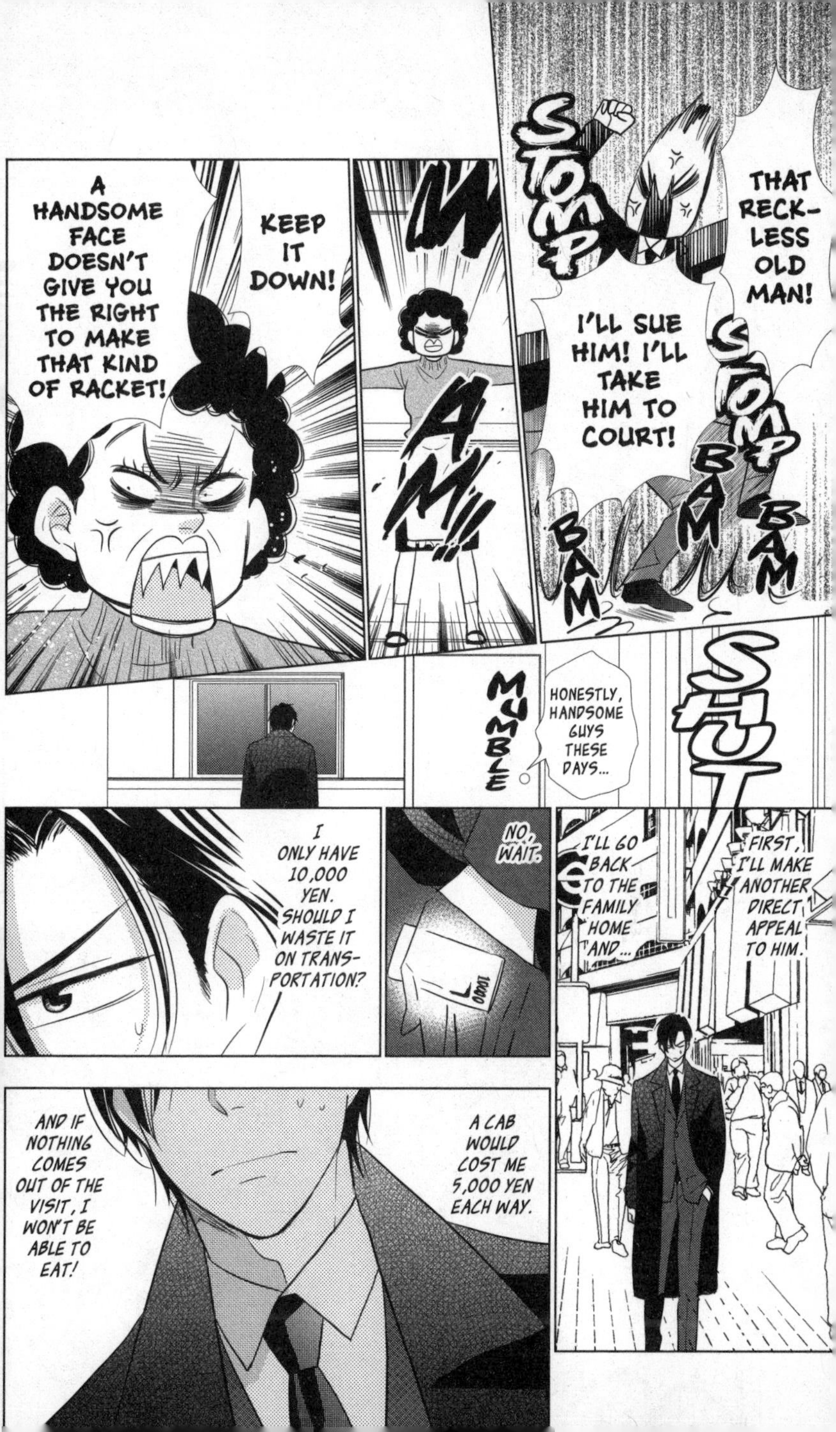

STOMP
THAT RECK-LESS OLD MAN!
I'LL SUE HIM! I'LL TAKE HIM TO COURT!
STOMP
BAM BAM BAM
BAM
MAM
KEEP IT DOWN!
A HANDSOME FACE DOESN'T GIVE YOU THE RIGHT TO MAKE THAT KIND OF RACKET!
SHUT
HONESTLY, HANDSOME GUYS THESE DAYS...
MUMBLE
FIRST, I'LL MAKE ANOTHER DIRECT APPEAL TO HIM.
I'LL GO BACK TO THE FAMILY HOME AND...
NO, WAIT.
10000
I ONLY HAVE 10,000 YEN. SHOULD I WASTE IT ON TRANS-PORTATION?
A CAB WOULD COST ME 5,000 YEN EACH WAY.
AND IF NOTHING COMES OUT OF THE VISIT, I WON'T BE ABLE TO EAT!

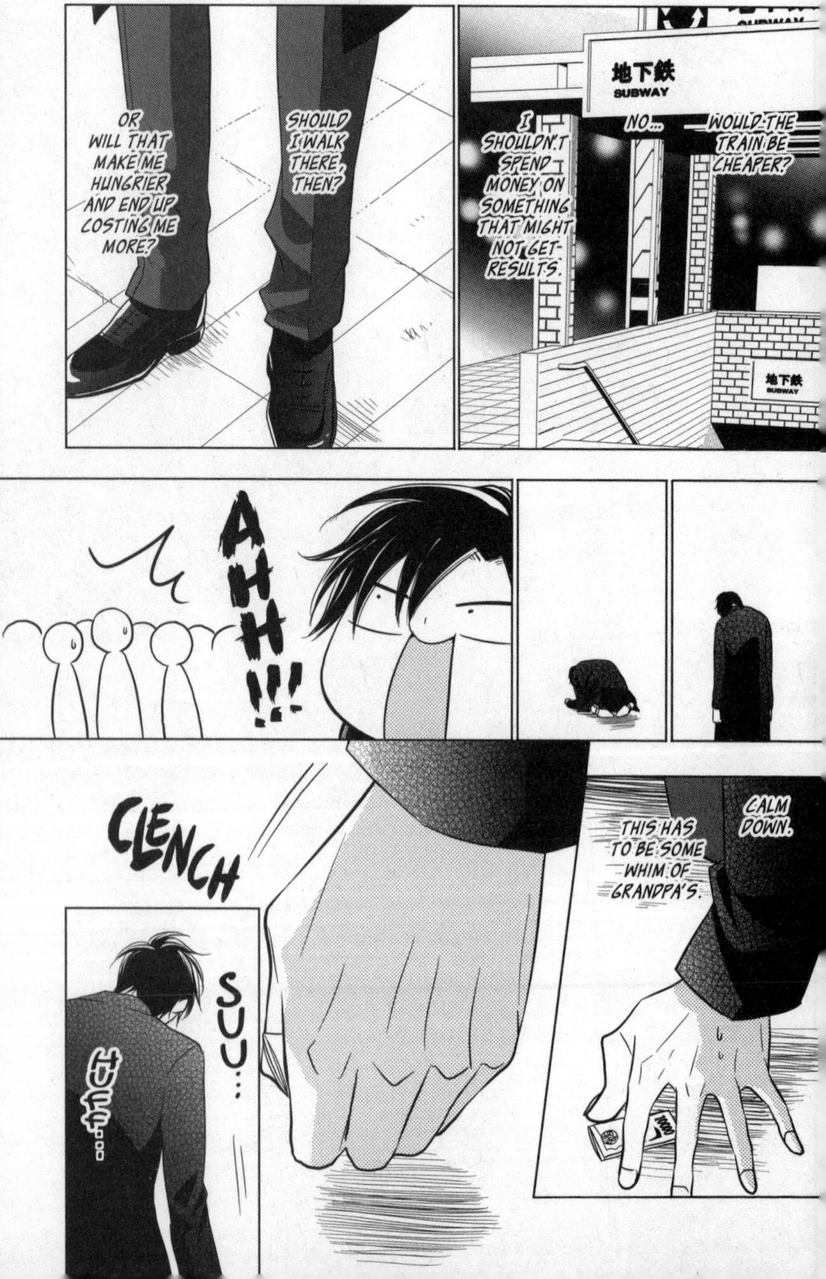
地下鉄
SUBWAY
WOULD THE TRAIN BE CHEAPER?
NO...
I SHOULDN'T SPEND MONEY ON SOMETHING THAT MIGHT NOT GET RESULTS.
地下鉄
SUBWAY
SHOULD I WALK THERE, THEN?
OR WILL THAT MAKE ME HUNGRIER AND END UP COSTING ME MORE?
AHH!!!
CALM DOWN.
THIS HAS TO BE SOME WHIM OF GRANDPA'S.
CLENCH
SUU...
HUFF...

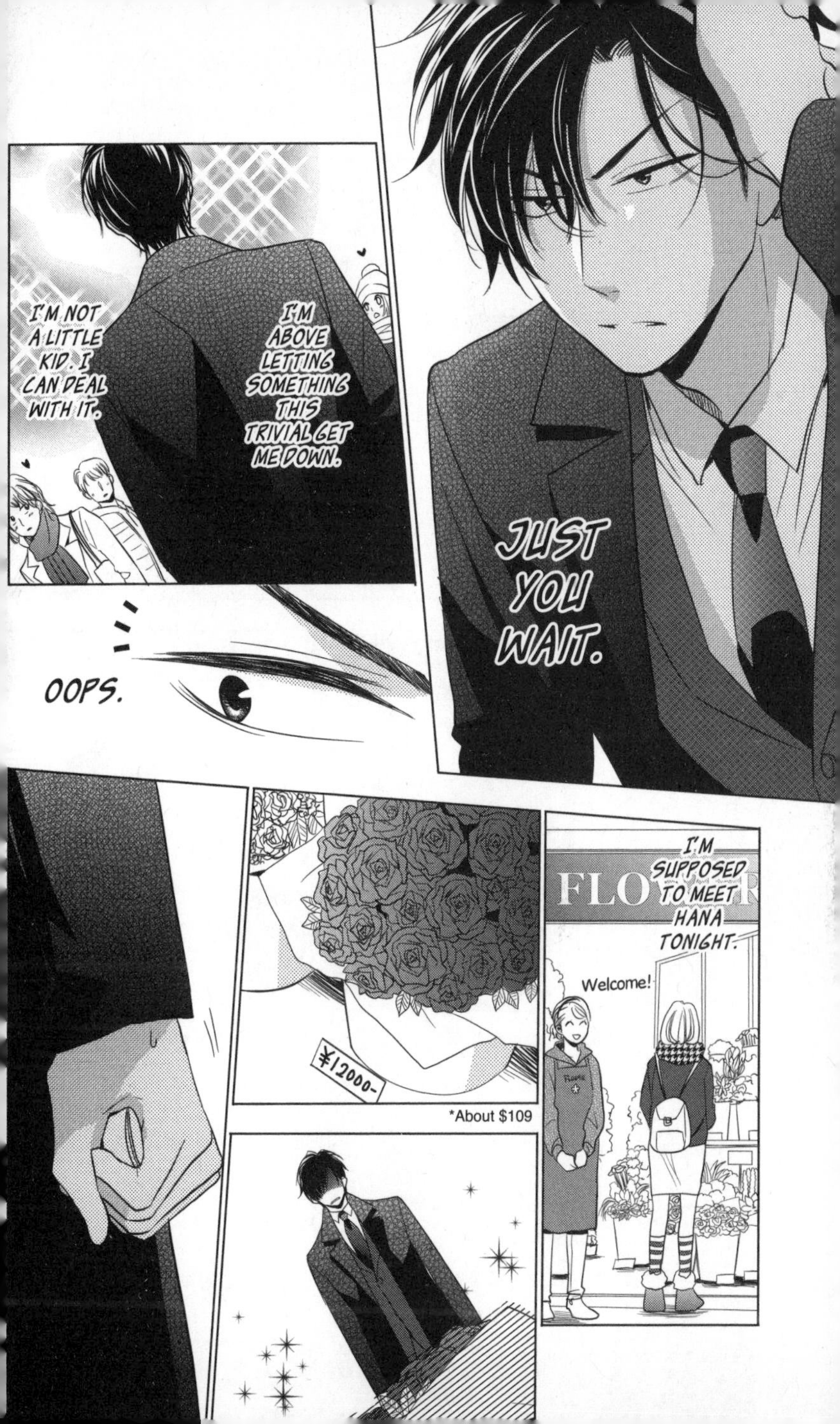
JUST YOU WAIT.
I'M ABOVE LETTING SOMETHING THIS TRIVIAL GET ME DOWN.
I'M NOT A LITTLE KID. I CAN DEAL WITH IT.
OOPS.
I'M SUPPOSED TO MEET HANA TONIGHT.
Welcome!
FLO
¥12000-
*About $109

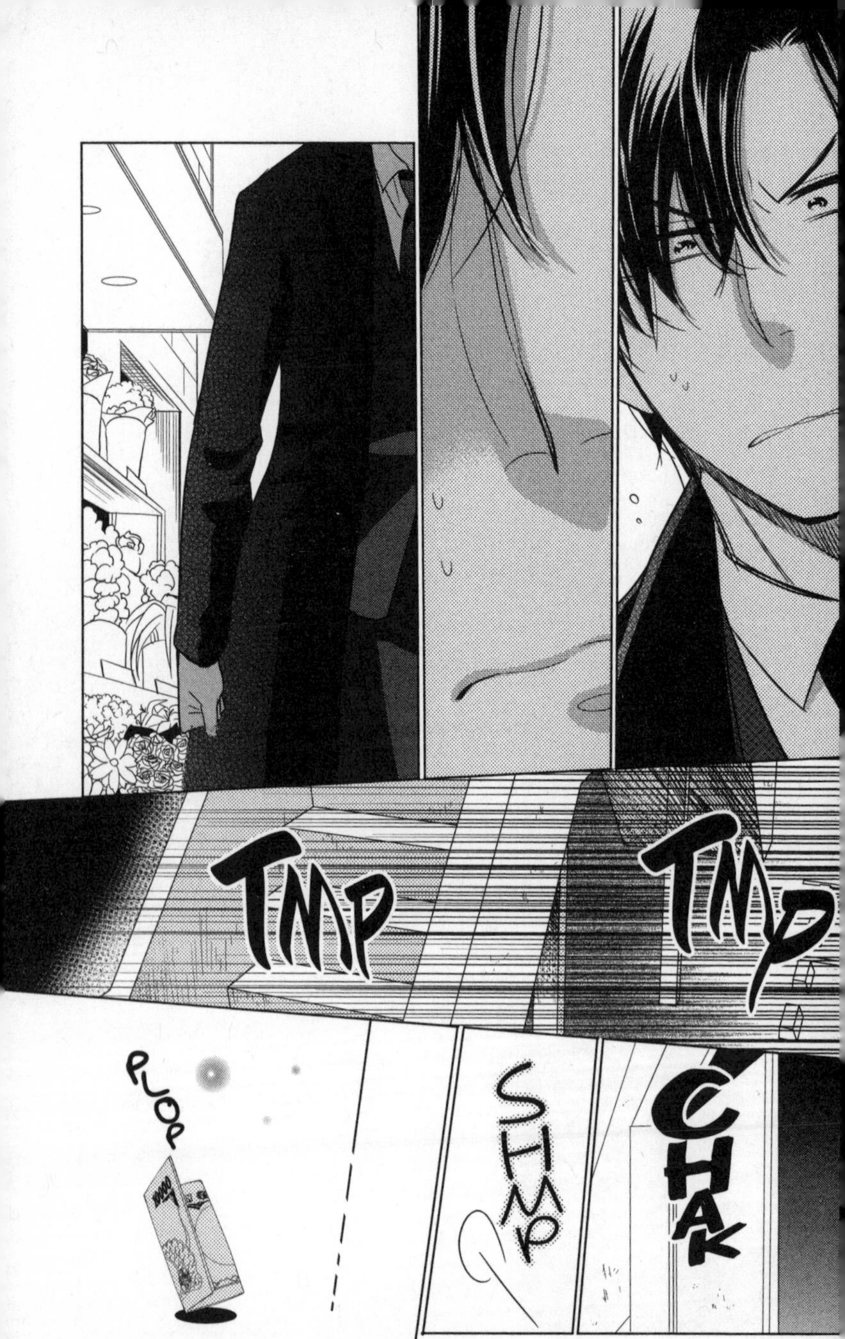
TMP
TMP
CHAK
SHMP
PLOP

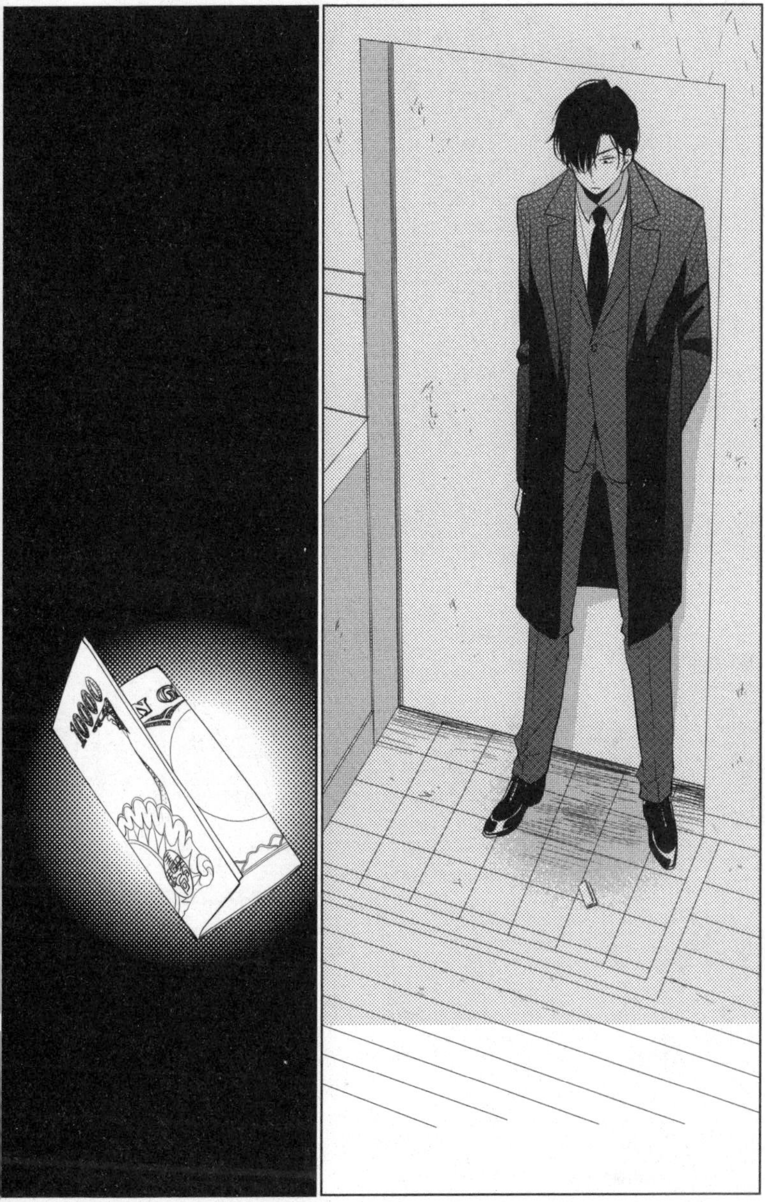

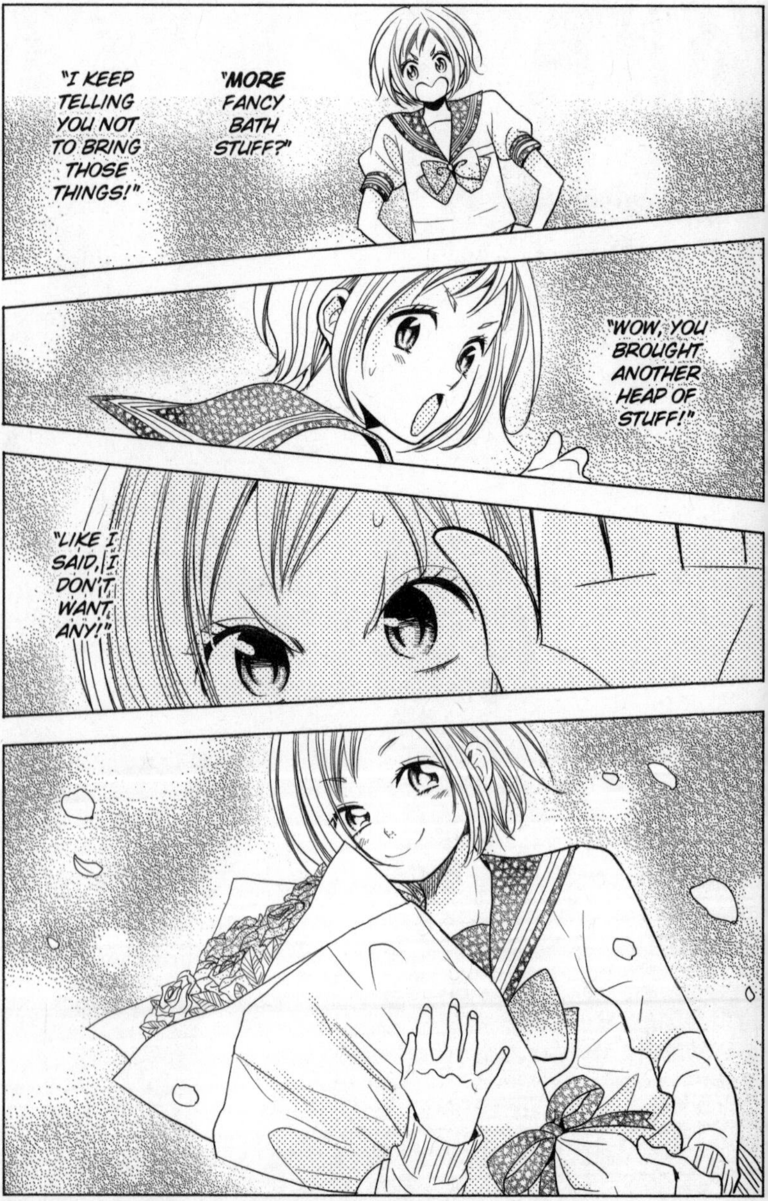
"MORE FANCY BATH STUFF?"
"I KEEP TELLING YOU NOT TO BRING THOSE THINGS!"
"WOW, YOU BROUGHT ANOTHER HEAP OF STUFF!"
"LIKE I SAID, I DON'T WANT ANY!"

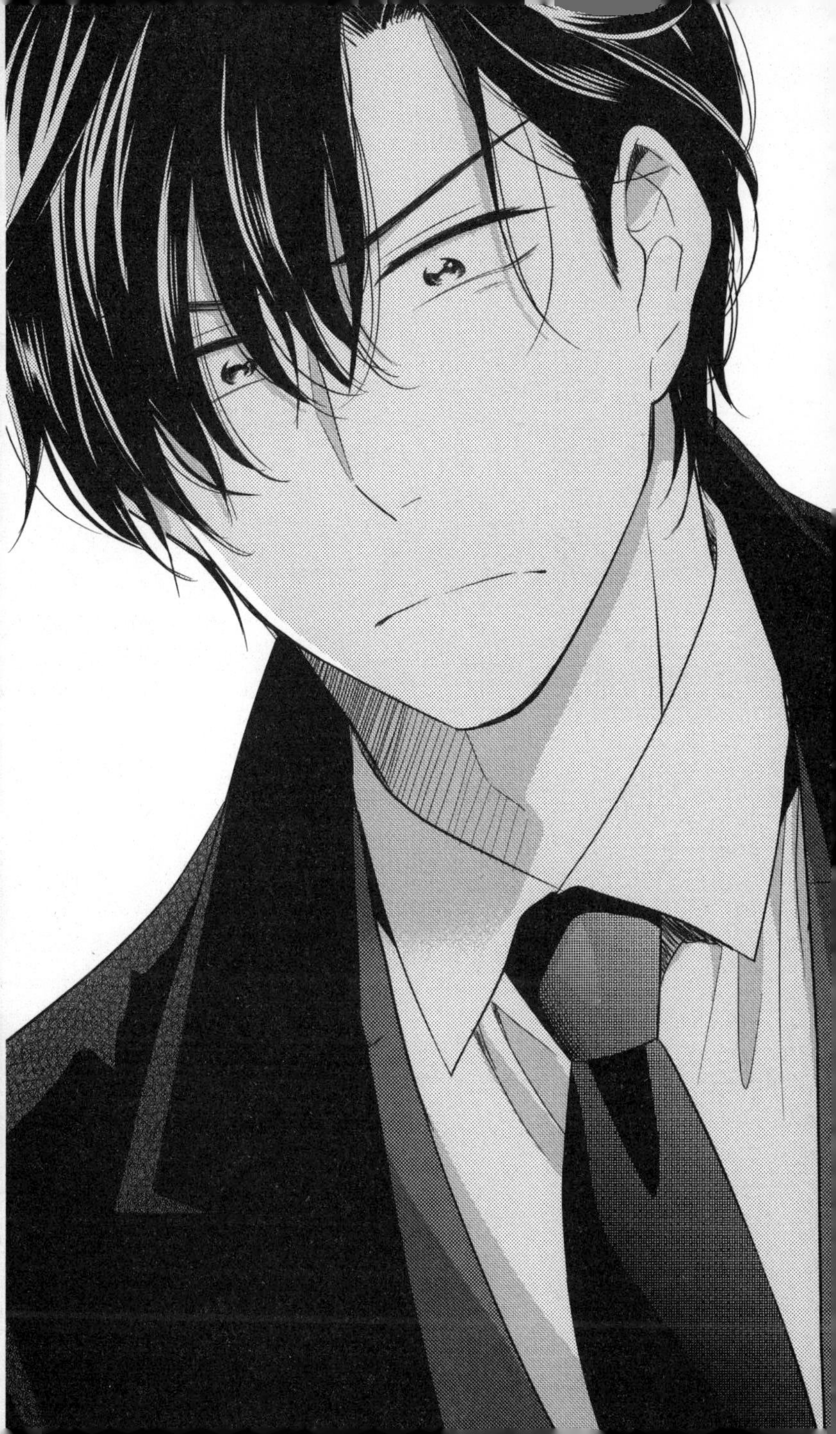

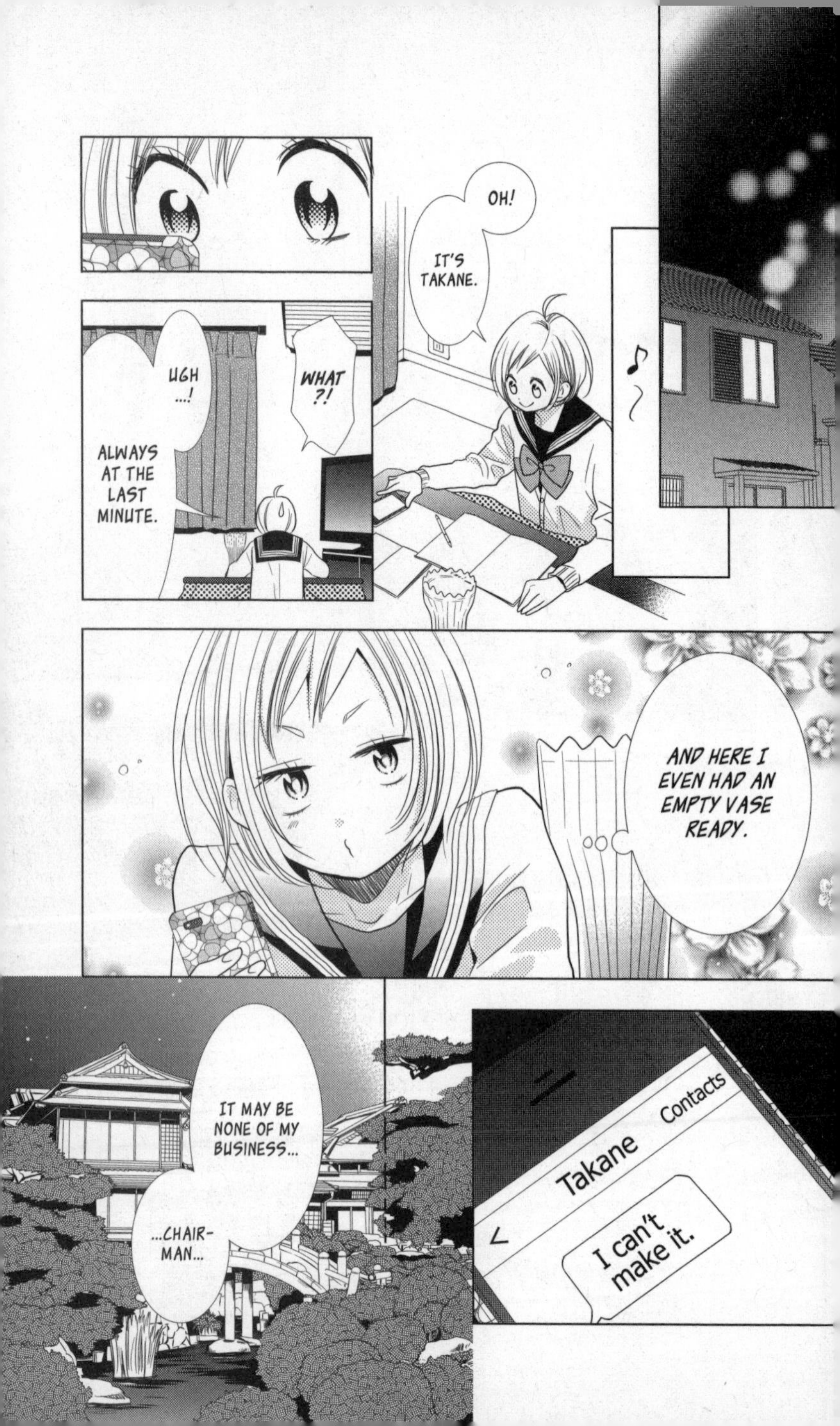
OH!
IT'S TAKANE.
WHAT?!
UGH...!
ALWAYS AT THE LAST MINUTE.
AND HERE I EVEN HAD AN EMPTY VASE READY.
Contacts
Takane
I can't make it.
IT MAY BE NONE OF MY BUSINESS...
...CHAIR-MAN...

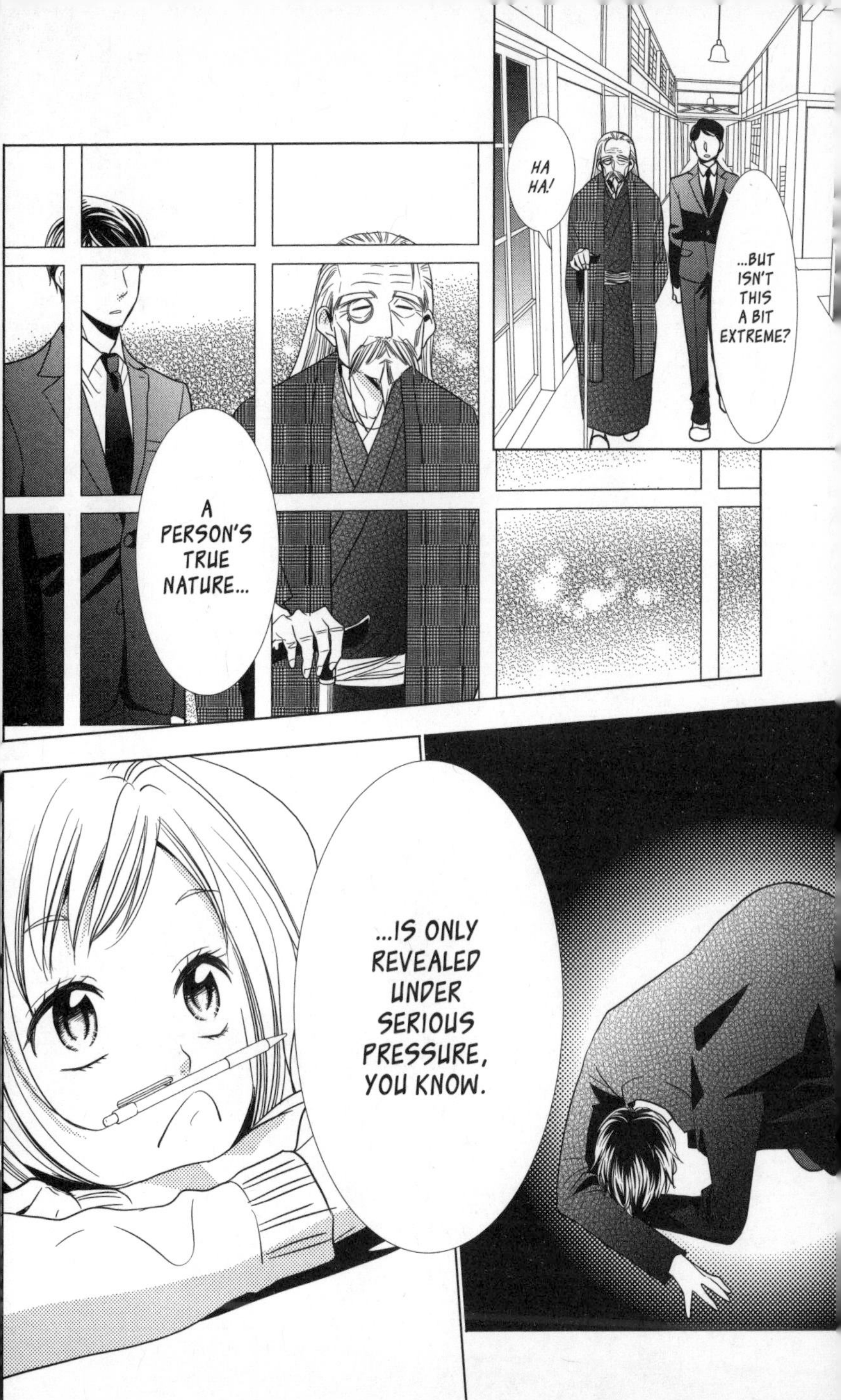
...BUT ISN'T THIS A BIT EXTREME?
HA HA!
A PERSON'S TRUE NATURE...
...IS ONLY REVEALED UNDER SERIOUS PRESSURE, YOU KNOW.

Special-Order Santa

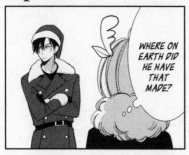

WHERE ON EARTH DID HE HAVE THAT MADE?

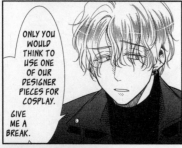

ONLY YOU WOULD THINK TO USE ONE OF OUR DESIGNER PIECES FOR COSPLAY.

GIVE ME A BREAK.

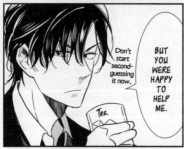

BUT YOU WERE HAPPY TO HELP ME.

Don't start second-guessing it now.

Tea.

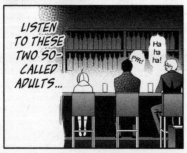

LISTEN TO THESE TWO SO-CALLED ADULTS...

Pfft!

Ha ha ha!

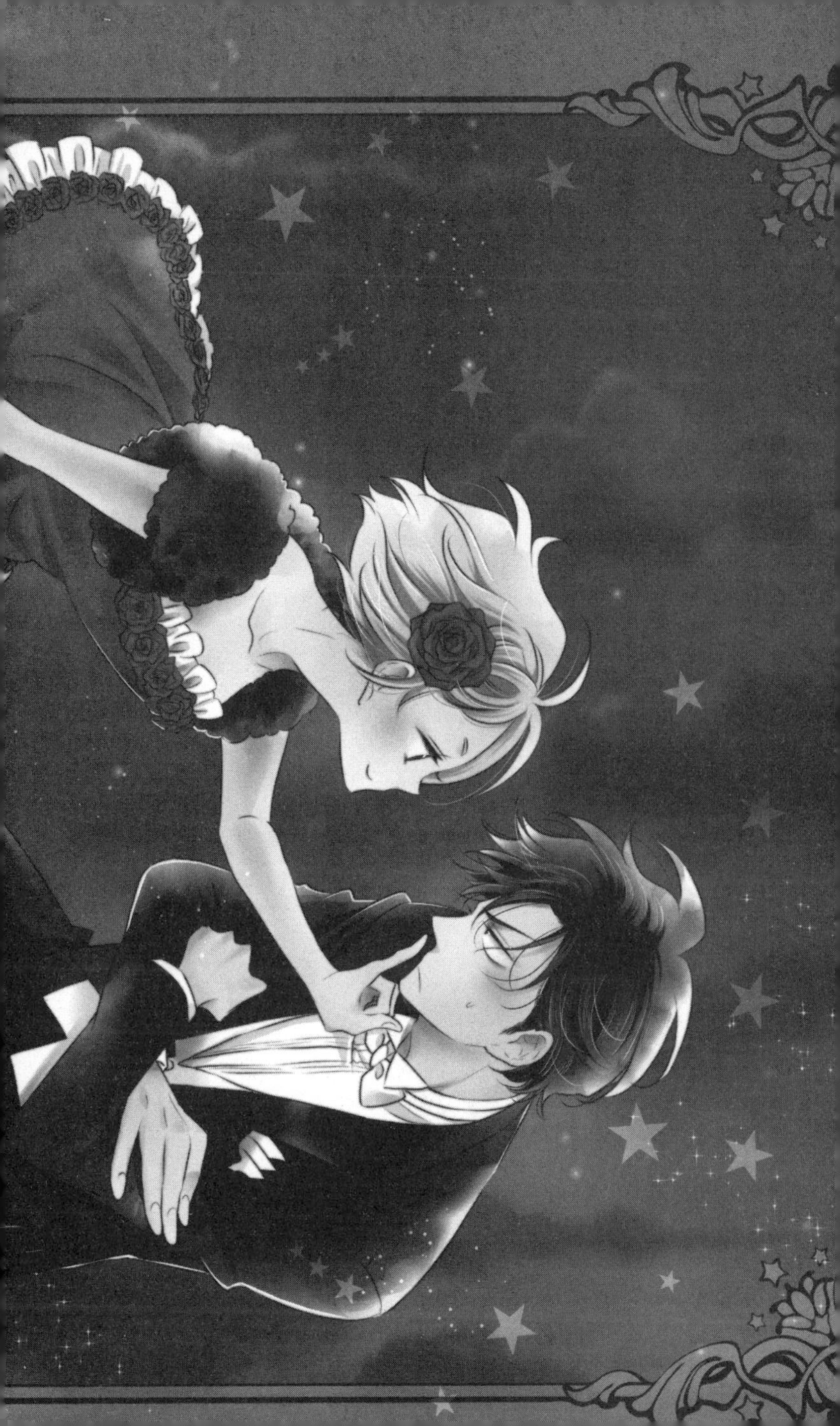

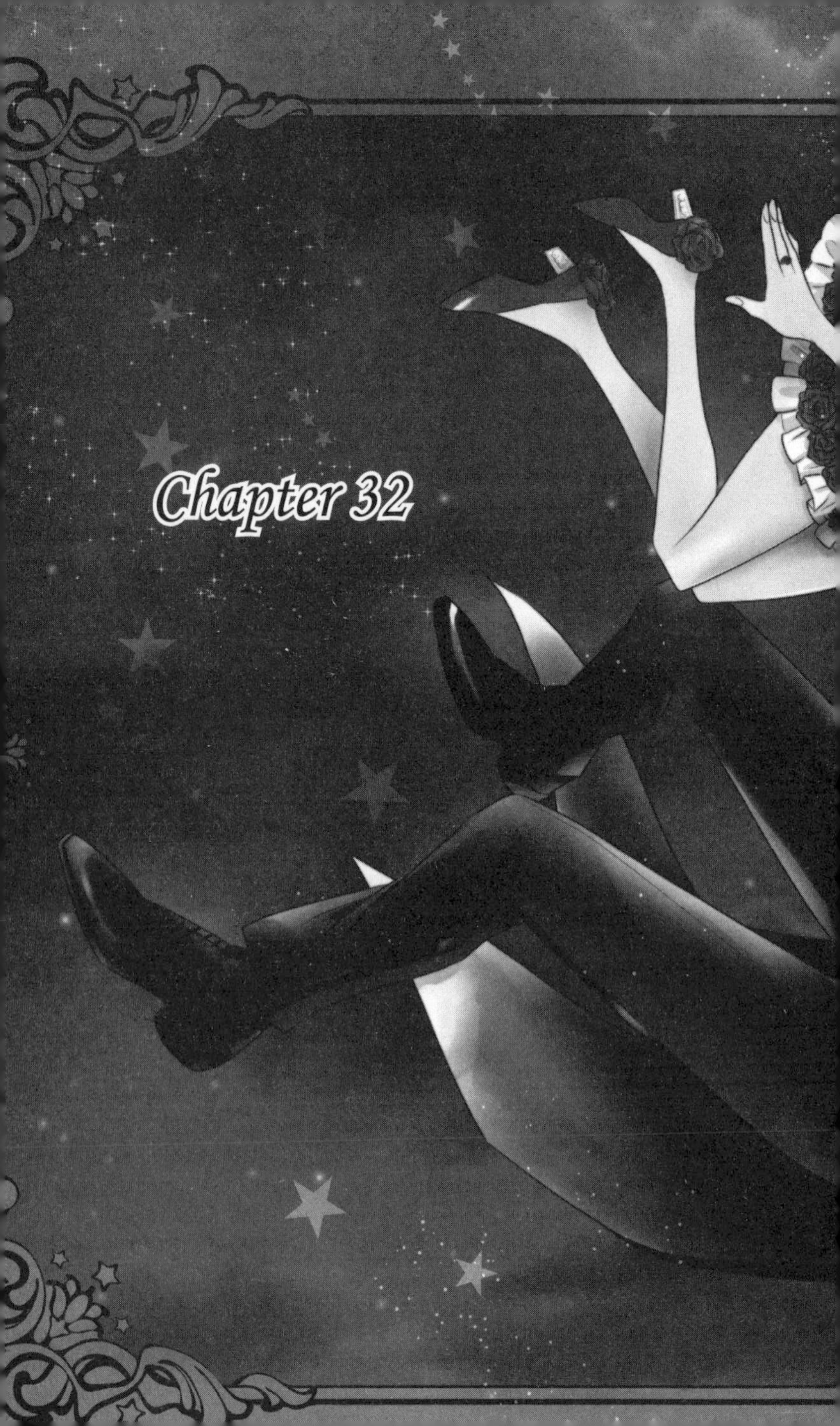
Chapter 32

The Middle

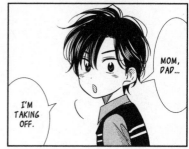

MOM, DAD...
I'M TAKING OFF.
RUMPLE RUMPLE
HIROMI, DON'T WEAR YOUR HAIR LIKE THAT.
PART IT IN THE MIDDLE.
THAT'S RIGHT, DEAR. IN THE MIDDLE.
HOW COULD YOU?! THAT STYLE TOOK ME TWO HOURS!!

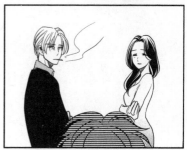

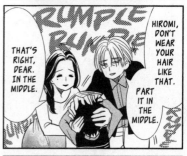

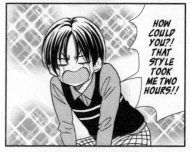

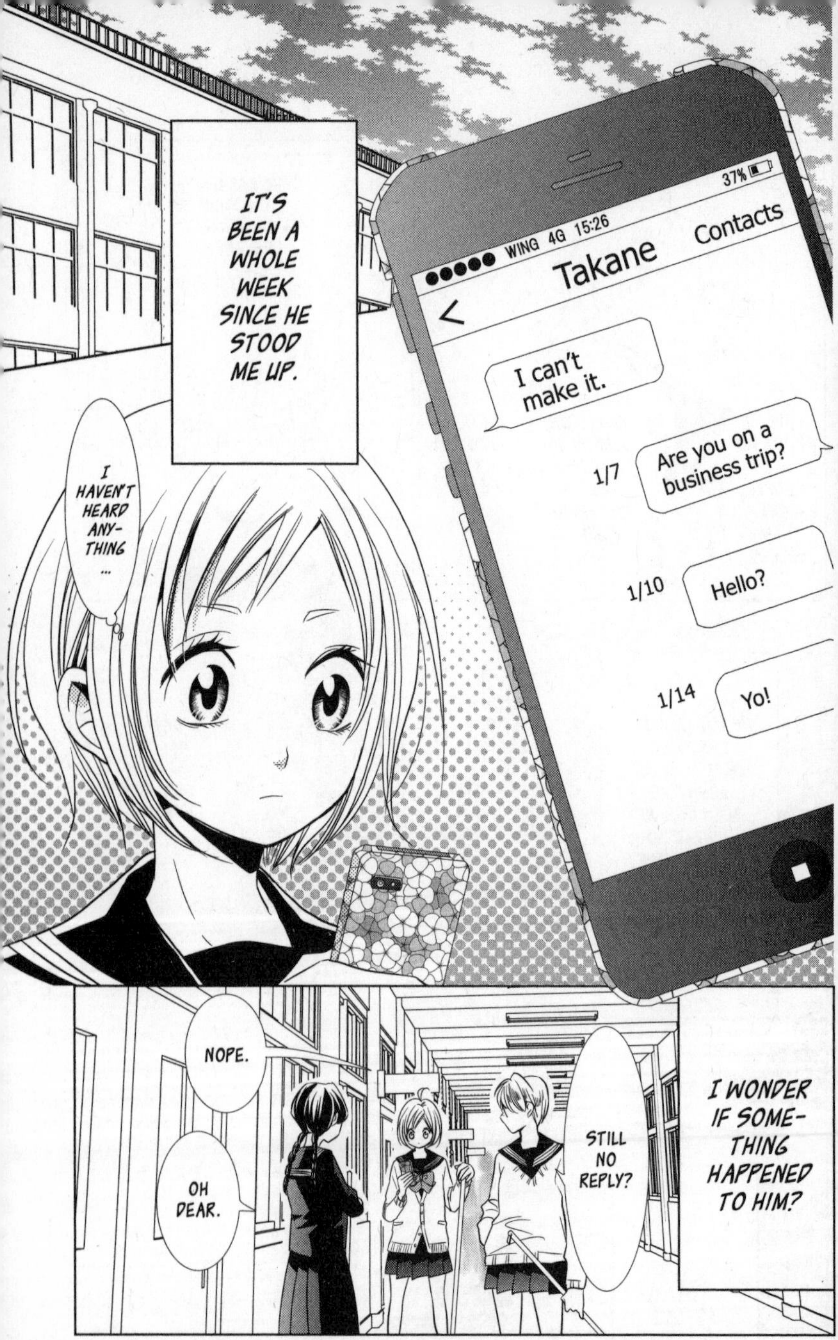

37%
●●●●● WING 4G 15:26
Contacts
<
Takane
I can't make it.
1/7
Are you on a business trip?
1/10
Hello?
1/14
Yo!
IT'S BEEN A WHOLE WEEK SINCE HE STOOD ME UP.
I HAVEN'T HEARD ANY-THING...
I WONDER IF SOME-THING HAPPENED TO HIM?
STILL NO REPLY?
NOPE.
OH DEAR.

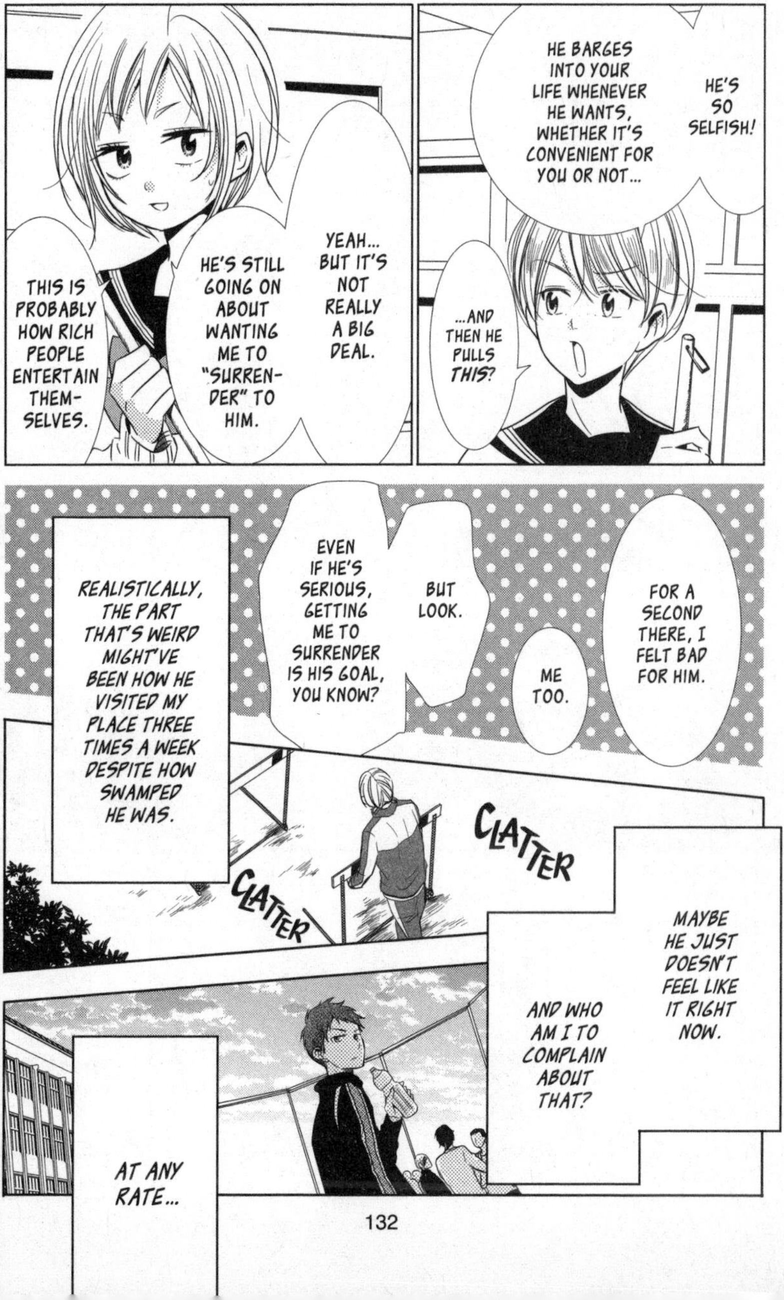
HE'S SO SELFISH!
HE BARGES INTO YOUR LIFE WHENEVER HE WANTS, WHETHER IT'S CONVENIENT FOR YOU OR NOT...
...AND THEN HE PULLS *THIS*?
YEAH... BUT IT'S NOT REALLY A BIG DEAL.
HE'S STILL GOING ON ABOUT WANTING ME TO "SURRENDER" TO HIM.
THIS IS PROBABLY HOW RICH PEOPLE ENTERTAIN THEMSELVES.
FOR A SECOND THERE, I FELT BAD FOR HIM.
ME TOO.
BUT LOOK.
EVEN IF HE'S SERIOUS, GETTING ME TO SURRENDER IS HIS GOAL, YOU KNOW?
REALISTICALLY, THE PART THAT'S WEIRD MIGHT'VE BEEN HOW HE VISITED MY PLACE THREE TIMES A WEEK DESPITE HOW SWAMPED HE WAS.
CLATTER
CLATTER
MAYBE HE JUST DOESN'T FEEL LIKE IT RIGHT NOW.
AND WHO AM I TO COMPLAIN ABOUT THAT?
AT ANY RATE...

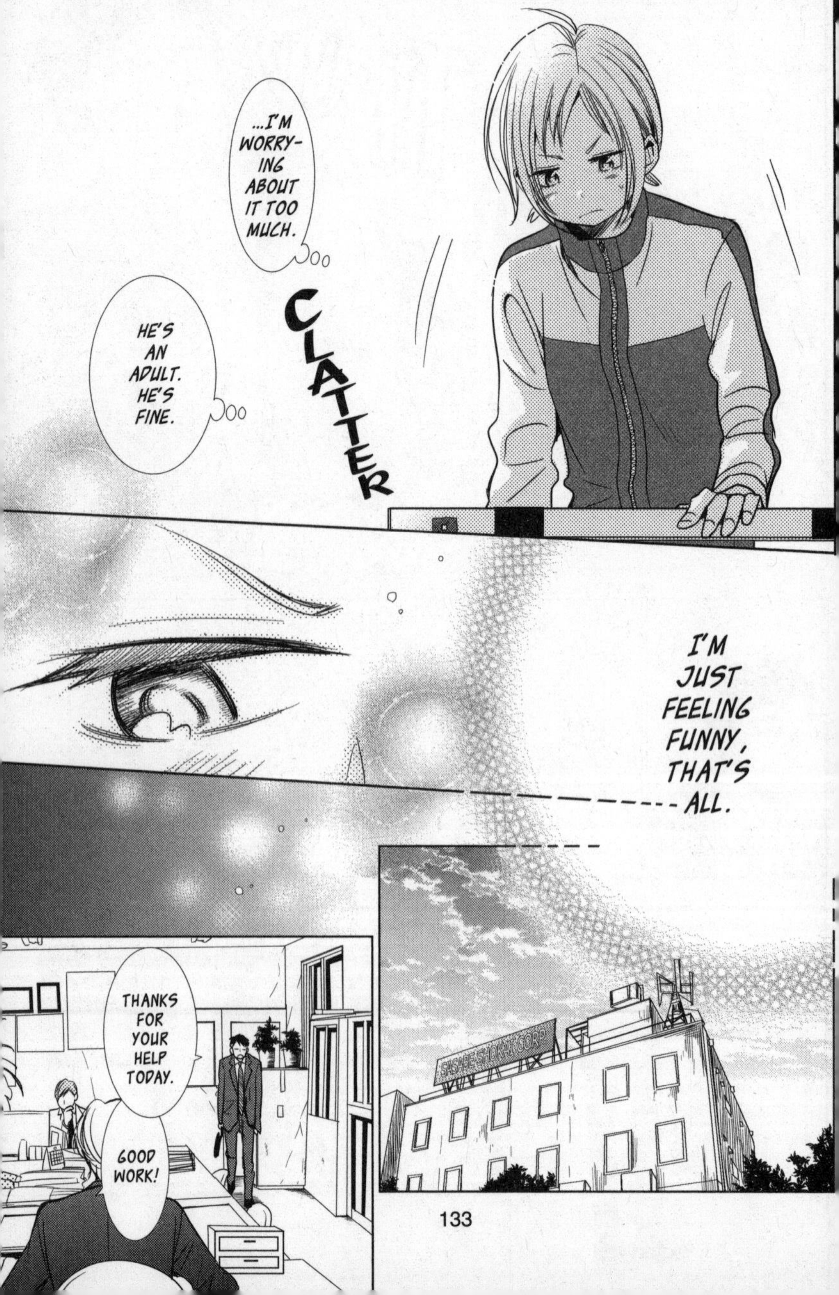
...I'M WORRYING ABOUT IT TOO MUCH.
HE'S AN ADULT. HE'S FINE.
CLATTER
I'M JUST FEELING FUNNY, THAT'S ALL.
SASABE SHOKAI CORP.
THANKS FOR YOUR HELP TODAY.
GOOD WORK!

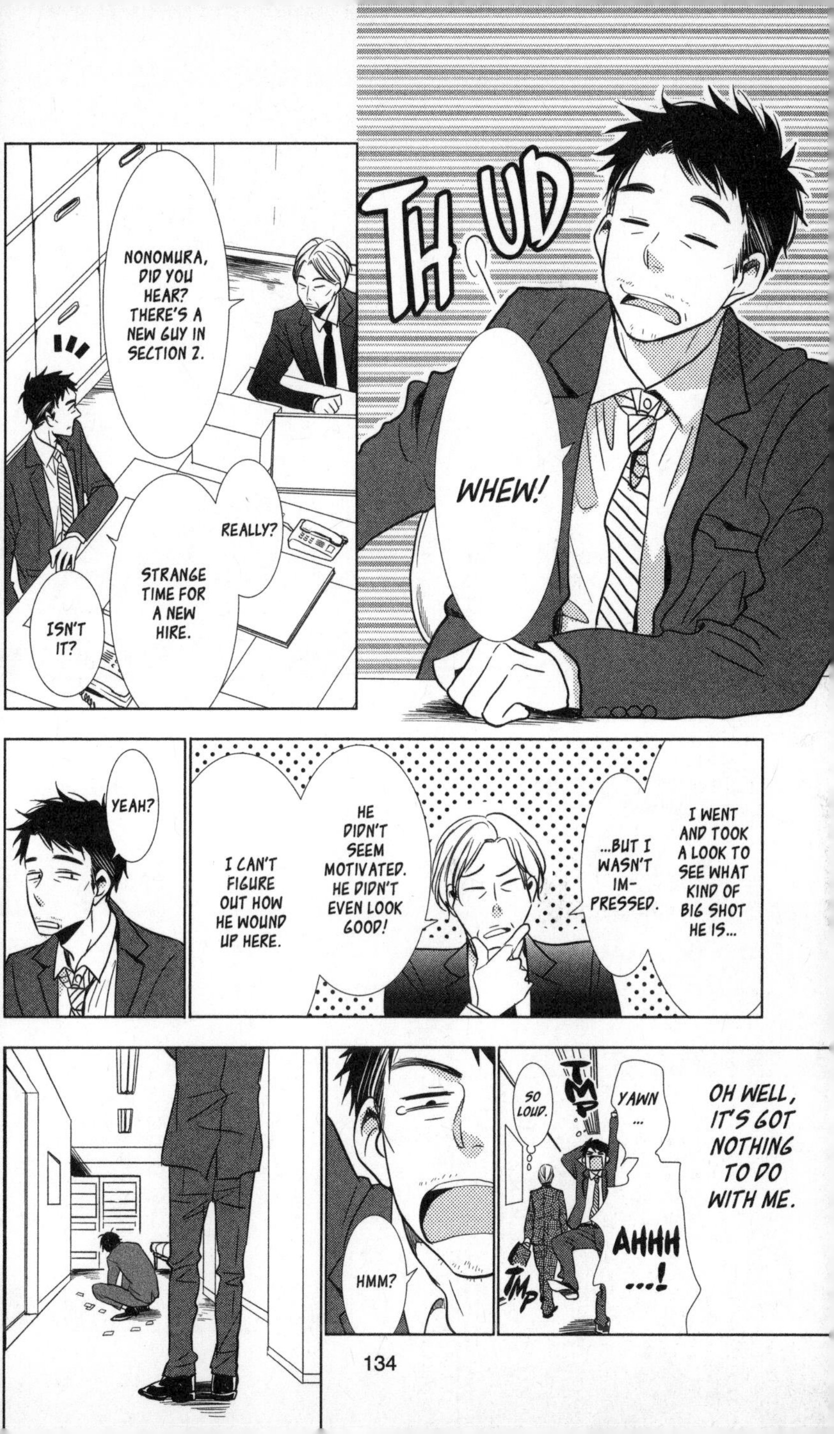
THUD
WHEW!
NONOMURA, DID YOU HEAR? THERE'S A NEW GUY IN SECTION 2.
REALLY?
STRANGE TIME FOR A NEW HIRE.
ISN'T IT?
I WENT AND TOOK A LOOK TO SEE WHAT KIND OF BIG SHOT HE IS...
...BUT I WASN'T IM-PRESSED.
HE DIDN'T SEEM MOTIVATED. HE DIDN'T EVEN LOOK GOOD!
I CAN'T FIGURE OUT HOW HE WOUND UP HERE.
YEAH?
OH WELL, IT'S GOT NOTHING TO DO WITH ME.
YAWN ...
TMP
SO LOUD.
AHHH ...!
TMP
HMM?

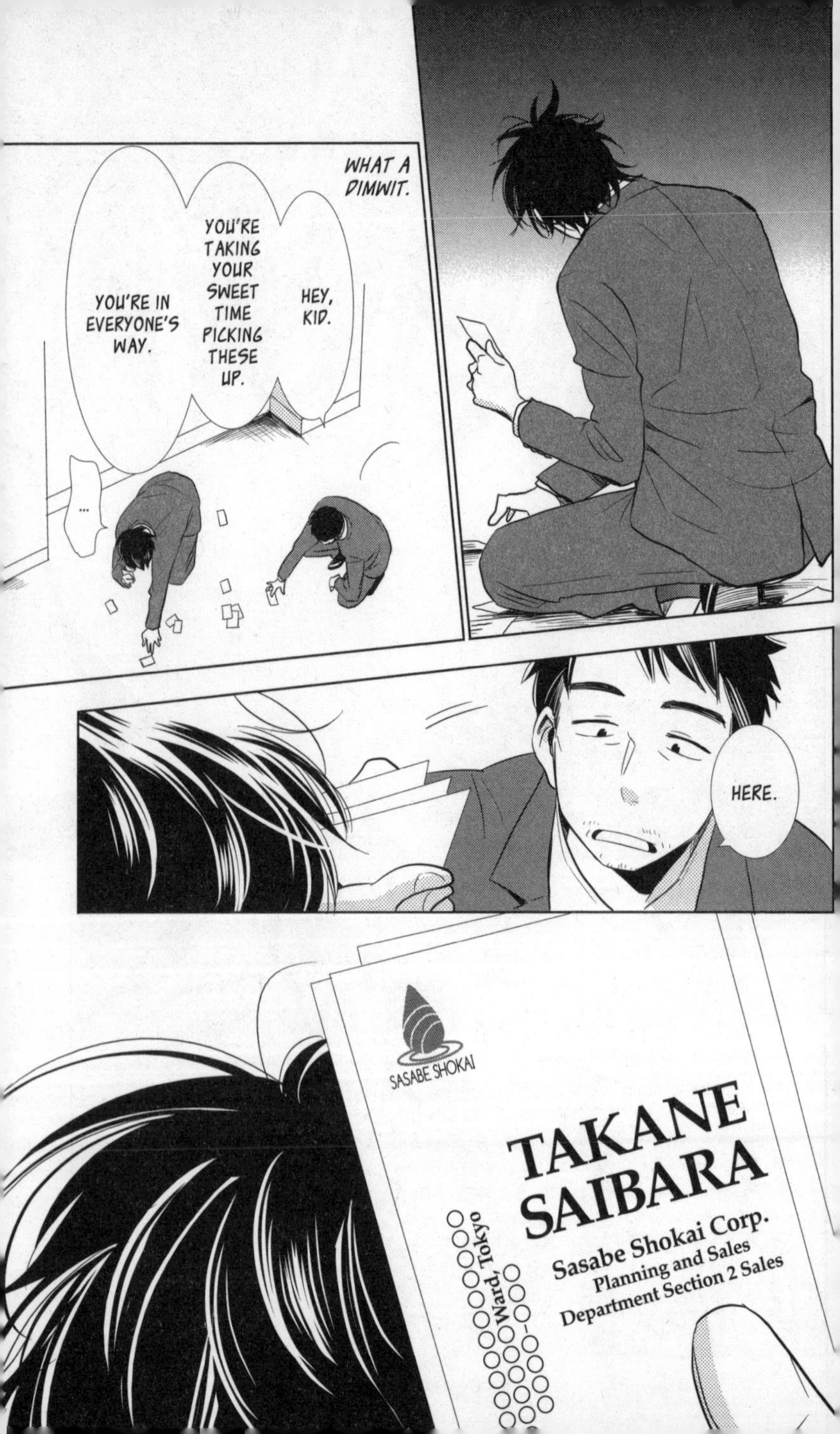
WHAT A DIMWIT.
HEY, KID.
YOU'RE TAKING YOUR SWEET TIME PICKING THESE UP.
YOU'RE IN EVERYONE'S WAY.
...
HERE.
SASABE SHOKAI
TAKANE SAIBARA
Sasabe Shokai Corp.
Planning and Sales
Department Section 2 Sales
○○○○○○○○ Ward, Tokyo
○○○○○-○○○○○

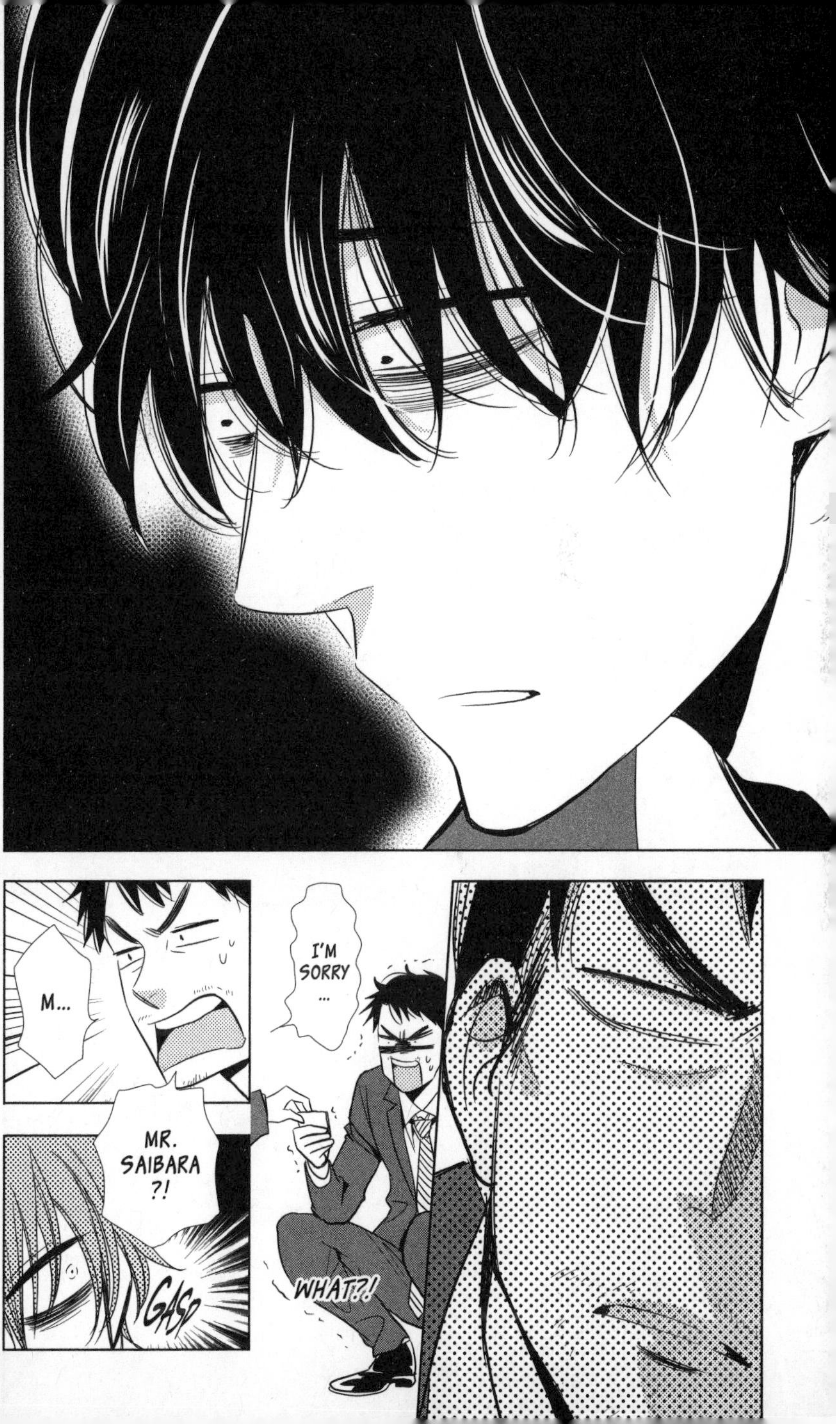
I'M SORRY ...
WHAT?!
M...
MR. SAIBARA ?!
GASP

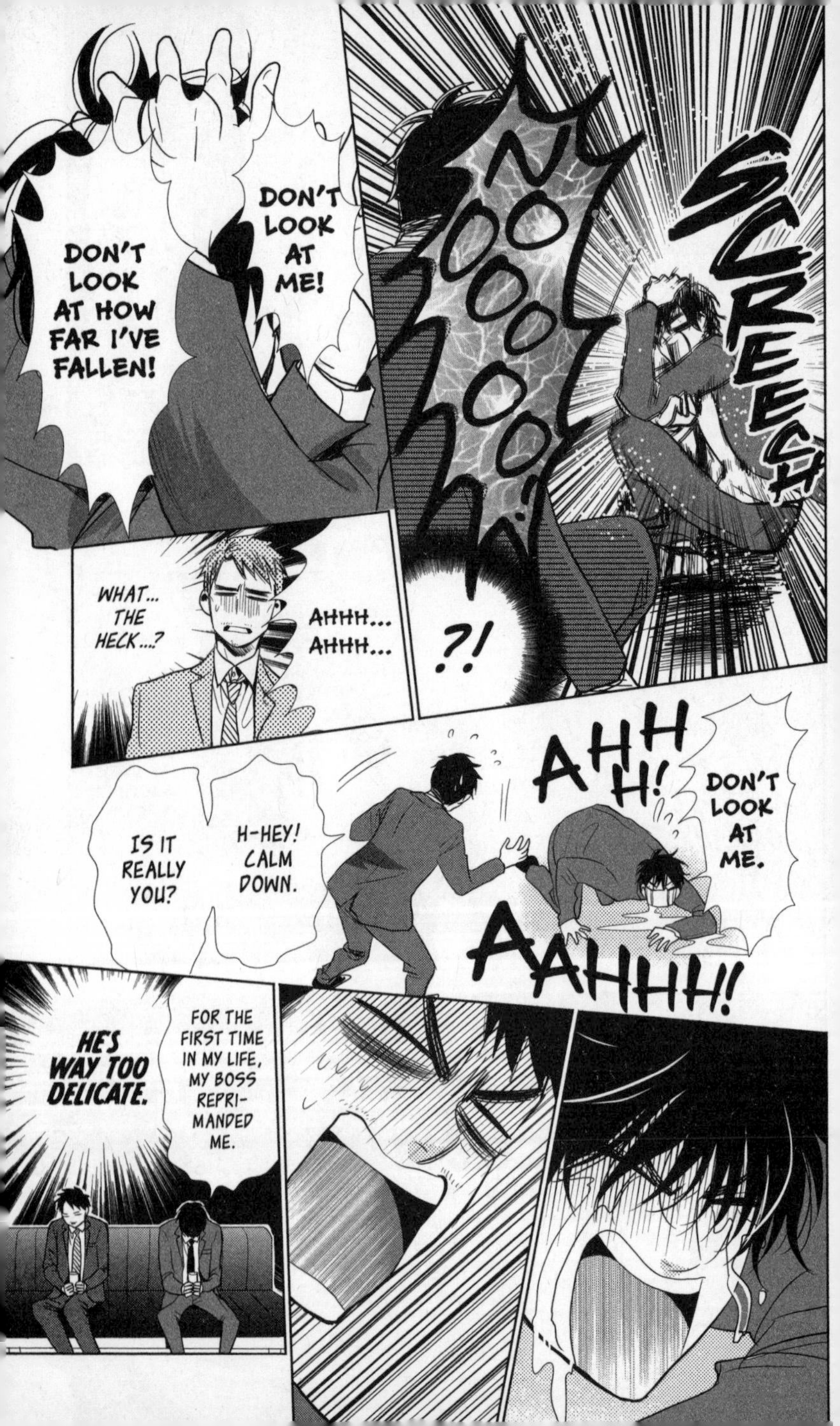
SCREECH
NOOOOOOOO?!
?!
DON'T LOOK AT ME!
DON'T LOOK AT HOW FAR I'VE FALLEN!
AHHH... AHHH...
WHAT... THE HECK...?
AHHH!
DON'T LOOK AT ME.
AAHHH!
H-HEY! CALM DOWN.
IS IT REALLY YOU?
FOR THE FIRST TIME IN MY LIFE, MY BOSS REPRIMANDED ME.
HE'S WAY TOO DELICATE.

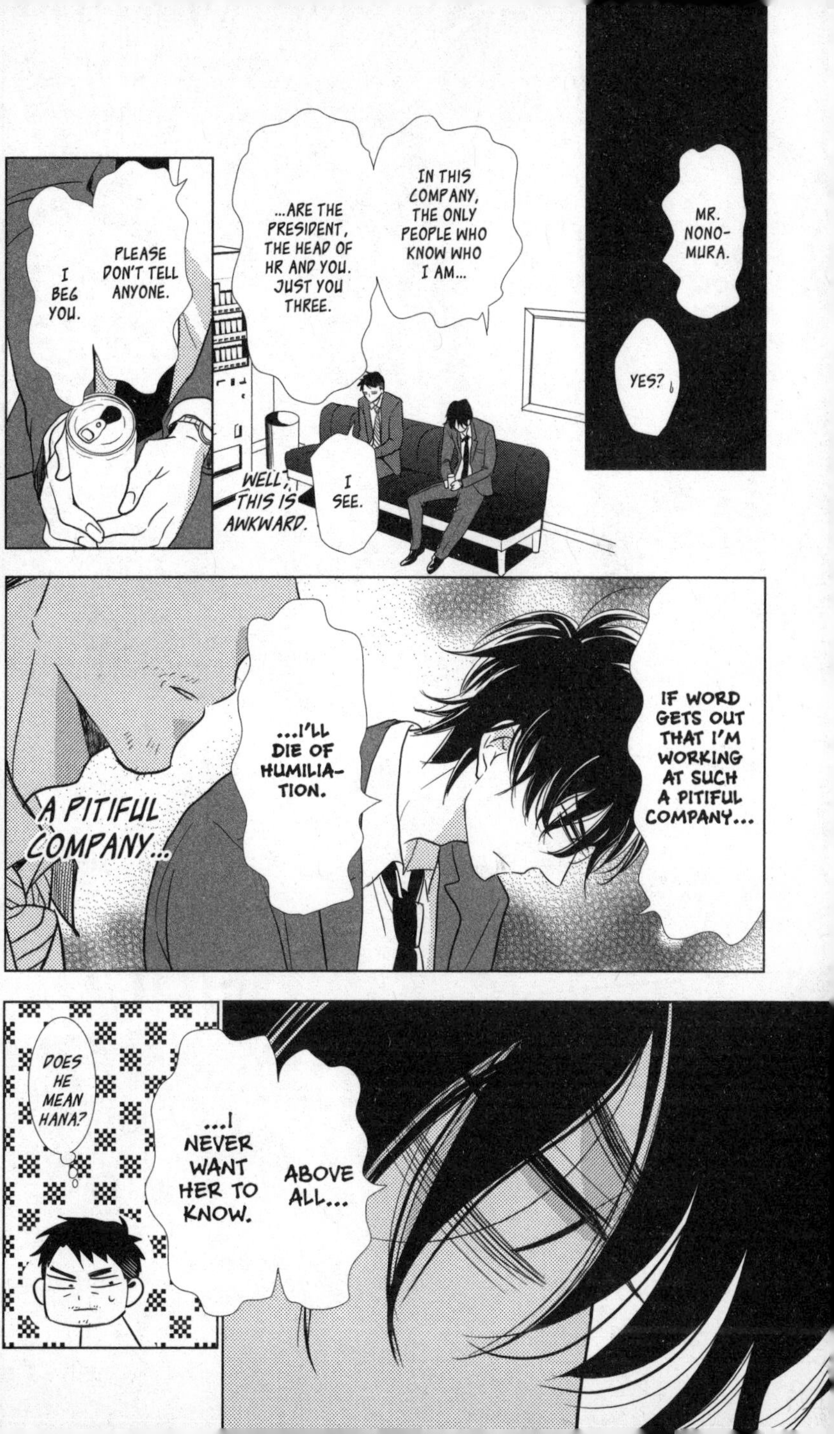
MR. NONO-MURA.
YES?
IN THIS COMPANY, THE ONLY PEOPLE WHO KNOW WHO I AM...
...ARE THE PRESIDENT, THE HEAD OF HR AND YOU. JUST YOU THREE.
I SEE.
WELL, THIS IS AWKWARD.
PLEASE DON'T TELL ANYONE.
I BEG YOU.
IF WORD GETS OUT THAT I'M WORKING AT SUCH A PITIFUL COMPANY...
...I'LL DIE OF HUMILIA-TION.
A PITIFUL COMPANY...
ABOVE ALL...
...I NEVER WANT HER TO KNOW.
DOES HE MEAN HANA?

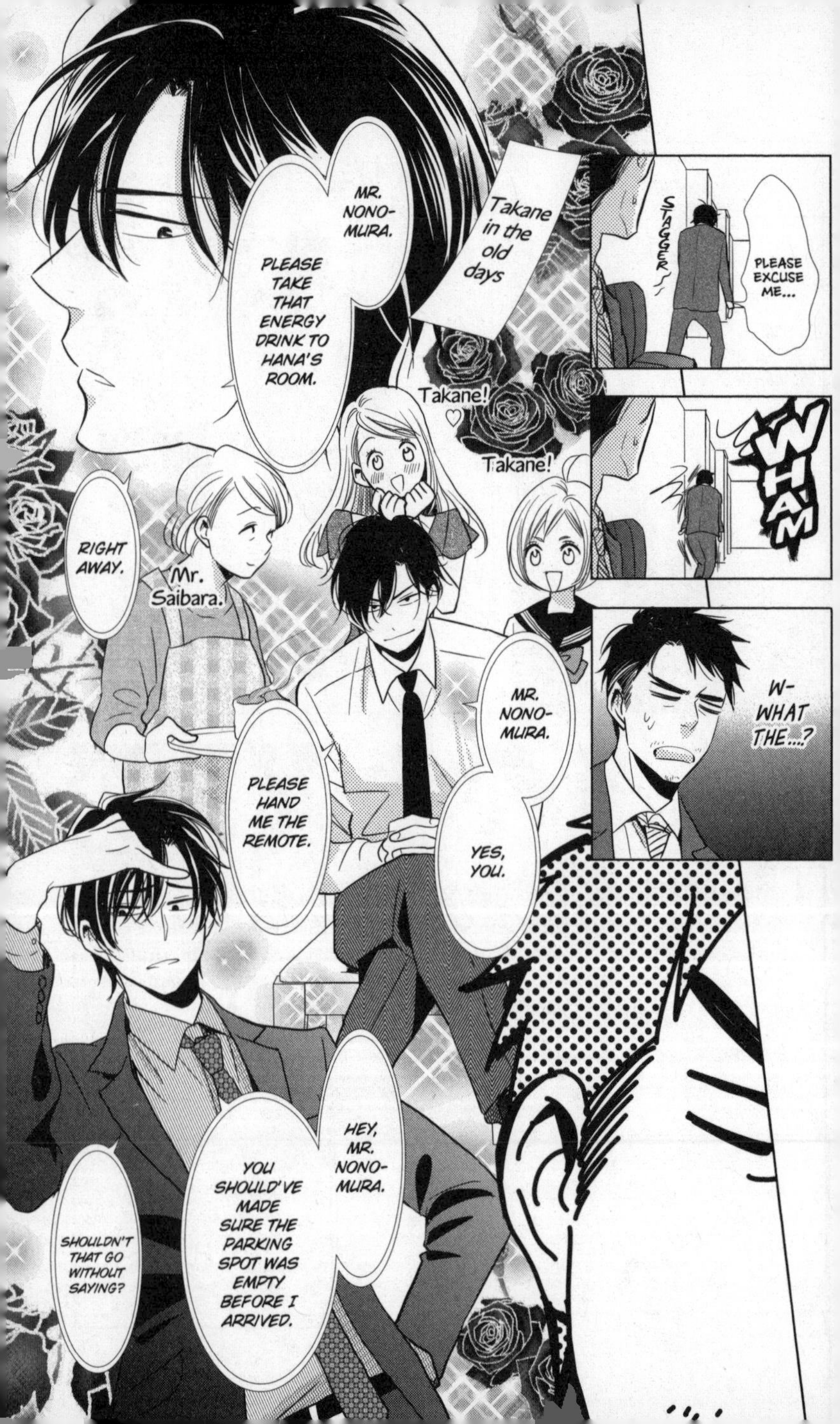
PLEASE EXCUSE ME...
STAGGER
WHAM
W-WHAT THE...?
Takane in the old days
MR. NONOMURA.
PLEASE TAKE THAT ENERGY DRINK TO HANA'S ROOM.
Takane! ♡
Takane!
Mr. Saibara.
RIGHT AWAY.
MR. NONOMURA.
YES, YOU.
PLEASE HAND ME THE REMOTE.
HEY, MR. NONOMURA.
YOU SHOULD'VE MADE SURE THE PARKING SPOT WAS EMPTY BEFORE I ARRIVED.
SHOULDN'T THAT GO WITHOUT SAYING?

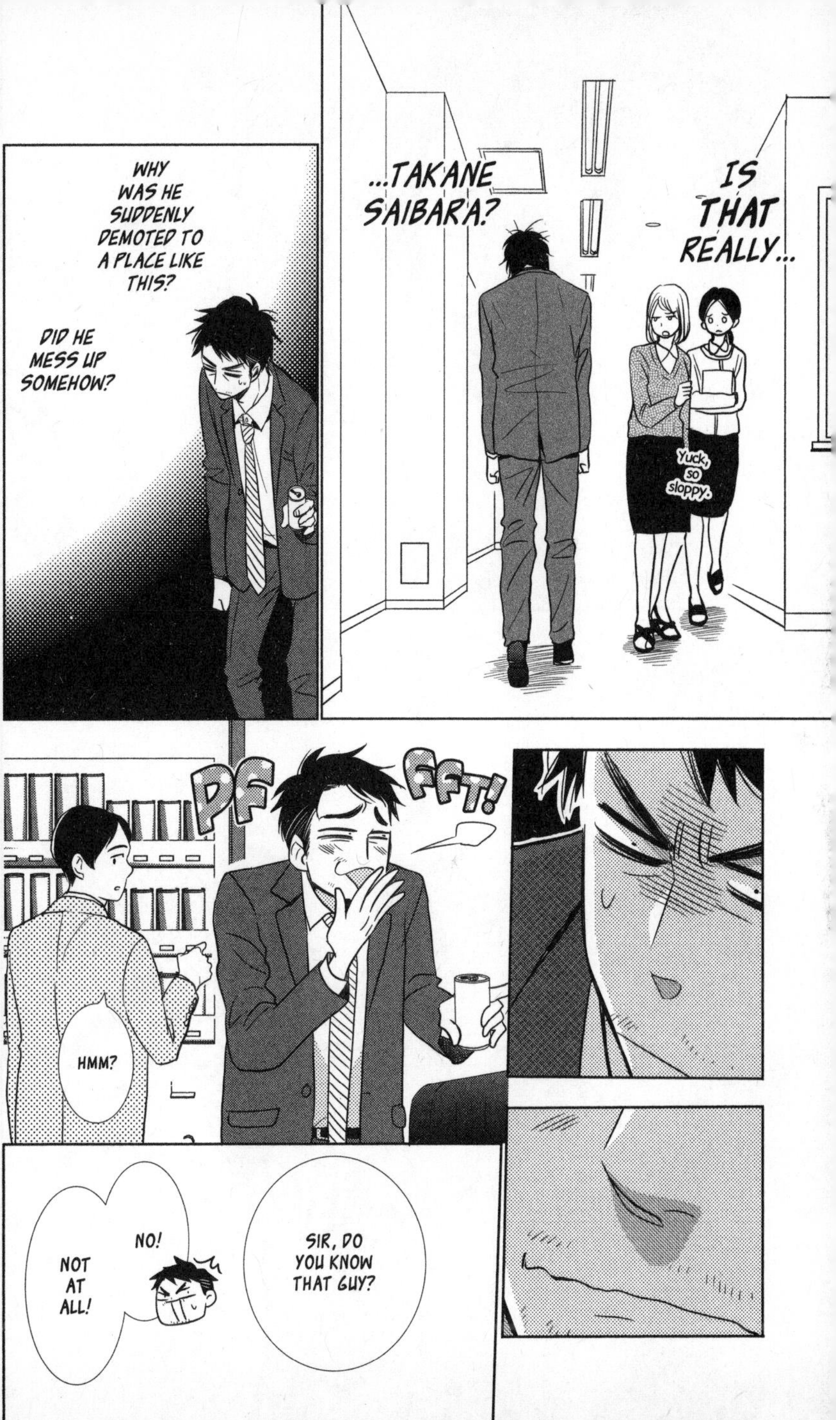
IS THAT REALLY...
...TAKANE SAIBARA?
Yuck, so sloppy.
WHY WAS HE SUDDENLY DEMOTED TO A PLACE LIKE THIS?
DID HE MESS UP SOMEHOW?
PFFFT!
HMM?
SIR, DO YOU KNOW THAT GUY?
NO! NOT AT ALL!

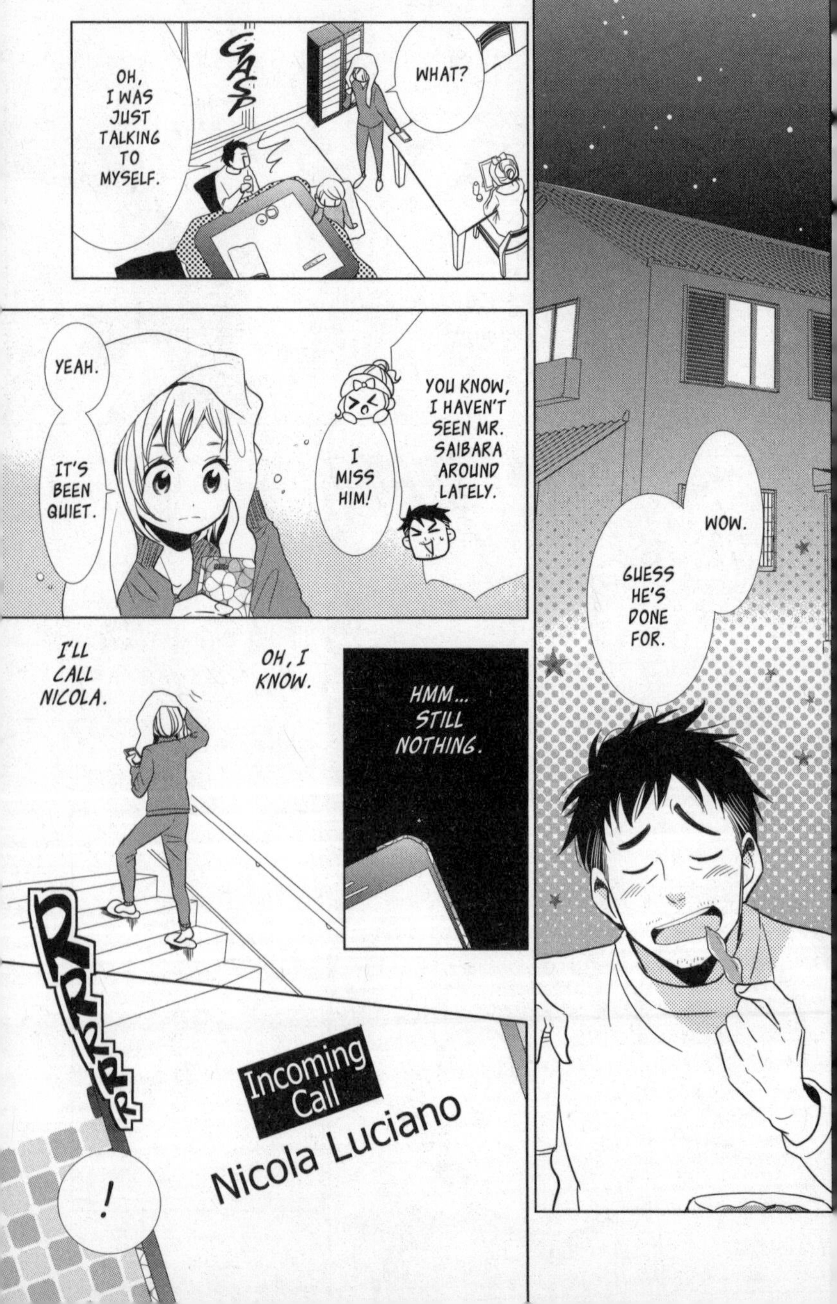
WOW.
GUESS HE'S DONE FOR.
WHAT?
GASP
OH, I WAS JUST TALKING TO MYSELF.
YOU KNOW, I HAVEN'T SEEN MR. SAIBARA AROUND LATELY.
I MISS HIM!
YEAH.
IT'S BEEN QUIET.
HMM... STILL NOTHING.
OH, I KNOW.
I'LL CALL NICOLA.
Incoming Call
Nicola Luciano
RRRRRR
!

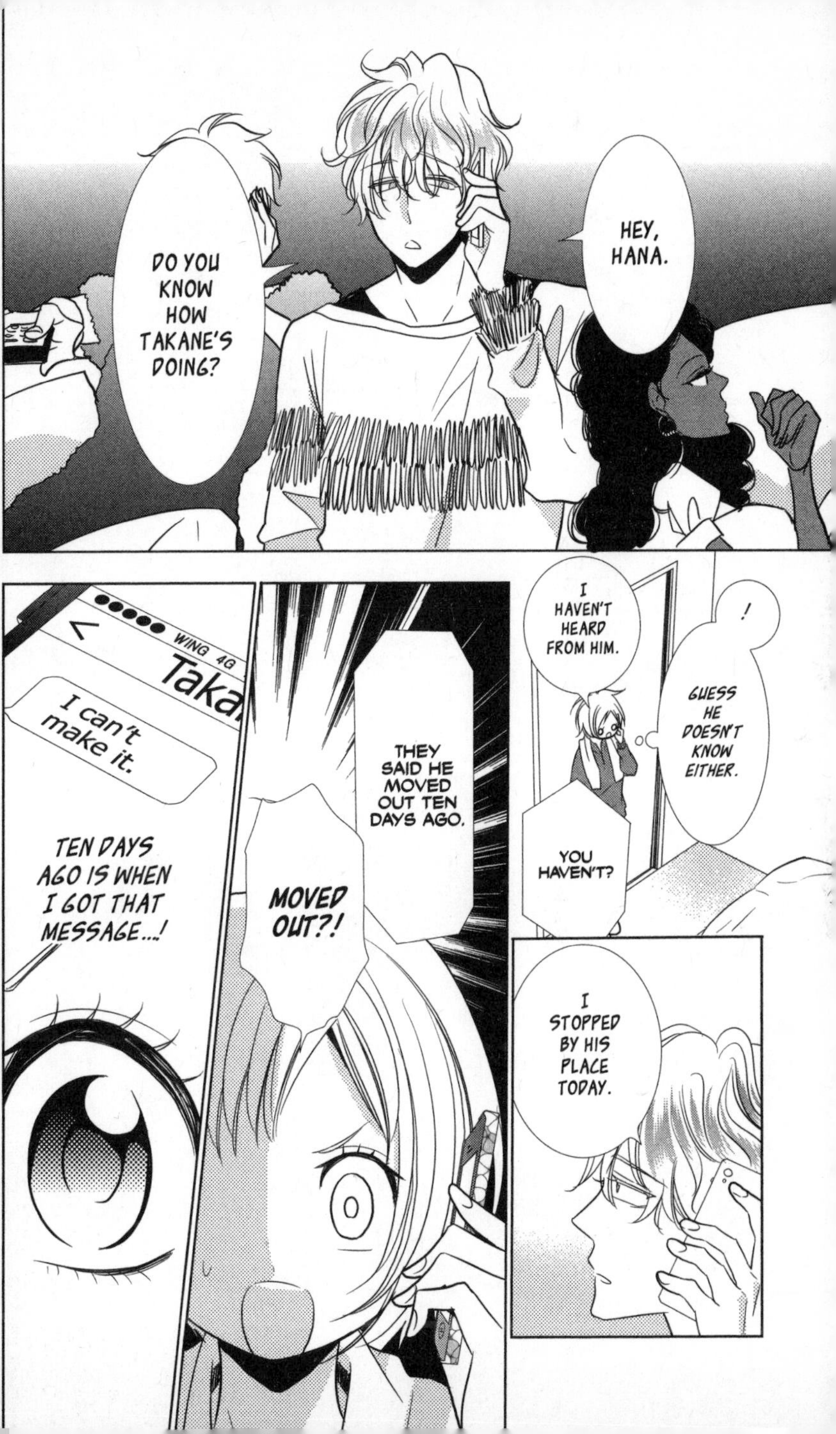
HEY, HANA.
DO YOU KNOW HOW TAKANE'S DOING?
I HAVEN'T HEARD FROM HIM.
YOU HAVEN'T?
!
GUESS HE DOESN'T KNOW EITHER.
I STOPPED BY HIS PLACE TODAY.
THEY SAID HE MOVED OUT TEN DAYS AGO.
MOVED OUT?!
WING 4G
I can't make it.
TEN DAYS AGO IS WHEN I GOT THAT MESSAGE...!

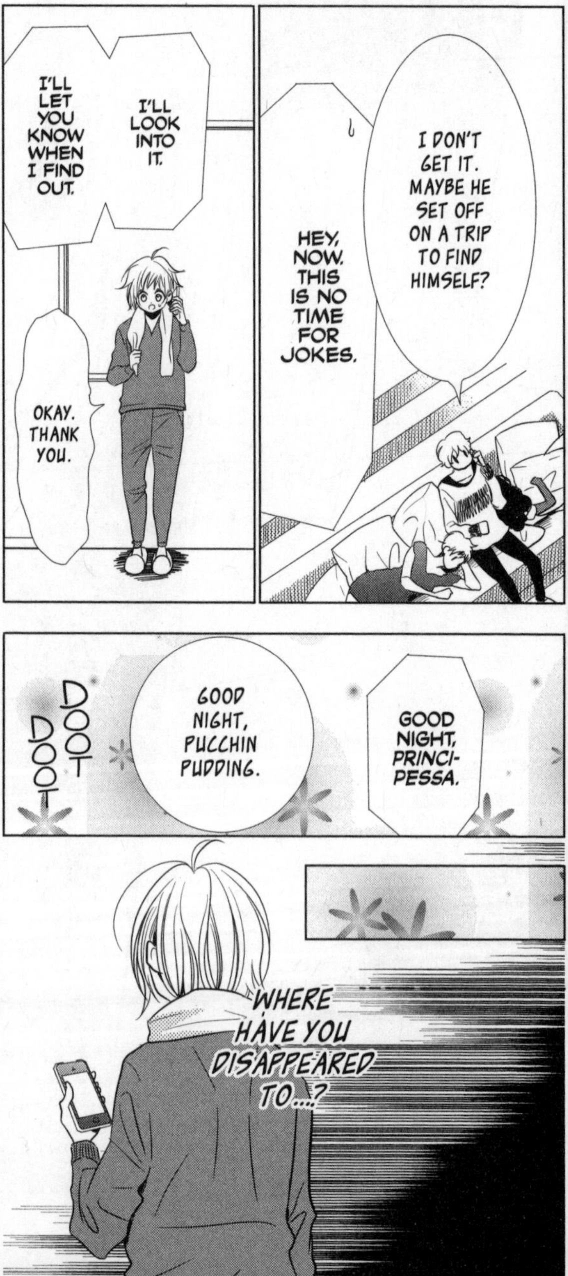
I DON'T GET IT. MAYBE HE SET OFF ON A TRIP TO FIND HIMSELF?
HEY, NOW. THIS IS NO TIME FOR JOKES.
I'LL LOOK INTO IT.
I'LL LET YOU KNOW WHEN I FIND OUT.
OKAY. THANK YOU.
GOOD NIGHT, PRINCI-PESSA.
GOOD NIGHT, PUCCHIN PUDDING.
DOOT DOOT
WHERE HAVE YOU DISAPPEARED TO...?

The "Takane in Trouble" Arc

It's finally here! Now that I've created a rich character, this was bound to happen! I'm nervous about writing such a major story line. Even my editor, who I always rely on, seemed a little worried and said, "I've never worked with a hero who sank this low before..." (*Ha ha*)

Takane's charm as a character as seen from an outside perspective versus his charm as a girls' manga hero as seen by those directly involved... It's a struggle trying to find a balance. (You could say I'm always struggling.)

I'm taking my time and telling this story with great care. I hope you'll see it through! You can do this, Takane!

"When the last tree is cut down, the last stream polluted..." This is a famous Native American saying. You may be obsessed with money, but in the end, it's nothing but paper. If you destroy nature and kill our food sources, then that paper is nothing but trash.

I think the saying means something like "What is truly important in this world?" I apologize if I'm totally off base.

SASABE SHOKAI

Sasabe Shokai's logo. A sparrow's teardrop motif. I actually get the biggest kick out of coming up with these trivial things.

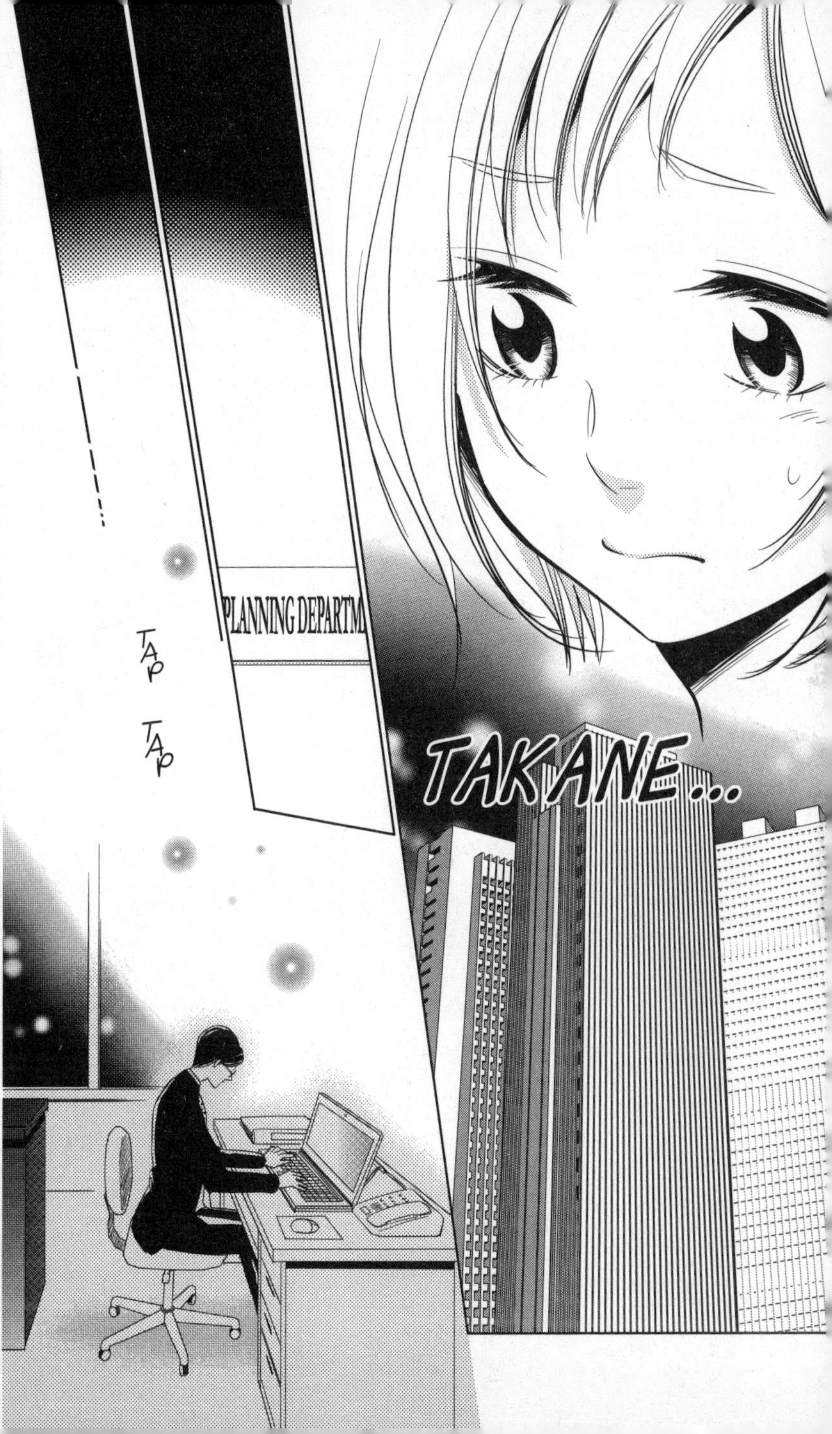
TAKANE...
PLANNING DEPARTM
TAP
TAP

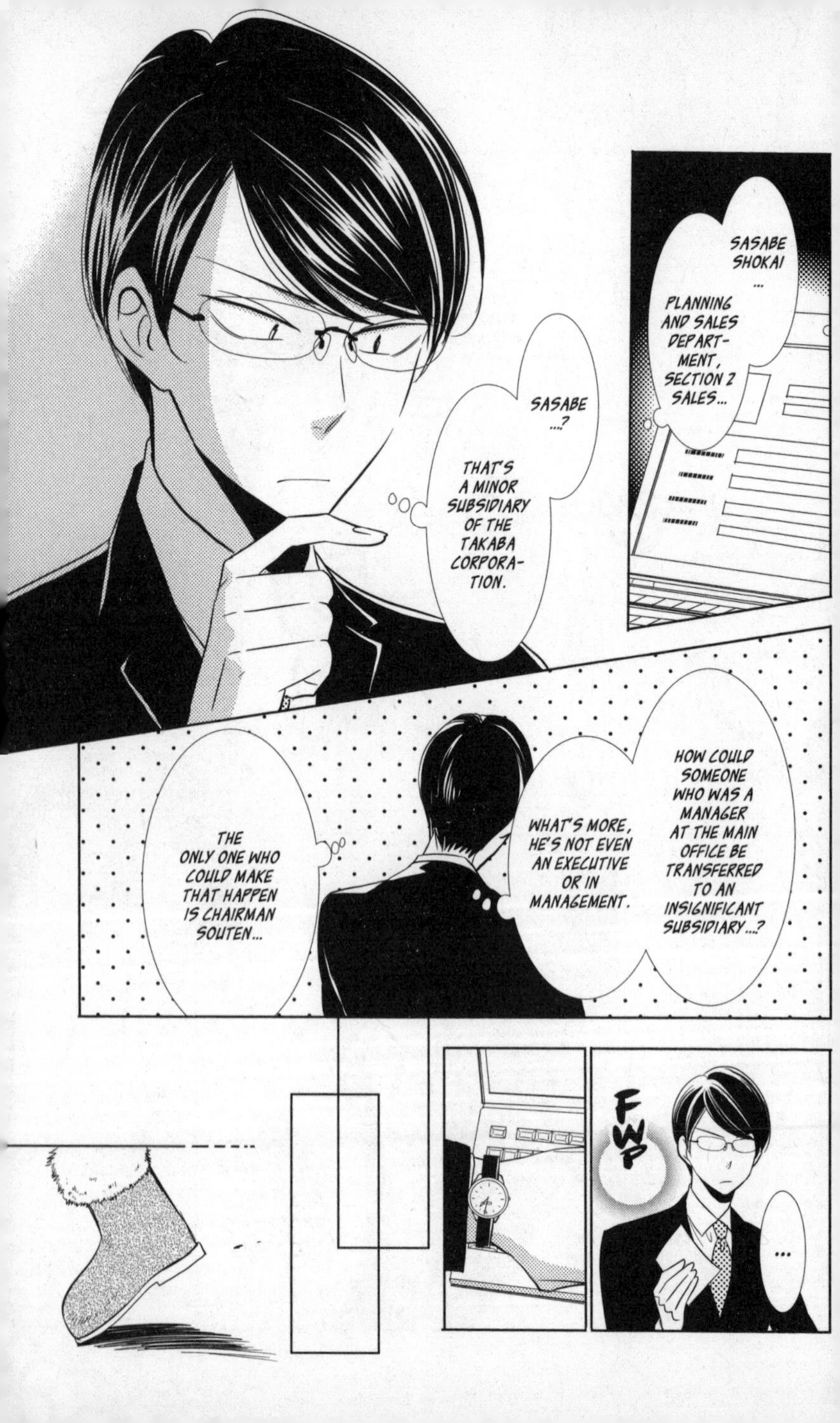
SASABE SHOKAI ...
PLANNING AND SALES DEPART-MENT, SECTION 2 SALES...
SASABE ...?
THAT'S A MINOR SUBSIDIARY OF THE TAKABA CORPORA-TION.
HOW COULD SOMEONE WHO WAS A MANAGER AT THE MAIN OFFICE BE TRANSFERRED TO AN INSIGNIFICANT SUBSIDIARY...?
WHAT'S MORE, HE'S NOT EVEN AN EXECUTIVE OR IN MANAGEMENT.
THE ONLY ONE WHO COULD MAKE THAT HAPPEN IS CHAIRMAN SOUTEN...
FWP
...

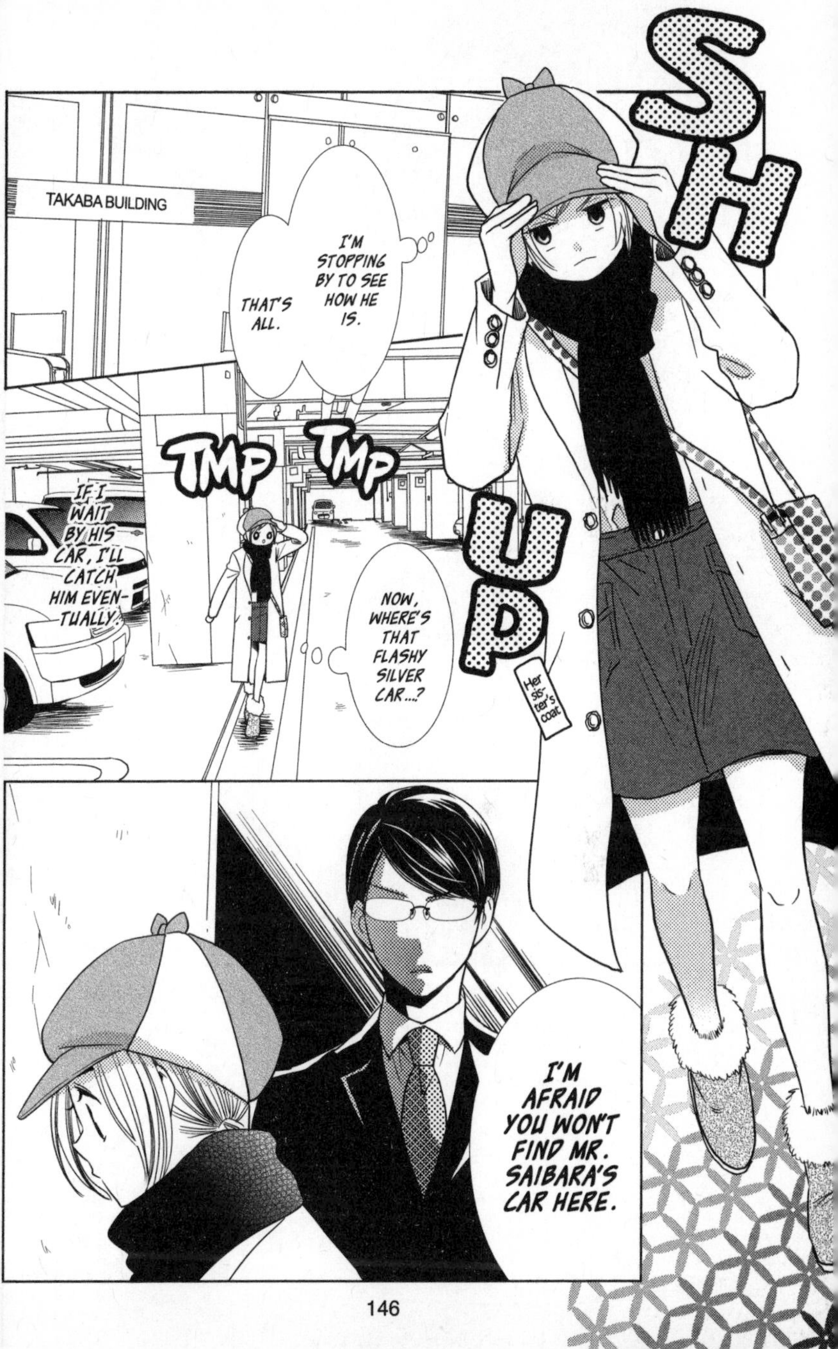
SHUP
Her sister's coat
TAKABA BUILDING
I'M STOPPING BY TO SEE HOW HE IS.
THAT'S ALL.
TMP TMP
NOW, WHERE'S THAT FLASHY SILVER CAR...?
IF I WAIT BY HIS CAR, I'LL CATCH HIM EVEN-TUALLY.
I'M AFRAID YOU WON'T FIND MR. SAIBARA'S CAR HERE.

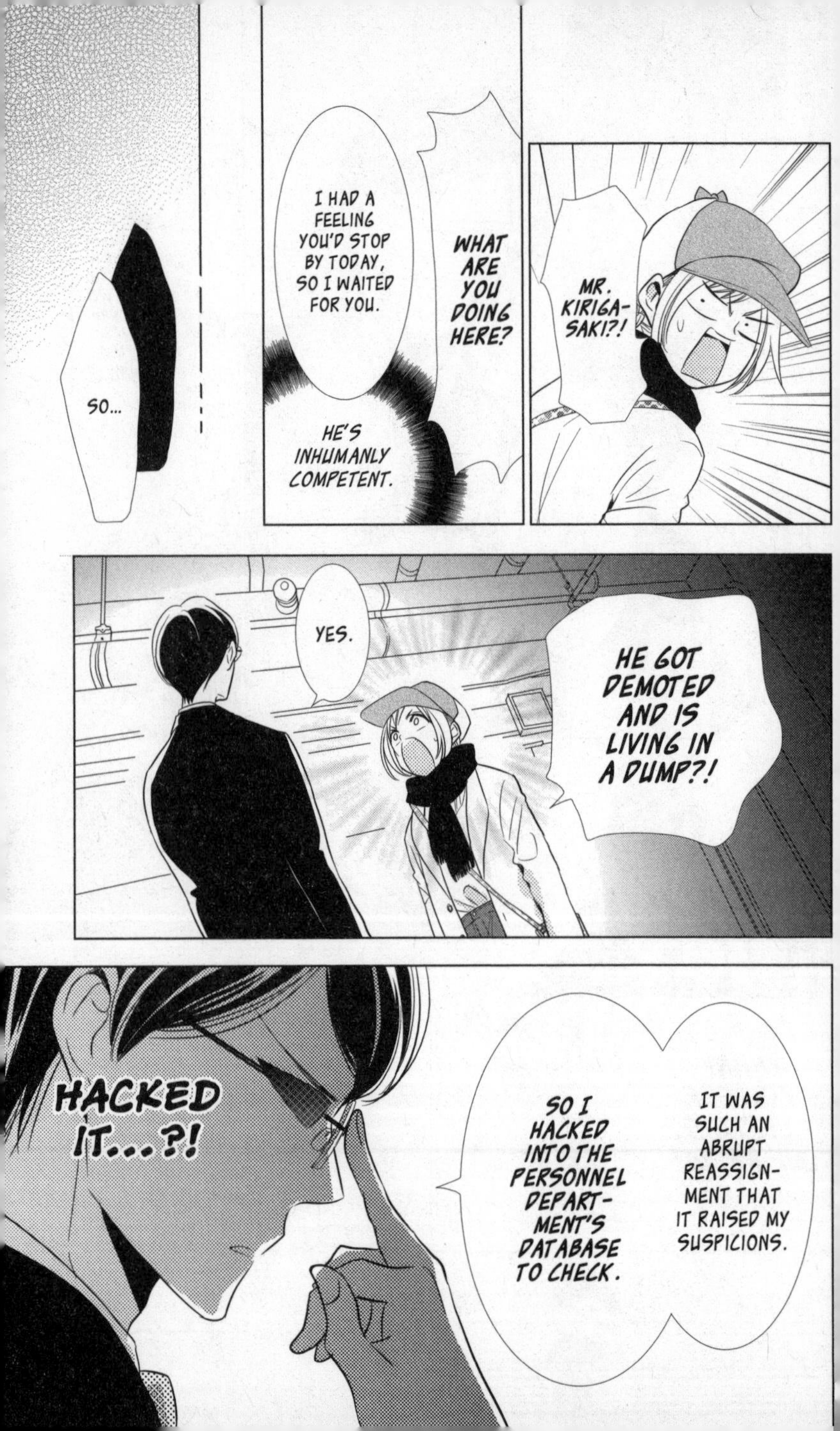
MR. KIRIGA-SAKI?!
WHAT ARE YOU DOING HERE?
I HAD A FEELING YOU'D STOP BY TODAY, SO I WAITED FOR YOU.
HE'S INHUMANLY COMPETENT.
SO...
HE GOT DEMOTED AND IS LIVING IN A DUMP?!
YES.
IT WAS SUCH AN ABRUPT REASSIGN-MENT THAT IT RAISED MY SUSPICIONS.
SO I HACKED INTO THE PERSONNEL DEPART-MENT'S DATABASE TO CHECK.
HACKED IT...?!

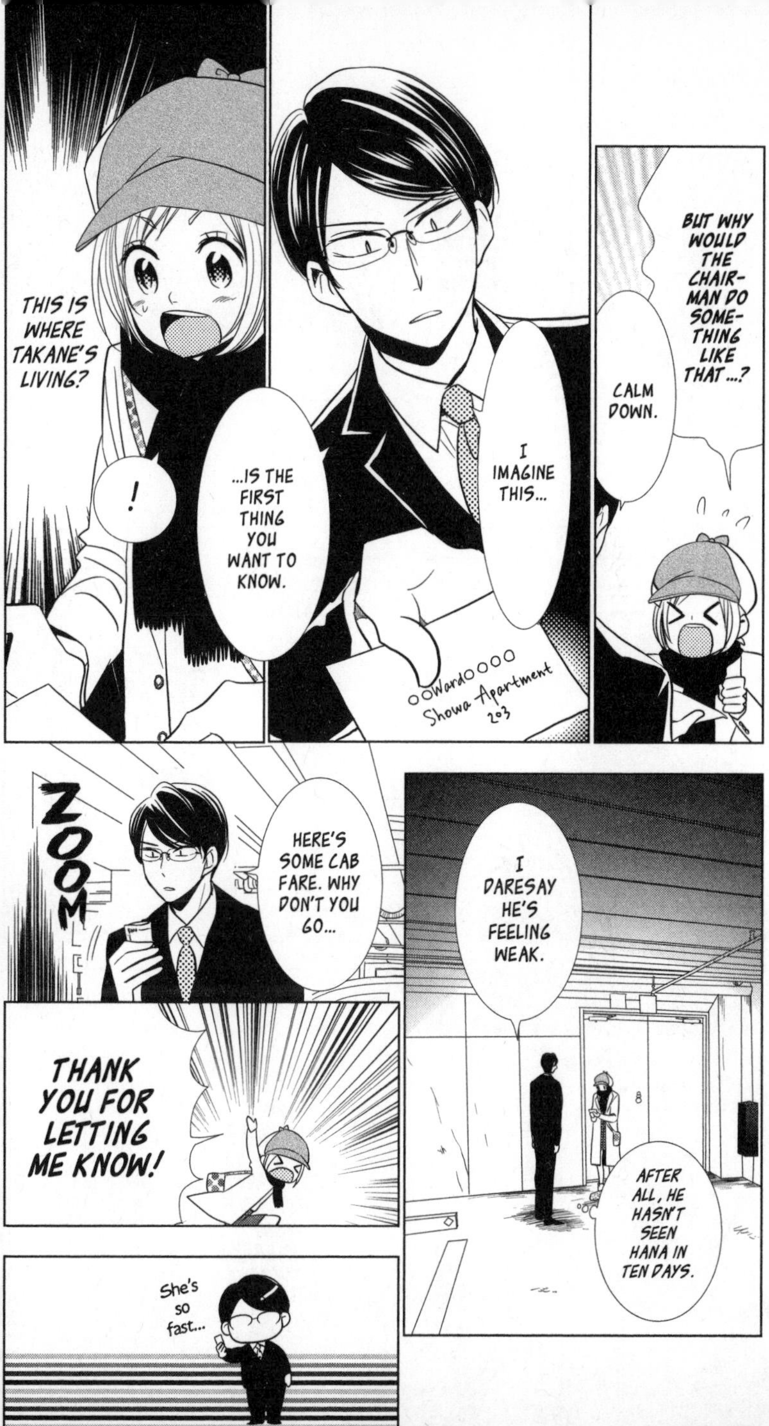
BUT WHY WOULD THE CHAIRMAN DO SOMETHING LIKE THAT ...?
CALM DOWN.
I IMAGINE THIS...
...IS THE FIRST THING YOU WANT TO KNOW.
○○Ward○○○○ Showa Apartment 203
!
THIS IS WHERE TAKANE'S LIVING?
I DARESAY HE'S FEELING WEAK.
AFTER ALL, HE HASN'T SEEN HANA IN TEN DAYS.
HERE'S SOME CAB FARE. WHY DON'T YOU GO...
ZOOM
THANK YOU FOR LETTING ME KNOW!
She's so fast...

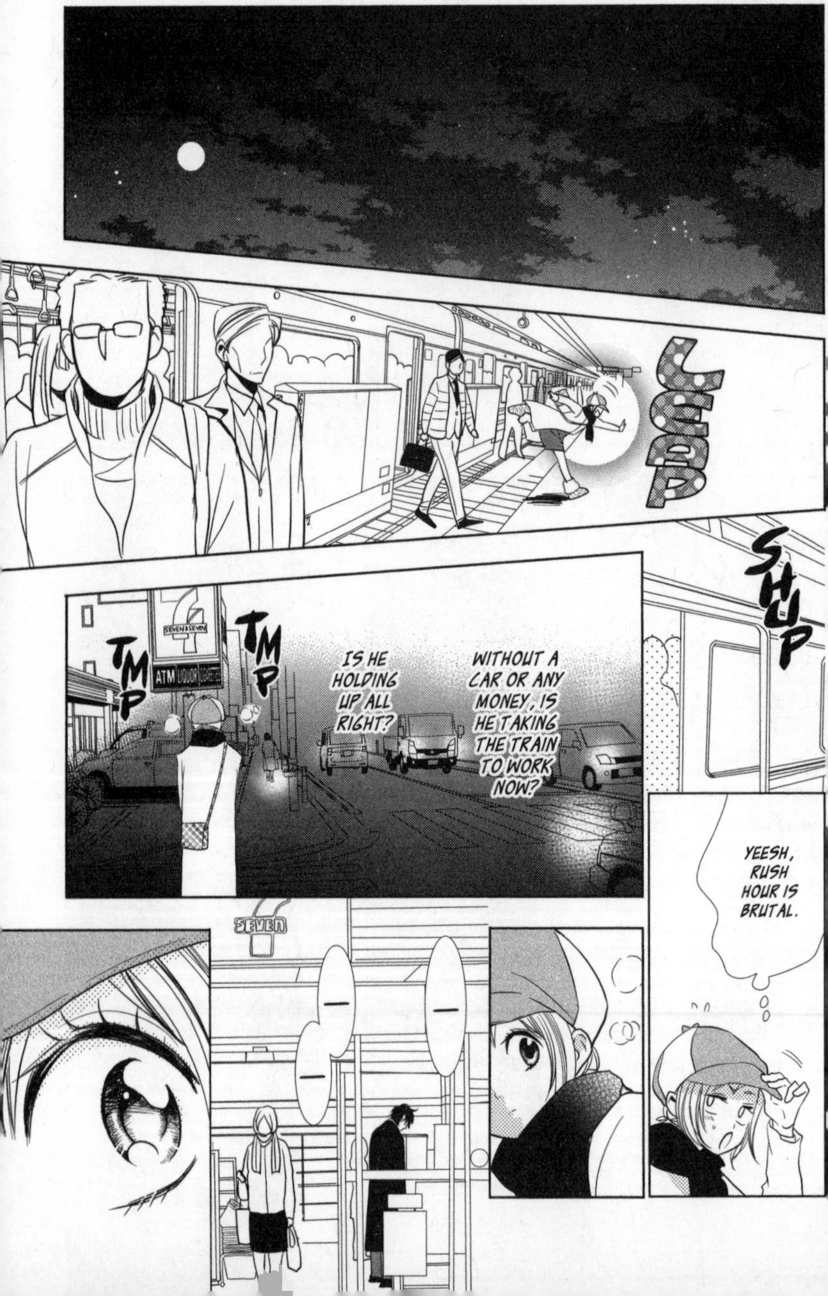
LEAP
SHUP
IS HE HOLDING UP ALL RIGHT?
WITHOUT A CAR OR ANY MONEY, IS HE TAKING THE TRAIN TO WORK NOW?
TMP
TMP
SEVEN&SEVEN
ATM
LIQUOR
YEESH, RUSH HOUR IS BRUTAL.
SEVEN
—
—
—

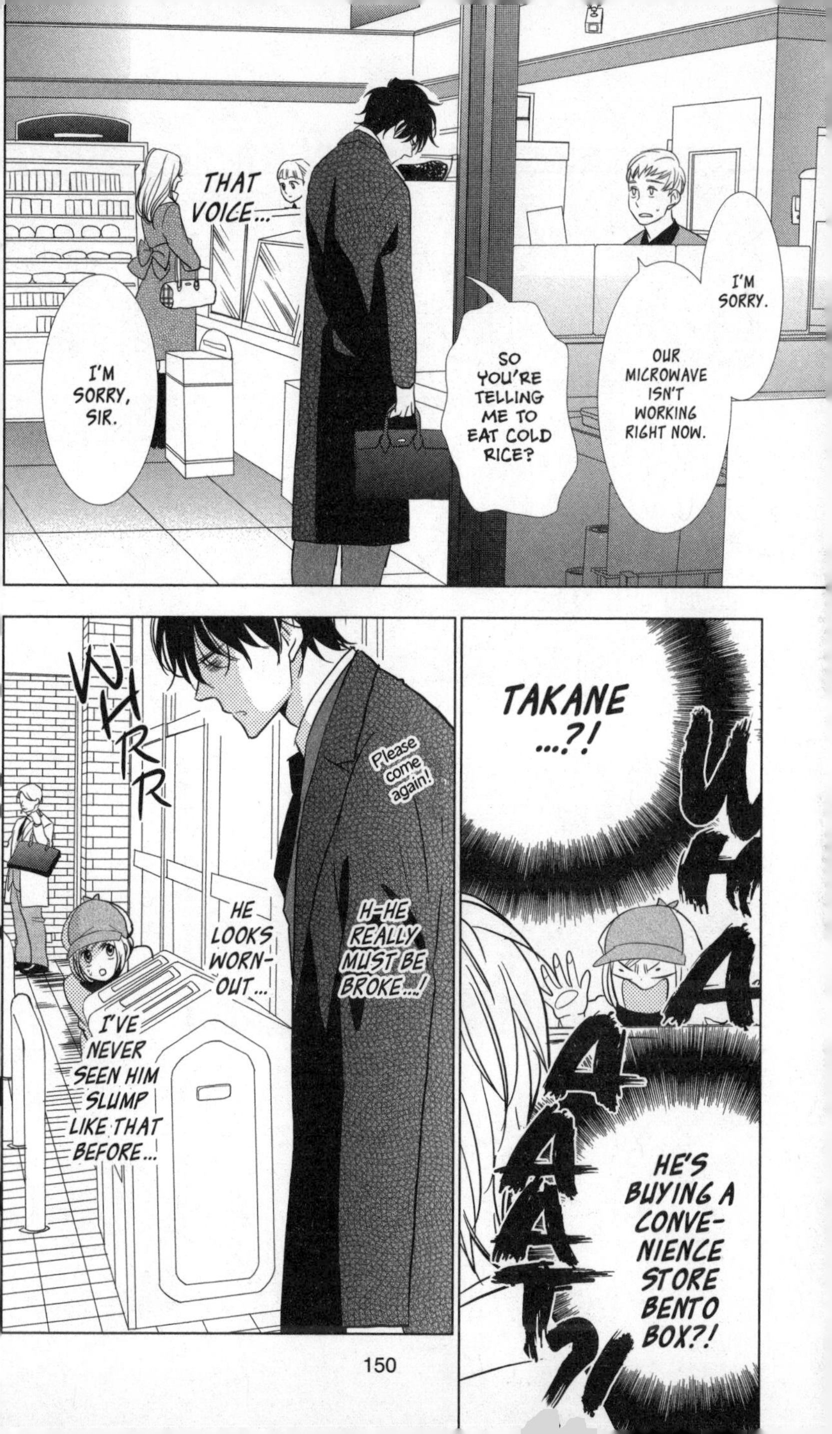
I'M SORRY.
OUR MICROWAVE ISN'T WORKING RIGHT NOW.
SO YOU'RE TELLING ME TO EAT COLD RICE?
THAT VOICE...
I'M SORRY, SIR.
TAKANE ...?!
WHAAAAAT?!
HE'S BUYING A CONVE-NIENCE STORE BENTO BOX?!
WHRR
Please come again!
H-HE REALLY MUST BE BROKE...!
HE LOOKS WORN-OUT...
I'VE NEVER SEEN HIM SLUMP LIKE THAT BEFORE...

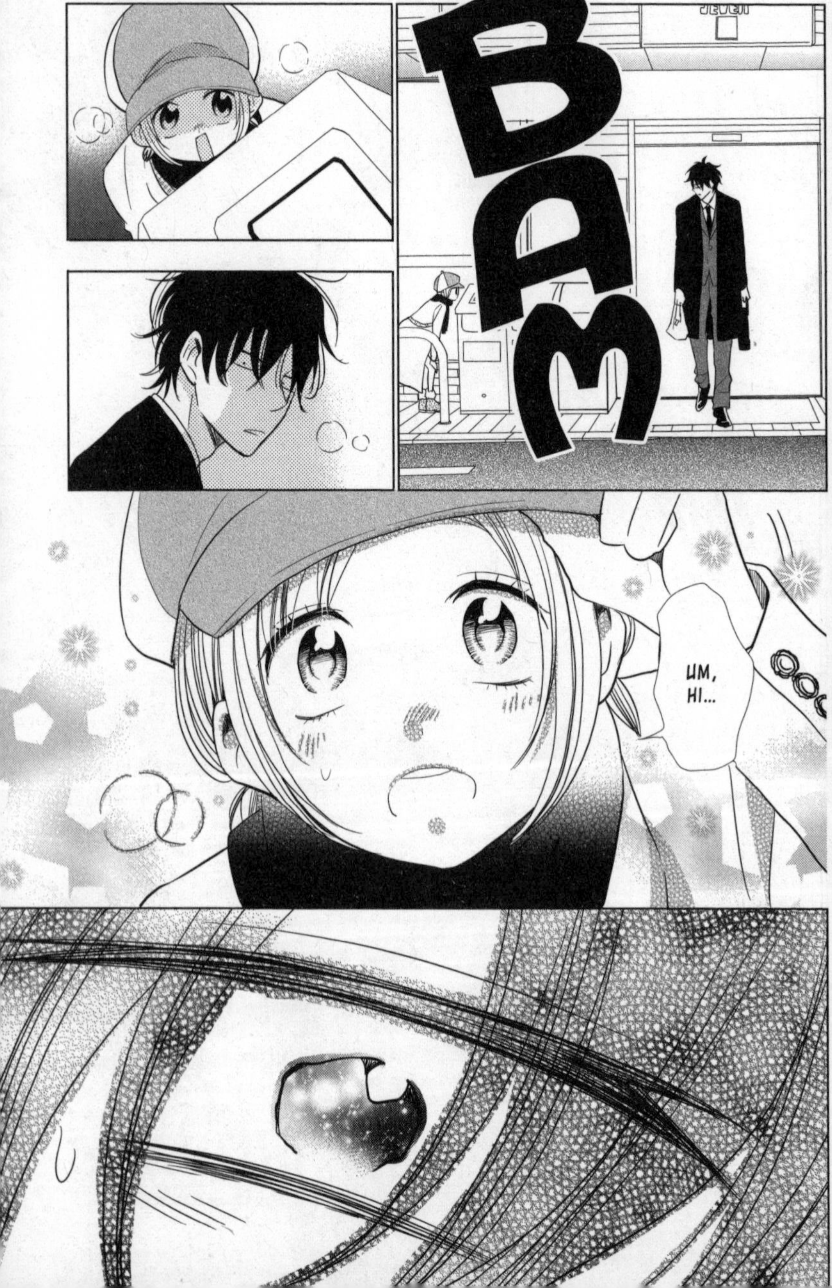
BAM
UM, HI...

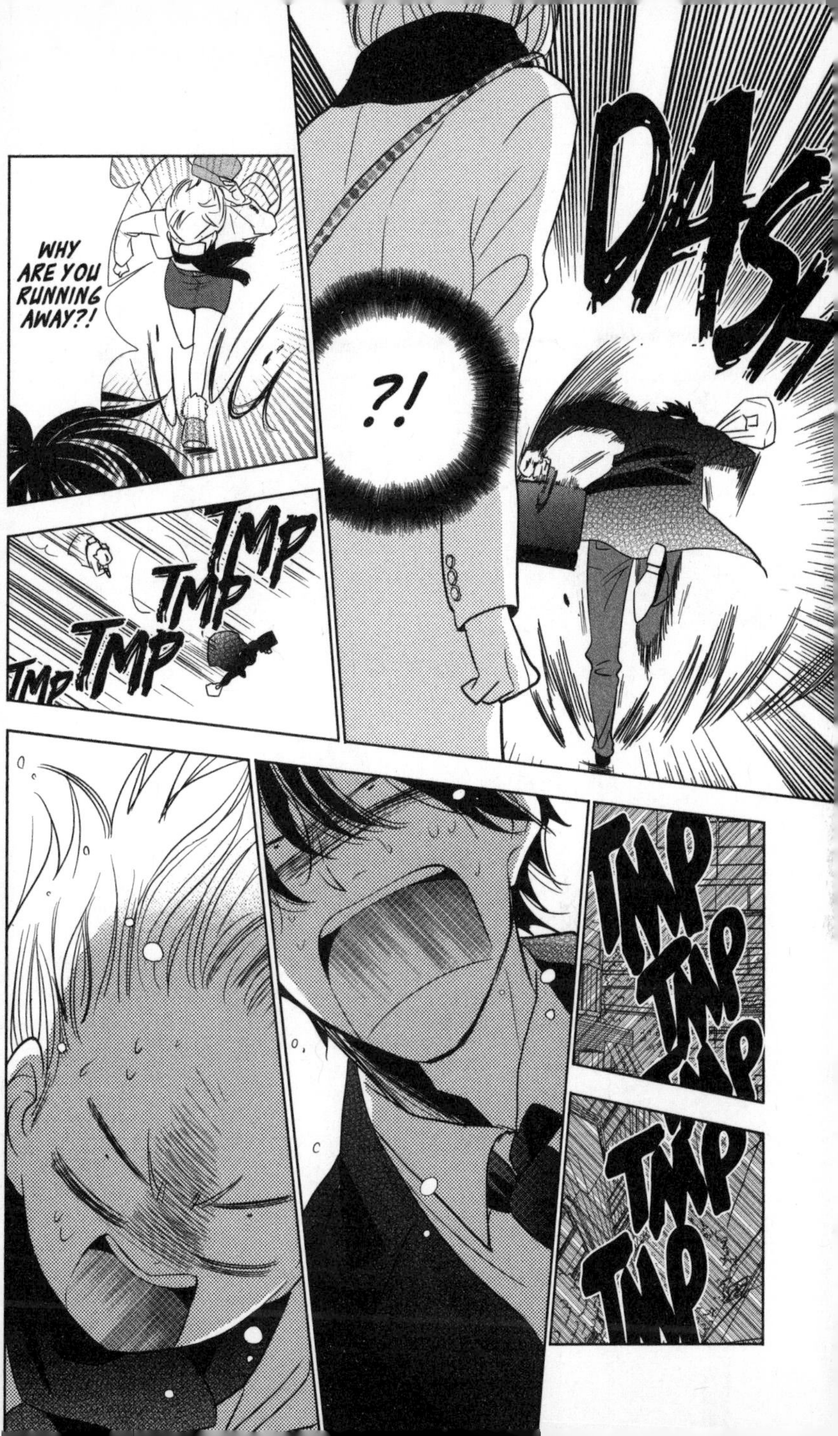
DASH
?!
WHY ARE YOU RUNNING AWAY?!
TMP TMP TMP TMP
TMP TMP TMP
TMP TMP

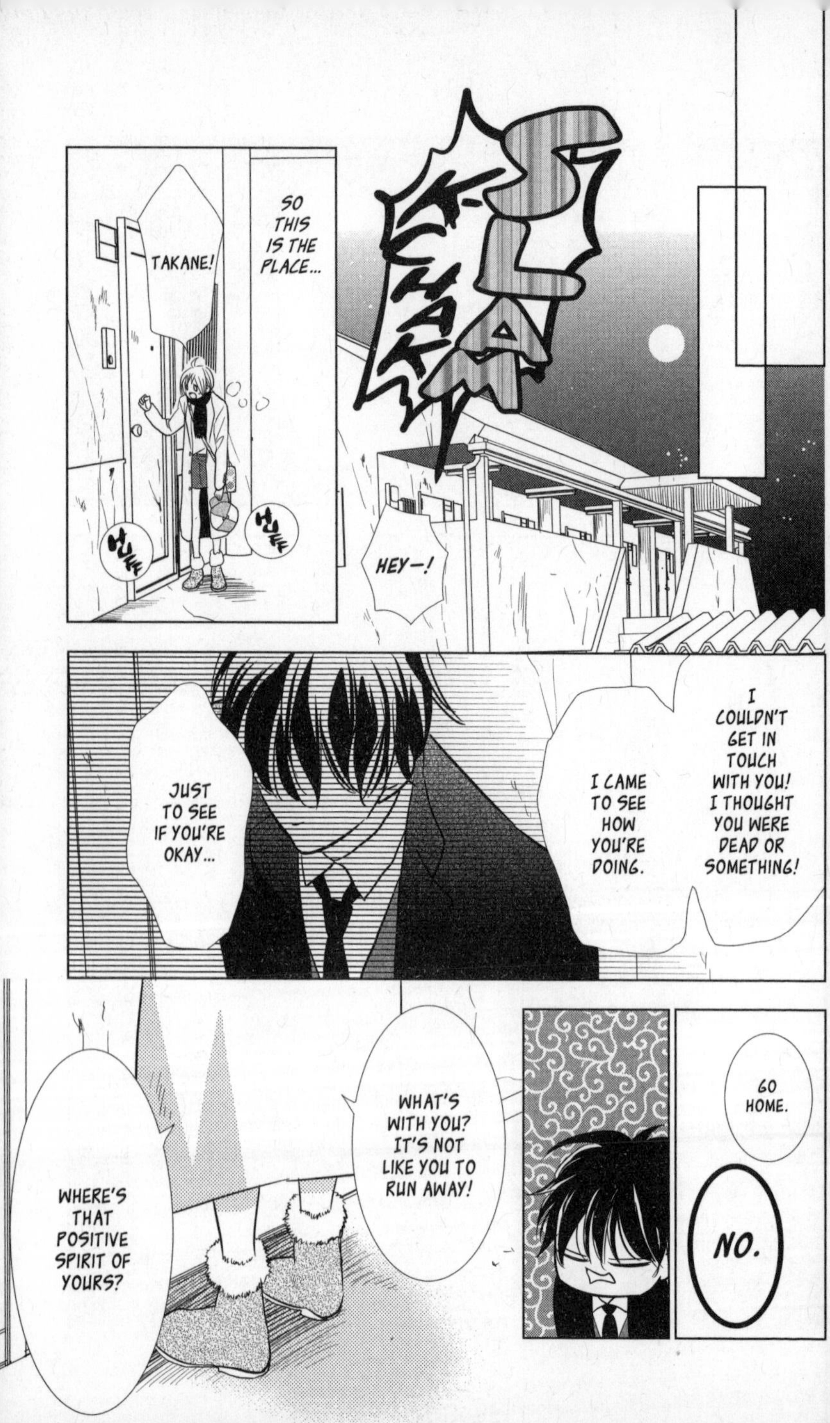
KA-CHAK
HEY—!
SO THIS IS THE PLACE...
TAKANE!
HUFF
HUFF
I COULDN'T GET IN TOUCH WITH YOU! I THOUGHT YOU WERE DEAD OR SOMETHING!
I CAME TO SEE HOW YOU'RE DOING.
JUST TO SEE IF YOU'RE OKAY...
GO HOME.
NO.
WHAT'S WITH YOU? IT'S NOT LIKE YOU TO RUN AWAY!
WHERE'S THAT POSITIVE SPIRIT OF YOURS?

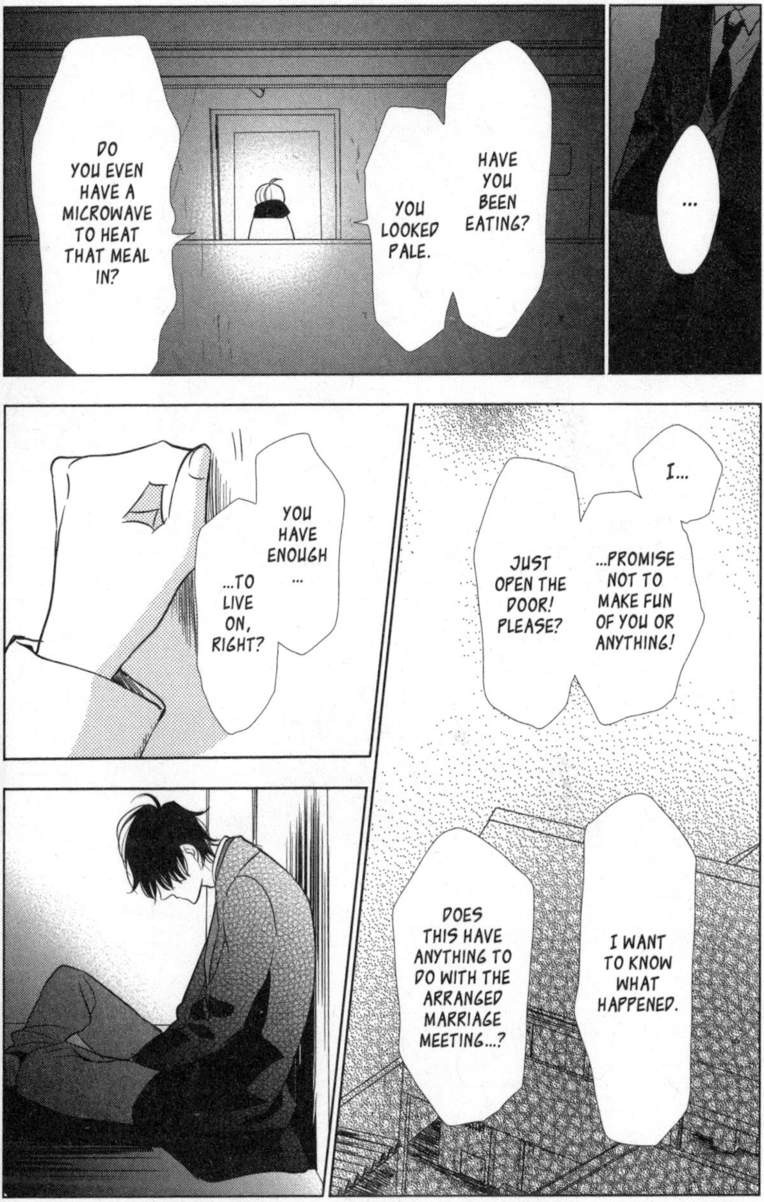
...
HAVE YOU BEEN EATING?
YOU LOOKED PALE.
DO YOU EVEN HAVE A MICROWAVE TO HEAT THAT MEAL IN?
I...
...PROMISE NOT TO MAKE FUN OF YOU OR ANYTHING!
JUST OPEN THE DOOR! PLEASE?
I WANT TO KNOW WHAT HAPPENED.
DOES THIS HAVE ANYTHING TO DO WITH THE ARRANGED MARRIAGE MEETING...?
YOU HAVE ENOUGH...
...TO LIVE ON, RIGHT?

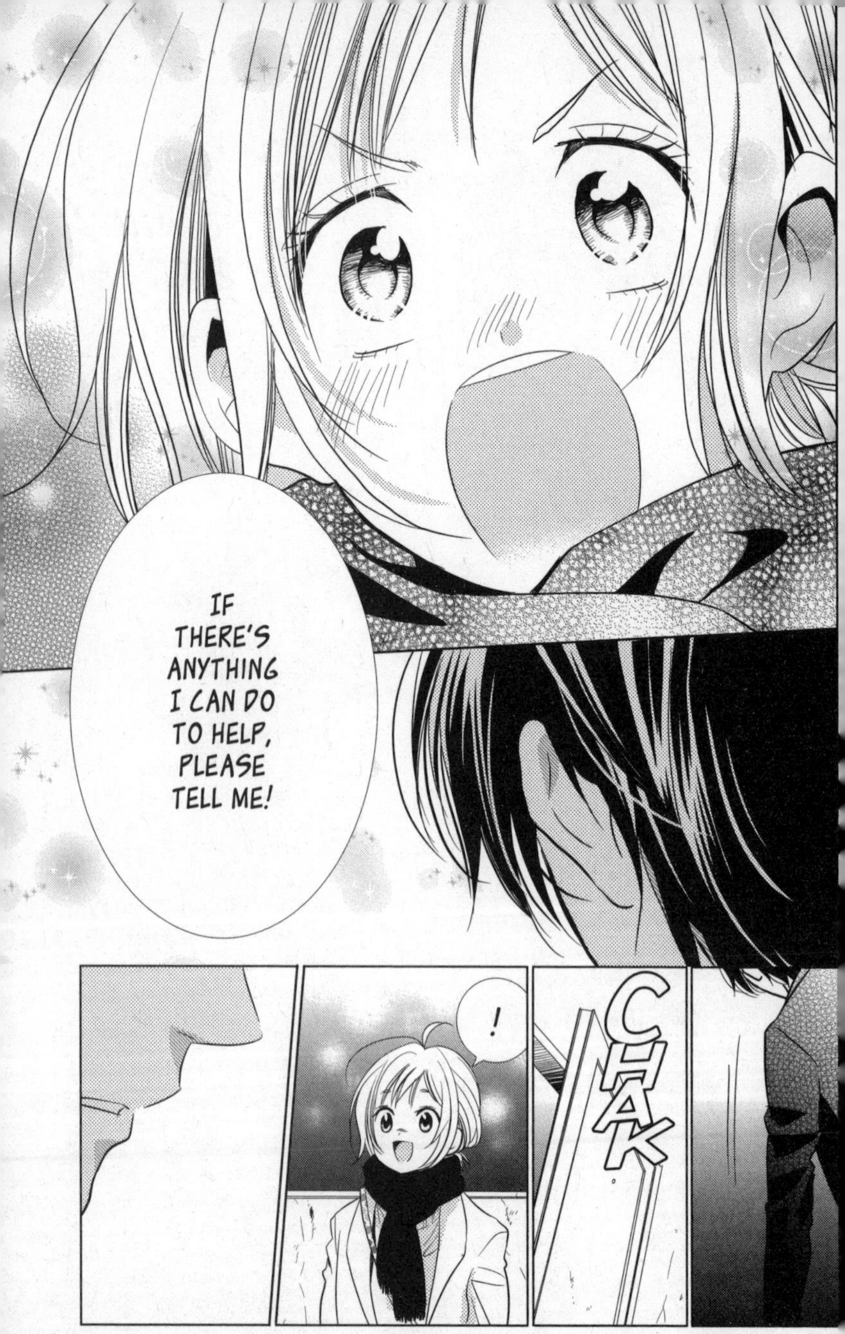
IF THERE'S ANYTHING I CAN DO TO HELP, PLEASE TELL ME!
CHAK
!

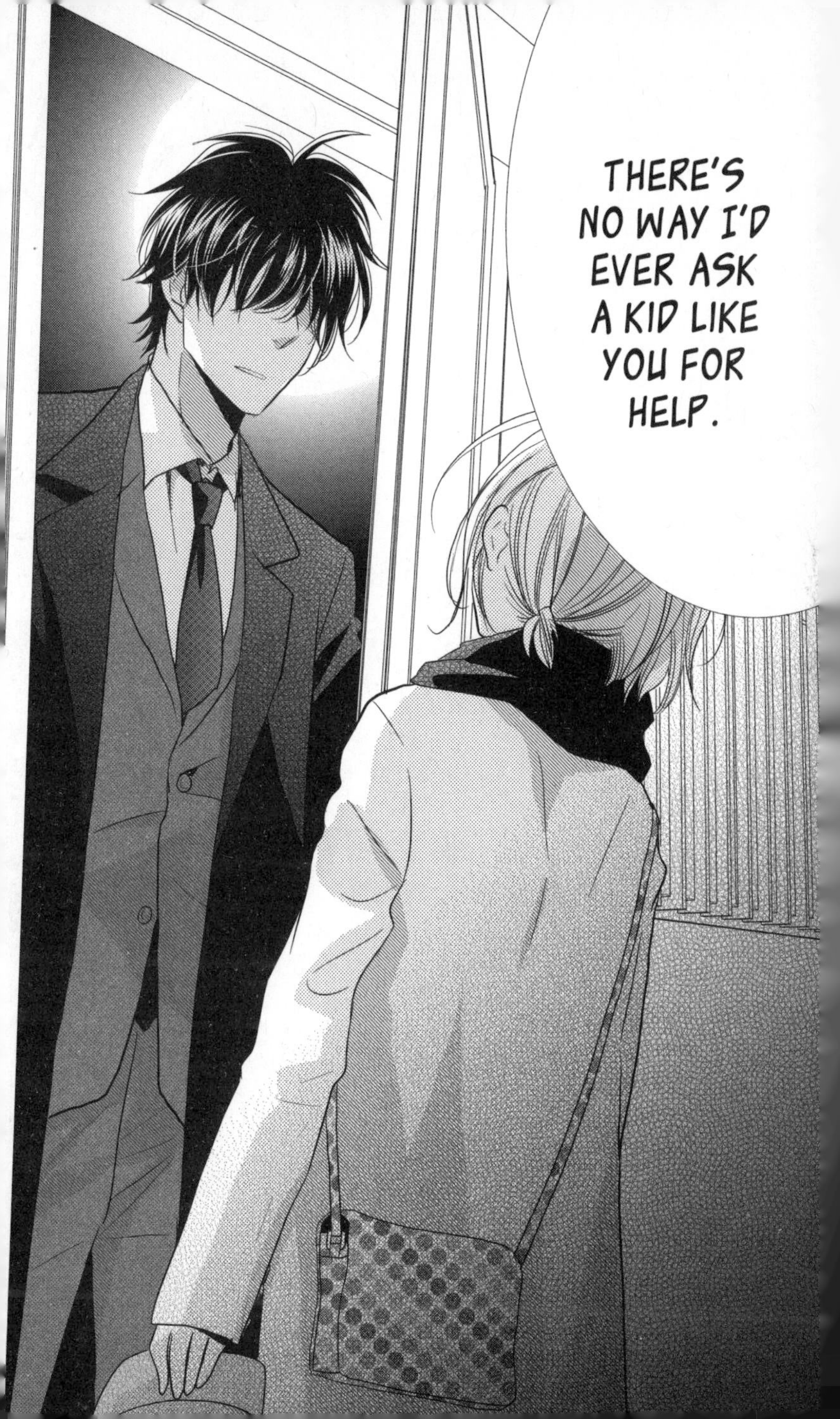
THERE'S NO WAY I'D EVER ASK A KID LIKE YOU FOR HELP.

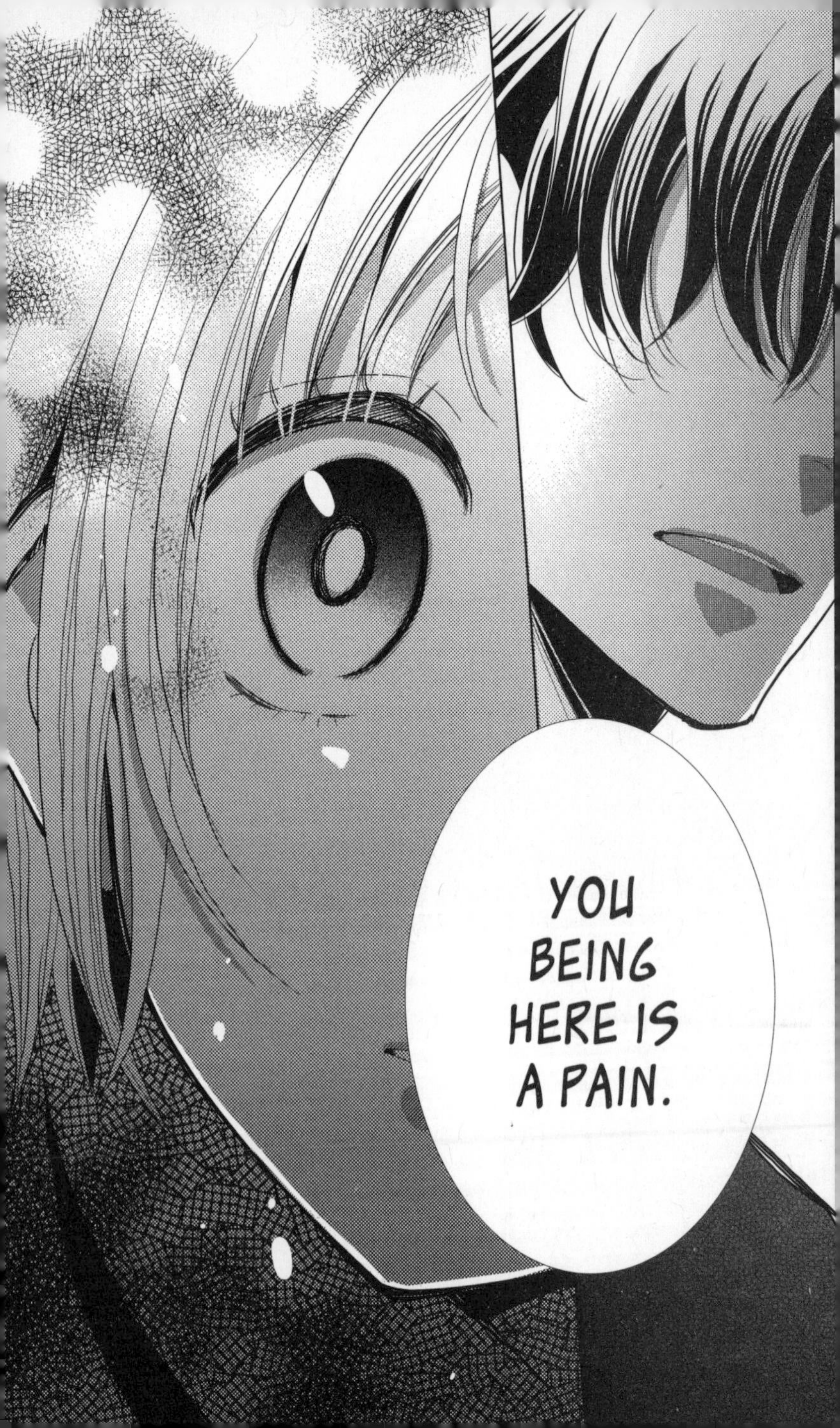
YOU BEING HERE IS A PAIN.

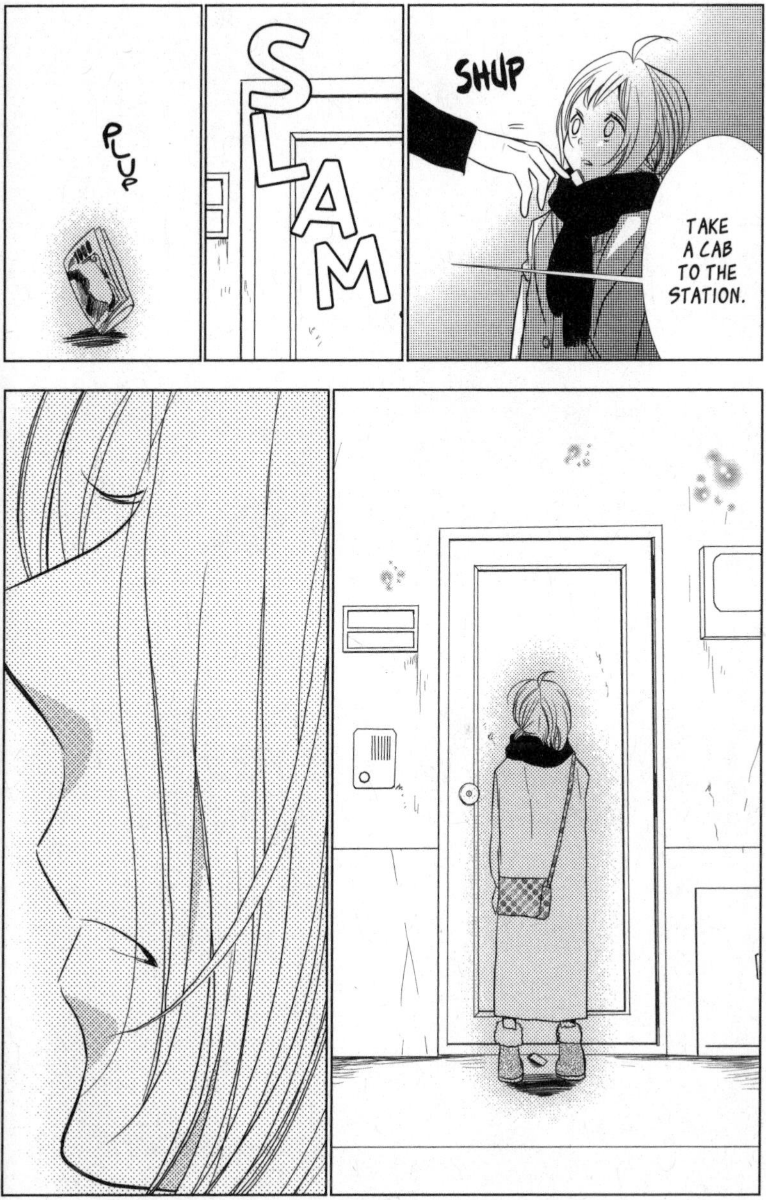
SHUP
TAKE A CAB TO THE STATION.
SLAM
PLUP

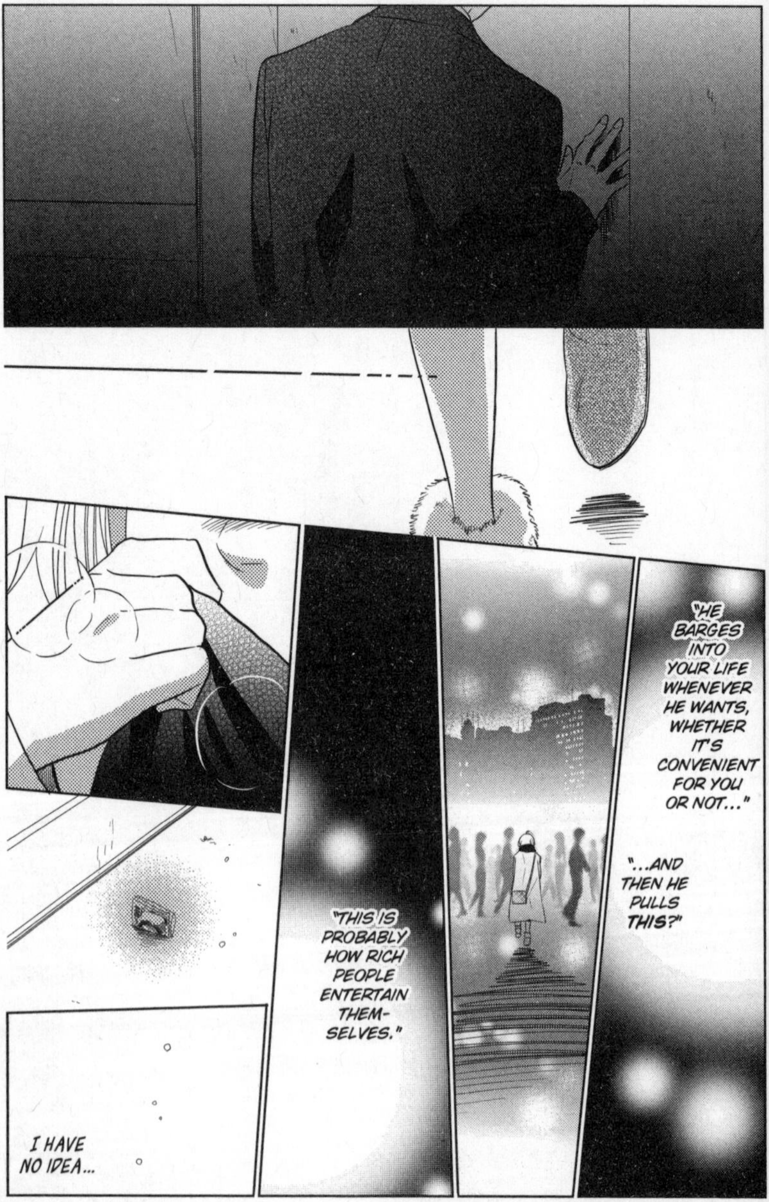
"HE BARGES INTO YOUR LIFE WHENEVER HE WANTS, WHETHER IT'S CONVENIENT FOR YOU OR NOT..."
"...AND THEN HE PULLS THIS?"
"THIS IS PROBABLY HOW RICH PEOPLE ENTERTAIN THEM-SELVES."
I HAVE NO IDEA...

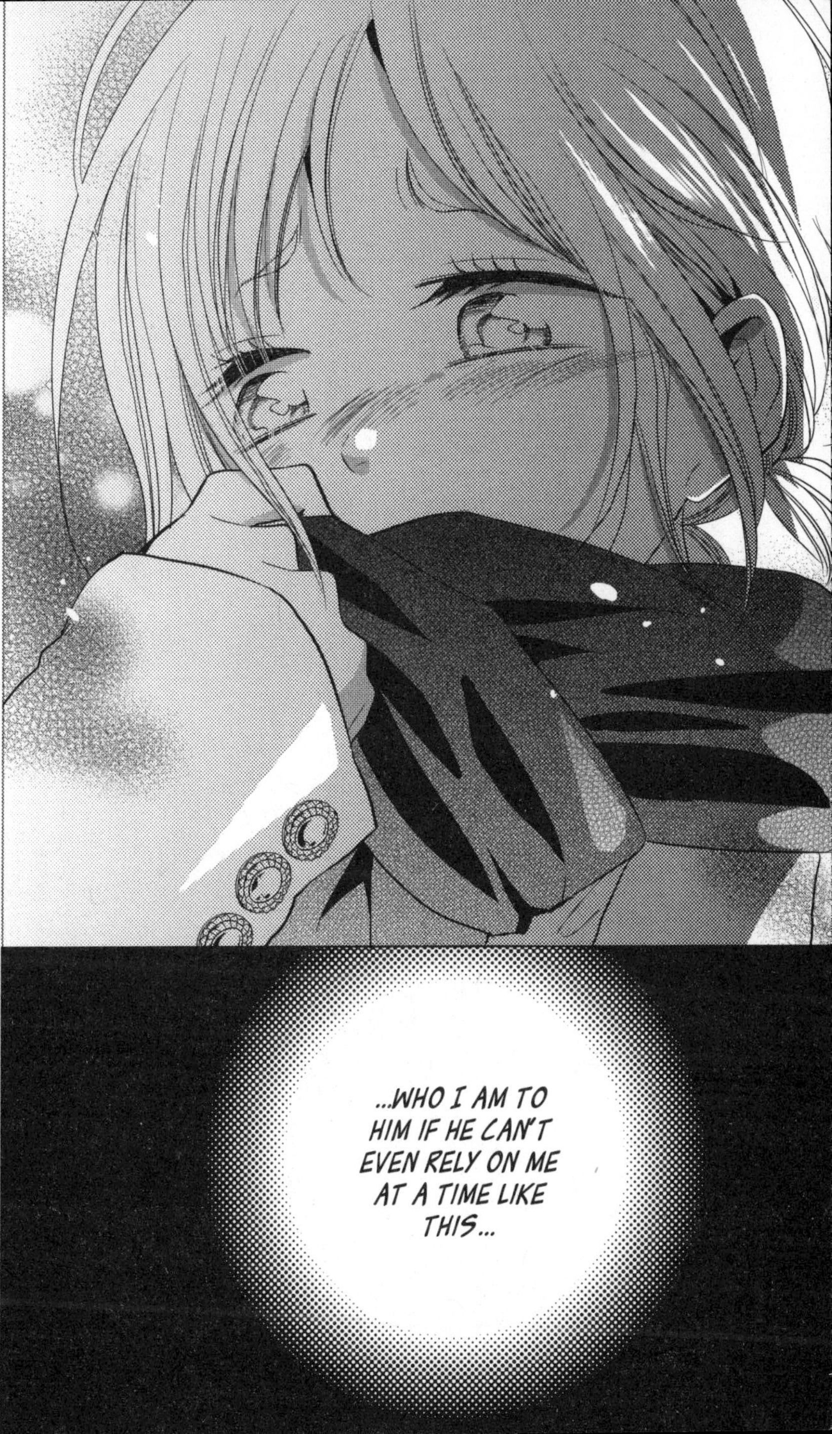
...WHO I AM TO HIM IF HE CAN'T EVEN RELY ON ME AT A TIME LIKE THIS...

Chapter 33

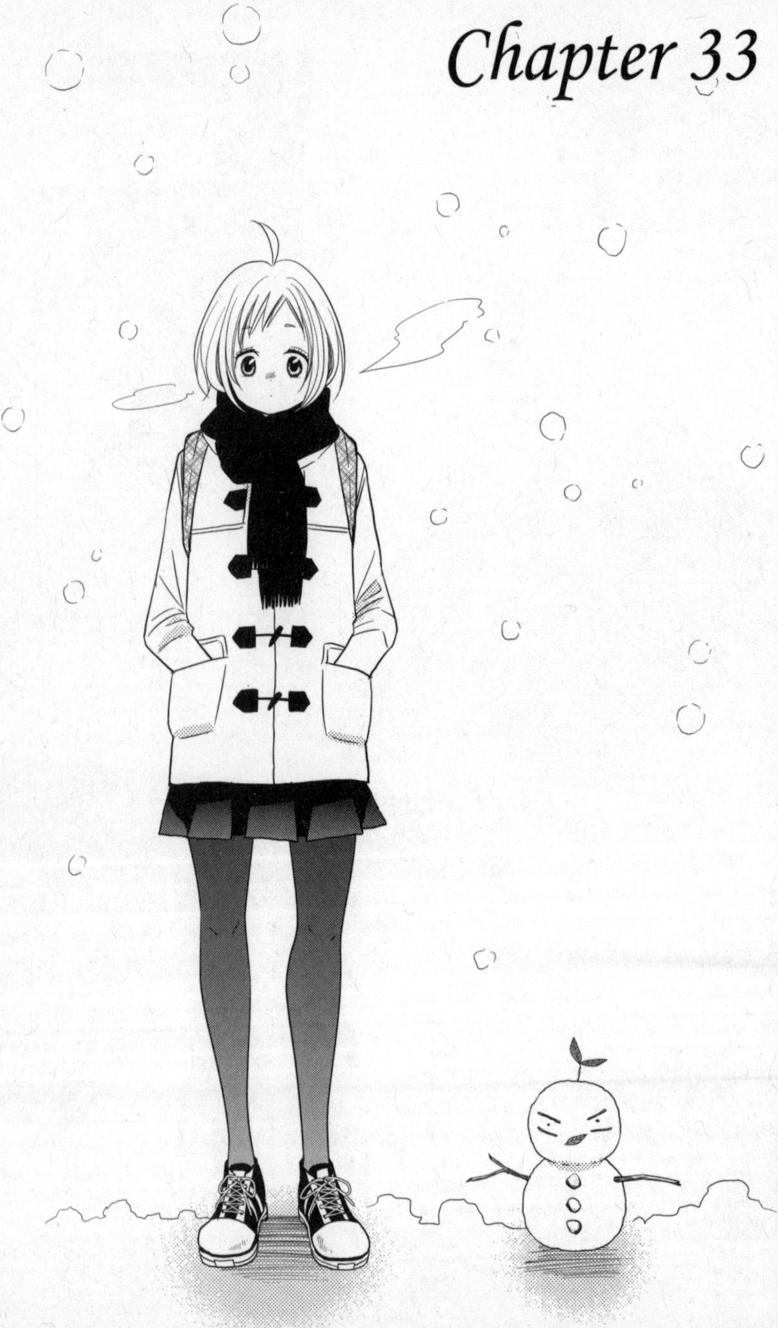

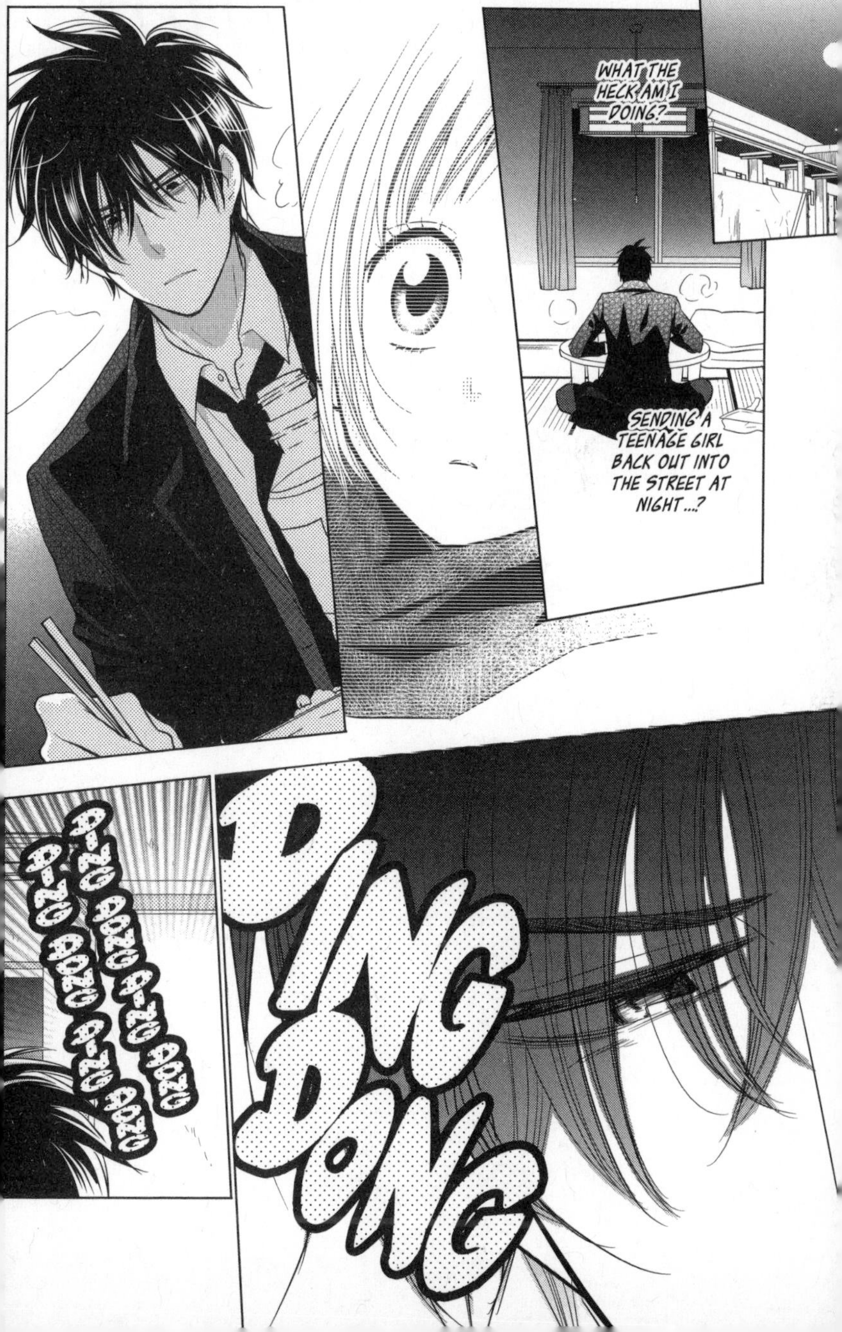
WHAT THE HECK AM I DOING?
SENDING A TEENAGE GIRL BACK OUT INTO THE STREET AT NIGHT...?
DING DONG
DING DONG DING DONG DING DONG DING DONG

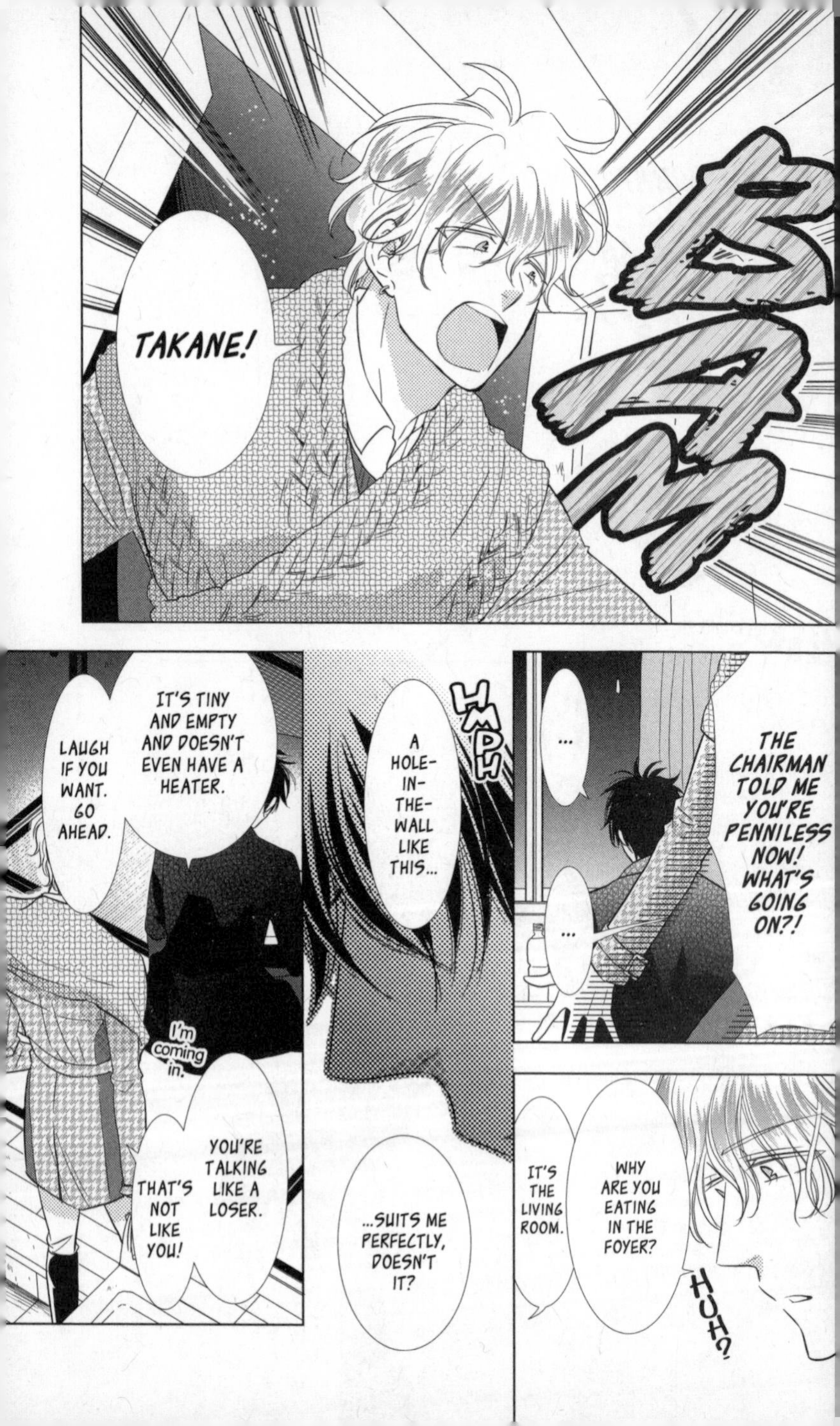

TAKANE!
THE CHAIRMAN TOLD ME YOU'RE PENNILESS NOW! WHAT'S GOING ON?!
...
...
WHY ARE YOU EATING IN THE FOYER?
IT'S THE LIVING ROOM.
HUH?
HMPH
A HOLE-IN-THE-WALL LIKE THIS...
...SUITS ME PERFECTLY, DOESN'T IT?
IT'S TINY AND EMPTY AND DOESN'T EVEN HAVE A HEATER.
LAUGH IF YOU WANT. GO AHEAD.
I'm coming in.
YOU'RE TALKING LIKE A LOSER.
THAT'S NOT LIKE YOU!

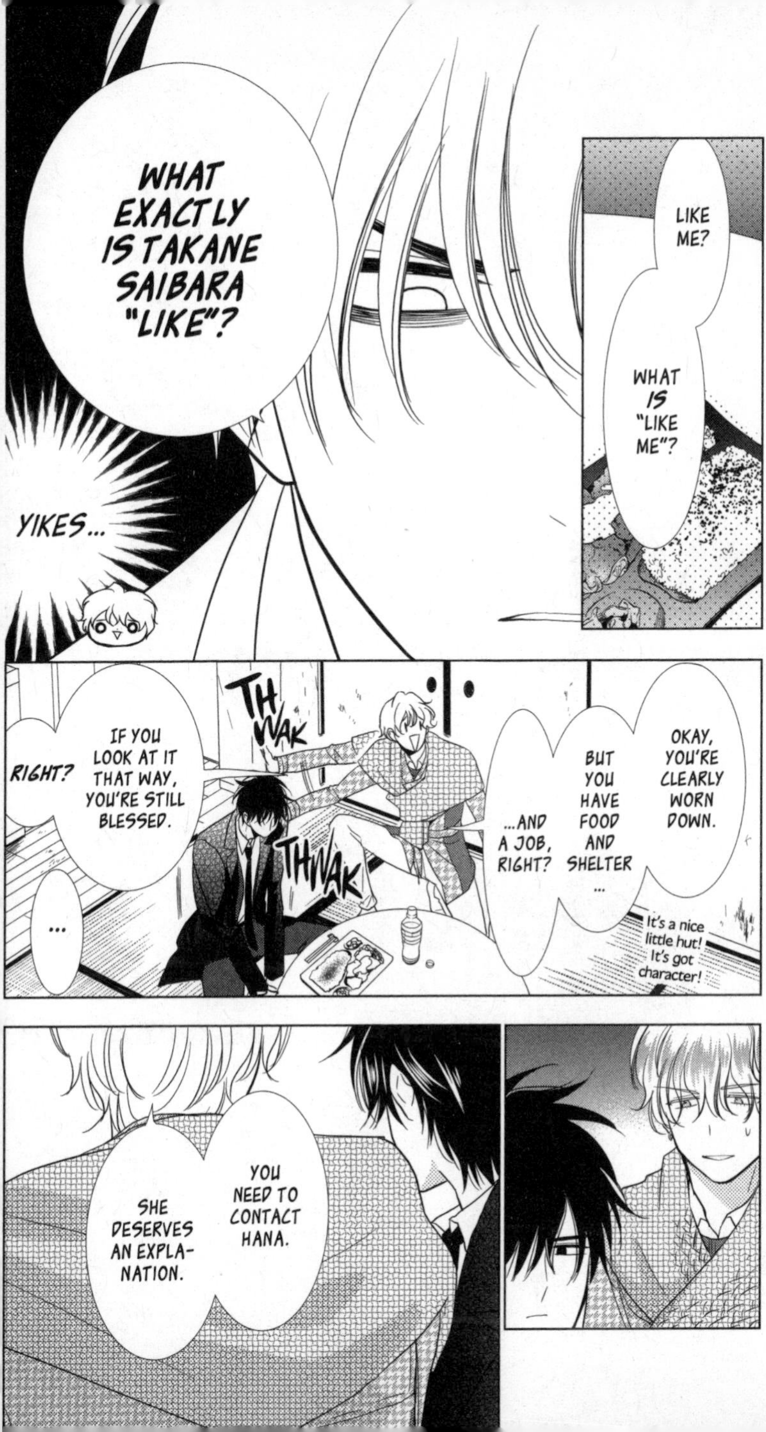
LIKE ME?
WHAT *IS* "LIKE ME"?
WHAT EXACTLY IS TAKANE SAIBARA "LIKE"?
YIKES...
OKAY, YOU'RE CLEARLY WORN DOWN.
BUT YOU HAVE FOOD AND SHELTER...
...AND A JOB, RIGHT?
It's a nice little hut! It's got character!
THWAK
THWAK
IF YOU LOOK AT IT THAT WAY, YOU'RE STILL BLESSED.
RIGHT?
...
YOU NEED TO CONTACT HANA.
SHE DESERVES AN EXPLANATION.

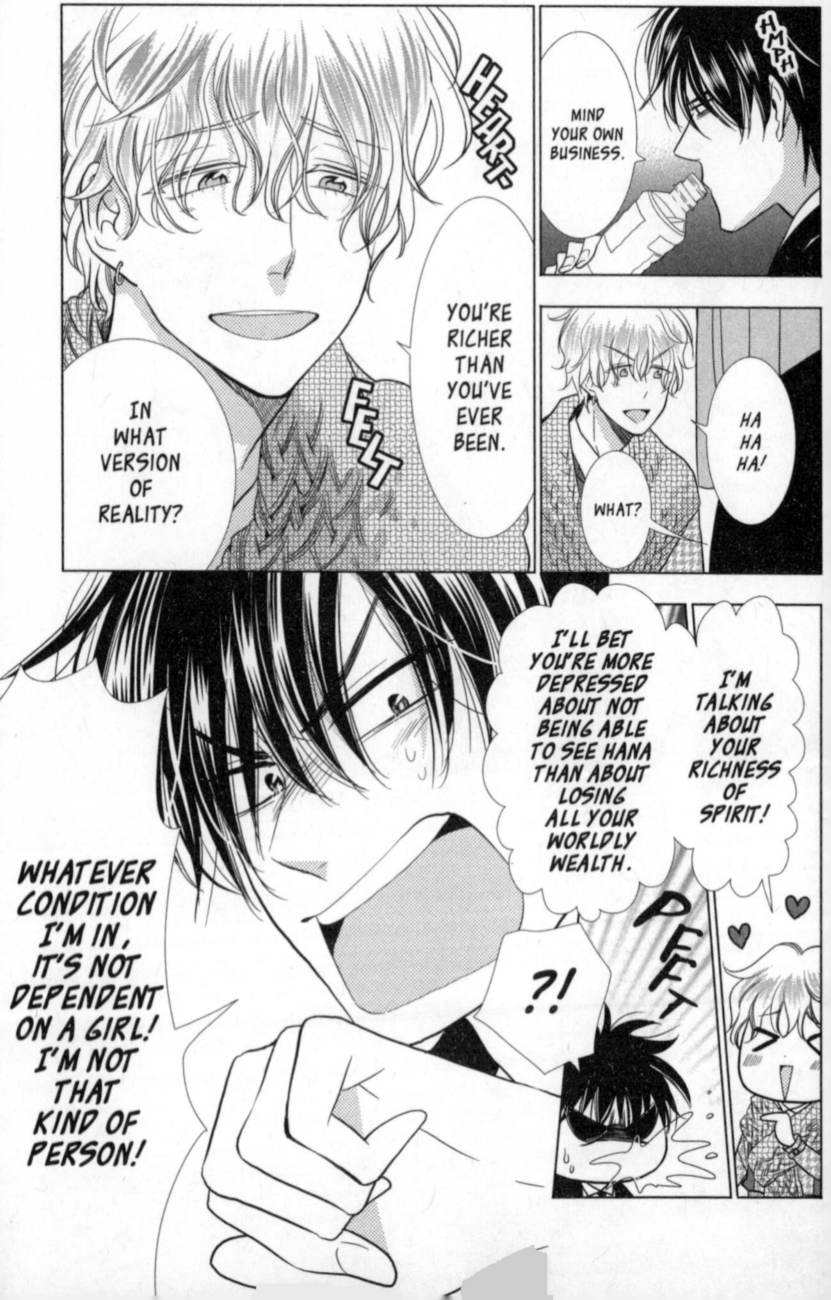
HMPH
MIND YOUR OWN BUSINESS.
HA HA HA!
WHAT?
HEART-FELT
YOU'RE RICHER THAN YOU'VE EVER BEEN.
IN WHAT VERSION OF REALITY?
I'M TALKING ABOUT YOUR RICHNESS OF SPIRIT!
I'LL BET YOU'RE MORE DEPRESSED ABOUT NOT BEING ABLE TO SEE HANA THAN ABOUT LOSING ALL YOUR WORLDLY WEALTH.
PFFT
?!
WHATEVER CONDITION I'M IN, IT'S NOT DEPENDENT ON A GIRL! I'M NOT THAT KIND OF PERSON!

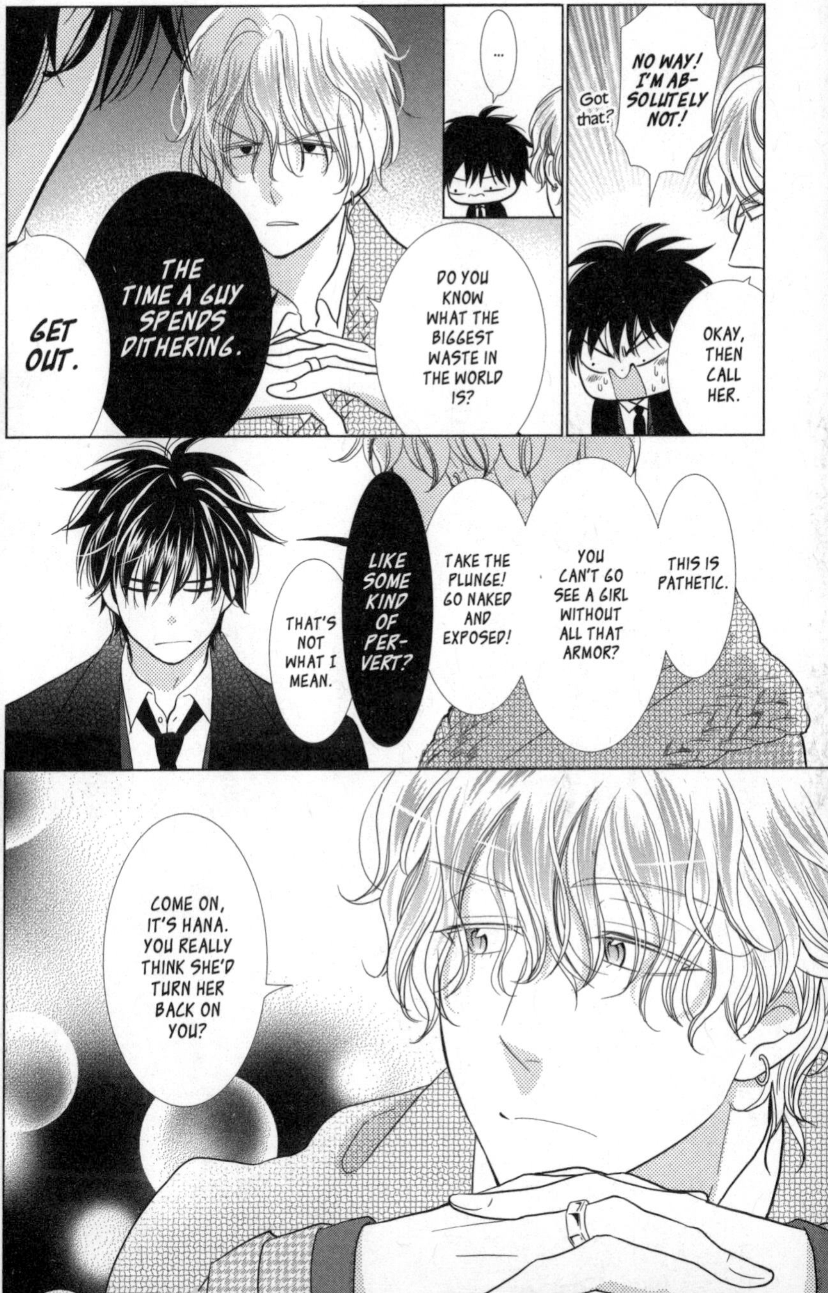
NO WAY! I'M ABSOLUTELY NOT!
Got that?
OKAY, THEN CALL HER.
...
DO YOU KNOW WHAT THE BIGGEST WASTE IN THE WORLD IS?
THE TIME A GUY SPENDS DITHERING.
GET OUT.
THIS IS PATHETIC.
YOU CAN'T GO SEE A GIRL WITHOUT ALL THAT ARMOR?
TAKE THE PLUNGE! GO NAKED AND EXPOSED!
LIKE SOME KIND OF PERVERT?
THAT'S NOT WHAT I MEAN.
COME ON, IT'S HANA. YOU REALLY THINK SHE'D TURN HER BACK ON YOU?

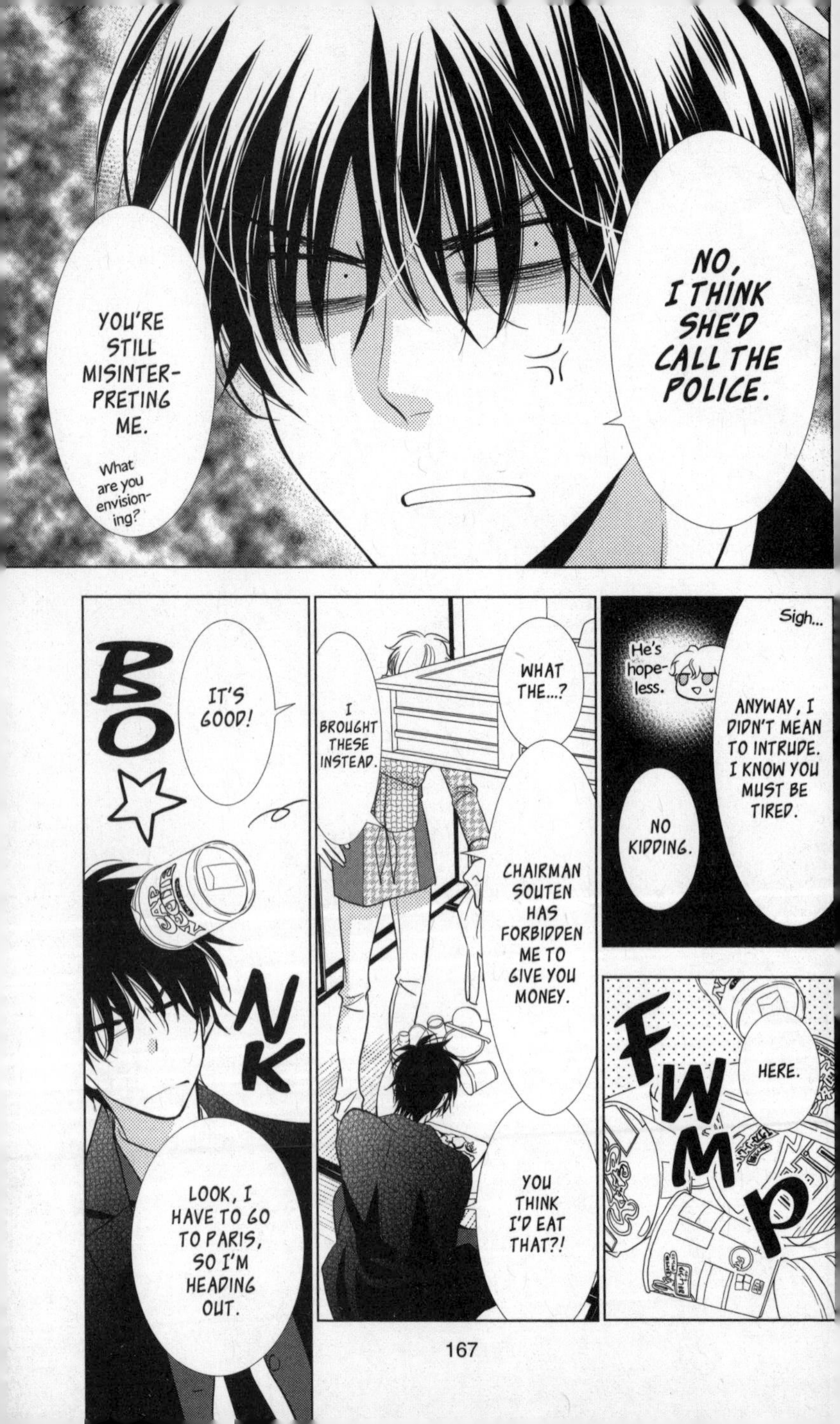
NO, I THINK SHE'D CALL THE POLICE.
YOU'RE STILL MISINTERPRETING ME.
What are you envisioning?
Sigh...
ANYWAY, I DIDN'T MEAN TO INTRUDE. I KNOW YOU MUST BE TIRED.
He's hopeless.
NO KIDDING.
FWMP
HERE.
WHAT THE...?
I BROUGHT THESE INSTEAD.
CHAIRMAN SOUTEN HAS FORBIDDEN ME TO GIVE YOU MONEY.
YOU THINK I'D EAT THAT?!
IT'S GOOD!
BONK
LOOK, I HAVE TO GO TO PARIS, SO I'M HEADING OUT.

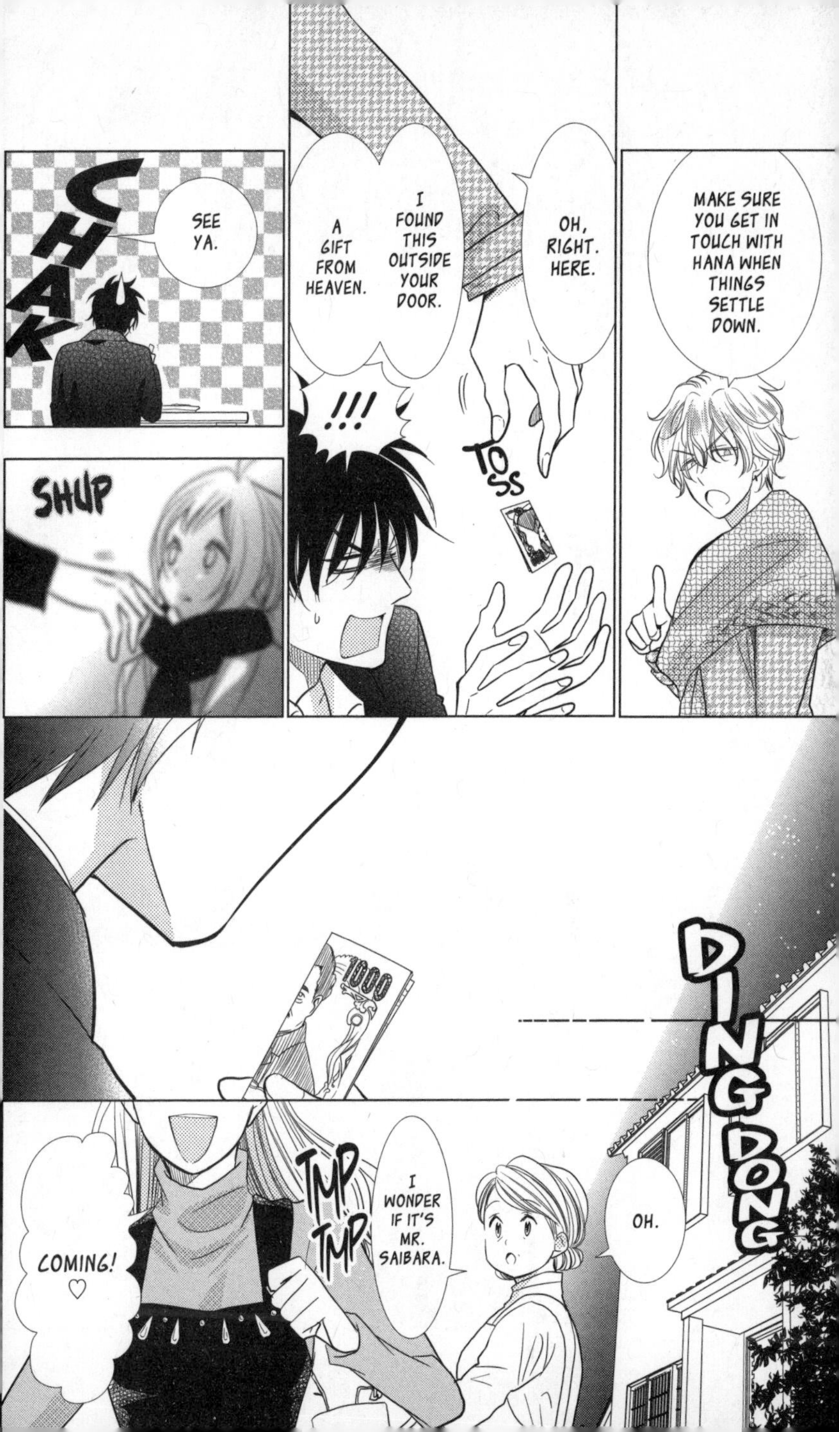
MAKE SURE YOU GET IN TOUCH WITH HANA WHEN THINGS SETTLE DOWN.
OH, RIGHT. HERE.
I FOUND THIS OUTSIDE YOUR DOOR.
A GIFT FROM HEAVEN.
!!!
TOSS
CHAK
SEE YA.
SHUP
DING DONG
1000
OH.
I WONDER IF IT'S MR. SAIBARA.
TMP TMP
COMING! ♡

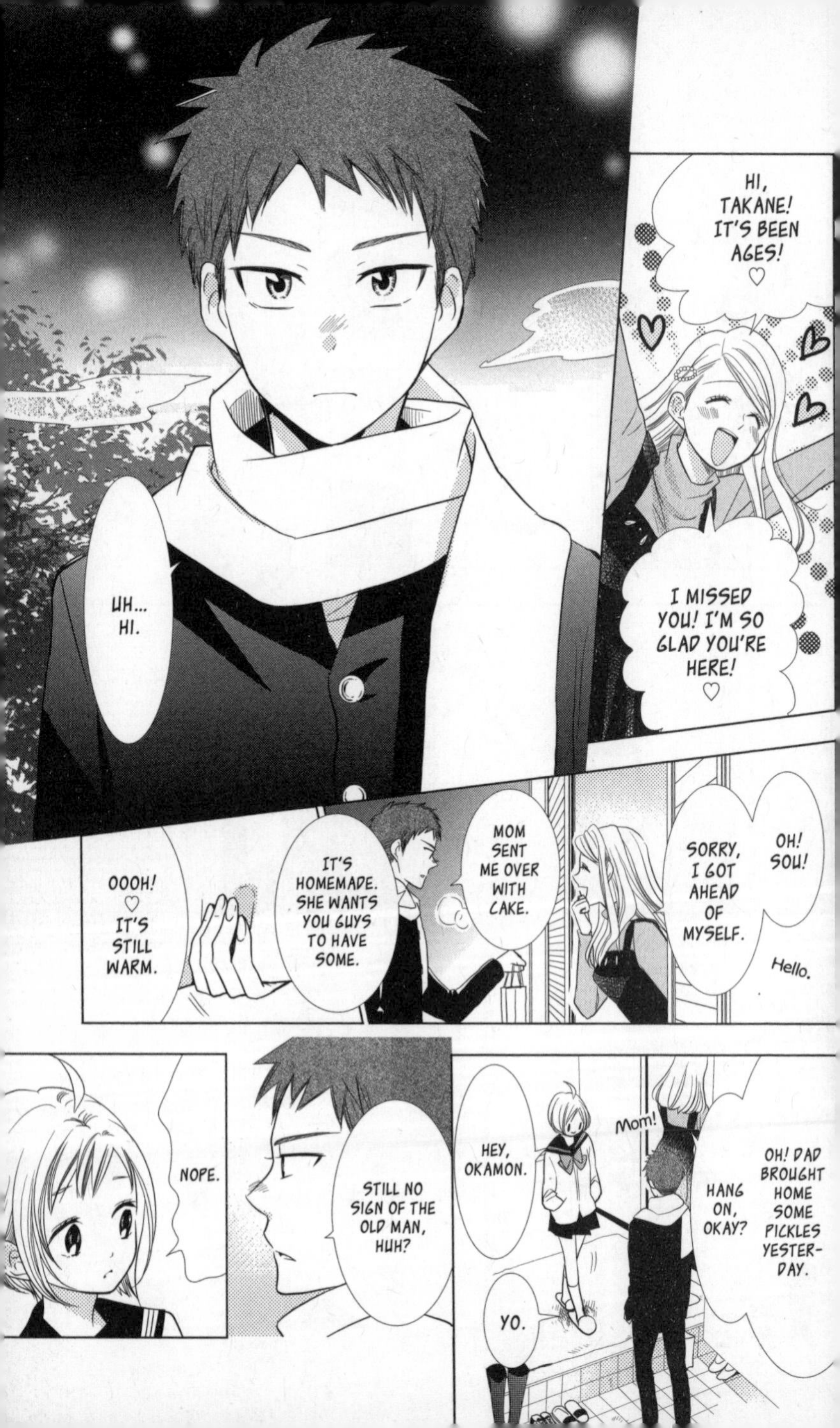
HI, TAKANE! IT'S BEEN AGES! ♡
I MISSED YOU! I'M SO GLAD YOU'RE HERE! ♡
UH... HI.
OH! SOU!
SORRY, I GOT AHEAD OF MYSELF.
Hello.
MOM SENT ME OVER WITH CAKE.
IT'S HOMEMADE. SHE WANTS YOU GUYS TO HAVE SOME.
OOOH! ♡ IT'S STILL WARM.
OH! DAD BROUGHT HOME SOME PICKLES YESTER-DAY.
HANG ON, OKAY?
Mom!
HEY, OKAMON.
YO.
STILL NO SIGN OF THE OLD MAN, HUH?
NOPE.

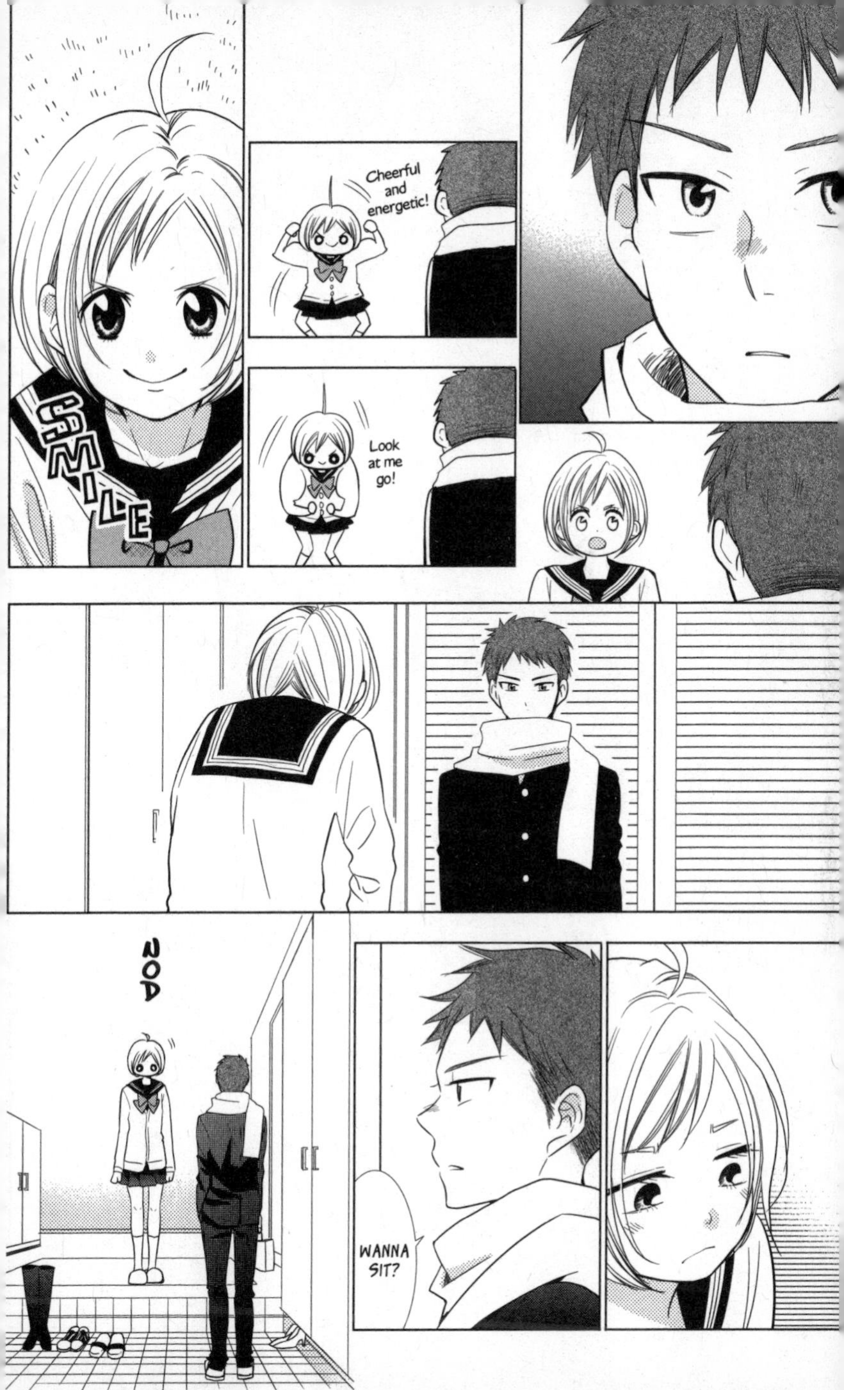
Cheerful and energetic!
Look at me go!
SMILE
WANNA SIT?
NOD

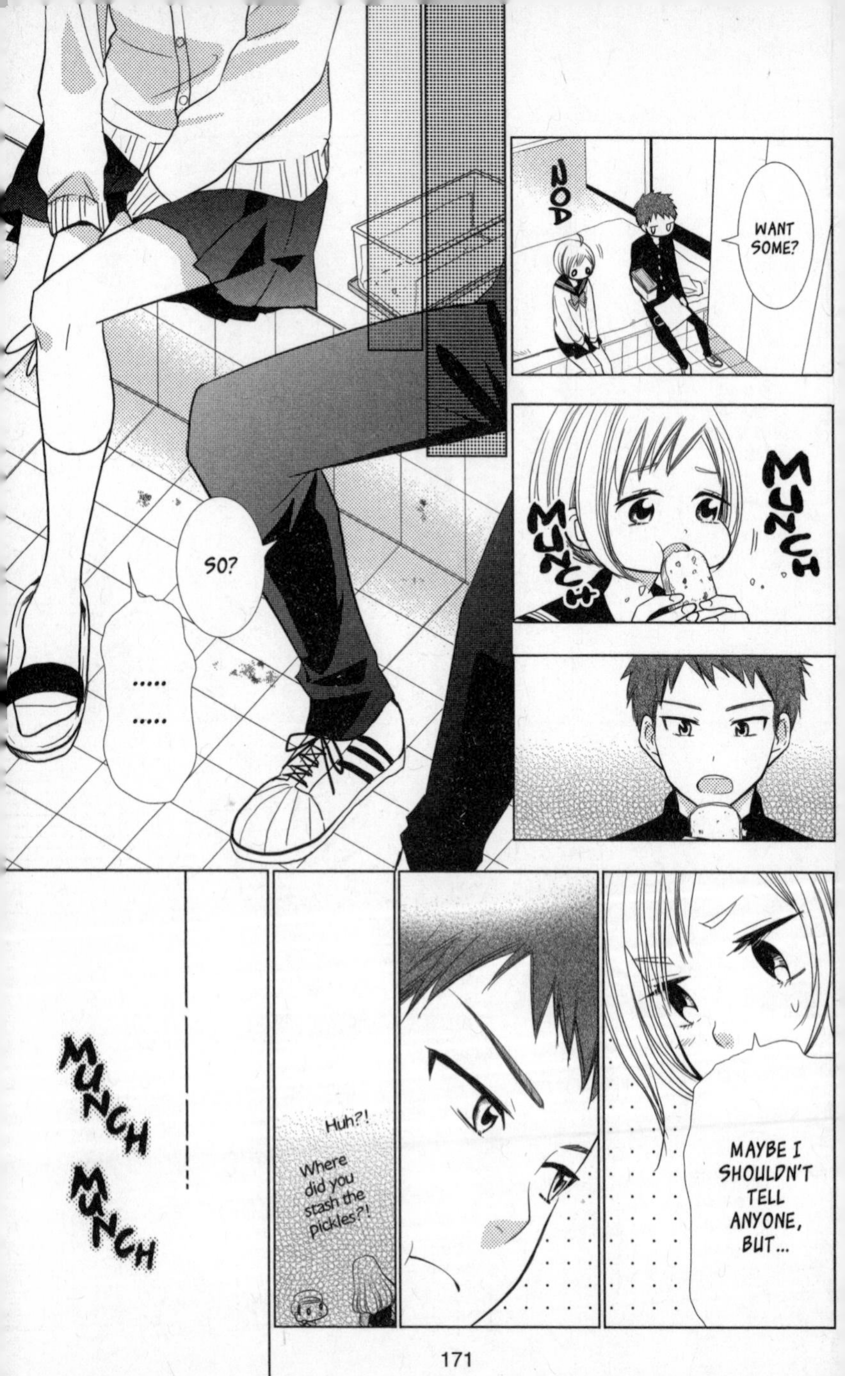
WANT SOME?
NOD
MUNCH
MUNCH
SO?
....
MAYBE I SHOULDN'T TELL ANYONE, BUT...
Huh?!
Where did you stash the pickles?!
MUNCH MUNCH

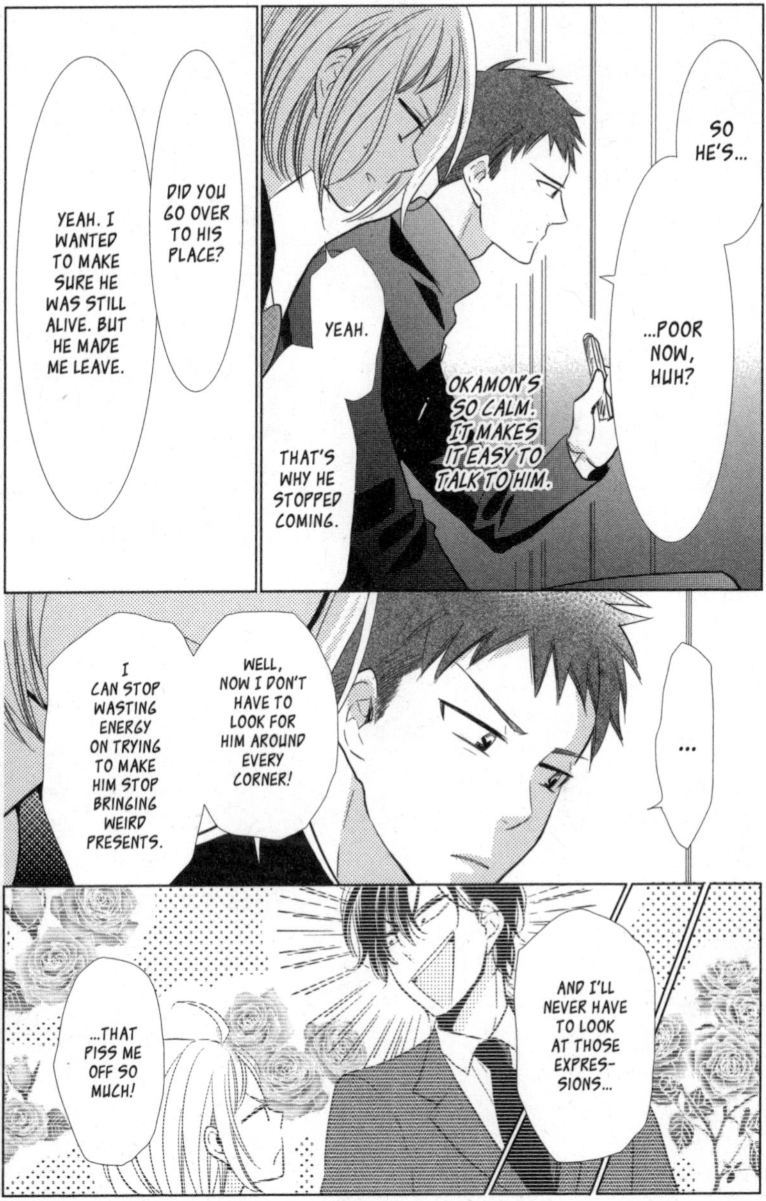
SO HE'S... ...POOR NOW, HUH?
YEAH.
OKAMON'S SO CALM. IT MAKES IT EASY TO TALK TO HIM.
THAT'S WHY HE STOPPED COMING.
DID YOU GO OVER TO HIS PLACE?
YEAH. I WANTED TO MAKE SURE HE WAS STILL ALIVE. BUT HE MADE ME LEAVE.
...
WELL, NOW I DON'T HAVE TO LOOK FOR HIM AROUND EVERY CORNER!
I CAN STOP WASTING ENERGY ON TRYING TO MAKE HIM STOP BRINGING WEIRD PRESENTS.
AND I'LL NEVER HAVE TO LOOK AT THOSE EXPRES- SIONS...
...THAT PISS ME OFF SO MUCH!

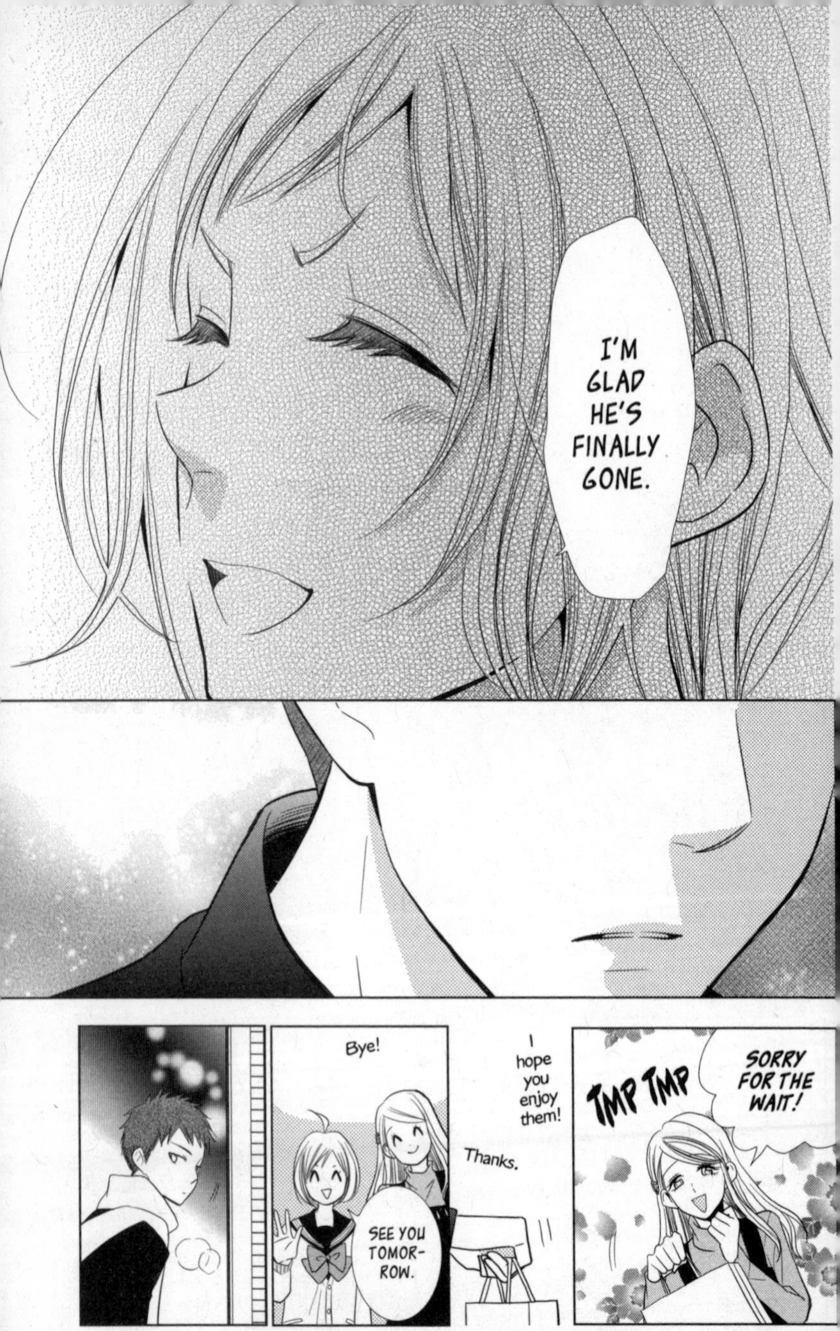
I'M GLAD HE'S FINALLY GONE.
TMP TMP
SORRY FOR THE WAIT!
I hope you enjoy them!
Thanks.
Bye!
SEE YOU TOMOR-ROW.

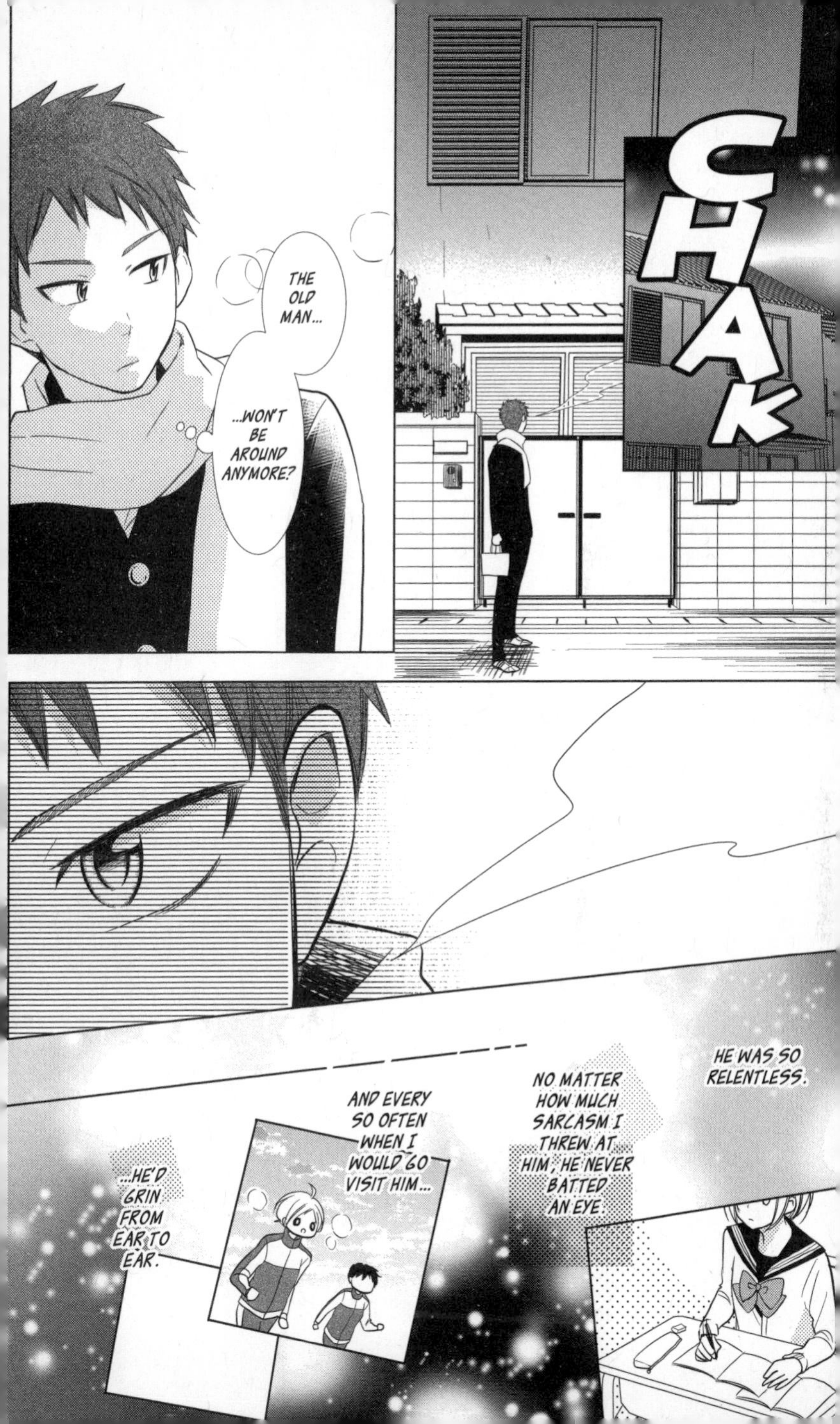
CHAK
THE OLD MAN...
...WON'T BE AROUND ANYMORE?
HE WAS SO RELENTLESS.
NO MATTER HOW MUCH SARCASM I THREW AT HIM, HE NEVER BATTED AN EYE.
AND EVERY SO OFTEN WHEN I WOULD GO VISIT HIM...
...HE'D GRIN FROM EAR TO EAR.

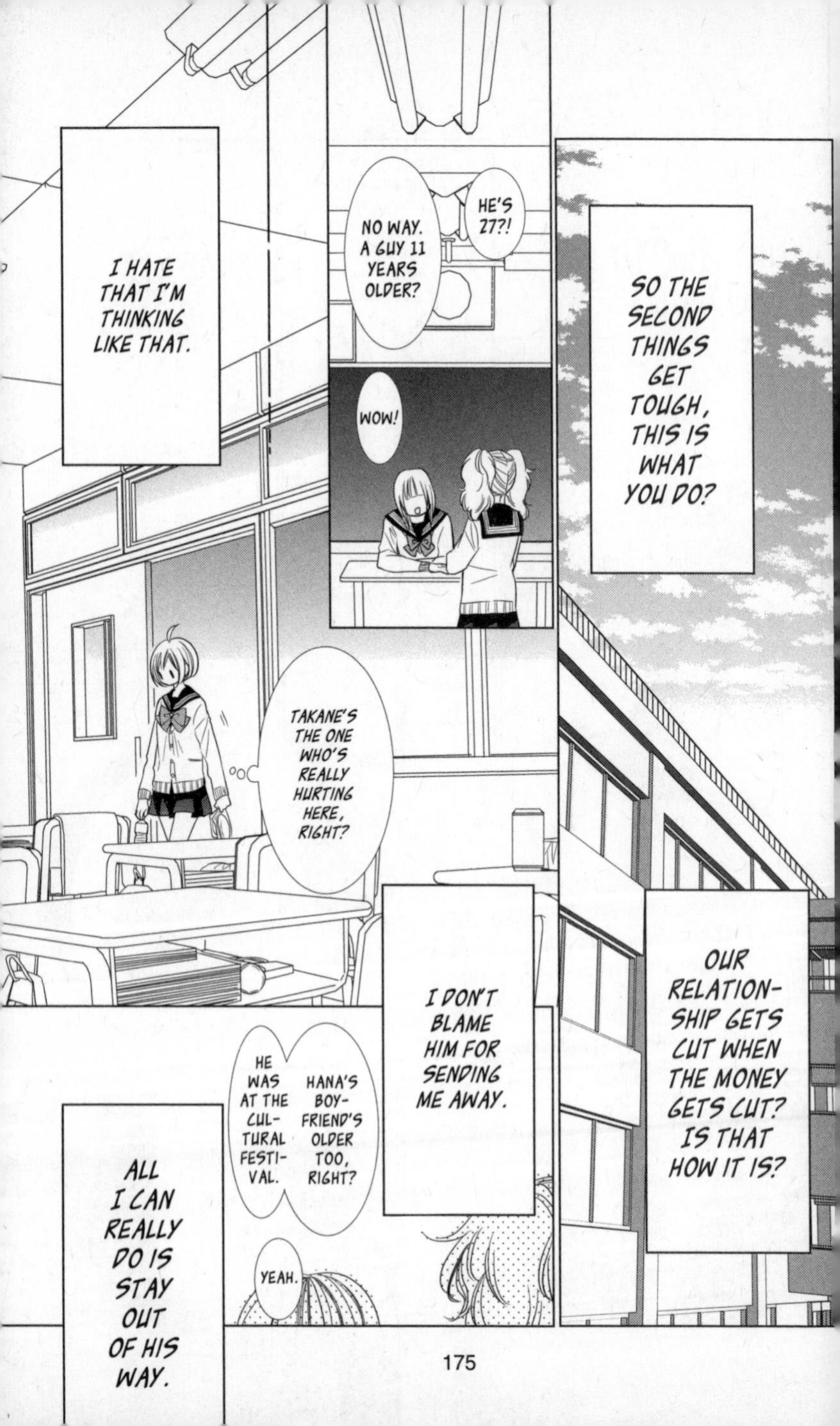
SO THE SECOND THINGS GET TOUGH, THIS IS WHAT YOU DO?
OUR RELATIONSHIP GETS CUT WHEN THE MONEY GETS CUT? IS THAT HOW IT IS?
HE'S 27?!
NO WAY. A GUY 11 YEARS OLDER?
WOW!
I HATE THAT I'M THINKING LIKE THAT.
TAKANE'S THE ONE WHO'S REALLY HURTING HERE, RIGHT?
I DON'T BLAME HIM FOR SENDING ME AWAY.
HANA'S BOYFRIEND'S OLDER TOO, RIGHT?
HE WAS AT THE CULTURAL FESTIVAL.
YEAH.
ALL I CAN REALLY DO IS STAY OUT OF HIS WAY.

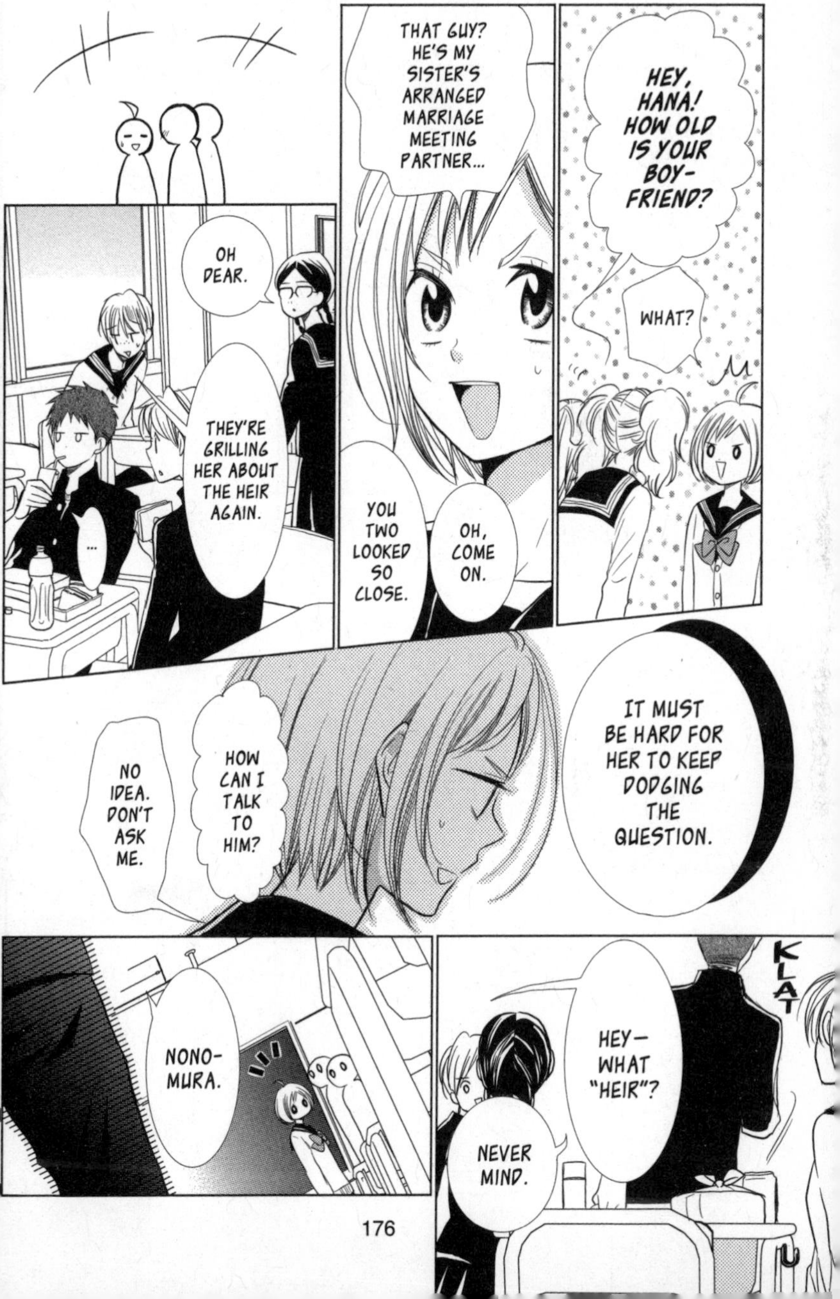
HEY, HANA! HOW OLD IS YOUR BOY-FRIEND?
WHAT?
THAT GUY? HE'S MY SISTER'S ARRANGED MARRIAGE MEETING PARTNER...
OH, COME ON.
YOU TWO LOOKED SO CLOSE.
OH DEAR.
THEY'RE GRILLING HER ABOUT THE HEIR AGAIN.
...
IT MUST BE HARD FOR HER TO KEEP DODGING THE QUESTION.
HOW CAN I TALK TO HIM?
NO IDEA. DON'T ASK ME.
KLAT
HEY— WHAT "HEIR"?
NEVER MIND.
NONO-MURA.

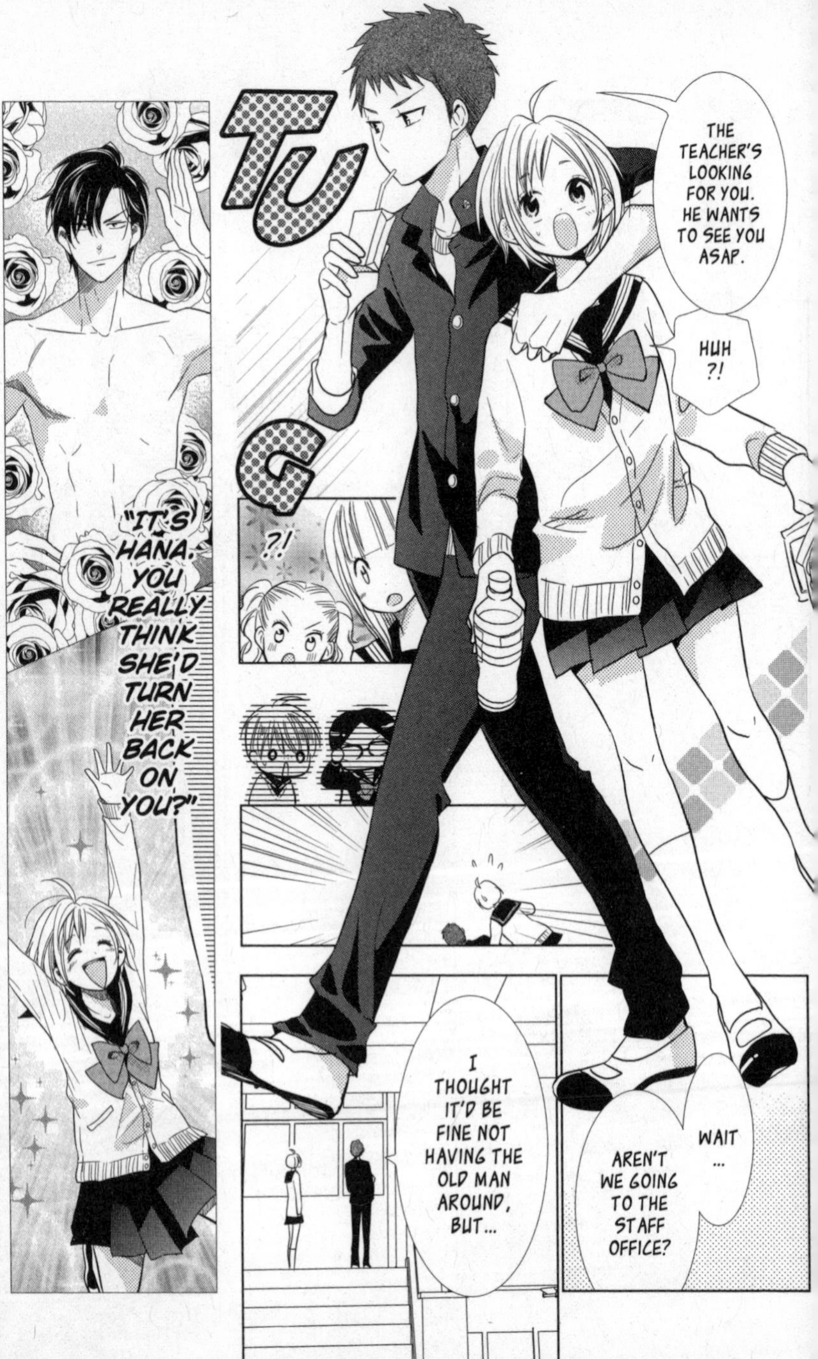
THE TEACHER'S LOOKING FOR YOU. HE WANTS TO SEE YOU ASAP.
HUH ?!
TUG
?!
WAIT ...
AREN'T WE GOING TO THE STAFF OFFICE?
I THOUGHT IT'D BE FINE NOT HAVING THE OLD MAN AROUND, BUT...
"IT'S HANA. YOU REALLY THINK SHE'D TURN HER BACK ON YOU?"

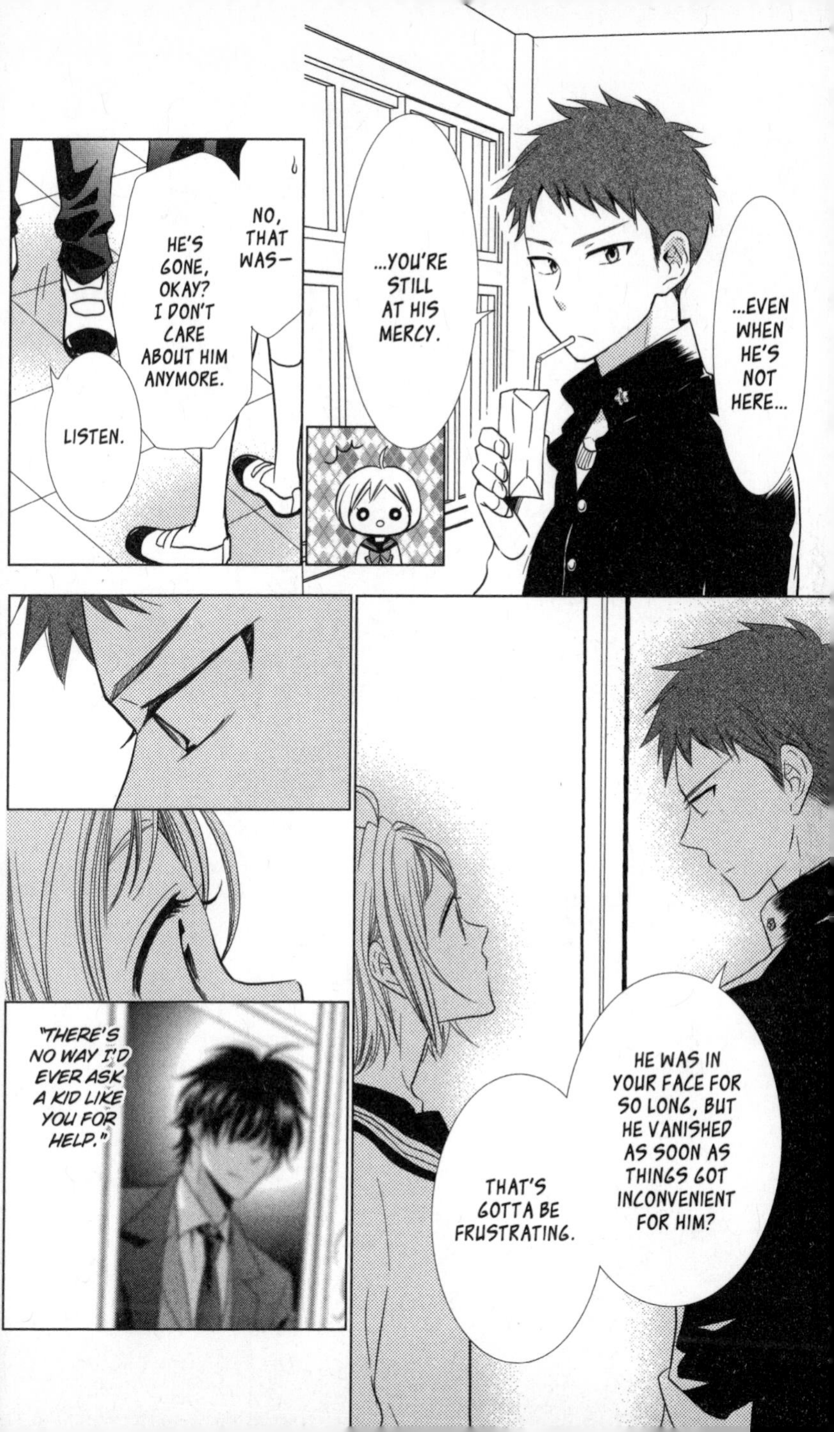
...EVEN WHEN HE'S NOT HERE...
...YOU'RE STILL AT HIS MERCY.
NO, THAT WAS—
HE'S GONE, OKAY? I DON'T CARE ABOUT HIM ANYMORE.
LISTEN.
HE WAS IN YOUR FACE FOR SO LONG, BUT HE VANISHED AS SOON AS THINGS GOT INCONVENIENT FOR HIM?
THAT'S GOTTA BE FRUSTRATING.
"THERE'S NO WAY I'D EVER ASK A KID LIKE YOU FOR HELP."

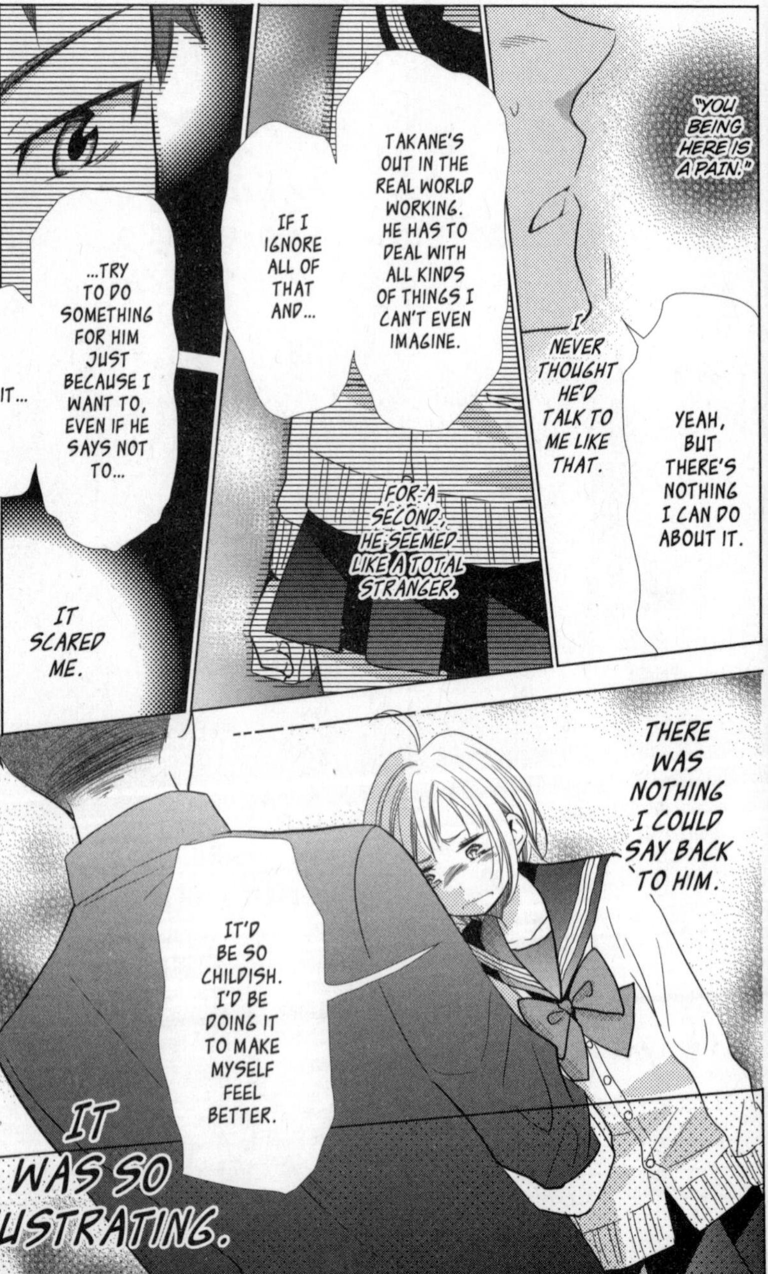
"YOU BEING HERE IS A PAIN."
I NEVER THOUGHT HE'D TALK TO ME LIKE THAT.
YEAH, BUT THERE'S NOTHING I CAN DO ABOUT IT.
TAKANE'S OUT IN THE REAL WORLD WORKING. HE HAS TO DEAL WITH ALL KINDS OF THINGS I CAN'T EVEN IMAGINE.
IF I IGNORE ALL OF THAT AND...
FOR A SECOND, HE SEEMED LIKE A TOTAL STRANGER.
...TRY TO DO SOMETHING FOR HIM JUST BECAUSE I WANT TO, EVEN IF HE SAYS NOT TO...
...IT...
IT SCARED ME.
THERE WAS NOTHING I COULD SAY BACK TO HIM.
IT'D BE SO CHILDISH. I'D BE DOING IT TO MAKE MYSELF FEEL BETTER.
IT WAS SO FRUSTRATING.

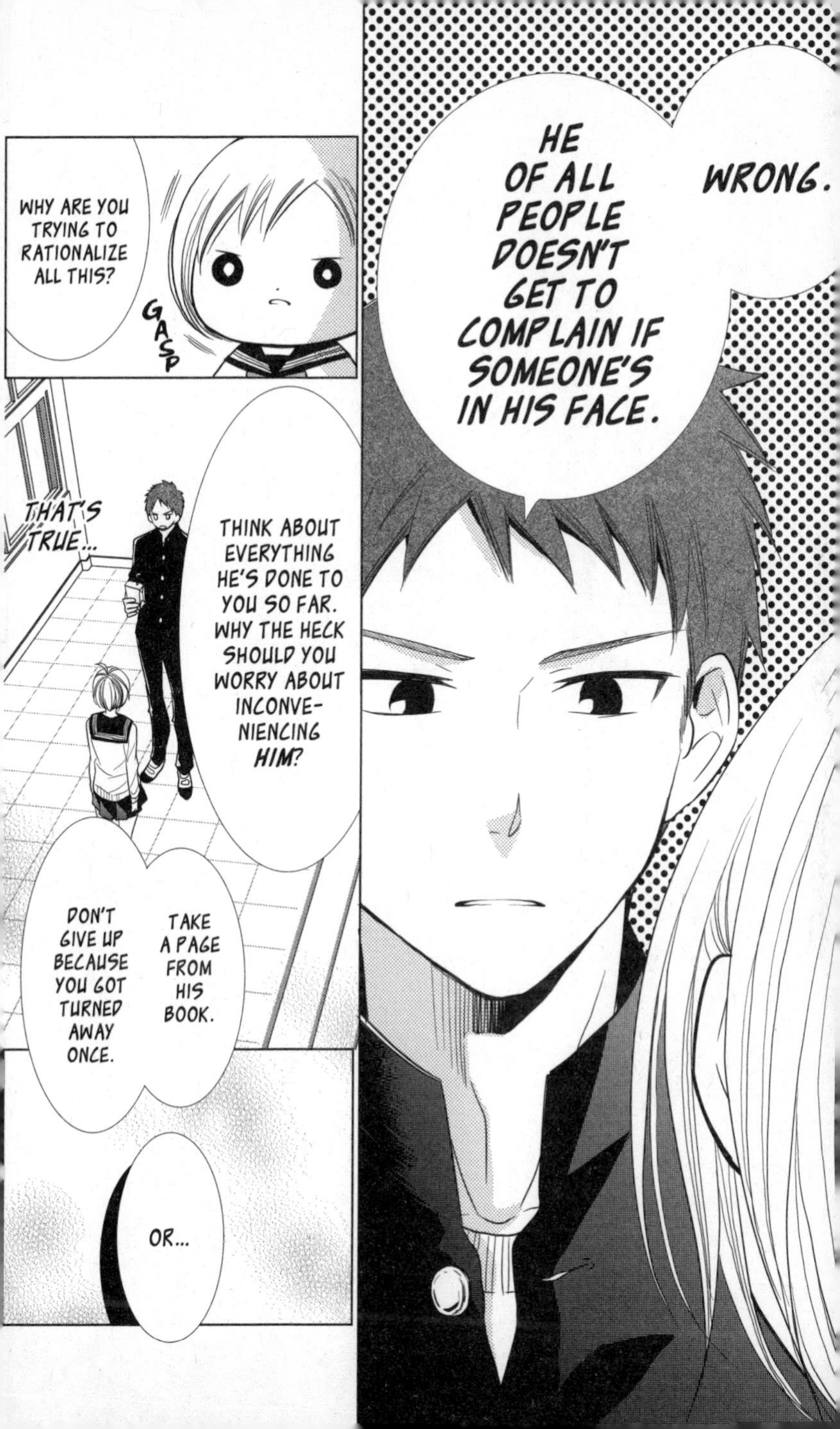
WRONG.
HE OF ALL PEOPLE DOESN'T GET TO COMPLAIN IF SOMEONE'S IN HIS FACE.
WHY ARE YOU TRYING TO RATIONALIZE ALL THIS?
GASP
THINK ABOUT EVERYTHING HE'S DONE TO YOU SO FAR. WHY THE HECK SHOULD YOU WORRY ABOUT INCONVE-NIENCING HIM?
THAT'S TRUE...
TAKE A PAGE FROM HIS BOOK.
DON'T GIVE UP BECAUSE YOU GOT TURNED AWAY ONCE.
OR...

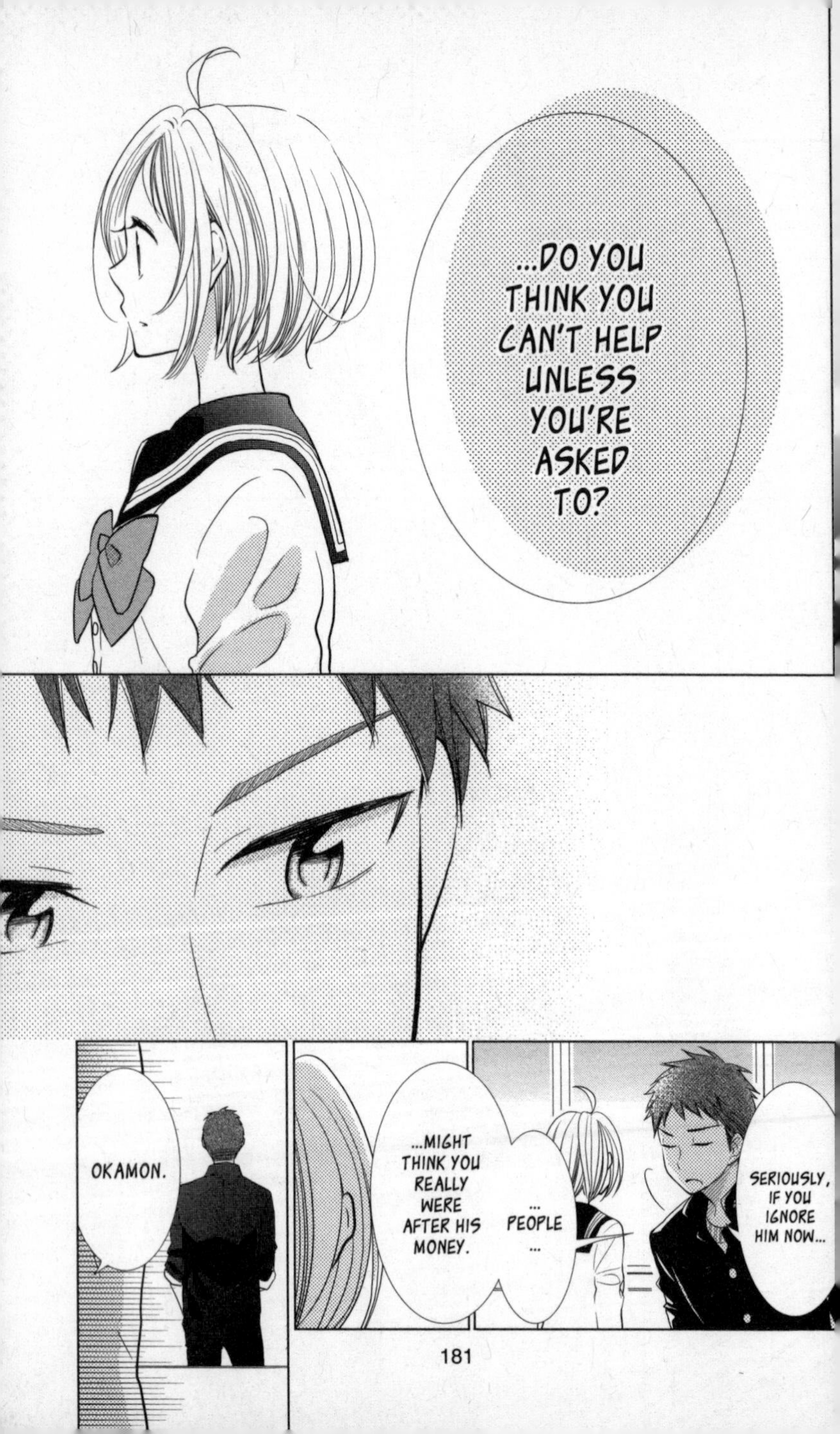
...DO YOU THINK YOU CAN'T HELP UNLESS YOU'RE ASKED TO?
SERIOUSLY, IF YOU IGNORE HIM NOW...
... PEOPLE ...
...MIGHT THINK YOU REALLY WERE AFTER HIS MONEY.
OKAMON.

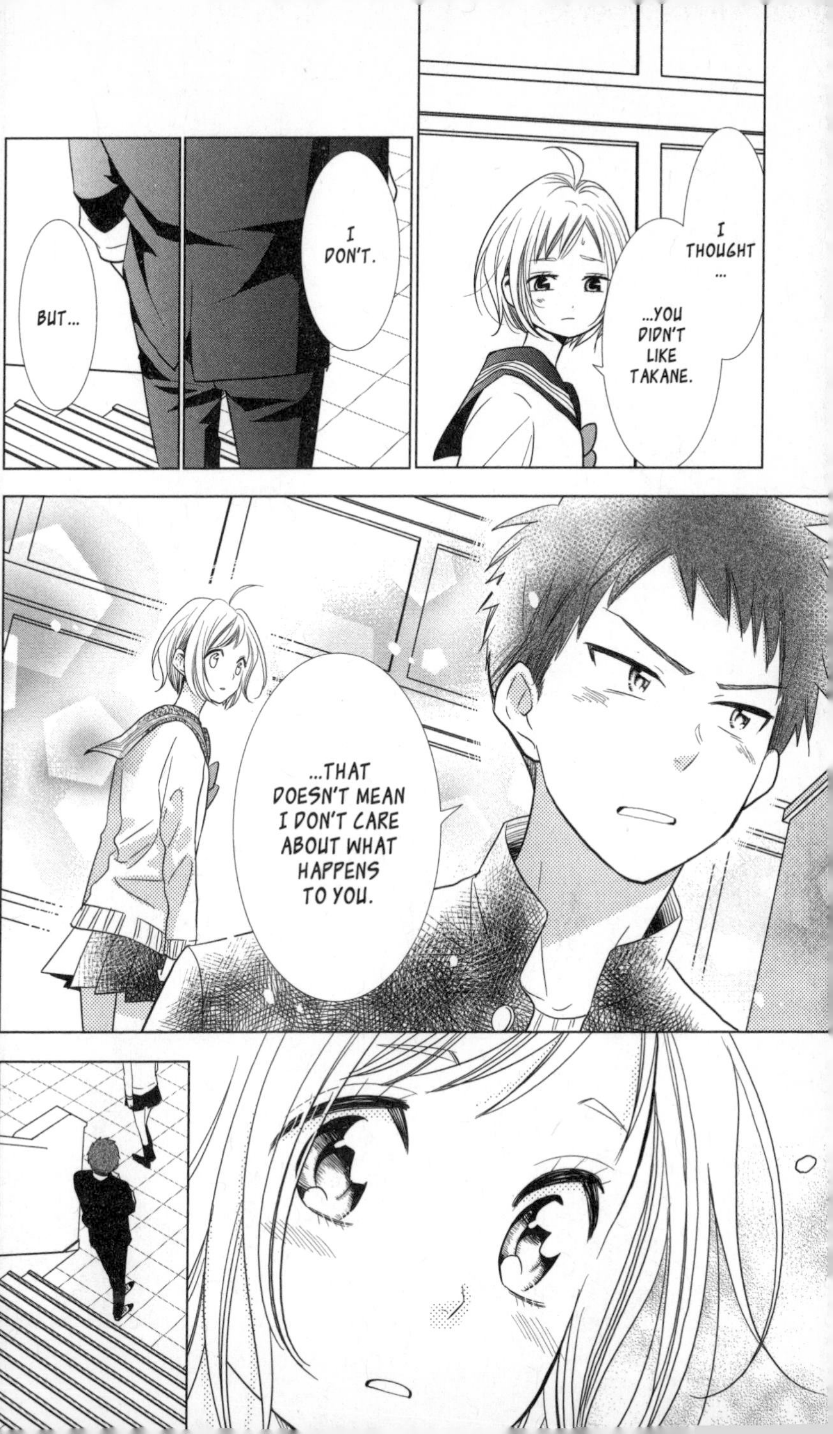
I THOUGHT ...
...YOU DIDN'T LIKE TAKANE.
I DON'T.
BUT...
...THAT DOESN'T MEAN I DON'T CARE ABOUT WHAT HAPPENS TO YOU.

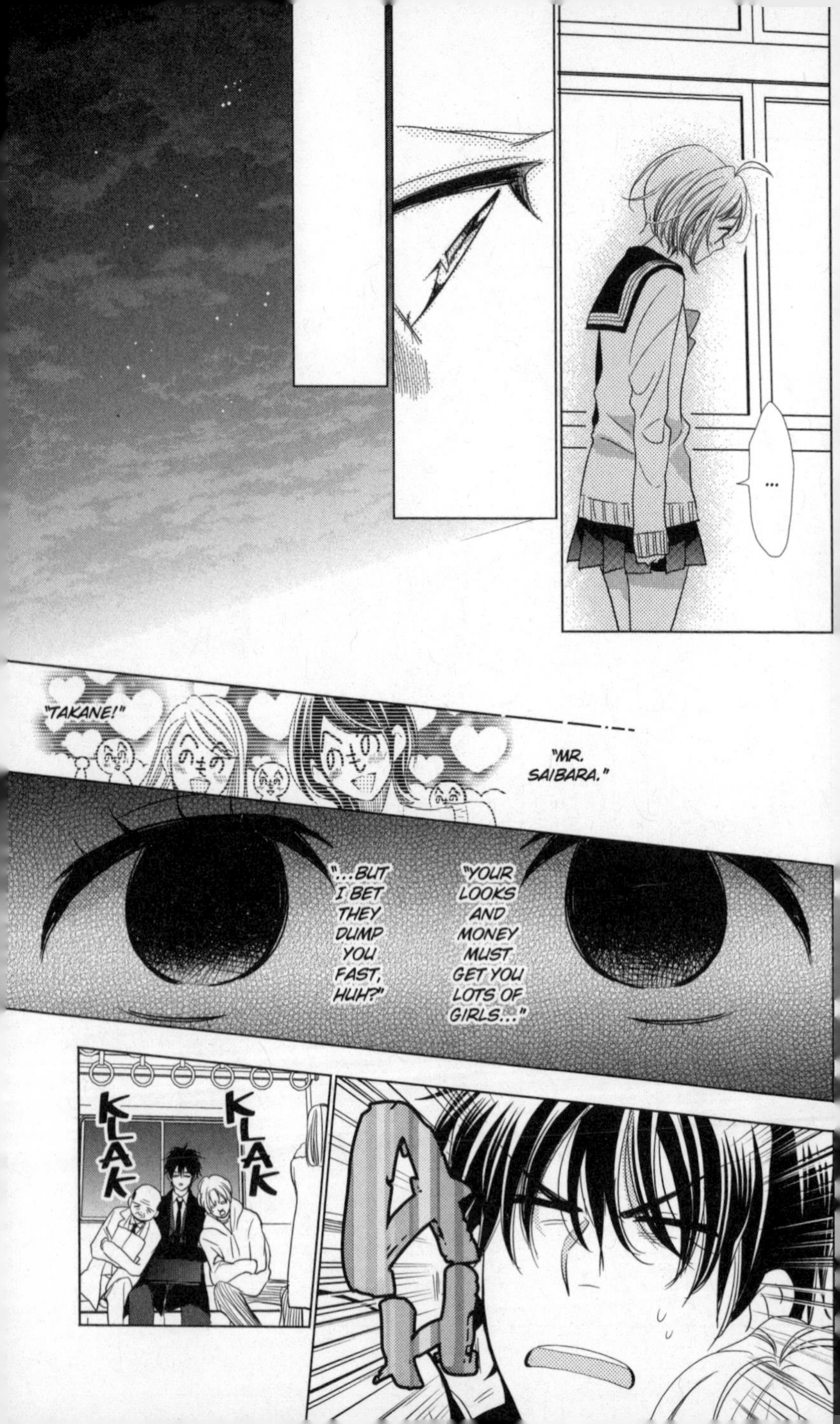
...
"MR. SAIBARA."
"TAKANE!"
"YOUR LOOKS AND MONEY MUST GET YOU LOTS OF GIRLS..."
"...BUT I BET THEY DUMP YOU FAST, HUH?"
KLAK
KLAK

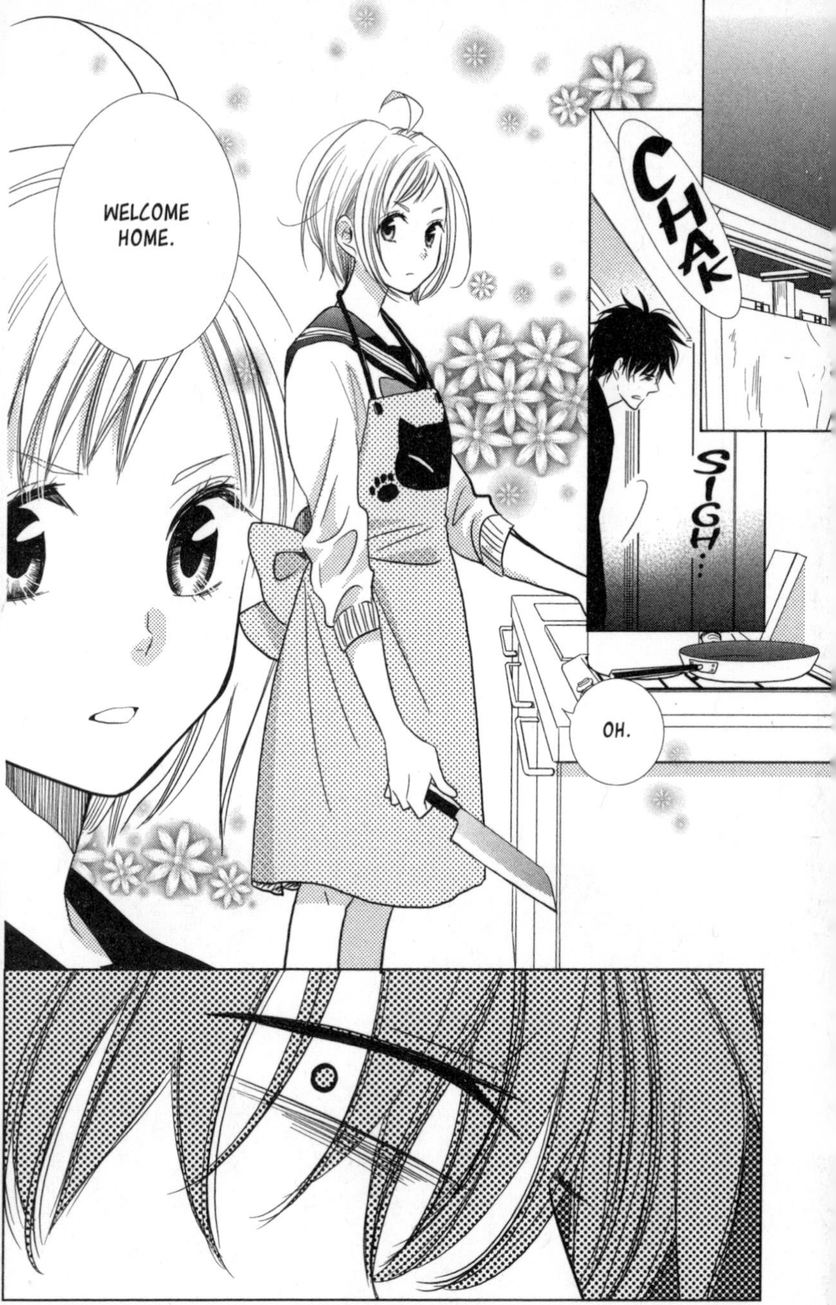
CHAK
SIGH...
OH.
WELCOME HOME.

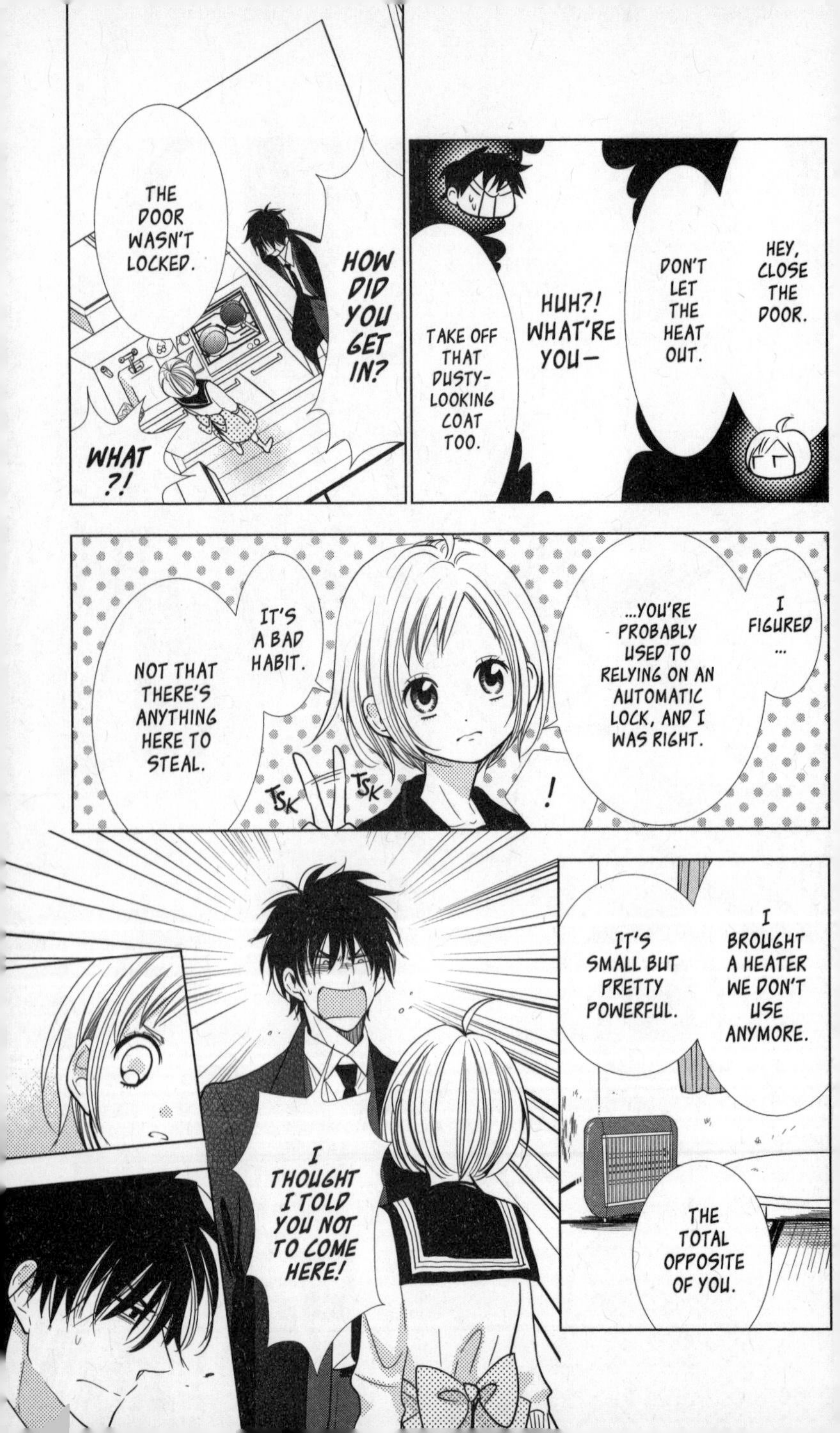
HEY, CLOSE THE DOOR.
DON'T LET THE HEAT OUT.
HUH?! WHAT'RE YOU—
TAKE OFF THAT DUSTY-LOOKING COAT TOO.
HOW DID YOU GET IN?
THE DOOR WASN'T LOCKED.
WHAT?!
I FIGURED ...
...YOU'RE PROBABLY USED TO RELYING ON AN AUTOMATIC LOCK, AND I WAS RIGHT.
!
IT'S A BAD HABIT.
TSK TSK
NOT THAT THERE'S ANYTHING HERE TO STEAL.
I BROUGHT A HEATER WE DON'T USE ANYMORE.
IT'S SMALL BUT PRETTY POWERFUL.
THE TOTAL OPPOSITE OF YOU.
I THOUGHT I TOLD YOU NOT TO COME HERE!

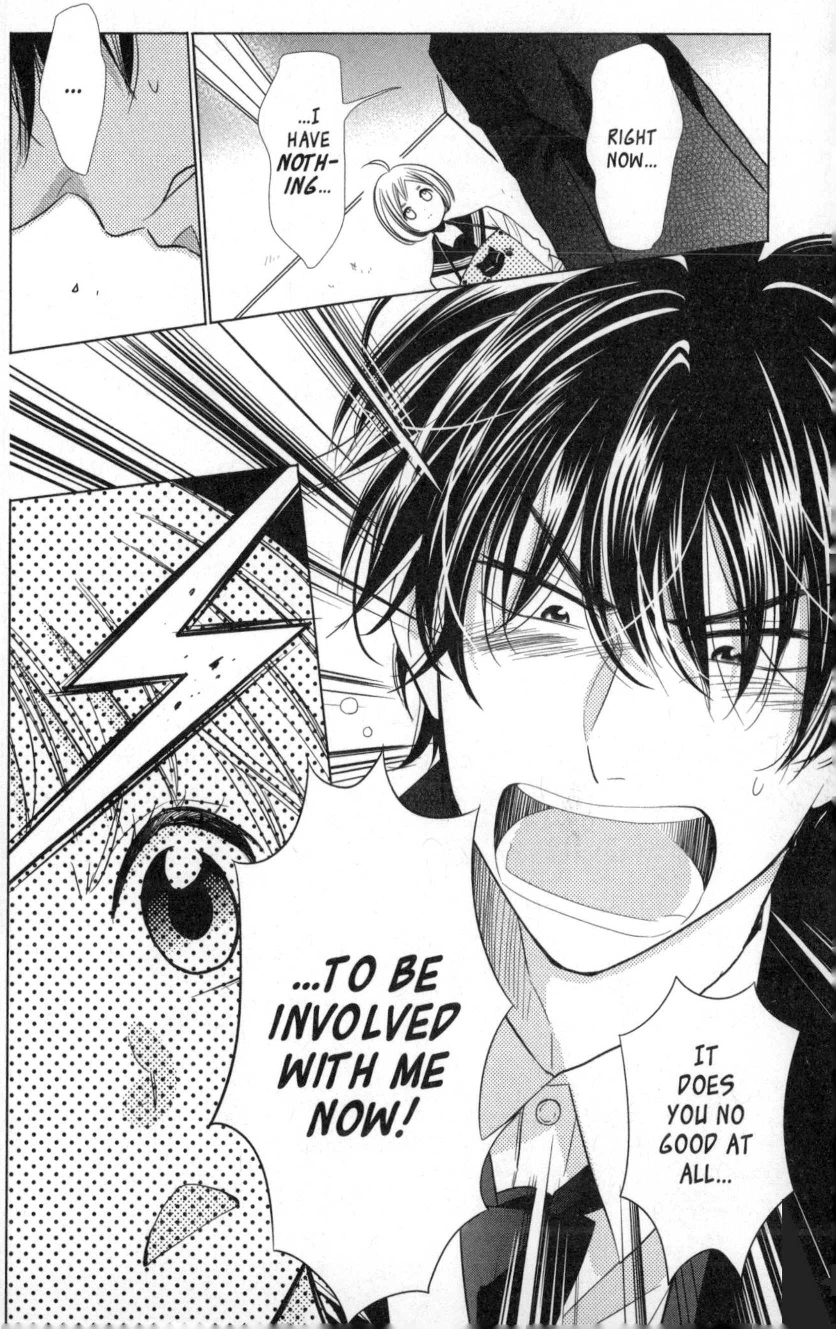
RIGHT NOW...
...I HAVE NOTHING...
...
IT DOES YOU NO GOOD AT ALL...
...TO BE INVOLVED WITH ME NOW!

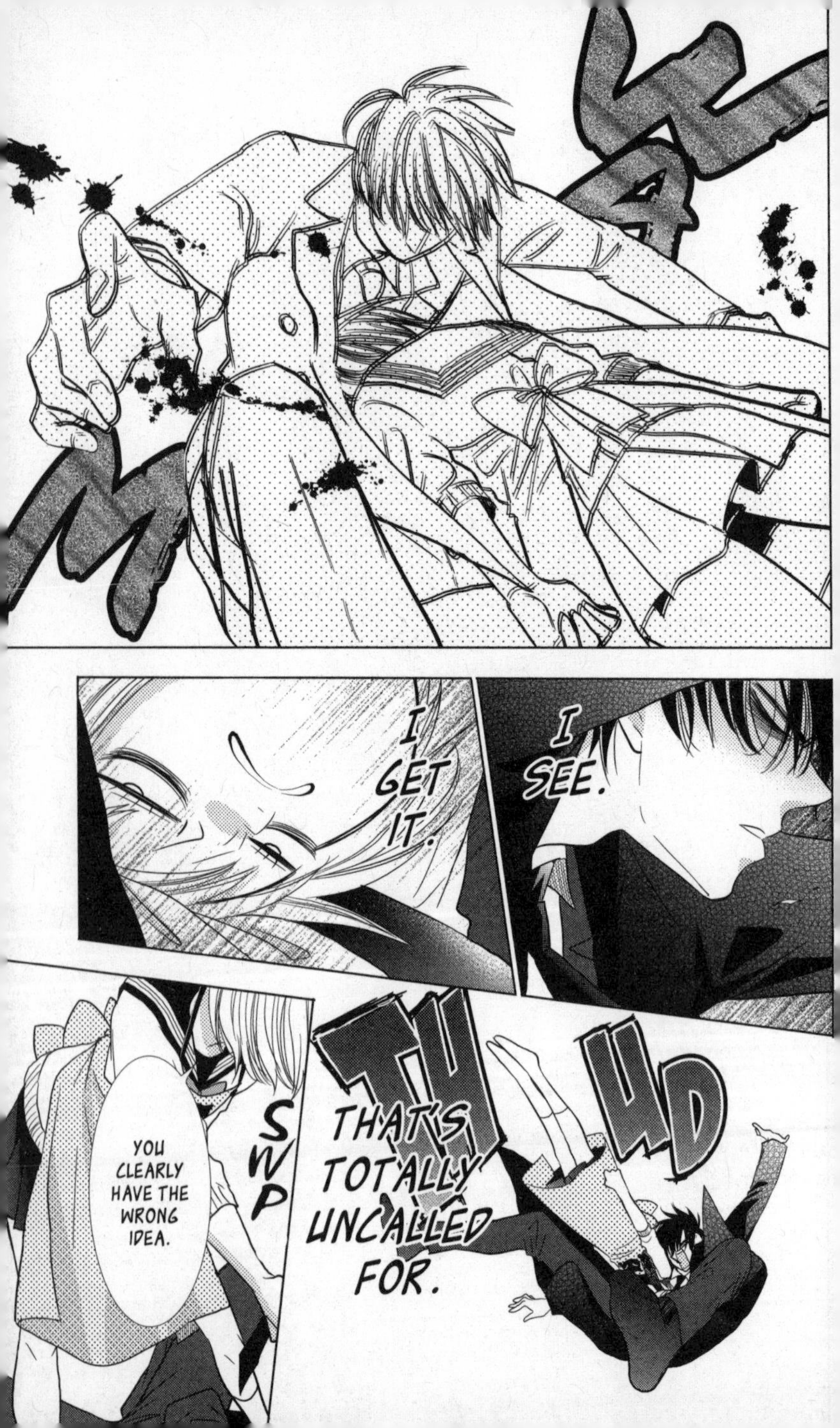
I SEE.
I GET IT.
THUD
THAT'S TOTALLY UNCALLED FOR.
SWP
YOU CLEARLY HAVE THE WRONG IDEA.

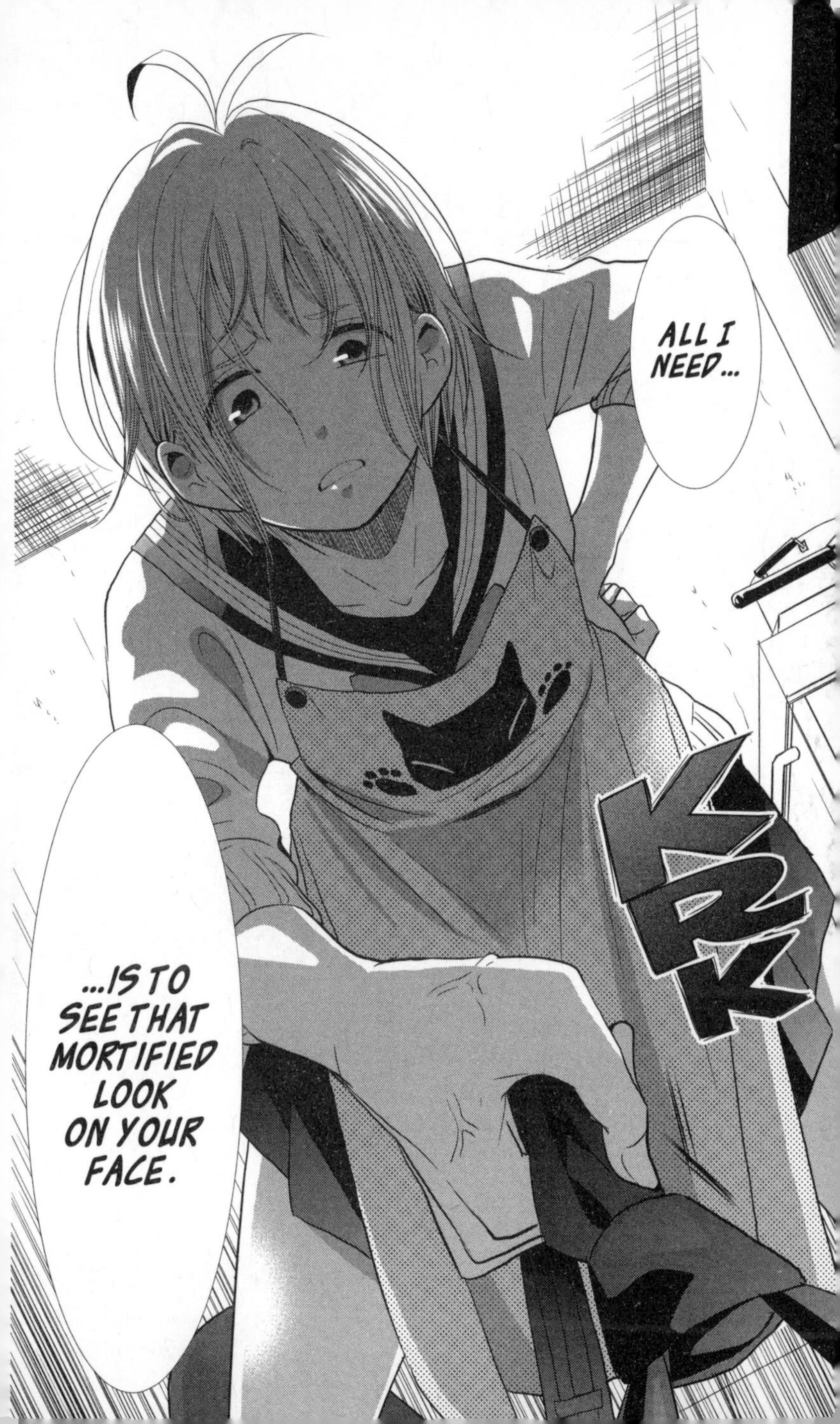
ALL I NEED...
KRAK
...IS TO SEE THAT MORTIFIED LOOK ON YOUR FACE.

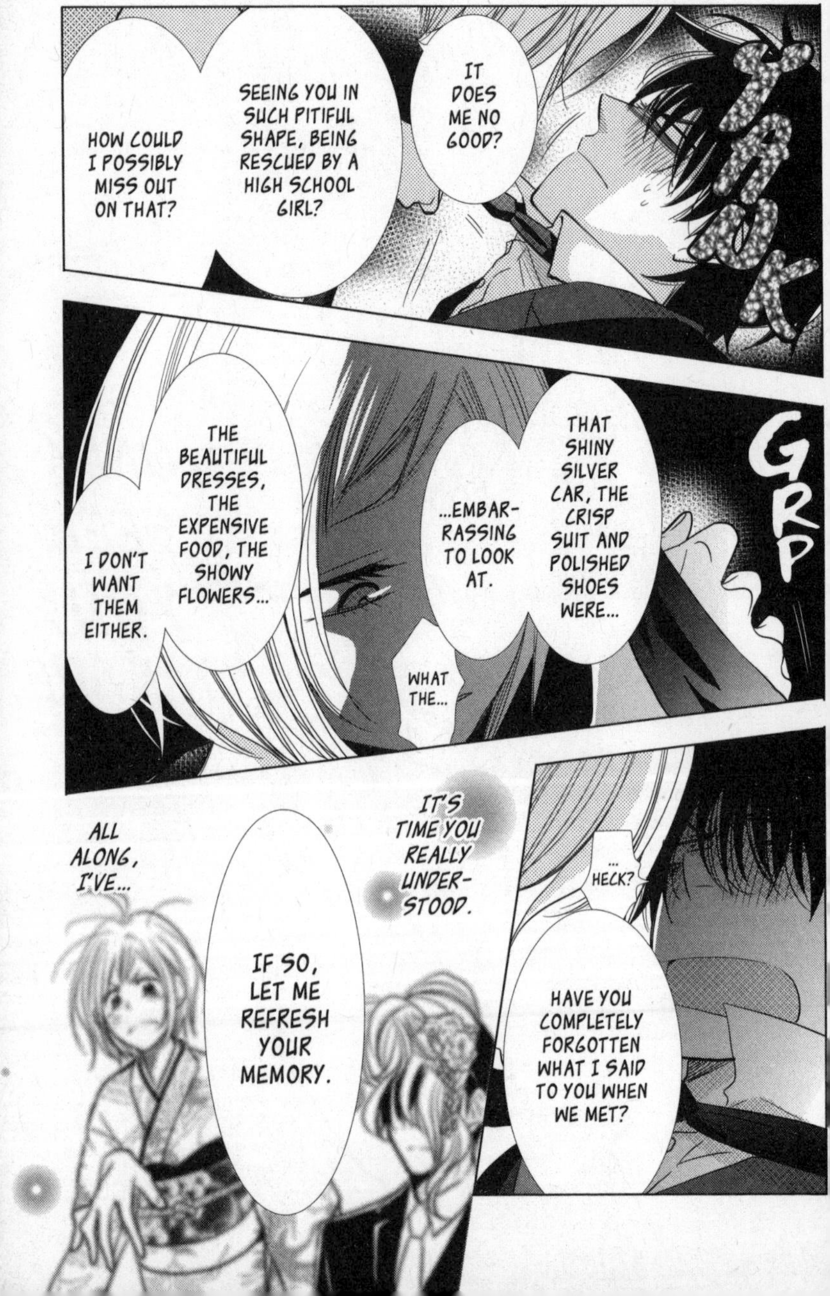
TAAK
IT DOES ME NO GOOD?
SEEING YOU IN SUCH PITIFUL SHAPE, BEING RESCUED BY A HIGH SCHOOL GIRL?
HOW COULD I POSSIBLY MISS OUT ON THAT?
GRP
THAT SHINY SILVER CAR, THE CRISP SUIT AND POLISHED SHOES WERE...
...EMBAR-RASSING TO LOOK AT.
WHAT THE...
THE BEAUTIFUL DRESSES, THE EXPENSIVE FOOD, THE SHOWY FLOWERS...
I DON'T WANT THEM EITHER.
...HECK?
HAVE YOU COMPLETELY FORGOTTEN WHAT I SAID TO YOU WHEN WE MET?
IT'S TIME YOU REALLY UNDER-STOOD.
IF SO, LET ME REFRESH YOUR MEMORY.
ALL ALONG, I'VE...

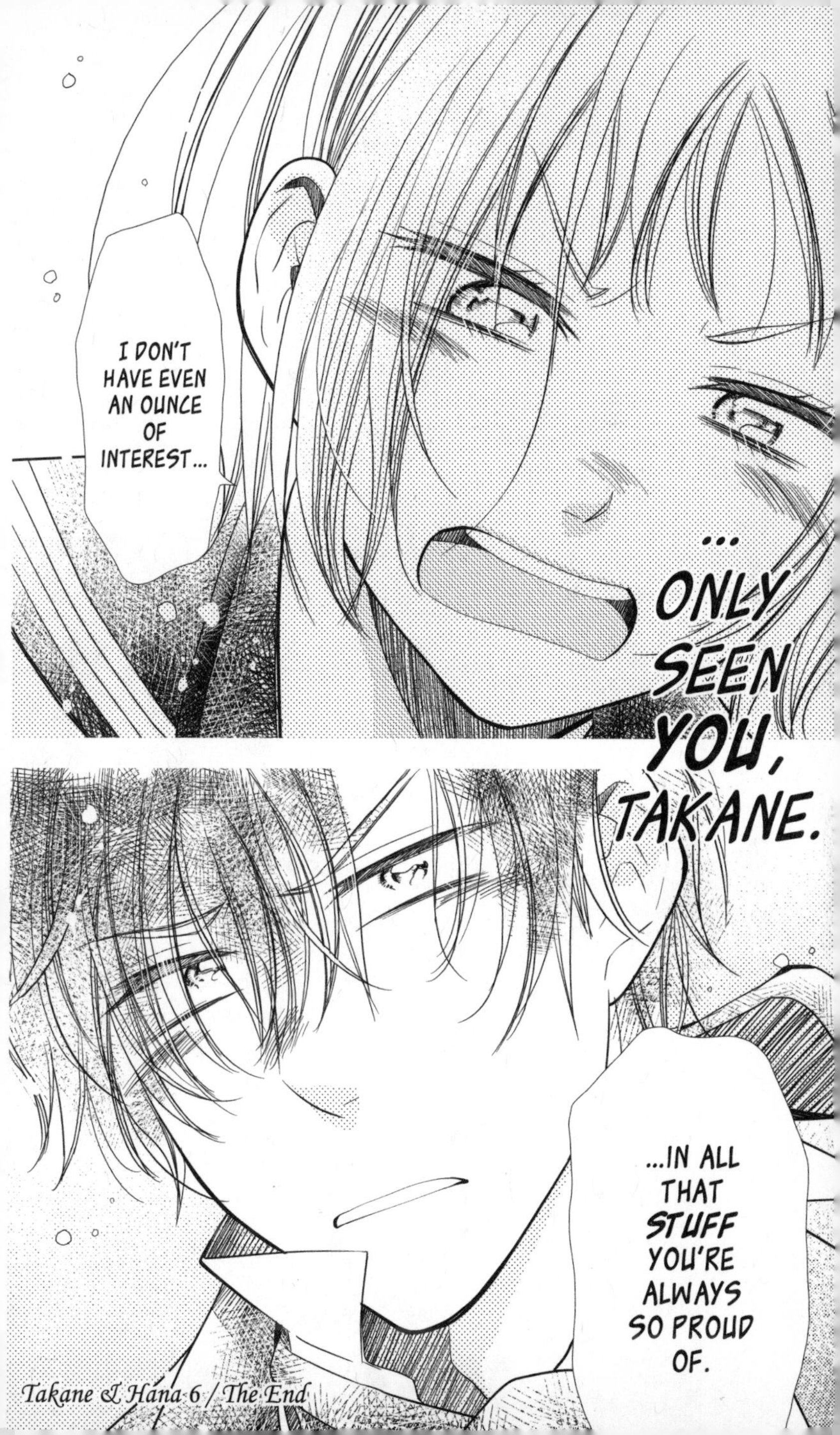
I DON'T HAVE EVEN AN OUNCE OF INTEREST...
...IN ALL THAT STUFF YOU'RE ALWAYS SO PROUD OF.
...ONLY SEEN YOU, TAKANE.

Takane & Hana 6 / The End

The Middle ②

SOB
YOU STILL LOOK COOL WITH YOUR HAIR PARTED IN THE MIDDLE!
HEARING THAT FROM YOU DOESN'T HELP, YOU DUMMY!
I'M NOT A DUMMY!

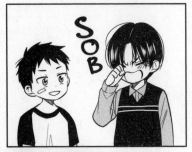

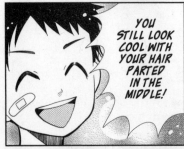

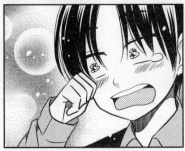

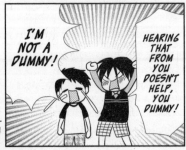

He apologized later.

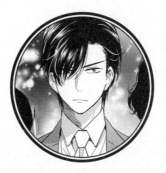

If you find Hikune on the street,
please gently warm him up.

—YUKI SHIWASU

Born on March 7 in Fukuoka Prefecture, Japan,
Yuki Shiwasu began her career as a manga artist
after winning the top prize in the Hakusensha Athena
Newcomers' Awards from *Hana to Yume* magazine. She
is also the author of *Furou Kyoudai* (Immortal Siblings),
which was published by Hakusensha in Japan.

Takane &Hana

VOLUME 6
SHOJO BEAT EDITION

STORY & ART BY YUKI SHIWASU

ENGLISH ADAPTATION **Ysabet Reinhardt MacFarlane**
TRANSLATION **JN Productions**
TOUCH-UP ART & LETTERING **Annaliese Christman**
DESIGN **Shawn Carrico**
EDITOR **Amy Yu**

Takane to Hana by Yuki Shiwasu
© Yuki Shiwasu 2016
All rights reserved.
First published in Japan in 2016 by HAKUSENSHA, Inc., Tokyo.
English language translation rights arranged with HAKUSENSHA, Inc., Tokyo.

The stories, characters and incidents mentioned
in this publication are entirely fictional.

Printed in the U.S.A.

Published by VIZ Media, LLC
P.O. Box 77010
San Francisco, CA 94107

10 9 8 7 6 5 4 3 2 1
First printing, December 2018

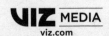

VIZ MEDIA
viz.com

shojobeat.com

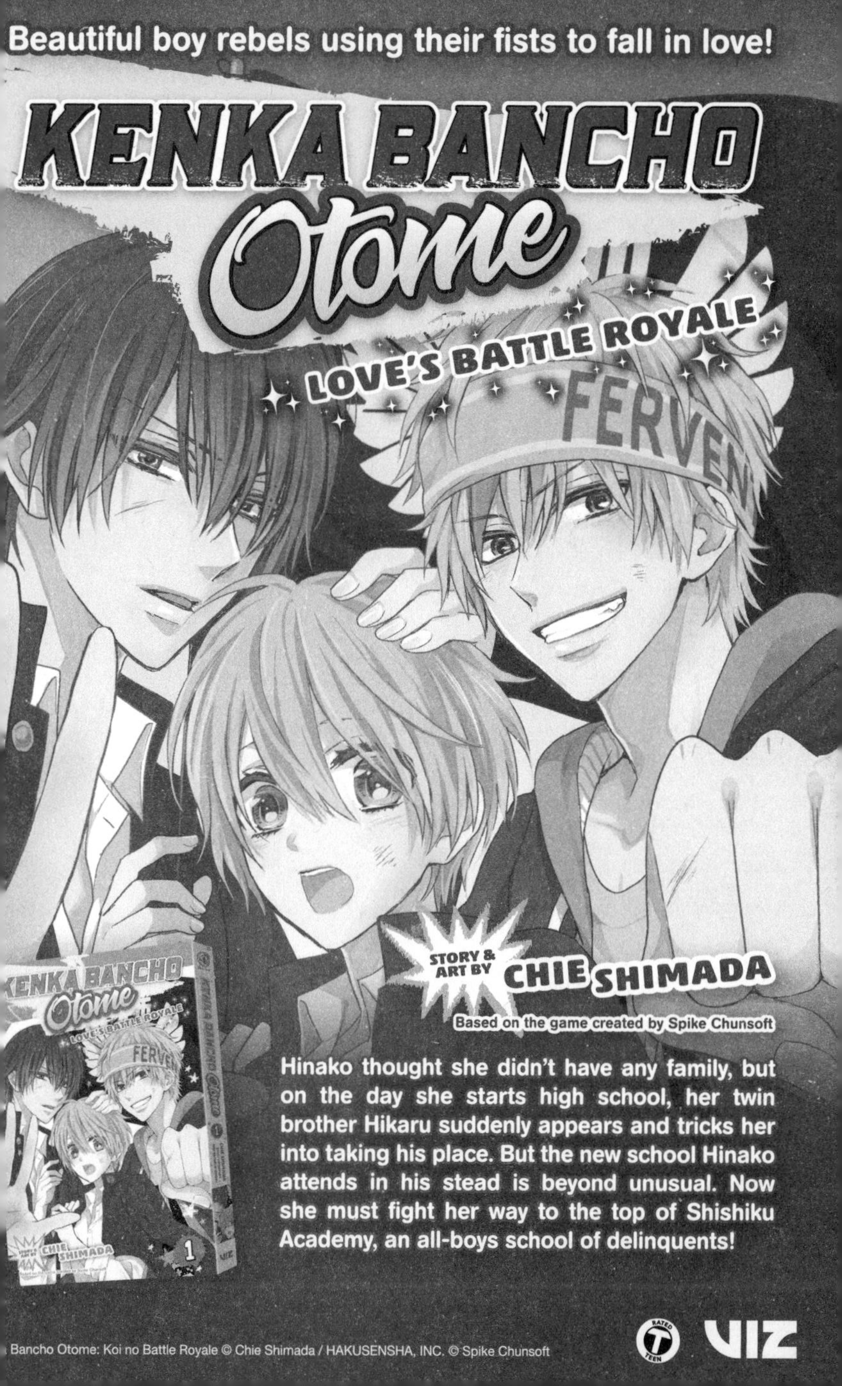

Beautiful boy rebels using their fists to fall in love!
KENKA BANCHO
Otome
LOVE'S BATTLE ROYALE
FERVEN
STORY & ART BY
CHIE SHIMADA
Based on the game created by Spike Chunsoft
Hinako thought she didn't have any family, but on the day she starts high school, her twin brother Hikaru suddenly appears and tricks her into taking his place. But the new school Hinako attends in his stead is beyond unusual. Now she must fight her way to the top of Shishiku Academy, an all-boys school of delinquents!
RATED T TEEN
VIZ
Bancho Otome: Koi no Battle Royale © Chie Shimada / HAKUSENSHA, INC. © Spike Chunsoft

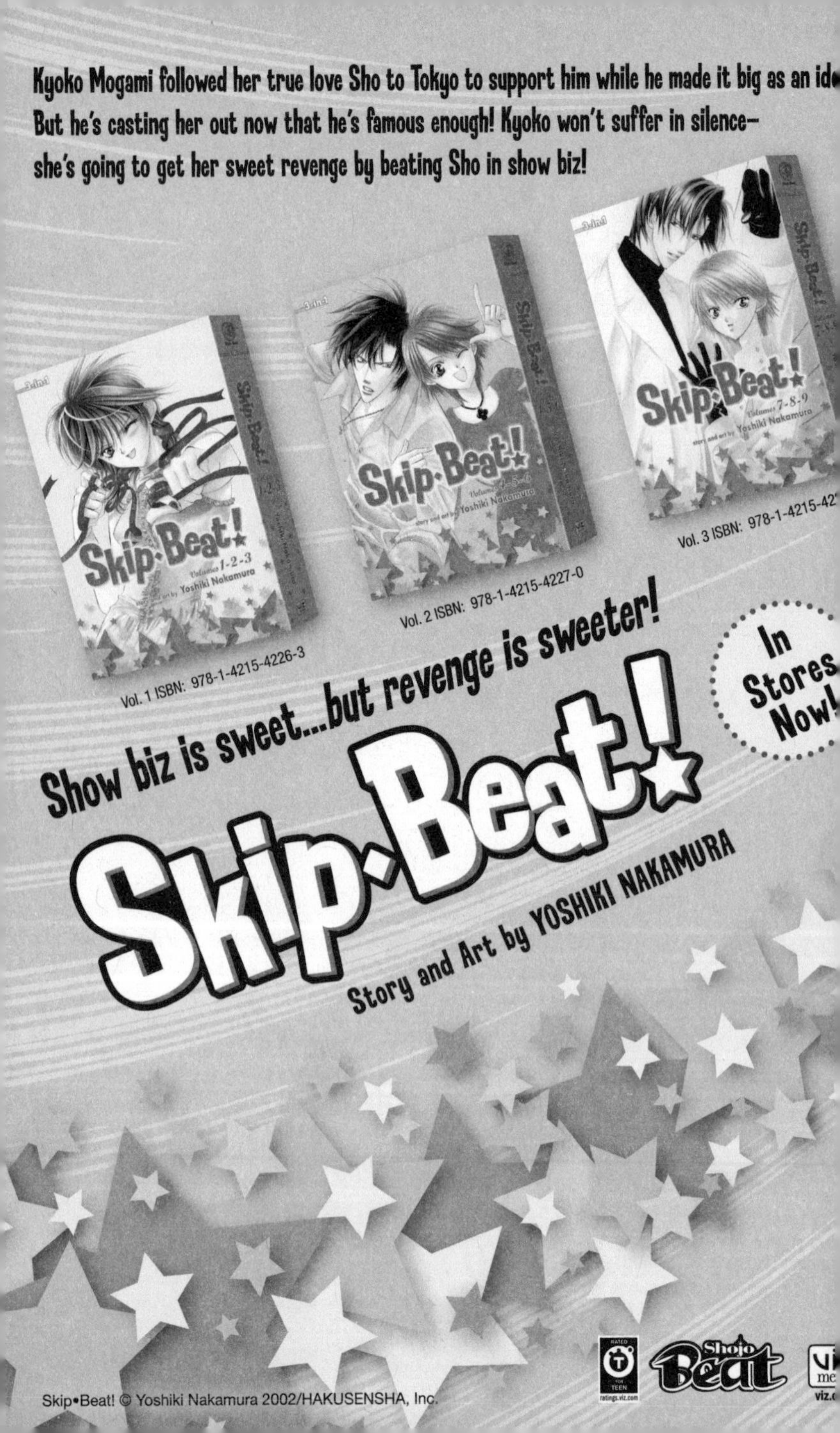
Kyoko Mogami followed her true love Sho to Tokyo to support him while he made it big as an ide
But he's casting her out now that he's famous enough! Kyoko won't suffer in silence—
she's going to get her sweet revenge by beating Sho in show biz!
Skip·Beat! Volumes 1-2-3 story and art by Yoshiki Nakamura
Vol. 1 ISBN: 978-1-4215-4226-3
Skip·Beat! Volumes 4-5-6 story and art by Yoshiki Nakamura
Vol. 2 ISBN: 978-1-4215-4227-0
Skip·Beat! Volumes 7-8-9 story and art by Yoshiki Nakamura
Vol. 3 ISBN: 978-1-4215-42
In Stores Now!
Show biz is sweet...but revenge is sweeter!
Skip·Beat!
Story and Art by YOSHIKI NAKAMURA
RATED T FOR TEEN ratings.viz.com
Shojo Beat
Skip•Beat! © Yoshiki Nakamura 2002/HAKUSENSHA, Inc.

IDOL dreams

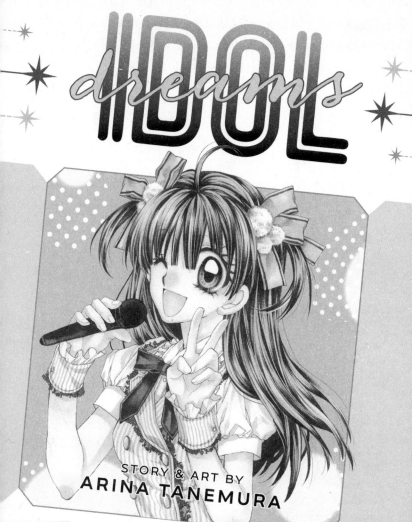

STORY & ART BY
ARINA TANEMURA

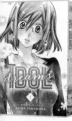

At age 31, office worker Chikage Deguchi feels she missed her chances at love and success. When word gets out that she's a virgin, Chikage is humiliated and wishes she could turn back time to when she was still young and popular. She takes an experimental drug that changes her appearance back to when she was 15. Now Chikage is determined to pursue everything she missed out on all those years ago—including becoming a star!

 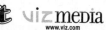

www.viz.com

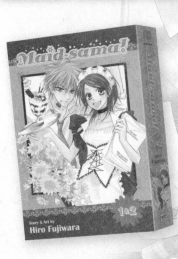

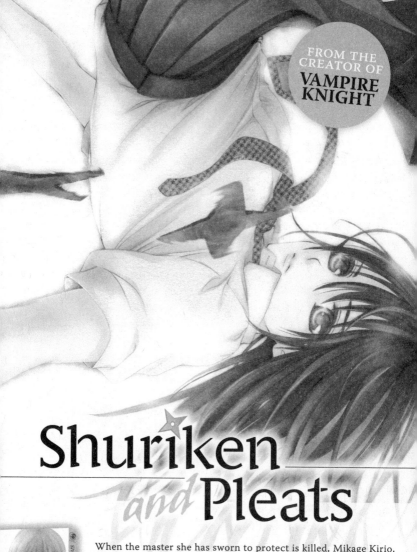

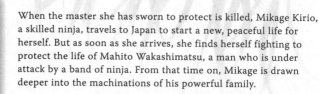
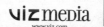

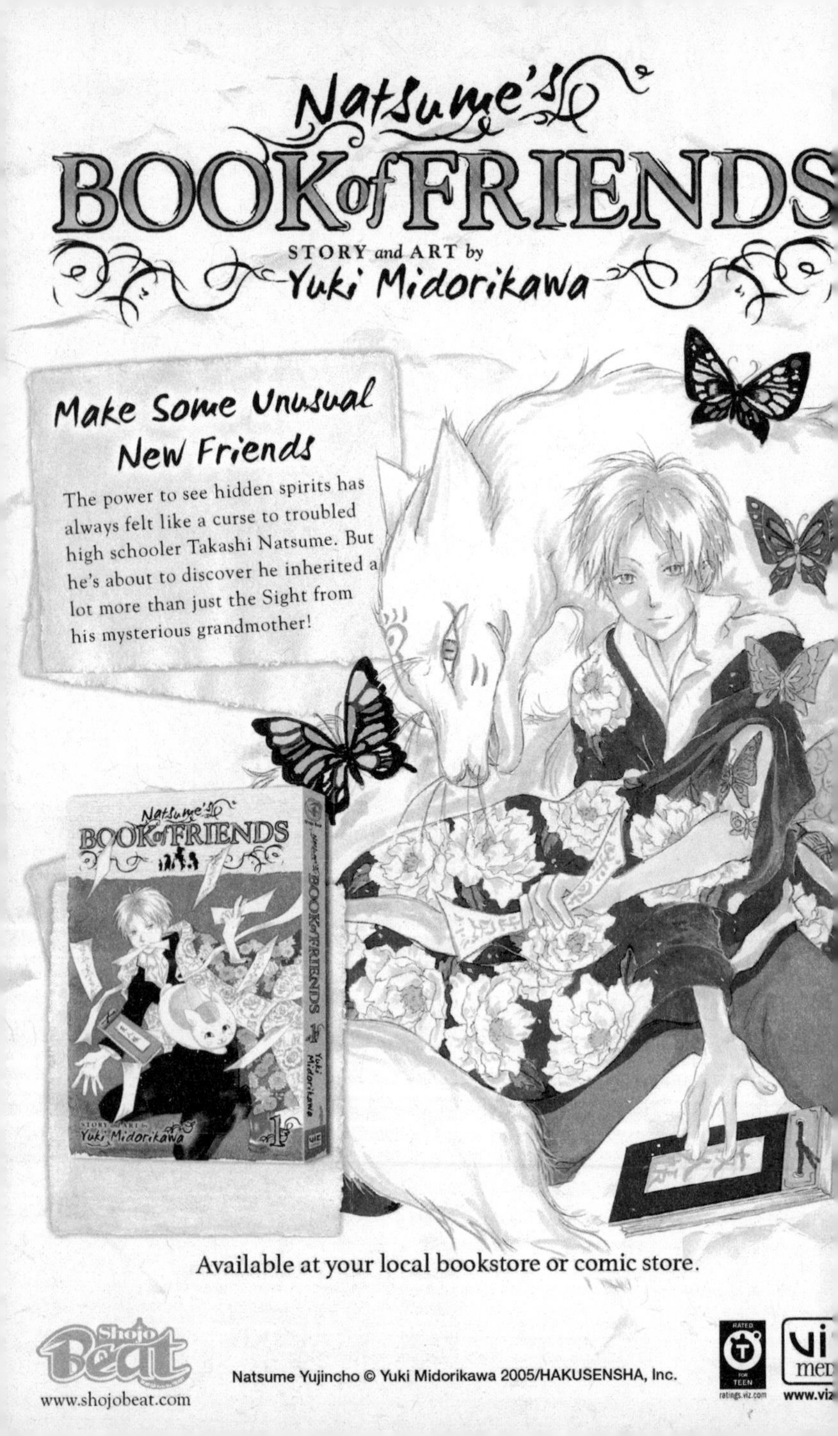
Natsume's
BOOK of FRIENDS
STORY and ART by
Yuki Midorikawa
Make Some Unusual New Friends
The power to see hidden spirits has always felt like a curse to troubled high schooler Takashi Natsume. But he's about to discover he inherited a lot more than just the Sight from his mysterious grandmother!
Available at your local bookstore or comic store.
Shojo Beat
www.shojobeat.com
Natsume Yujincho © Yuki Midorikawa 2005/HAKUSENSHA, Inc.
RATED T FOR TEEN
ratings.viz.com
www.viz

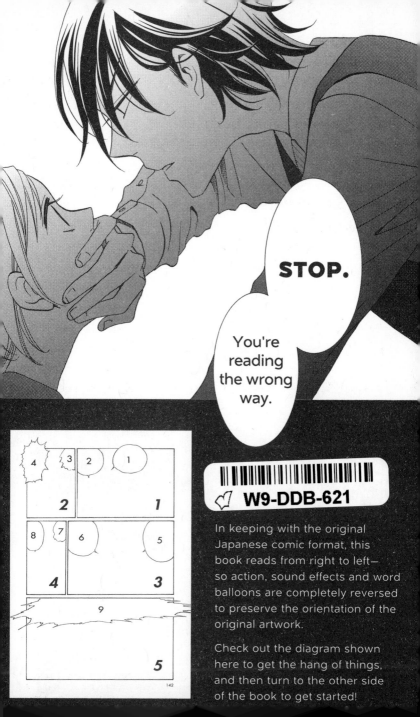

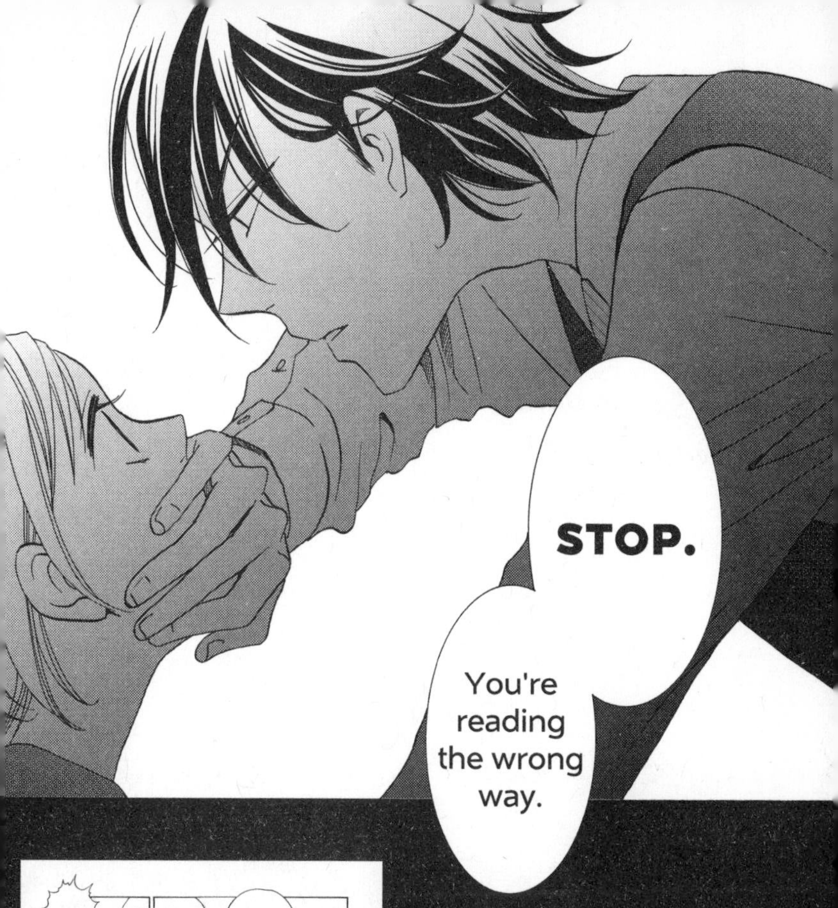
STOP.
You're reading the wrong way.

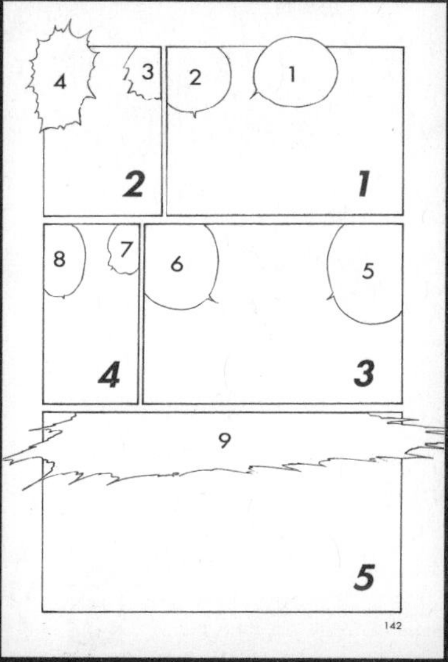
1
2
3
4
1
2
5
6
7
8
3
4
9
5
142

In keeping with the original Japanese comic format, this book reads from right to left—so action, sound effects and word balloons are completely reversed to preserve the orientation of the original artwork.

Check out the diagram shown here to get the hang of things, and then turn to the other side of the book to get started!